O9-BTO-825

The Ecology of Games

This book was made possible by grants from the John D. and Catherine T. MacArthur Foundation in connection with its grant making initiative on Digital Media and Learning. For more information on the initiative visit www.macfound.org.

The John D. and Catherine T. MacArthur Foundation Series on Digital Media and Learning

Civic Life Online: Learning How Digital Media Can Engage Youth, edited by W. Lance Bennett
Digital Media, Youth, and Credibility, edited by Miriam J. Metzger and Andrew J. Flanagin
The Ecology of Games: Connecting Youth, Games, and Learning, edited by Katie Salen
Digital Youth, Innovation, and the Unexpected, edited by Tara McPherson
Learning Race and Ethnicity: Youth and Digital Media, edited by Anna Everett
Youth, Identity, and Digital Media, edited by David Buckingham

The Ecology of Games

Connecting Youth, Games, and Learning

Edited by Katie Salen

The MIT Press
Cambridge, Massachusetts
London, England

For information about special quantity discounts, please email special_sales@mitpress.mit.edu.

This book was set in Stone sans and Stone serif by Aptara, Inc.

Printed and bound in the United States of America.

Library of Congress Cataloging-in-Publication Data

The ecology of games : connecting youth, games, and learning / edited by Katie Salen.
p. cm.—(The John D. and Catherine T. Macarthur Foundation series on digital media and learning)
Includes bibliographical references and index.
ISBN 978-0-262-19575-1 (hardcover : alk. paper)—ISBN 978-0-262-69364-6 (pbk. : alk. paper)
1. Video games—Social aspects. I. Salen, Katie.
GV1469.3.E325 2008
794.8—dc22 2007029495

10 9 8 7 6 5 4 3 2 1

CONTENTS

Foreword vii
Series Advisors

Toward an Ecology of Gaming 1
Katie Salen

PART I: LEARNING ECOLOGIES
Learning and Games 21
James Paul Gee

In-Game, In-Room, In-World: Reconnecting Video Game Play to the Rest of Kids' Lives 41
Reed Stevens, Tom Satwicz, and Laurie McCarthy

E Is for Everyone: The Case for Inclusive Game Design 67
Amit Pitaru

PART II: HIDDEN AGENDAS
Education vs. Entertainment: A Cultural History of Children's Software 89
Mizuko Ito

The Rhetoric of Video Games 117
Ian Bogost

The Power of Play: The Portrayal and Performance of Race in Video Games 141
Anna Everett and S. Craig Watkins

PART III: GAMING LITERACIES
Open-Ended Video Games: A Model for Developing Learning for the Interactive Age 167
Kurt Squire

Why *I Love Bees*: A Case Study in Collective Intelligence Gaming 199
Jane McGonigal

Education Unleashed: Participatory Culture, Education, and Innovation in *Second Life* 229
Cory Ondrejka

Why Johnny Can't Fly: Treating Games as a Form of Youth Media Within a Youth Development Framework 253
Barry Joseph

Glossary 267

Games Index 275

Foreword

In recent years, digital media and networks have become embedded in our everyday lives, and are part of broad-based changes to how we engage in knowledge production, communication, and creative expression. Unlike the early years in the development of computers and computer-based media, digital media are now *commonplace* and *pervasive*, having been taken up by a wide range of individuals and institutions in all walks of life. Digital media have escaped the boundaries of professional and formal practice, and the academic, governmental, and industry homes that initially fostered their development. Now they have been taken up by diverse populations and non-institutionalized practices, including the peer activities of youth. Although specific forms of technology uptake are highly diverse, a generation is growing up in an era where digital media are part of the taken-for-granted social and cultural fabric of learning, play, and social communication.

In 2005, The John D. and Catherine T. MacArthur Foundation began a new grant-making initiative in the area of digital media and learning. An initial set of exploratory grants in the study of youth practices and the development of digital literacy programs has expanded into a major initiative spanning research, educational reform, and technology development. One component of this effort is the support of this book series. As part of the broader MacArthur Foundation initiative, this series is aimed at timely dissemination of new scholarship, fostering an interdisciplinary conversation, and archiving the best research in this emerging field. Through the course of producing the six initial volumes, the foundation convened a set of meetings to discuss the framing issues for this book series. As a result of these discussions we identified a set of shared commitments and areas of focus. Although we recognize that the terrain is being reshaped even as we seek to identify it, we see these as initial frames for the ongoing work to be put forward by this series.

This book series is founded upon the working hypothesis that those immersed in new digital tools and networks are engaged in an unprecedented exploration of language, games, social interaction, problem solving, and self-directed activity that leads to diverse forms of learning. These diverse forms of learning are reflected in expressions of identity, how individuals express independence and creativity, and in their ability to learn, exercise judgment, and think systematically.

The defining frame for this series is not a particular theoretical or disciplinary approach, nor is it a fixed set of topics. Rather, the series revolves around a constellation of topics investigated from multiple disciplinary and practical frames. The series as a whole looks at the relation between youth, learning, and digital media, but each book or essay might deal with only a subset of this constellation. Erecting strict topical boundaries can exclude some of the most important work in the field. For example, restricting the content of the series only to people of a certain age means artificially reifying an age boundary when the phenomenon demands otherwise. This becomes particularly problematic with new forms of online participation where one important outcome is the mixing of participants of different ages. The same goes for digital media, which are increasingly inseparable from analog and earlier media forms.

In the case of learning, digital media are part of the redefinition and broadening of existing boundaries of practice and our understanding of what learning means. The term *learning* was chosen rather than *education* in order to flag an interest in settings both within and outside the classroom. Many of the more radical challenges to existing learning agendas are happening in domains such as gaming, online networks, and amateur production that usually occur in informal and non-institutional settings. This does not mean we are prejudiced against learning as it happens in the classroom or other formal educational settings. Rather, we hope to initiate a dialog about learning as it spans settings that are more explicitly educational and those that are not.

The series and the MacArthur Foundation initiative respond to certain changes in our media ecology that have important implications for learning. Specifically, these are new forms of media *literacy* and changes in the modes of media *participation*. Digital media are part of a convergence between interactive media (most notably gaming), online networks, and existing media forms. Navigating this media ecology involves a palette of literacies that are being defined through practice but require more scholarly scrutiny before they can be fully incorporated pervasively into educational initiatives. Media literacy involves not only ways of understanding, interpreting, and critiquing media, but also the means for creative and social expression, online search and navigation, and a host of new technical skills. The potential gap in literacies and participation skills creates new challenges for educators who struggle to bridge media engagement inside and outside the classroom.

The shift toward interactive media, peer-to-peer forms of media communication, and many-to-many forms of distribution relate to types of participation that are more bottom-up and driven by the "user" or "consumer" of media. Audiences have always had the opportunity to "talk back" to corporate media or to create their own local media forms. However, the growing dominance of gaming as a media format, the advent of low-cost digital production tools, and online distribution means a much more dynamic range in who participates and how they participate in the production and distribution of media. Gamers expect that media are subject to player control. Add to this the fact that all forms of media are increasingly being contextualized in an online communication ecology where creative production and expression is inseparable from social communication. Finally, new low-cost digital production tools mean that amateur and casual media creators can author, edit, and distribute video and other rich media forms that were once prohibitively expensive to produce and share with others.

We value the term *participation* for the ways in which it draws attention to situated learning theory, social media literacies, and mobilized forms of media engagement. Digital media networks support existing forms of mass media distribution as well as smaller publics and collectivities that might center on peer groups or specialized niche interests. The presence of social communication, professional media, and amateur niche media in shared online spaces introduces a kind of leveling effect, where small media players gain new visibility and the position of previously authoritative media is challenged. The clash between more socially driven or niche publics and the publics defined by professional forms of media is playing out in high-profile battles in domains such as intellectual property law, journalism, entertainment, and government. For our purposes, the questions surrounding knowledge and credibility and young people's use of digital media to circumvent adult authority are particularly salient.

The emerging power shift, where smaller and edge players are gaining more visibility and voice, is particularly important to children and youth. If we look at children and youth through the lens of digital media, we have a population that has been historically subject to a high degree of systematic and institutional control in the kinds of information and social communication to which they have access. This is one reason why the alchemy between youth and digital media has been distinctive; it disrupts the existing set of power relations between adult authority and youth voice. While many studies of children, youth, and media have for decades stressed the status of young people as competent and full social subjects, digital media increasingly insist that we acknowledge this viewpoint. Not only must we see youth as legitimate social and political actors, but we must also recognize them as potential innovators and drivers of new media change.

This does not mean that we are uncritical of youth practices or that we believe that digital media necessarily hold the key to empowerment. Rather, we argue against technological determinism, stressing the need for balanced scholarship that recognizes the importance of our current moment within the context of existing structures and unfolding histories. This means placing contemporary changes within a historical context as well as working to highlight the diversity in the landscape of media and media uptake. Neither youth nor digital media are monolithic categories; documenting how specific youth take up particular forms of media with diverse learning outcomes is critical to this series as a whole. Digital media take the form they do because they are created by existing social and cultural contexts, contexts that are diverse and stratified.

As with earlier shifts in media environments, this current turn toward digital media and networks has been accompanied by fear and panic as well as elevated hopes. This is particularly true of adult perception of children and youth who are at the forefront of experimentation with new media forms, and who mobilize digital media to push back at existing structures of power and authority. While some see "digital kids" as our best hope for the future, others worry that new media are part of a generational rift and a dangerous turn away from existing standards for knowledge, literacy, and civic engagement. Careful, socially engaged, and accessible scholarship is crucial to informing this public debate and related policy decisions. Our need to understand the relation between digital media and learning is urgent because of the scale and the speed of the changes that are afoot. The shape and uses of digital media are still very much in flux, and this book series seeks to be part of the definition of our sociotechnical future.

Mizuko Ito
Cathy Davidson
Henry Jenkins
Carol Lee
Michael Eisenberg
Joanne Weiss
Series Advisors

Toward an Ecology of Gaming

Katie Salen

Institute of Play; Parsons the New School for Design, Design and Technology

A time is marked not so much by ideas that are argued about as by ideas that are taken for granted.
—Jonathan Letham[1]

1954. West Germany gains an unexpected 3-2 victory over Hungary in the World Cup, known from then on as The Miracle of Bern. Officials announce that an American hydrogen bomb test had been conducted on Bikini Atoll in the Pacific Ocean. Marilyn Monroe weds Joe DiMaggio. The Geneva Conference partitions Vietnam into North Vietnam and South Vietnam. Mathematician Alan Turing commits suicide. "Gaming as a Technique of Analysis" is released, praising games as designed models with which to think.

When viewed from this perspective, 1954 looks a lot like 2007: a year of instability and transformation on the world stage, a year shadowed by the promise and threat of competing ideologies, a year colored by fear, hope, and the advent of new technology. 1954 was also a year, like this year, when games entered the popular lexicon and *man the player* was seized upon as a harbinger of change. By 1954, Piaget had mapped the moral judgment of a child through a study of his or her coming to know the rules of a game;[2] Turing had contributed

Connie Yowell of the MacArthur Foundation was an early champion of video games, game design, and game studies as valuable players in the digital media and learning conversation. This volume, and much of the research it contains, would simply not exist without her support or that of the MacArthur Foundation. An amazing duo—Michael Carter and Ruth Rominger of the Monterey Institute for Technology and Education—provided invaluable advice, guidance, and editorial support throughout the process. Joanne Weiss lent her sharp eye and expertise to many of the early drafts, and both Tara McPherson and Anna Everett contributed immensely to my thinking over the course of the project.

I'd also like to thank the participants of "Everywhere Now: Kids, Games, and Learning," a three-week online dialogue that did much to enliven and enrich this volume; they shared ideas, anecdotes, and research that deepened my own thinking, as well as that of the contributing authors. In an era in which time is a most precious commodity, all of these remarkable individuals gave of theirs freely, and the volume is much the richer for it. Contributors included Matteo Bittanti, Douglas Rushkoff, Jane Pinkard, Kallen Tsikalas, Wagner James Au, Mary Flanagan, Tracy Fullerton, Lizbeth Goodman, Justin Hall, Toby Miller, Michael Nitsche, Jane Park, Clay Shirky, Betty Hayes, Constance Steinkuhler, Eric Zimmerman, Andrew Burn, Diane Carr, Victoria Carrington, Mechelle De Craene, Jay Lemke, Mark Marino, Linda Polin, Bernie DeKoven, Jason Della Rocca, Nichole Pinkard, Brian Thompson, Joe Beckmann, Phil Bell, Carrie Heeter, Joel Josephson, Reid Kimball, Beth Kolko, and Robert Torres. Lastly, tremendous thanks to the other editors in the MacArthur Series—Lance Bennett, David Buckingham, Tara McPherson, Anna Everett, Andrew Flanagin, and Miriam Metzger—for their support, intellect, and generosity.

to "Digital Computers Applied to Games, of Faster than Thought";[3] Huizinga had released his seminal study of play, *Homo Ludens*[4] sixteen years earlier, setting the stage for Caillois's *Les Jeux et Les Hommes* in 1958; and two analysts from the Rand Corporation, A. M. Mood and R. D. Specht, chose 1954 as the year to present "Gaming as a Technique of Analysis"[5] as part of a symposium on the use and value of war game methods. Interested in the role which players could play in modeling the behavior of a complex system, upon closer inspection the two scientists found something more: "A virtue of gaming that is sometimes overlooked by those seeking grander goals . . . is its unparalleled advantages in training and educational programs. A game can easily be made fascinating enough to put over the dullest facts. To sit down and play through a game is to be convinced as by no argument, however persuasively presented."[6] An idea that to many seems new today turns out to have graced the lips of researchers some fifty-odd years ago.

What was missing in 1954, however, was the presence of a generation of kids who knew no time untouched by the promises and pitfalls of digital technology. Born into a world where concepts like copyright, mastery, civic engagement, and participation are seamlessly negotiated and redefined across highly personalized networks spanning the spaces of Facebook, *Yu-Gi-Oh*, and YouTube, today's kids are crafting learning identities for themselves—hybrid identities—that seemingly reject previously distinct modes of being. Writer, designer, reader, producer, teacher, student, gamer—all modes hold equal weight. Where we used to call them *player-producers, prosumers,* or even *multitaskers,* we now just call them *kids.* The phrase that best explains this change comes from Mikey, a participant in one of our contributors' studies, who in talking about games said, "It's what we do." The "we" to which he was referring was kids these days, the young people of his generation.

It is this condition of digital "kidness" as it pertains to games, which serves as the focus of *Ecology of Games.* Part of the MacArthur Foundation Series on Digital Media and Learning, its authors explore many of the core issues arising from a consideration of the impact of games and gaming within social, cultural, and learning domains. Four main questions guide the work throughout:

- What forms of participatory practices do games and gaming engender for youth; which forms of learning are present, missing, or reinforced through gaming?
- What *gaming literacies,* or families of practice produced by games and gaming attitudes, do we see emerging?
- How does gaming act as a point of entry or departure for other forms of knowledge, literacies, and social organization?
- What barriers of entry into gaming and game communities exist, and what are the implications for those who haven't been invited to play?

Although there has been a considerable amount written on games and young people's use of them, there has been little work done to establish an overall "ecology" of gaming, game design, and play, in the sense of how all of the various elements—from code to rhetoric to social practices and aesthetics—cohabit and populate the game world. Purposefully broad in scope and multidisciplinary in perspective, *Ecology of Games* is intended to complexify a debate around the value of games and gaming that has been, to date, overly polemic and surprisingly shallow. The language of the media is replete with references to the devil (and heavy metal) when it comes to the ill-found virtues of video games, while a growing movement in K–12 education casts them as a Holy Grail in the uphill battle to keep kids learning. While many credit game play with fostering new forms of social organization and alternative ways of thinking and interacting, more work needs to be done to situate these forms of learning within a dynamic media ecology that has the participatory and social nature of gaming at its core. My goal, and that of the authors selected for inclusion, is to pepper this often black-and-white mix with shades of gray, pointing toward a more sophisticated understanding of the myriad ways in which gaming could and should matter to those considering the future of learning.

Structure of the Volume

Three sections organize the collection: "Learning Ecologies," "Hidden Agendas," and "Gaming Literacies." While this tripartite structure may set up an expectation of separation or even of progression across chapters, this is due more to publication within a traditional book format and less to any real conceptual division between them. With that said, the three sections do bring together a subset of chapters to thematically organize what is, admittedly, a wide-ranging collection. This breadth comes both from an attempt to map gaming as an ecology of concerns drawn from a range of contexts and from a series of disciplinary perspectives. Contributors come from education, the learning sciences, film studies, technology, anthropology, game design, performance studies, computer science, and youth development. Such a diversity of perspectives leads to a condition of both wealth and poverty. Wealth comes in the form of new frameworks, methodologies, and alternate histories that enrich the dialogue with multiple points of view; poverty comes in the choice of breadth over depth and in the challenge of locating a common vocabulary. We could not even decide on a shared name to refer to our object of study—games, digital games, video games? In the end we decided to use them all; each name came with subtleties and distinctions that would have been lost within a unifying framework.

The development process gained an additional dimension with the inclusion of an online dialogue entitled, "Everywhere Now: Kids, Games, and Learning,"[7] which brought together experts from around the world to discuss how, if, and why kids were infusing their gaming with learning, or vice versa. This online conversation benefited all those involved in writing for this volume, as the dialogue provided an excellent test bed for ideas and arguments. I came away from it having gained an even greater respect for the challenges and complexities of the subject at hand.

Learning Ecologies

Contributions from James Paul Gee, Reed Stevens, Tom Satwicz, Laurie McCarthy, and Amit Pitaru explore the spaces of intersection between gaming, the design of dynamic and player-driven learning spaces, and the role each plays for kids familiar with or coming to know video games. These chapters articulate a form of *learning ecology* present in the way kids game. The volume opens with "Learning and Games." In this chapter, Gee takes on the intersection of game design and good learning, choreographing potential sites of engagement between the two by drawing on contemporary work in the learning sciences. Well established as an authority within the video games, learning, and literacy space, Gee creates a useful foundation upon which many of the other authors in the volume draw.

Stevens, Satwicz, and McCarthy follow with "In-Game, In-Room, In-World"—a captivating ethnography of young people in different families playing video games in their own homes.

Based on previous research work in everyday cognition and informal learning, they came to this study by way of an interest in how children spend their time and what they learn in the process. Rather than holding to a *separate worlds* view, which posits that game play takes place in a world separate from other activities, the authors instead argue that the culture of video game play is one deeply "tangled up" with other cultural practices. These practices include relations with siblings and parents, patterns of learning at home and school, as well as imagined futures for oneself. Given the relative scarcity of empirical research on video game play, this study creates a model for how such work might be done in the future. While it remains to be seen whether the frameworks of "separate" and "tangled up" are truly opposed, Stevens, Satwicz, and McCarthy take a strong step toward refining our understanding of each.

Designer Amit Pitaru concludes Section 1, providing an overview of his work with the Henry Viscardi School in adapting mainstream video games for play by children with disabilities. Arguing for a larger ecology of accessible design for players who have traditionally been barred from entry into gaming, he traces the impact of coming to learn to game on the educational, social, and therapeutic life of a child with special needs. The accessibility mandate outlined by Pitaru goes beyond impacting kids with special developmental or cognitive needs, however. He argues that making digital games accessible to a wider audience benefits everyone by providing opportunities for play across communities. He cites a closed captioning mod for *Doom-3* that provides auditory information in the form of text (or other) visuals. Rather than simply allowing players who may be hard of hearing to increase their quality of play, the mod has been taken up and used by many English language learners to help them learn and understand English better.[8]

Within the commercial gaming industry, there have been few attempts to address issues of accessibility in video gaming despite the fact that more and more people are beginning to recognize that the right to play is a developmental right. As kids get left out—not only of video game play but also of other digitally based experiences popular among their peers—they will continue to fall further and further beyond. Pitaru's piece provides a much-needed call to action supported, in part, by the increasing work in the IGDA, Games for Health, and Serious Games initiatives; significantly, any change requires buy-in from the game development community too, if the situation is to be affected.

Hidden Agendas

The link between games and learning is not a contemporary phenomenon, nor a digital one. Long before *Math Blaster* or *Oregon Trail* hit the market, games have been used as learning tools. Members of the volunteer Militia of Rhode Island played *American Kriegsspiel* in the years following the Civil War, theater games like *Sibling Rivalry* were used in contexts ranging from activism to acting, and Fröebel's invention of kindergarten in 1840 was premised in large part on the integration of learning through games and play. Attempts to use computer technologies to enhance learning began with the efforts of pioneers such as Atkinson, Morningstar, and Suppes in 1968; the presence of computer technology in classrooms has increased dramatically since that time, including the use of games and simulations.[9]

In "Education V. Entertainment" Mizuko Ito acknowledges this history and argues that it is critical to understand not only the historical conditions under which a digital game has been produced, but also how it gets taken up and regulated in different contexts of play. Ito uses the concepts of *media production* and *participation genres* to read across the circuits of culture influencing styles of representation, practice, and institutional structure in children's software development. In order to build an agenda for how video games could contribute to systemic change in learning and education, Ito suggests it is "necessary—but not sufficient—to analyze representational content and play mechanics."[10] Her chapter outlines a framework for doing so, which is then built upon both by Ondrejka and by Everett and Watkins elsewhere in the volume.

"The Rhetoric of Video Games," by Ian Bogost, focuses on video games as contexts for the circulation, interpretation, and deployment of meaning. Bogost introduces the concept of *procedural rhetoric,* the art of persuasion through rule-based representations and interactions. Bogost is part of a growing body of researchers, many from the realms of computer science and design more generally, who recognize games as process-based systems that produce models and representations algorithmically through player interaction. This perspective is significant because it points to a quality distinguishing video games from other media (like films, television, and books), beyond their status as interactive or participatory systems. More specifically, citing games like *Animal Crossing, Bully,* and *America's Army,* Bogost looks at the systemic approach used by video games to construct arguments about the way social or cultural systems work in the world. Players learn to interpret these arguments and eventually make arguments of their own. Such a perspective opens up the possibility for defining a set of new literacies associated with reading, producing, and playing games, a set of *gaming literacies* further explored in Section 3 of this volume. According to Bogost,

> Playing video games is a kind of literacy. Not the literacy that helps us read books or write term papers, but the kind of literacy that helps us make or critique the systems we live in. . . . When we learn to play games with an eye toward uncovering their procedural rhetorics, we learn to ask questions about the models such games present. (p. 136)

Anna Everett and S. Craig Watkins actively put this rhetorical framework to work in their chapter "The Power of Play," which considers how race and gender are codified, constructed, and performed within a gaming ecology. In what ways, they ask, do young people's interactions with video games influence how and what they learn about race and gender? Can games facilitate learning that is antisocial? Taking on popular video game titles like *Saint's Row, Bully,* and *NBA Street,* they show that by striving to locate players in what are often promoted as graphically real and culturally "authentic" environments, urban/street games produce some of the most powerful, persistent, and problematic lessons about race in American culture. Like Ito, Everett and Watkins locate the issue of representation as an important voice within the ongoing conversation regarding the digital divide. They conclude their chapter by advocating the need to expand the discussion of games and learning to include concerns about access to and participation in digital media culture, communities, and user-generated content.

Gaming Literacies

Whereas education in the early part of the twentieth century focused on the acquisition of basic literacy skills—simple reading, writing, and calculating—many believe that education in the twenty-first century must focus on high literacy skills such as the ability to think, read, and interact critically, to solve complex problems in mathematics and science, and to express oneself persuasively through language and media. The meaning of *knowing* today has "shifted from being able to remember and repeat information to being able to find and use it."[11] Designing pedagogical approaches to support this form of knowing involves deep changes not only in the ways instruction is delivered, but also in the tools and technologies involved. The work of John Bransford, Roy Pea, Brigid Barron, and others has been particularly instructive in this respect, as has that of researchers like Colin Lankshear, Michele Knobel, and Rebecca Black, who have studied the acquisition of new literacies in contexts such as fan fiction, blogging, and video remixing.[12] Computer scientists Seymour Papert and Mitchel Resnick pioneered thinking about how the acquisition of a programming language empowers kids to model knowledge within learner-driven contexts. This approach has been mirrored over the years in the development of products like Mindstorms®, and open-source tools and programming languages like Logo©, Squeak©, Scratch©, and Alice©, designed to teach procedural thinking, problem solving, and logic.

Taken in sum it is clear that contemporary research influencing the games and learning space has started to move beyond an analysis of media as a way to become literate about it, and toward an emphasis on creative production and the principles of design as a starting place and main area of emphasis with kids. Former digital kid Justin Hall has said that he "continues to believe that literacy, language, and personal expression will stem from increasing exposure to flexible rule sets and iterative systems for solving small problems."[13] Like Hall, the contributors to this volume, each in his or her own way, shares in the belief that exposure to the flexible rule sets and iterative, cyclical play embodied in both design and gaming practices are critical for thinking about literacy in the twenty-first century.

Gaming Literacies, the final section in the volume, builds on this belief, refining a thread that runs through the volume as a whole. Each of its four chapters offers a case study of a specific type or genre of video game—sandbox or simulation games, alternate reality games, online casual games, and virtual worlds. I felt it was important to conclude the volume with a number of studies that put theory into practice, as a way to illuminate some of the real difficulties that arise around activating games as learning frameworks. Specific in focus, each study defines clear limitations as to the applicability of its proposed model. While Kurt Squire discusses the learning merits of open-ended simulation or sandbox games, he does not suggest that his model will work in the same way for players of the alternate reality games Jane McGonigal makes the focus of her research. Cory Ondrejka looks closely at the way certain design-oriented gaming literacies are supported in *Second Life*, but makes no claims for any standardized outcomes. In fact, each author argues for the distinctiveness of learning instigated and acquired by each participant *on his or her own terms*. It appears that to be literate within the family of practices activating the ecology of games is to achieve status as a unique and distinctive learner. This does not bode well for those seeking a silver bullet to slay the games and learning beast. It does suggest, however, that ongoing work will need to be done to design and support a *set* of gaming and learning frameworks for use by students, parents, teachers, and researchers.

Gaming Literacies begins with Squire's chapter, "Open-Ended Video Games," which attempts to take into account a set of disparate activities that partially define the current landscape of work around games and learning. These include studies of gamers and gaming culture, game design work modifying commercial computer games, and educational design research orchestrating social events around them. His chapter offers a theoretical model for video game-based learning environments as designed experiences, focusing on open-ended simulation games, modeled by both the *Grand Theft Auto* and *Civilization* series with which he has been working for a number of years. He ties together studies of gamers "in the wild," within school, and in afterschool programs designed specifically for learning. He concludes with an investigation of how such games develop players' *productive* literacies, an ability to use digital technologies to produce both meanings and tangible artifacts.[14] Squire's interest is in both observing and analyzing the learning occurring in these commercial, off-the-shelf games, and also in transforming this understanding into an effective and repeatable design framework.

Within the types of learning systems discussed by Squire, players are encouraged to develop specific areas of expertise, separate from one another and perhaps even from those of their mentors or teachers. Squire shows that as students progress, they develop new interests, which then propel them out of the community of practice toward new areas of interest, such as game design or ancient history.[15] Recognizing that such an approach is antithetical to the way most schools currently operate, Squire looks to video games not only as contexts for gaming but as doorways or catalysts for the acquisition of knowledge. Squire's work shows that the value of gaming may not only be in the recruiting of productive, gaming literacies, but in driving kids to discover and nurture interests they may not know they have.

This theme is taken up by Jane McGonigal in "Why *I Love Bees*," a case study on massively multiplayer alternate reality games. These search and analysis style games operate for players as immersive tutorials in network collaboration and coordination. According to McGonigal, players of such games develop a new kind of digital network literacy, one specifically tuned to the techniques, challenges, and rewards of massively scaled collaboration. Using the game *I Love Bees* as her model, she explores how real-time game design, or "puppet mastering," can be used to support and further develop the multiple tracks of engagement that emerge from players' diverse perspectives.

McGonigal notes that as massively social experiences, alternate reality games are especially well suited to encouraging metalevel reflection on the skills and processes that players use to meet new challenges. Being part of a massively multiplayer game community, she argues, means sharing your thoughts and experiences with your fellow players. Further, she demonstrates that games like *I Love Bees* are part of a larger cultural trend toward an age of powerful networked collaboration. If this is the case, we must take care to prepare students for entry into these networks. As Henry Jenkins has noted, "We are just learning how to exercise that power—individually and collectively—and fighting to define the terms under which we will be allowed to participate."[16]

In "Education Unleashed," Cory Ondrejka uses the history of virtual worlds as a context for building an argument around the role new technology is playing in defining when, where, and how kids learn. Chief Technology Officer for Linden Lab (the creators of *Second Life*), Ondrejka is an unapologetic advocate for the use of virtual worlds as a building block of the future of learning. Connecting the cost of learning to innovation and knowledge creation, he suggests that it is the lower cost of learning in virtual worlds that is transformative. "For the first time, geography is not the primary determining factor in who can learn together or who can teach" (p. 243).

Ondrejka points to the heterogeneous, scaffolded, and peer-supported pedagogy that has emerged from *Second Life*, a model echoed in the work of a number of game studies researchers. According to Constance Steinkuhler "Online technologies provide new opportunities for 'anytime/anywhere' social interaction, and the number of innovative curricular designs that incorporate online collaborative environments has been steadily increasing since such technology first emerged."[17]

This fact is supported by the breadth and depth of styles of learning that Ondrejka has witnessed in *Second Life*, from in-world classes in the scripting language to mixed-reality conferences about the future of broadcasting. As Ondrejka shows, a tremendous variety of both amateurs and experts is currently leveraging *Second Life* as a platform for learning.

Barry Joseph, in "Why Johnny Can't Fly," rounds out the volume with an overview of how his organization, Global Kids, treats gaming as a form of youth media. Joseph's chapter is distinctive in its documentation of missteps and successes in working within a youth development context. In his work we see a grappling with the "problem of pedagogy" around game-based learning that infuses so much of the work represented here. Through a playful description of a series of innovative programs, Joseph offers a peek into Global Kids' attempts to develop critical thinking skills that are not necessarily designed for passing standardized tests. While No Child Left Behind[18] is rarely mentioned in these pages, its specter continues to be felt by all.

As these case studies show, understanding the ways in which the structures of games themselves elicit particular attitudes toward action, interaction, and knowing is endlessly beneficial. Acknowledging that games *already* operate as robust learning systems forces a focus on the intrinsic qualities and characteristics that guide the types of learning and new literacies gaming and games advance. Learning to "read" a game system in order to play with it points toward a specific kind of gaming literacy connected, in part, to the ability of a player to understand how systems operate, and how they can be transformed. Modding and world-building, which form the basis for much of the play of MMOs and virtual worlds (for example), might be another such gaming literacy, while learning how to navigate a complex system of out-of-game resources—from game guides, FAQs, walkthroughs, and forums to peer-to-peer learning—might represent another. A third gaming literacy might be seen in the learning that takes place in negotiating the variable demands of fair play: players must become literate in the social norms of a specific gaming community, learning what degree of transgression is acceptable and when a player has crossed the line. A fourth is learning how to collaborate within a multiplayer space, where knowledge is distributed and action is most often collective.

Yet the circuits of production, distribution, and play of games involve ongoing tensions between industry relations, distribution infrastructure, patterns of player/viewer engagement, genres of representation, social agendas, and educational philosophies. These tensions affect how we think about which literacies an ecology of gaming supports and which it potentially denies. Bertram C. Bruce sums this situation up when he writes,

> Adolescents need to learn how to integrate knowledge from multiple sources, including music, video, online databases, and other media. They need to think critically about information that can be found nearly instantaneously through out the world. They need to participate in the kinds of collaboration that new communication and information technologies enable, but increasingly demand. Considerations of globalization lead us toward the importance of understanding the perspective of others, developing a historical grounding, and seeing the interconnectedness of economic and ecological systems.[19]

Gaming can allow players to experience various perspectives. In his framing of games as procedural systems, Bogost offers just such a consideration. "Video games are not just stages that facilitate cultural, social, or political practices; they are also media where cultural values themselves can be represented—for critique, satire, education, or commentary" (p. 119). Can we teach players (and their parents and teachers) how to read games in order to ask questions about the models they represent? Absolutely, and Bogost offers the beginnings of a framework to do so. Is this a way that kids learn how to debate or do history or math? Not necessarily. This is where the real work needs to be done to better understand the connections between forms of gaming and certain kinds of acquired knowledge and practice. Such work must be studied at the level of discourse and lived, embodied practices, as these are the levels on which games live.[20] Some of the most innovative research currently being done in this area focuses on assessment and the need to develop models that take into account the conditions leading to the literacies previously described.[21]

Discovering what literacies are general and specific to games may lead to new approaches to the creation of both games and other learning environments.

Beyond Game

The concept of *gaming* as it is used in the following pages goes beyond games, in the same way that *learning* goes beyond the configuration of a classroom. Gaming constitutes the sum total of activities, literacies, knowledge, and practices activated in and around any instance of a game. Gaming is play across media, time, social spaces, and networks of meaning; it includes engagement with digital FAQs, paper game guides, parents and siblings, the history of games, other players, as well as the games themselves. It requires players to be fluent in a series of connected literacies that are multimodal, performative, productive, and participatory in nature. It requires an attitude oriented toward risk taking, meaning creation, nonlinear navigation, problem solving, an understanding of rule structures, and an acknowledgment of agency within that structure, to name but a few.[22]

Gaming also requires what Jay Lemke and others have referred to as a "stance of playfulness," a cognitive attitude tied directly to the creative, improvisational, and subversive qualities of play. Huizinga would call this the *lusory attitude*, the attitude required of players in order to play.[23] To play a game is, in many ways, an act of faith that invests the game with special meaning—without willing players the game is a formal system waiting to be inhabited, like a recipe for baking or choreographer's score. As designed systems, games offer certain terms of engagement, rules of play that engender stylized forms of interaction. Gamers not only follow rules, but push against them, testing the limits of the system in often unique and powerful ways. Yet it is in the moment when "pushing against" is transformed into a metareflective "questioning about" that learning truly takes place, as Squire points out in his study of Apolyton U, an informal online community of players founded to extend players' interest and learning while playing *Civilization III*.

> Here players are parsing not only the underlying rule system of the game, but the complex set of interrelationships which make up this rule system. Players dissect the game system, modify the underlying rule set for various purposes... design their own scenarios to communicate particular ideas, and run their own courses on specific ideas. (p. 185)

A study of how learning works in such communities provides an opportunity to push on existing concepts of what virtuosity means within such systems.

As Stevens, Satwicz, and McCarthy note,

> Practices—even practices like video game play that constitute a seemingly separate world—substantially acquire meanings for people not because they have this or that property (e.g., interactivity or narrative engagement), but by the ways that particular practices are in circulation with others. (p. 64)

Ito makes a similar point in her chapter discussing the history of children's software, noting that this history "emerged as an experimental media category, and its subsequent uptake by various social and political actors—including kids, parents, educators, and various commercial enterprises—is a microcosm for the social and cultural contestations surrounding new technology, children, and education" (p. 89). The story of technical and design innovation to transform the conditions of learning and play is shared as a cautionary tale about the difficulties of reforming existing social and cultural structures even with the best of intentions and innovative new technologies.

Similarly, despite the range of perspectives offered, there is an implicit assumption carried on every page of this volume of a need to identify the kinds of questions not yet asked, the kinds of research not yet done—the failings, in other words—of the current approach to a field that is only now beginning to take shape. With regard to this point, there are a number of simple, yet often overlooked premises that have shaped the volume as a whole. I list them in abbreviated form here by way of quick introduction:

- Gaming can include interaction with nondigital media. While video games dominate the discourse around game-based learning, many qualities of games as learning systems are present in nondigital games as well, and many games take both digital and nondigital forms. Play across media is one way games are mobilized within everyday activity.[24]
- The relationship between games and learning has a history that predates the advent of modern video games, including a rich history in the design of children's software.
- Learning *about* games and learning *with* games take place simultaneously. One cannot learn about or from games without engaging in their play.
- There is no "one" game: the individual, social, and cultural motivations of any player affect what is experienced through play, and no two players ever experience the "same" game. This creates a challenge for those looking to games to provide a standardized context for learning.
- All play means something: games, like other forms of media, are systems of meaning that are read, interpreted, and performed by players.
- Players determine how they learn. The productivity of gaming environments lies in the fact that kids among themselves are free to figure out and create learning and teaching arrangements that work for them. So while it is important to understand how the qualities of games themselves support learning, it is equally critical to address how players take on active roles in determining how, when, and why they learn.

Through an emphasis on gaming-as-ecology I pushed the authors to explore the design and behavior of games *as systems* in which young people participate as gamers, producers, and learners. This systemic bias comes from my own status as a game designer who has theorized games in this way, and represents just one of many possible approaches. I acknowledge that there are limitations to this perspective, as there are with any that might be used. Similarly, while I tried to include as broad a range of topics as possible, there are obvious holes. Nowhere in the volume is there a chapter explicitly on video games and violence, nor one on *World of Warcraft* or *The Sims*, each representative of topics popular among the media and game scholars more generally. It is because of their popularity, in fact, that I decided to forgo their inclusion, in favor of less present voices and games. The historical time line included at the end of the volume gives an overview of the range of games referenced throughout; a great deal of ground was covered within the limitations of the series' guidelines.

In addition, because the MacArthur series was conceived as a set of six related volumes, it was important to ensure that video games were represented in volumes outside of this one. Any argument made here to support a gaming ecology would be weakened if work on gaming were exclusive to the "video game" volume. Happily, chapters like Douglas Thomas's on *Diablo II* and the crafting of transnational identity and Henry Lowood's on the political uses of machinima, for example, enrich their respective volumes.[25] This collection is certainly stronger for their parallel engagement.

Having kept each of these concerns in mind, I did my best to create a volume that supported complementary and contradictory perspectives without the weight of too much conceptual prejudice. In so doing, I hope the collection brings a more sophisticated and informed awareness of the meaning, significance, and practicalities of gaming in young people's lives. This awareness does not presuppose that all effects are positive, nor does it assume that no challenges exist in transforming this knowledge into practical strategies. As Ito notes, "the problem of 'using games to make learning fun' cannot be addressed simply as a research or software design problem. Although . . . we may recognize the learning potential of games, this recognition alone does not change the structural conditions that insist on the bifurcation between entertainment and education and correlate only academic content with educational success" (p. 114). The challenges of overcoming these conditions are many and deep. I repeat *the challenges are many and deep.* It does posit, however, that gaming represents an ecology that is tangled up in a range of other ecologies—social, technological, economic, political—and that learning how to activate gaming as one node within a larger network holds promise for those willing to engage.

Litmus Test

I once saw game designer Will Wright give a talk in which he described two key moments that would occur during the demonstration of a new game with a group of players, if the game was well designed. He looked for these moments for they helped him to assess a game's ability to engage players. Key moment Number One comes when a player unconsciously reaches for the game controller or mouse and asks, "Can I try?" This request reveals several things: the player is excited by the game and can't wait to try it (the sooner this happens in the demo, the better!); the player understands what to do; and the player also feels confident in his or her ability to play. This last point is critical, for a player who lacks confidence will rarely choose to play, in the same way that a student who lacks confidence in his or her ability to read will tend to shy away from reading, and most certainly will refrain from demonstrating that ability in front of others. Key moment Number One requires *clarity* on the part of design.

Several authors in the volume address key moment Number One quite explicitly. Joseph's "Why Johnny Can't Fly" explores the implications of gaming within a youth development framework, arguing that the power of games to create numerous "Can I try?" moments is one reason his program, Global Kids, has seen success with gaming as a trigger for learning. Stevens, Satwicz, and McCarthy look at the range of kid-created learning arrangements that naturally embed support for such moments within a peer group, extending the design of the game to include the design of the environment in which it is played. And Pitaru, with his focus on allowing kids to act on their own ideas through independent or mediated play, notes that games do so in a way that improves a sense of self-reliance and self-esteem. In his case study of *Tetris*, he frames the question of "Can I try?" as a conduit for social inclusion. As Kate, an Occupational Therapist writes, "Even when a kid is playing a game at home, he's actually participating indirectly with a social activity because that's what they'll be talking about tomorrow morning—eventually they will sit in front of the game together, eventually the kid will be able to show what he's achieved through practice."[26] Thus "Can I try" is not only a marker of design success, but one of learning too.

Key moment Number Two arrives the moment a player turns to ask, "Can I save it?" This request records the moment that the player feels *invested* in the experience. Not only does he or she feel like the time spent playing is both valuable and meaningful, but he or she is anticipating playing again. Key moment Number Two can bring tears of joy to designers' eyes, for it means they have crafted an experience over which the player feels ownership. This sense of *productive* agency is a quality discussed by several authors within this volume—Gee, Ondrejka, Squire, and Joseph among them—as critical to gaming. Gee, for example, writes that

> From a learning perspective, what is important about video games is not interactivity per se, but the fact that in many games players come to feel a sense of agency or ownership. . . . In good games, players feel that their actions and decisions—and not just the designers' actions and decisions—cocreate the world they are in and shape the experiences they are having. Their choices matter. What they do matters. (p. 35)

Much of this material is covered in other volumes in the series, so I won't duplicate it here, but what is clear is that—for this generation of kids—gaming as a productive literacy drives feelings of personal agency, affecting both life and thought. As Everett and Watkins posit, "empowering young people on the social and economic margins to create content not only diversifies what content they consume; it also holds the promise of expanding how they learn and reproduce race for public consumption for generations to come" (p. 160). What matters a great deal within this model of agency is the network of social creation and critical reflection it offers, and the community of collaboration, which results. Key moments One and Two are requirements of any good learning system, digital or otherwise. As a teacher I often measure the quality of my own instruction within this framework. Key moment Number Two requires *depth* on the part of design.

Although I only remember Will defining two key moments, I believe there is another equally important one, which grows out of the context of gaming as a socially embedded practice. Key moment Number Three occurs when a player turns to another and asks, "Want me to show you?" This form of learning may take place on a micro- or macroscale—one player to another or one player to thousands—but in each case there is an implicit understanding of a player's desire to teach another. Pitaru describes a scene between two wheelchair-bound adolescents playing a modified version of *Tetris* together:

> Jonah had never played the game before, and Eric started explaining it to him. We did not intervene. This mentorship went on for over thirty minutes, with a growing sense of excitement. With every shape that fell into place Jonah became more visibly excited—occasionally turning around to us with a huge smile but mostly laughing audibly at the screen, at times shouting—*"I love this!"* Eric, who picked up on Jonah's joy, became even more motivated to provide Jonah with strategies. Despite the fact that it took Jonah a considerable amount of effort and time to operate the buttons, not once did Eric take over the controls. (p. 81)

Key moment Number Three requires support of *reflection* and *interpretation* on the part of designers.

And there is a fourth key moment as well. One metatheme that emerges again and again across chapters is the power peer-to-peer learning affords the evolution of a knowledge system, and the range of guises in which such learning is currently cloaked. Ondrejka points to moment Number Three's logical counterpart in his description of *Second Life*. "The 'Welcome Area' is often full of residents displaying their newest and most impressive creations. While sometimes confusing to new arrivals, these displays provide a powerful demonstration... and often lead to the most critical of questions: 'How did you do that?'" Key moments 1–4 infuse the ecology of gaming, creating feedback loops that cycle through levels of engagement, agency, mastery, expertise, and back again. Key moment Number Four requires support of a *community of practice* on the part of design.

So where does this emphasis on key moments get us? For me, these moments point to one of the most basic reasons that games are recognized, without reservation, by players as learning systems—*trust*. Players trust that the game system will teach them everything they need to know in order to play. When games don't do this, players walk away. The term *system* refers not just to the game itself, but to the entire tool-set available to the player within a gaming practice, including FAQs or strategy guides, cheats, forums, and other players in and out of multiplayer settings. Unlike a cell phone, computer operating system, or set of directions from IKEA, a game has to communicate successfully to its players how to play, or it will, in some sense, fail to exist fully. A game without players is nothing more than a rule set. Significantly, this contract of trust represents a fundamental change in the way people relate to systems, particularly technological systems. Ask someone who has not grown up with games to play a game like *Super Mario Bros.* for the DS and he or she will spend the first thirty minutes pouring over the instruction book. Gamers know this is a waste of time since reading a line like "If Mario gets hit by an enemy when he's not shell dashing, he'll lose his shell and become Super Mario" means nothing out of context, which is the play of the game. Designers of cell phones, operating systems, and new learning spaces would do well to learn from games. When the stakes are so high, a system can't afford not to teach.

Games invite learning through a reputation based on trust, which is being extended into kids' attitudes toward technology more generally. Betty Hayes's work around games as trajectories of IT expertise demonstrates that games can become pathways for players toward an interest in computer science and the mastery of skills in programming.[27] The efforts to engage more girls in the field of Computer Science, for example, have often involved the use of games—or game technology—to do so.[28] Yet, if it is important to try to grasp the impact and implications of games for a generation of kids that considers them a second skin, it is critical to understand better how players come to games in the first place, and the different pathways they take once games become a part of their lives. Technology may be one of those pathways as the distinction between technological spaces and gaming spaces continues to erode. What might be others?

Games are currently used by players/teachers/parents in many different ways. Games can function as doorways into specific content, offer an introduction to a specific skill set (learning probability by playing *Dungeons & Dragons*, for example), or operate as a node within a larger learning system, as is the case in science museums or libraries. Games can be used to occasion family interaction or to escape from the social fold. Squire's work with *Civilization III* suggests that many kids use games as gateways toward the acquisition of new interests. Stevens, Satwicz, and McCarthy suggest that games offer kids pathways toward professional identities. But as both Everett and Watkins and Pitaru show, entry into a broad ecology of gaming is never a given. Many barriers to entry exist. As Nichole Pinkard notes:

> Pathways into gaming is one question that I have been pondering lately as I attempt to figure out the role of game playing in our Digital Youth Afterschool Program. Our program serves a 99 percent African American audience of 6th through 9th graders who each have a laptop computer. I have been struck by the lack of MMOG game playing by our kids. Our kids play Xbox, Sega and Playstation but for the most part they use their laptops to create movies and music, to engage in social networking sites such as

MySpace, Tagged or view videos on YouTube. The students that play MMOGs such as *World of Warcraft*, are few and far between. What accounts for this reality especially in situations where the digital divide in relationship to access has been addressed? I hypothesize that our kids have not taken up MMOGs because they are not surrounded by peers or mentors who play MMOGs and can support them in their play.[29]

Access to a network of both peers and mentors who can model what it might mean to participate in a gaming space affects kids' entry into games and learning. In the same way that kids need teachers to model effectively the activity of "being a good student," they need access to others actively engaged in communities of practice across gaming genres.

Envisioning a future that looks to pedagogies and practices drawn from games requires finding ways to provide models and mentors for those who have not had equal access to either. Helping teachers and parents learn how to take on such roles within a gaming context is equally critical. New platforms such as the Nintendo Wii, and games that invite intergenerational play, like *Animal Crossing*, *Karaoke Revolution*, and *World of Warcraft*, point to strategies for inclusion on this level. Other "triggers" into gaming exist as well. Phil Bell, in his group's study of everyday learning as it relates to science and technology, has found several complex and fascinating social contexts that provide reinforcing conditions initiating (and sustaining) the gaming that is present.

We have a Filipino mother and her fifth grade daughter who does a fair amount of Nintendo DS gaming. We have learned that there is an extended parenting network of sorts—made up of four sets of formal godparents and a handful of additional adults that go by the honorary title of "aunt" and "uncle"—who regularly interact with the daughter on specific domains or interests. They describe it as being common in Filipino culture. One godmother helps the girl with her math learning. Another is actually her "technology godmother"—who bought her the DS and her cell phone—so that the girl can have access and learn how to use technology. This strikes us as a fascinating social organization where adults with particular interests/backgrounds/resources can serve as targeted learning brokers for the children.[30]

While it is true that many kids game, it is not true of all kids, and certainly not true of those who have been looked to in the past to lead their education. It is also true that teachers and other school personnel have very few resources for bringing gaming (and many other everyday activities) into school, and so it is very difficult to create policies that make sensible use of digital media. It is not yet clear what routes to policy change will be the most effective, but it is an area that must be engaged if any real difference is to be made.

Conclusion

If, as Jonathan Letham writes, "a time is marked not so much by ideas that are argued about as by ideas that are taken for granted," then we must look closely at what is not new, or seemingly new, in the arguments we make.[31] What is it that we purport to know? We know, for example, that play is iterative as is good learning, and that gaming is a practice rooted in reflection in action, which is also a quality of good learning. We know games are more than contexts for the production of fun and deliver just-in-time learning, the development of specialist language, and experimentation with identity and point of view. We know games are procedurally based systems embedded within robust communities of practice. We know that video games and gaming have done much to shape our understanding and misunderstanding of the post-Nintendo generation, and hold a key place in the minds of those looking to empower educators and learners. Beyond their value as entertainment media, games and game modification are currently key entry points for many young people into productive literacies, social communities, and digitally rich identities. This we know, and yet history seems slow.

It seems slow because, despite our desire to change the way kids think and learn, we are bound constantly by old tensions—tensions in distinction between the real and the virtual, in school and out of school, formal and informal, learning and teaching, knowing and being. We are bound by old thinking that says what is new here is the games, when what is new is the attitude and tools of the players. We are bound by believing that to understand the meanings of game play we can simply look at the rules when we, in fact, need to look at players' performance and understand *their* understandings of them.[32]

Increasingly, we are bound by a failure to see that a game is not a commodity but a *gift*, a thing not gotten by our own efforts, but something given and received freely. This is not to say that no money is exchanged nor effort exerted, but rather that the game defines itself not by this transaction, but by the contract it establishes with players when they accept its rule set and enter into the space of play. We see players take on the burden of learning so easily; a game makes a connection. But it, like a gift, has demands too, for its giving is not unconditional. A game demands that something be given back, that players do their very best to receive increasing levels of challenge and to succeed. A game desires to be played, to be shared, to be critiqued. It demands that players compete, exploit any weakness, and teach others how to do the same. A game demands, finally, that it be beaten, so that it may be given as a gift to another. It is here, then, in the name of a gift, that games will help us change.

The gift of this volume is in the many questions it leaves unanswered, providing new pathways for work in the field.

a. In what ways are games and gaming shaping kids' lives? How are they shaping, misshaping, or transforming kids' approach to learning?

b. What forms of knowledge, literacy, and social organization are being supported by a broad ecology of gaming?

c. What forms of learning do we see emerging from the specific qualities of games (i.e., their status as play experiences, procedural systems, interactive and visual systems, etc.)? Which forms are emerging from the qualities, characteristics, and social practices of digital media more generally? And which from players' status as kids?

d. Are video games presenting new pedagogies to be explored and developed? Are video games employing existing pedagogy, but in an unfamiliar context? Are video games transforming or reinterpreting old pedagogies into new forms?

e. What strategies have we missed that might validate, exemplify, or discount connections between video games and learning? Is there a fundamental difference, for example, in the way kids game? If so, what are those differences, and why do they matter to a larger discussion around games and learning?

Notes

1. Jonathan Letham, The Ecstasy of Influence, *Harper's Magazine* (February 2007), 59–71.

2. Jean Piaget, *The Moral Judgment of the Child* (New York: Free Press, 1966).

3. B. V. Bowden, ed., *Digital Computers Applied to Games, of Faster than Thought* (London: Pitman, 1953).

4. Johan Huizinga, *Homo Ludens: A Study of the Play Element in Culture* (Boston: Beacon Press, 1971).

5. Alexander Mood and R. D. Specht, *Gaming as a Technique of Analysis*, Paper 579 (Santa Monica, CA: Rand Corporation, 1954).

6. Ibid., 32.

7. Katie Salen, ed., *Everywhere Now: Kids, Games, and Learning*, Online dialogue, 2006.

8. Katie Salen, Gaming Literacies: What Kids Learn Through Design, *Journal of Educational Multimedia and Hypermedia (JEMH)* 16, no. 3 (2003): 301–22.

9. John Bransford, Ann Brown, and Rodney Cocking, eds., *How People Learn: Brain, Mind, Experience, and School* (Washington, DC: National Academy Press, 2000).

10. Mizuko Ito, Mobilizing the Imagination in Everyday Play: The Case of Japanese Media Mixes, in *International Handbook of Children, Media, and Culture*, eds. Sonia Livingstone and Kirsten Drotner, forthcoming.

11. Herbert Simon, Observations on the Sciences of Science Learning, *Journal of Applied Developmental Psychology* 21, no. 1 (January 2000): 115–21.

12. Colin Lankshear, Michele Knobel, Chris Bigum, and Michael Peters, eds., *A New Literacies Sampler* (New York: Peter Lang, 2007); Rebecca Black, Online Fanfiction: What Technology and Popular Culture Can Teach Us About Writing and Literacy Instruction, *New Horizons for Learning Online Journal* 11, no. 2 (Spring 2005). http://www.newhorizons.org/strategies/literacy/black.htm. Accessed February 11, 2007.

13. Salen, Gaming Literacies, 47.

14. Henry Jenkins, *Convergence Culture: Where Old and New Media Collide* (New York: New York University Press, 2006).

15. Kurt Squire, Open-Ended Video Games: A Model for Developing Learning for the Interactive Age, in *The Ecology of Games: Connecting Youth, Games, and Learning*, ed. Katie Salen (Cambridge, MA: The MIT Press, 2007), 167–198.

16. Jenkins, *Convergence Culture*, 245.

17. Constance Steinkuhler, Cognition and Learning in Massively Multiplayer Online Games, A Critical Approach (Ph.D. diss., University of Wisconsin–Madison, 2005), 82.

18. See http://www.ed.gov/nclb. Accessed March 7, 2007.

19. Bertram Bruce, Diversity and Critical Social Engagement: How Changing Technologies Enable New Modes of Literacy in Changing Circumstances, in *Adolescents and Literacies in a Digital World*, ed. Donna Alvermann (New York: Peter Lang, 2002), x. Several good articles include: Cindy Hmelo, Douglas Holton, and Janet Kolodner, Designing to Learn About Complex Systems, *The Journal of the Learning Sciences* 9, no. 3 (2000): 247–98; and Ann Brown, Design Experiments: Theoretical and Methodological Challenges in Creating Complex Interventions in Classroom Settings, *The Journal of the Learning Sciences* 2, no. 2 (1992): 141–78.

20. James Paul Gee, *Games and Learning: Issues, Perils, and Potentials: A Report to the Spencer Foundation*, Spencer Foundation Report, 2006.

21. Ito, Mobilizing the Imagination in Everyday Play.

22. Gee, *Games and Learning*; Salen, Gaming Literacies.

23. Huizinga, *Homo Ludens.*

24. Ito, Mobilizing the Imagination in Everyday Play.

25. Douglas Thomas, KPK, Inc.: Place, Nation, and Emergent Culture in Online Games, in *Learning Race and Ethnicity: Youth and Digital Media,* ed. Anna Everett (Cambridge, MA: The MIT Press, 2007); Henry Lowood, Found Technology: Players as Innovators in the Making of Machinima, in *Digital Youth, Innovation, and the Unexpected,* ed. Tara McPherson (Cambridge, MA: The MIT Press, 2007).

26. Amit Pitaru, E Is for Everyone: The Case for Inclusive Game Design, in *The Ecology of Games: Connecting Youth, Games, and Learning,* ed. Katie Salen (Cambridge, MA: The MIT Press, 2007), 67–86.

27. Elizabeth Hayes, Becoming a (Virtual) Skateboarder: Communities of Practice and the Design of E-Learning, Under review for publication in *Adult Education Quarterly.*

28. See the Alice project (www.alice.org) from Carnegie Mellon, as well as Rapunsel (www.rapunsel.org) from Hunter College and NYU.

29. Salen, Everywhere Now, 94.

30. Ibid., 96.

31. Letham, The Ecstasy of Influence, 63.

32. Squire, Open-Ended Video Games.

PART I: LEARNING ECOLOGIES

Learning and Games

James Paul Gee

Arizona State University, Literary Studies

Experience and Learning

In this chapter, I want to argue that good video games recruit good learning and that a game's design is inherently connected to designing good learning for players.[1] Good game design has a lot to teach us about good learning, and contemporary learning theory has something to teach us about how to design even better and deeper games. Let's start with contemporary learning theory.[2] When today's learning scientists talk about the mind, it sometimes seems as if they are talking about video games. Earlier learning theory argued that the mind works like a calculating device, something like a digital computer. On this view, humans think and learn by manipulating abstract symbols via logiclike rules. Newer work, however, argues that people primarily think and learn through *experiences* they have had, not through abstract calculations and generalizations.[3] People store these experiences in memory—and human long-term memory is now viewed as nearly limitless—and use them to run simulations in their minds to prepare for problem solving in new situations. These simulations help them to form hypotheses about how to proceed in the new situation based on past experiences.

However, things are not quite that simple. There are conditions experiences need to meet in order to be truly useful for learning.[4] Since I will later argue that video games offer players experiences and recruit learning as a form of pleasure and mastery, I will argue as well that these conditions are properties of a well-designed game.

First, experiences are most useful for future problem solving if the experience is structured by specific goals. Humans store their experiences best in terms of goals, and how these goals did or did not work out.

Second, for experiences to be useful for future problem solving, they have to be interpreted. Interpreting experience means thinking—in action and after action—about how our goals relate to our reasoning in the situation. It means, as well, extracting lessons learned and anticipating when and where those lessons might be useful.

Third, people learn best from their experiences when they get immediate feedback during those experiences so that they can recognize and assess their errors and see where their expectations have failed. It is important too that they are encouraged to explain their errors and why their expectations failed, along with what they could have done differently.

Fourth, learners need ample opportunities to apply their previous experiences—as interpreted—to similar new situations, so they can "debug" and improve their interpretations of these experiences, gradually generalizing them beyond specific contexts.

Fifth, learners need to learn from the interpreted experiences and explanations of other people, including both peers and more expert people. Social interaction, discussion, and sharing with peers, as well as mentoring from others who are more advanced, are important. Debriefing after an experience—that is, talking about why and how things worked in the accomplishment of goals—is important. Mentoring is best done through dialogue, modeling, worked examples, and certain forms of overt instruction, often "just in time" (when the learner can use it) or "on demand" (when the learner is ready).

One way to look at what is going on here is this: When the above conditions are met, people's experiences are organized in memory in such a way that they can draw on those experiences as from a data bank, building simulations in their minds that allow them to prepare for action.[5] They can test out things in their minds before they act, and they can adjust their predictions after they have acted and gotten feedback. They can play various roles in their own simulations, seeing how various goals might be accomplished, just like a gamer playing a video game. The simulations we humans run—and there are various neural accounts of how this works[6]—are composites of our interpreted experiences built to prepare us to predict, act, and assess. Interpreted experiences are the engine from which we build simulations.

A Piece of Research: Action, Simulation, and Reading

One interesting line of research that exemplifies these points is Glenberg et al.[7] This study describes an experiment in which young children read a passage and manipulate plastic figures so that they can portray the actions and relationships in the passage. By manipulating the figures, the children get a structured, embodied experience with a clear goal (portray the action in the text). After some practice doing this, the children were asked to simply imagine manipulating the figures. This is a request to engage in simulation in their heads. As a posttest, the children read a final passage without any prompting.

Children who completed the sequence of embodied experience then simulation were better at remembering and drawing inferences about the new passage, as compared to children who received no training. They were better as well, compared to children who were instructed to only imagine the passage. And, most interestingly, they were better compared to children who manipulated the figures without the intermediate instructions to imagine manipulating. Encouraging simulation through the initial use of physical enactment helped the children learn a new reading comprehension strategy, namely a strategy whereby they called on their experiences in the world to build simulations for understanding a text in specific ways.

Social Identity and Learning

Modern learning theory tends to stress the social and cultural more than I have done so far.[8] The reason for this is that the elements of good learning experiences—namely goals, interpretations, practice, explanations, debriefing, and feedback—have to come from someplace. In fact, they usually flow from participation in, or apprenticeship to, a social group, or what are sometimes called "communities of practice"[9] or affiliation groups.[10] For instance, I am a bird-watcher and I have lots of experience looking for birds. But my experiences in this domain have been greatly shaped by other people and institutions devoted to birds and bird watching.

What we might call a "social identity" is crucial for learning. For example, consider learning to be a SWAT team member. The sorts of goals one should have in a given situation; the ways in which one should interpret and assess one's experiences in those situations; the sorts of feedback one should receive and react to; the ways in which one uses specific tools and technologies—all of these flow from the values, established practices, knowledge, and skills of experienced SWAT team members. They all flow from the identity of being or seeking to become such a person.

What is true of being a SWAT team member is equally true of being a bird-watcher, teacher, carpenter, elementary school student, scientist, community activist, soccer player, gang member, or anything else. Social groups exist to induct newcomers into distinctive experiences, and ways of interpreting and using those experiences, for achieving goals and solving problems. Today, of course, social groups can engage in interactions at a distance via the Internet and other technological devices, so the role of face-to-face interaction is, in many cases, changing, and new forms of social organization around identity are emerging.[11]

Good learning requires participation—however vicarious—in some social group that helps learners understand and make sense of their experience in certain ways. It helps them understand the nature and purpose of the goals, interpretations, practices, explanations, debriefing, and feedback that are integral to learning.

Having discussed good learning, I now turn to good game design, arguing that game design is also design for good learning, since good games are, at their heart, learning and problem-solving experiences.

Game Design

What's a video game? In many cases—for example, in the case of games like *SWAT4*, *Deus Ex*, *Half Life*, or *Chibi Robo*—a video game is a set of experiences a player participates in from a particular perspective, namely the perspective of the character or characters the player controls. Of course, not all games offer the player an avatar; although this fact is important, I will deal with it later, where we will see that having an avatar is just one way of achieving "microcontrol," one of the defining features of video games. For the moment, I will stick with games played from a first- or third-person perspective.

Video games like those I have just mentioned are designed to set up certain goals for players, but often leave players free to achieve these goals in their own ways. The game may also allow players to construct their own goals, but only within the rule-space designed into the game (e.g., you can interact with enemies in different ways in *Thief*, but robust hand-to-hand combat is not one of them). Level design ensures that players get lots of practice applying what they have learned earlier both in similar situations (within a level) and in somewhat less similar situations (across levels). Feedback is given moment by moment, and often summarily at the end of a level or in boss battles, which require players to integrate many of the separate skills they have picked up in prior battles with lesser enemies. Within such a structure, a number of our learning conditions are met as a matter of the basic design of the game.

Such games also encourage players to interpret their experiences in certain ways and to seek explanations for their errors and expectation failures. Such encouragement works through in-game features like the increasing degrees of difficulty that a player faces as the levels of a game advance, or when facing a boss that requires rethinking what one has already learned. However, it is precisely here that talking about "games"—and not "gaming" as a social practice—falls short. A good deal of reflection and interpretation stems from the social settings and practices within which games are situated.

Reflection and interpretation are encouraged, not just through in-game design features, but also through socially shared practices like FAQs and strategy guides, cheats, forums, and other players (in and out of multiplayer settings). Gamers often organize themselves into communities of practice that create social identities with distinctive ways of talking, interacting, interpreting experiences, and applying values, knowledge, and skill to achieve goals and solve problems. This is a crucial point for those who wish to make so-called serious games: to gain these sorts of desired learning effects will often require as much care about the social system (the learning system) in which the game is placed as the in-game design itself.

Because this last point is crucial, let me distinguish between what I will call the *game*, with a little *g*, and the *Game*, with a big *G*.[12] The "game" is the software in the box and all the elements of in-game design. The "Game" is the social setting into which the game is placed, all the interactions that go on around the game. I will write "game/Game" when I mean both together.

Both games and Games are crucial for good learning and, I would argue, good game design. But let me first talk directly about game design (in-game design), not Game design (the design of the interactions around the game). Video games offer people experiences in a virtual world (which, we will see below, is linked tightly to the real world), and they use learning, problem solving, and mastery for engagement and pleasure. It should be noted that humans and other primates find learning and mastery deeply, even biologically, pleasurable under the right conditions, though often not the ones they face in school.[13] Thus, I want to argue that game design is not accidentally related to learning, but rather that learning is integral to it. Game design is applied learning theory, and good game designers have discovered important principles of learning without needing to be or become academic learning theorists.

The Situated Learning Matrix

One way in which game design and modern learning theory come together is in what I will call the "Situated Learning Matrix." First, consider that any learning experience has some *content*, that is, some facts, principles, information, and skills that need to be mastered. So the question immediately arises as to how this content ought to be taught? Should it be the main focus of the learning and taught quite directly? Or should the content be subordinated to something else and taught via that "something else"? Schools usually opt for the former approach, games for the latter. Modern learning theory suggests the game approach is the better one.[14]

One version of the game approach is what I call the Situated Learning Matrix. To see what I mean by this term, let's take a concrete case, the game *SWAT4*. There is a lot of content to be mastered in learning to be a SWAT team member, some of which is embedded in *SWAT4*. This content involves things like how a team should form up to enter a room safely, where to position oneself in an unsafe environment, how to subdue people with guns without killing them, and facts about the range and firing power of specific weapons, ammunition, grenades, and much else.

But the game does not start with or focus on this content, save for a tutorial that teaches just enough of it so that players can learn the rest by playing within the Situated Learning Matrix, which is the game itself. Rather, the game focuses first and foremost on an *identity*, that is, being a SWAT team member. What do I mean by calling this an "identity"? I mean a "way of being in the world" that is integrally connected to two things: first, characteristic *goals*, namely—in this case—goals of the sort a SWAT team characteristically has; and second, characteristic *norms* (composed of rules or principles or guidelines) by which to act and evaluate one's actions—in this case, these norms are those adopted by SWAT teams.

In some games—and this is true of *SWAT4*—the norms amount, in part, also to a value system, even a moral system (e.g., Don't shoot people, even if they have guns, until you have warned them you are a policeman). Without such norms, one does not know how to act and how to evaluate the results of one's actions as good or bad, acceptable or not. Of course, norms and goals are closely related in that the norms guide how we act on our goals and assess those attempts. In a game like *SWAT4*, I am who I am (a SWAT team member) because I have certain sorts of goals and follow certain norms and values that cause me to see the world, respond to the world, and act on the world in certain ways.

To accomplish goals within norms and values, the player/learner must master a certain set of skills, facts, principles, and procedures—must gain certain sorts of *content* knowledge. However, in a game like *SWAT4*, players are not left all alone to accomplish this content mastery. Rather, they are given various tools and technologies that fit particularly well with their goals and norms, and that help them master the content by using these tools and technologies in active problem-solving contexts. These tools and technologies mediate between—help explicate the connection between—the players' identity (goals and norms), on the one hand, and the content the player must master, on the other. The SWAT team's doorstop device (yes, it's just a little rubber doorstop) is a good example. This little tool integrally connects the team's goal of entering rooms safely and norm of doing so as nonviolently as possible, with the content knowledge that going in one door with other open doors behind you can lead to being blindsided and ambushed from behind—an ambush in which both you and innocent bystanders may be killed. Using the doorstop in specific situations enacts these connections. In turn, players have to reflect on these connections as they think of better and better ways of using the doorstop.

Let me be clear, though, what I mean by tools and technologies. I am using these terms expansively. First, in *SWAT4*, tools and technologies include types of guns, ammunition, grenades, goggles, armor, lightsticks, communication devices, doorstops, and so forth. Second, tools and technologies also include one's fellow SWAT team members—artificially intelligent nonplayer characters (NPCs)—to whom the player can issue orders and who have lots of built-in knowledge and skills to carry out those orders. This allows players initially to be more competent than they are all by themselves. (Players can perform before they are fully competent and attain competence through performance.) Further, it means that the NPCs model correct skills and knowledge for the player.

Third, tools and technologies include forms of built-in collaboration with the NPCs and, in multiplayer versions of the game, forms of collaboration, participation, and interaction with real people, at different levels of skill. These forms of collaboration go further when the player enters Web sites and chat rooms, or uses guides, as part of a community of practice built around the game. Thus, I am counting NPCs as smart tools—and real people as tools too—when players can coordinate themselves with other players' knowledge and skills.

So, tools and technologies (in all these senses) mediate the relationship between identity and content, rendering that content meaningful. I know why, for instance, I need to know about open doors behind me. This knowledge is not just a matter of isolated and irrelevant facts. It's a matter now of being and becoming a good SWAT team member. And as a player, I have the tool to connect the two—the doorstop.

But this mediation means, of course, that players always learn in specific contexts. That is, they learn through specific embodied experiences in the virtual world (the player has a bodily presence in the game through the character or characters he or she controls). And, indeed, one hears a lot these days about learning in context. However, contexts in a game like *SWAT4* are special. While they are richly detailed and specific, they are—in reality—not just any old contexts, but richly *designed problem spaces* containing problems that fall into a set of similar, but varied, challenges across the levels of the game.

Context here then means a *goal-driven problem space*. As players move through different contexts—each containing similar but varied problems—this movement helps them to interpret and, eventually, generalize their experiences. They learn to generalize—but always with appropriate customization for specific different contexts—their skills, procedures, principles, choices, and uses of information. This essentially solves the dilemma that learning in context can leave learners with knowledge that is too context-specific, but that learning out of context leaves learners with knowledge they cannot apply. Players come to see specific in-game solutions as part of more general types of approaches.

Below I give a diagrammatic representation of the Situated Learning Matrix. The Matrix has "Experience" on top, listing the conditions that render experience efficacious for learning. Good games—together with their associated Games—ensure that these conditions are met. However, in an educational context, things need to go further, since we want to be certain that we create Games (social systems) that ensure that experiences will be well interrogated in the game (the in-game play). This is where "teachers" and mentors (not necessarily official teachers in the school sense) become crucial. Such teachers and mentors help create an effective Game and game/Game combination.[15]

Situated Learning Matrix Experience: Goals, Interpretation, Feedback, Explanation, Practice, Social Interaction (Mentoring, Sharing, Debriefing)

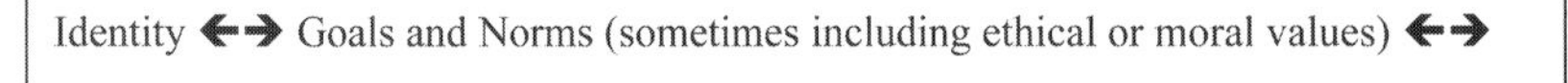

Identity ←→ Goals and Norms (sometimes including ethical or moral values) ←→ Tools and Technologies ←→ Context as Problem-Solving Space That Is One of a Set of Similar but Varied Problems ←→ Content

Why do I call this *a situated* learning matrix? Because content is rooted in experiences a person is having as part and parcel of taking on a specific identity (in terms of goals and norms stemming from a social group, like SWAT team members). Learning is situated in experience, but goal-driven, identity-focused experience.

Learning in video games—learning in terms of the Situated Learning Matrix—is not "anything goes," "just turn the learners loose to do their own thing."[16] There is a good deal of guidance in games: guidance from the game design itself, from the NPCs and the environment, from information given "just in time" and "on demand," from other players in and out of the game, and from the resources of communities of practice built up around the game.

Clearing Up Possible Misconceptions

By using *SWAT4* as my example, I may well have created a number of misconceptions. So, let me try to clear them up. All games have content, that is, facts, skills, and procedures that players must master. This content is crystal clear in *SWAT4* because the game is organized around a connection to a real-world domain. But consider a game like *Chibi Robo*. In this game, players take on the identity of a four-inch house-cleaning robot enjoined to make people happy. This identity defines and in turn flows from the goals of the game (e.g., solve problems in the house by cleaning and getting to hard-to-reach places where you can do or get something that will make people happy), and norms (e.g., you should do good, not bad, to the people and animated toys in the house; it is important to talk repeatedly to everyone; problems must be solved in a time-efficient way, since your battery—or "health"—lasts only so long). There are lots of skills and facts a player needs to master, all of them germane to being a four-inch robot, skills such as how to get to high places, and facts like falling from such high places will take a good deal off your allowable time to solve problems. And there are tools that connect your identity and these skills and facts, for example, a little rotor that you can use to soften your fall.

The same can be said of *Half-Life, Deus Ex, Civilization,* or any other such game. The skills and facts in these games are content, but usually not recognized as such unless they fall into a real-world domain like physics or SWAT teams.

Finally, using *SWAT4* as an example may lead to the conception that the Situated Learning Matrix is only germane to violence or, at least, to action-filled adventures. It can seem that content—knowledge—in a domain like science or art is much less connected to identities, goals, and values. However, ethnographic accounts of scientists learning and doing science, for instance, show this is not true.[17] And, for students in school, there is clear research that shows that content divorced from the Situated Learning Matrix is inert and unable to be applied in practice, however much the student may pass multiple choice tests.[18]

Models and Modeling

The Situated Learning Matrix leaves out one element that is crucial to both learning and games. What it leaves out is a particularly important type of knowledge-building and knowledge-transforming tool, namely "models."[19] A discussion of models also allows us to move beyond games played in the first- or third-person perspective with avatars.

I will be using the word *model* here in an extended sense from its everyday use, so let's start in familiar territory. Consider a child's model airplane. Real planes are big, complex, and dangerous. A child can safely play with the model plane, trying out things, imagining things, and learning about planes. Of course, models are always simpler than the things they model (since we use them to understand or deal with realities too complex or dangerous to deal with directly). Thus, different types of models capture different properties of the thing being modeled and allow different sorts of things to be tried out and learned. Even a child's toy plane may be more or less detailed.

Of course, model planes can be used by engineers and scientists as well. They can use the model plane in a wind tunnel, for example, to test things that are too dangerous or too expensive to do with real planes. They can make predictions based on the model and see if these procedures hold true for the real thing in real life. They can use the model to make plans about how to build a better real plane. The model plane is a tool for thought, learning, and action.

Models are just depictions of a real thing (like planes, cars, or buildings) or a system (like atomic structure, weather patterns, traffic flow, ecosystems, social systems, and so forth) that are simpler than the real thing, stressing some properties of the thing and not others. They are used for imaginative thought, learning, and action, when the real thing is too large, too complex, too expensive, or too dangerous to deal with directly.

A model plane usually resembles closely the thing it is modeling (a real plane). But models can be ranged on a continuum of how closely they resemble the things they are modeling. They can be, in this sense, more or less "abstract." One model plane may have lots of details. Another may be a simple balsa-wood wings-and-frame construction, no frills. Even more abstractly, the blueprint of the plane, on a piece of paper, is a model, useful for some purposes (e.g., planning and building) and not for others. The blueprint is a model that resembles the plane very little, but still corresponds to the real plane in a rule-governed way. It's an abstract picture.

We can go even further and consider a model of the plane represented as a chart. In the chart, each of the plane's different parts is listed in rows along the left column, with the remaining columns filled with numbers, representing degrees of stress. The intersection of a part and number would stand for the amount of stress each part is under during flight. For each part we can trace our finger along the row to find the corresponding number. This representation of the plane doesn't "look" like a plane, but is a model all the same. We can still map from pieces of the chart to pieces of the plane. The chart still represents some properties of the plane, though it offers a very abstract picture of the plane, indeed, one useful for a narrow purpose.

However, this type of model—at the very abstract end of the continuum of resemblance—shows us another important feature of models and modeling. The chart captures an invisible, relatively "deep" (that is, not so readily apparent) property of the plane, namely how parts interact with stress. Of course, we could imagine a much more user-friendly picture (model) of this property, perhaps a model plane all the parts of which are color coded (say, in degrees of red) for how much stress they must bear in flight. This is more user-friendly and it makes clear the mixture of what is readily apparent (the plane and its parts) and what is a deep (less apparent) property, namely stress on parts.

These are very basic matters. Models and modeling are basic to human play. They are basic to a great many other human enterprises as well, for example, science (a diagram of a cell), architecture (model buildings), engineering (model bridges), art (the clay figure the sculptor makes before making the real statue), video and film (storyboards), writing (outlines), cooking (recipes), travel (maps), and many more.

Models are basic to video games as well, and represent another point at which game design and the learning sciences intersect. Thinking about models brings us to the topic of how to think about different types of games. Earlier I mentioned that not all video games offer the player an avatar, but set that issue aside. There are scholars who believe that "video game" is a unitary concept, and they seek a uniform theory applicable to all video games.[20] I do not believe this. There are different types of video games, and they need to be understood in somewhat different, though linked, ways. Thinking about models in fact keys us in to two different large categories of video games (and, of course, there are still other categories). So let's look at these two different types of games.

The video games discussed thus far are simulations in which the player is inside the simulation, thanks to the presence of an avatar. And, of course, all simulations are models of what they are simulating. *World of Warcraft* simulates (models) a world of mountains, lakes, roads, buildings, creatures, and so forth that, although fantasy, is meant to resemble aspects of the real world. However, players (for the most part) pay very little attention to this modeling aspect of *World of Warcraft*, because it usually plays no important role in the game play. Rather, players concentrate on the embodied experiences of play, problem solving, and socialization that *World of Warcraft* offers. By and large, the fact that it models environments does not matter all that much to the game play, beyond providing a spatialized context in which to act.

However, sometimes in *World of Warcraft* this is not true; sometimes the modeling aspect comes to the fore. For example, when I get stuck trying to walk up the inclines and crevices of a mountain in *World of Warcraft*, I begin to think about how the game's mountain is representing (modeling) gravity and resistance in the real world. Sometimes this reflection is tinged with anger, because I realize the game does not model mountains well enough to ensure that I can climb them successfully. In other games, where one's character seems more than tall enough to jump over an obstacle, but can't, the player is well aware the model is a model and isn't working well. In games like *World of Warcraft*, the modeling aspect comes to the fore only when there are problems with being able to act in the world. Of course, models and modeling are present throughout the game, but are rarely the focus.

There are other games in which the modeling aspect of the simulation is crucial. Players in these games are having experiences, just as they are in *World of Warcraft* or *Half-Life*, but the modeling aspect is crucial at nearly all points, not just intermittently. In a game like *Civilization*, for instance, the depictions of landscapes, cities, and armies are not very realistic, not nearly as realistic as in *World of Warcraft*. For example, in *Civilization*, a small set of soldiers stands for a whole army and the landscape looks like a colorful map. However, given the nature of game play in *Civilization*, these components are clearly meant to be models of real things stressing only some of their properties (to see how game play works in *Civilization*, see videos at http://media.pc.ign.com/media/620/620513/vids_1.html). They are clearly meant to be used for quite specific purposes in the game—for example, modeling large-scale military interactions across time and space, and modeling the roles of geographical features in the historical development of different civilizations.

Models and modeling are integral to game play in *Civilization*—it's the point of the game, in one sense. Since a game like *Civilization* stresses modeling, it is not surprising that it is played with a top-down god's eye view, rather than the first-person, world-internal view of *Half-Life*. However, not all games that stress modeling as integral to game play have such a top-down view (though many do, e.g., *Zoo Tycoon*, *Rise of Nations*, and *The Sims*). A game like *SWAT4* is played with a first-person, world-internal view, and modeling is crucial to the game. The player is very aware that it matters how and why the game designers modeled the SWAT team members, their equipment, their social interactions, and the sorts of environments with which and in which they interact. This is after all a "toy" SWAT team in very much the way a model airplane is a toy. But it is more than a toy team—just as a model airplane can be more than a toy—since it models aspects of SWAT teams that are serious and interestingly complex. The game models not just objects, but behaviors as well, in support of the articulation of values. *Full Spectrum Warrior* is an example of another modeling-intensive game, like *SWAT4*, that is played from a close-in top-down perspective, much closer to the action than, say, in *Rise of Nations* or *Civilization*.

So we can distinguish between video games that stress player experiences but not modeling, and other games that, while offering experiences, stress modeling as well. Games in the first category are usually played in a first- or third-person up-close perspective, while those in the latter category can be played from such perspectives (as in *SWAT4*), but can also be played in a middle-distance top-down view (as in *Full Spectrum Warrior*) or a god's eye farther-distance top-down view (as in *Civilization* or *Rise of Nations*).

However, even in games where, at the "big picture" level, modeling is not integral to game play in terms of their overall virtual worlds—games like *World of Warcraft* or *Half-Life*—very often models appear ubiquitously *inside* the game to aid the player's problem solving. For example, most games have maps that model the terrain (and maps are pretty abstract models) and that allow players to navigate and plan. The bottom part of *World of Warcraft*'s interface screen includes a set of stats which provides an abstract model of the player's abilities and skills. Lots of games allow players to turn on and off a myriad of interface screens, which display charts, lists, and graphs depicting various aspects of game play, equipment, inventories, abilities, skills, histories, and accomplishments. In a first-person shooter, the interface displaying an inventory of all the guns a player has, their firing types, and their ammunition is a model of the game's weapon system, an abstract picture of it that is made for planning, strategizing, predicting, and problem-solving purposes.

Models inside games go further, much further. Players and player communities often build modifications of games that are models used to solve certain sorts of problems. For example, *World of Warcraft* players can download a model that displays a chart (during actual fighting) listing each player's class (e.g., Druid, Priest, Warrior, Mage, Paladin, etc.) and the amount of damage he or she is doing in a group raid inside a dungeon. This chart can be used to check—publicly—that each player is holding up his or her end of the group task (so Warriors better be doing lots of damage and healing Priests better not be—they had better be concentrating on healing rather than attacking). This is one of several models (almost all of them made by players) that help players solve a very real world problem, namely the problem of individuals attempting to take a free ride in a group or attempting to hide their lack of skill.

Models and modeling reach a new pitch in games like *Tony Hawk's Pro Skater 4* or *Tony Hawk's Underground*. First, in these cases, the whole game is a model of the practices and culture of skateboarders. Within that larger model, there are a myriad of models of boards, dress styles, tricks, and environments. However, players can readily design their own skaters, clothes, boards, tricks, points for tricks, and skate parks. That is, they can build their own models. When they build a model skate park, they interact with a set of more abstract models of environments (screens made up of grids and rotatable objects) that help them build the more specific and realistic-looking model skate park they want (like a toy plane). Indeed, as skating styles in the real world change, the models in the game and those made by players change in turn, each iteration trying to capture things that are seen by players as important or essential, all the while balancing a variety or criteria about fidelity to different things and systems. This is modeling with a vengeance. Here modeling is integral to game play at all levels.

So why, in the end, are models and modeling important to learning? Because while people learn from their interpreted experiences—as we have argued above—models and modeling allow specific aspects of experience to be interrogated and used for problem solving in ways that lead from concreteness to abstraction.[21] This is not the only way abstraction grows—we have already seen through several game examples that it grows as well from comparing and contrasting multiple experiences. But modeling is an important way to interrogate and generalize from experience. This is readily apparent in a game like *Tony Hawk's Underground*. Surely, players of this game, if they have made skate parks and shared them, have both an embodied experiential understanding of skating (as least as an in-game simulated activity) and a more abstract take on properties and features of skating and skate parks. Indeed, these two forms of understanding constantly interact with and feed off of each other.

On the other hand, why are models and modeling important to a game's design? Because in-game models are tools to facilitate, enrich, and deepen the problem solving the game designer is building. And because games like *Civilization*, *SWAT4*, *The Sims*, and *Tony Hawk's Underground*—games that stress modeling even at the larger level of the game-play experience—allow for a quite deep form of play. This is play-connected in complicated ways with the real world, though this is not to say, of course, that such games are necessarily more "fun" than other games. One can take note here as well of the beautiful video game *Okami* that models, in a myriad of ways, Japanese spiritual, cultural, and historical perspectives on the relationship between drawing (e.g., in writing in characters) and the world.

Games and Simulations: Microcontrol and Empathy for a Complex System

Simulations are regularly used at the cutting edge of science, especially to study complex systems—things like weather systems, atoms, cells, or the rise and fall of civilizations. This raises the question of what differences exist between simulations and video games. There are two key differences: one is that most (but not all) video games have a win state, and the other is that gamers don't just run a simulation, they microcontrol elements inside the simulation (e.g., an avatar in *Doom*, squads in *Full Spectrum Warrior*, armies and cities in *Rise of Nations*, and shapes and movement in *Tetris*).

Microcontrol has well-known cognitive effects.[22] Humans feel their bodies extend only so far as the space over which they have small-scale control, which for most of us is a space quite close to the body. Blind people have the feeling that their bodies extend out to the end of their canes, since the cane extends their space of small-scale control. When people use webcams to water plants in a far away place via the Internet, they feel that their bodies have extended into space—a novel feeling for humans, since it is one unavailable for most of human history. Video games also offer humans a new experience in history, namely microcontrol over objects in a virtual space. This gives us the feeling that our bodies and minds have extended into this virtual space and that the spaces of the real and the virtual are joined.

While scientists often do not have such microcontrol over elements in their simulations and graphs, it turns out that many scientists often talk and think *as if* they were inside not only the simulations they build, but even the graphs they draw and the models they build. They do this to gain a deeper feel for how variables are interacting in the system. For example, consider the following remark from a physicist talking to other physicists while looking and pointing to a graph (an abstract model) on a blackboard:[23] (Points to the right side of the diagram) "When (moves finger to left) I come down (moves finger to right) I'm in (moves finger to left) the domain state."[24]

Notice the "you's" and "I's." The scientist talks and acts as if he and his colleagues are moving their bodies not only inside the graph, but inside the complex system it represents as well. This is much like gamers who say "I died" in *Doom* or "my army was crushed" in *Rise of Nations*.

In science education too, research shows that students often find it helpful to identify with individual elements in a model, and then view phenomena from the perspective of this element. For example, Wilensky and Reisman[25] mention that a student building a model to understand how fireflies synchronized their light patterns found it useful to try to "think like" an individual firefly in the model.

Video games, under the right circumstances, may well be able to encourage (and actually help players to enact) an "attitude" or "stance" similar to the one taken by scientists studying complex systems. This stance involves a sort of "embodied empathy for a complex system" wherein a person seeks to enter imaginatively into a system, all the while seeing and thinking of it as a system, rather than as a group of local or random events. This does, indeed, seem similar to the stance players take when they play as Garrett in a game like *Thief* and seek to figure out the rule system that underlies the virtual world through which Garrett (and they) move. We can go on to ask whether video games could create such empathy for the sorts of complex systems relevant to academic and other domains outside of entertainment (e.g., urban planning, space exploration, or global cooperation among competing societies).

Distributed Intelligence and Cross-Functional Teams

The modern learning sciences have stressed the ways in which human thinking and learning go beyond the processes going on inside people's heads. One way in which they have done this is to focus on "distributed cognition" or "distributed knowledge."[26] These terms are meant to describe the ways in which people can act smarter when they combine or integrate their own individual knowledge with knowledge that is built into tools, technologies, environments, or other people. We have already seen in the discussion of *SWAT4* how some video games can distribute intelligence between the player and artificially intelligent virtual characters.

By distributing knowledge and skills between the virtual characters and the real-world player, a game like *SWAT4* guides and supports the player through the knowledge built into the virtual policemen. This off-loads some of the cognitive burden from the learner, placing it in smart tools (the virtual policemen) that can do more than the learner is currently capable of doing by him- or herself. It allows the player to begin to act, with some degree of effectiveness, before being really competent: "performance before competence."[27] The player thereby eventually comes to gain competence through trial, error, and feedback. Of course, when real people are involved in multiplayer games, this becomes a condition for a well-functioning team that can apprentice new members and guide new learning for each. This suggests an important question: whether and how we could model other "professions"—scientists, doctors, government officials, urban planners, political activists—and distribute their knowledge and skills as a deep form of value-laden learning. Learners could in turn compare and contrast different value systems as they play different games. Shaffer's[28] "epistemic games"—games which model sorts of professional practices—already give us a good indication that even young learners, through video games embedded inside a well-organized curriculum, can be inducted into professional practices as a form of value-laden deep learning that transfers to school-based skills and conceptual understandings.

Another way in which the modern learning sciences have stressed that thinking and learning go beyond individuals' isolated thought processes is in regard to the social and collaborative nature of learning and knowledge building. Indeed, researchers of the modern workplace have become intensely interested in how people can work together as a group to be and act smarter than any individual in the group.[29] This is really a question of how people can distribute knowledge and learning between themselves, requiring them to move beyond tools and technologies to include as well the organization of the group itself as a tool to leverage deep learning and high performance.

One form of group organization has played a major role in modern workplaces, so-called cross-functional teams.[30] They have also played a major role in activist groups like Greens, advocating for particular causes. On such teams, each member must have deep expertise in a specific area, that is, specialized knowledge (their "function"). At the same time, each team member must have a good knowledge of each other team member's special skills, both so that he or she can integrate with that person smoothly in practice and so that he or she can carry out some of the team member's functions even if one or another team member is missing (crossing functions). That is, each team member must have extensive knowledge in addition to intensive knowledge.

One of the fascinating things about modern video gaming is that game designers have discovered that people find great pleasure, excitement, and fun in organizing themselves into cross-functional teams, however boring the concept sounds at an institutional level. Though such teams have given rise to high stress and a lot of tensions in workplaces, millions play on such teams for pleasure in games like *World of Warcraft*.

In *World of Warcraft*, a hunting group might be composed of a Hunter, Warrior, Druid, Mage, and Priest. Each of these types of characters has quite different skills and plays the game in a different way. Each group member must learn to be good at his or her special skills and also learn to integrate these skills as a team member into the performance of the group as a whole. Each team member must also share some common knowledge about the game and game play with all the other members of the group—including some understanding of the specialist skills of other player types—in order to achieve a successful integration. So each member of the group must have specialist knowledge (intensive knowledge) and general common knowledge (extensive knowledge), including knowledge of the other member's functions.

Anyone who has played *World of Warcraft* knows that a good many groups have solved a major social problem that crops up in business and education: the free-rider problem—that is, the problem that, in groups, individuals can try to take a free ride by letting all the others do the work. Free riders in a *World of Warcraft* dungeon quest get noticed, castigated, and removed quickly. There are readily available information tools (as we saw above) that can display quite clearly what contribution each member of the group is making, and each group member is well aware of whether the others are effectively using their specialized skills to good purpose for the group as a whole. They know this, not just because of the information available to them through such tools, but also because they have "cross-functional" understandings learned through play. Many a Druid, for instance, has also played as a Priest or Mage and knows what Priests or Mages ought to be doing.

The workings of *World of Warcraft* groups can get to be pretty stressful. Groups can often have very high performance expectations, which they enforce in a range of ways (e.g., by not grouping with someone who has misbehaved in the past). The game itself sets problems for small groups and larger one (raids) that can sometimes be extremely demanding in terms of the need for tight organization, the expression of specific and well-executed individual skills, and the quick and smooth integration of those skills.[31] While it doesn't sound like much fun, millions pay to do it.

At a more general level, widely popular games like *World of Warcraft* and *GuildWars* have made a game out of social planning and organization itself. For example, in *World of Warcraft*, small groups organize into larger groups to go on challenging raids in dungeons. Each large group is composed of five-person cross-functional teams, and each of these teams has to function well as a team while also integrating quickly and smoothly with other teams in the group to produce a well-choreographed raid. Raids require intricate preplanning, lots of practice, and skilled orchestration. They require levels of leadership from top-level planners to team leaders, and they demand both excellent vertical (top-down) and horizontal (across all participants) communication.

In part because of these demands, people very often organize into large guilds of dozens or several hundred people in games like *GuildWars* or *World of Warcraft*. (How guilds and groups work has changed somewhat with *World of Warcraft's* expansion, *The Burning Crusade*.) Guilds orchestrate organization, planning, and the enforcement of norms and values at a high level—for example, choosing who goes on what raids and how specialized skills (like being a Priest) are to be learned and played-out in practice. From guilds to raids to hunting parties (groups), *World of Warcraft* is all about social organization for high performance of just the sort that workplaces pay consultants to refine, and workers find stressful. Such games hold out the potential for the discovery of new forms of social organization, new ways of solving social problems (e.g., the free-rider problem), and new ways of researching and testing collaborative learning, knowledge building, and performance.

We saw above that what is important for learning—and, indeed, for mastery in game play—is not just the game (software) but also the Game (the social system in which the game is embedded). The identities, goals, norms, tools, and technologies that form the core of the Situated Learning Matrix flow from social groups (e.g., SWAT teams). In massively multiplayer games like *World of Warcraft*, social groups organically grow their own identities, norms, tools, and technologies, which intersect with and transform those built into the game.[32] Big "G" Game and little "g" game become evermore tightly knit together, as the game/Game becomes a learning, knowledge building, design community.

Motivation and Ownership

An issue that comes up repeatedly when considering games and learning is the fact that video games appear to be deeply motivating to young people in ways in which much of school, say, is not. It is clearly a profoundly important subject for research to understand the source (or sources) of this motivation.

There are certainly features connected to video games that help explain both the motivation they recruit and the learning they enable. One key feature is the role of failure. The role of failure is very different in video games than it is in school. In good games, the price of failure is lowered—when players fail, they can, for example, start over at their last saved game. Furthermore, failure—for example, a failure to kill a boss—is often seen as a way to learn the underlying pattern and eventually to win. These features of failure in games allow players to take risks and try out hypotheses that might be too costly in places where the cost of failure is higher or where no learning stems from failure.

Every gamer and game scholar knows that a great many gamers, including young ones, enjoy competition with other players in games, either one-on-one or team-based. It is striking that many young gamers see competition as pleasurable and motivating in video games, but not in school.[33] Why this is so ought to be a leading question for research on games and learning.

One thing that seems evident is that competition in video games is seen by gamers as social and is often organized in ways that allow people to compete with people at their own levels or as part and parcel of a social relationship that is as much about gaming as about winning and losing. Furthermore, gamers highly value collaborative play, for example, two people playing *Halo* together to beat the game, or the grouping in massive multiplayer games like *World of Warcraft*. Indeed, collaboration and competition often seem to be closely related and integrated in gaming, though not in school.

Many have connected the motivation video games recruit with their status as interactive, and hence *active*, systems. But, from a learning perspective, what is important about video games is not interactivity per se, but the fact that in many games players come to feel a sense of agency or ownership. In a video game, players make things happen; they don't just consume what the "author" (game designer) has placed before them. In good games, players feel that their actions and decisions—and not just the designers' actions and decisions—cocreate the world they are in and shape the experiences they are having. Their choices matter. What they do matters. I would argue that all deep learning involves learners feeling a strong sense of ownership and agency, as well as the ability to produce and not just passively consume.

Emotion

Traditional work on learning viewed human thinking in almost entirely rational and intellectual terms, ignoring the role of emotion. However, recent research in neuroscience has clearly demonstrated that both thinking and learning depend on emotions.[34] Learning involves not just the cortex (or "higher" intellectual functions), but the whole brain, including the amygdalae, the limbic system, and the cortex. Emotion appears to be a key source of motivation for driving thinking, learning, and problem solving. Video games, as a form of entertainment, are good at attaching emotion to problem solving, just as films are good at attaching emotion to stories.

Emotion plays a variety of important roles in thinking and learning. First, when we are processing information, we store it more deeply and integrate with our prior knowledge better when that new information has an emotional charge for us, when we feel something is at stake or matters. Thus, emotion plays an important role in the organization of long-term memory. Second, emotions can often help us to both focus our attention on what is important or matters to us and retrieve information from long-term memory.

Third, emotions assist us in evaluating information and action. When we act in the world, we get feedback from the world, and something happens. But we have to know how to evaluate or assess the meaning, import, and usefulness of this result. While this most certainly involves rational judgments based on norms, it also involves weighted choices of what to do next in terms of how we feel, what we care about among those choices. If a person has no such emotional weighting, he or she can be paralyzed in choosing among equally good possibilities and left unable to act or decide.

Of course, while emotions can facilitate thinking and learning, they can also frustrate thinking and learning. High stress, too much frustration, powerful anger, or intense fear can overwhelm our thinking and shut down our learning. Some theorists have talked about people having an "affective filter"[35]—that is a filter that shuts out input from the world when a person is fearful, emotionally resistant, frustrated, or otherwise emotionally overburdened. When this happens, input does not become intake for learning in the human mind (e.g., when someone is trying to learn a foreign language, but is fearful of failing and looking silly).

Good game design gives an emotional charge to the thinking, problem solving, and learning it recruits. This is sometimes done partly in terms of players' attachment to the identities of their avatars—characters they come to care about. It is sometimes done through elements of storytelling, as well as the norms and values the game associates with identity and action (as in *SWAT4*). It is sometimes done as well through the player's caring about accomplishing goals, not dying or otherwise failing, and winning the game. At the same time, good games keep the player below a level of frustration that will trigger an affective filter to go up. Failure is not so consequential that the player is so fearful of failure that he or she can't act and explore. Help is available in a variety of forms (difficulty levels, hints, FAQs, cheats, other players, and forums).

Situated Meaning

Video games deal with language and literacy in ways that also tie to research on deep learning in the learning sciences. One concern of this research is that so many students in school cannot apply the knowledge they are learning in practice, even when they can pass verbal paper-and-pencil tests.[36] One reason for this is that students very often do not know what the words (and other symbols) in an area like physics mean at the level of application to real problem solving, rather than just as words they can define in terms of other words (as in a dictionary).

People acquire what I will call "situated meanings"[37] for words—that is, meanings that they can apply in actual contexts of use for action and problem solving—only when they have heard these words in interactional dialogue with people more expert than themselves[38] and when they have experienced the images and actions to which the words apply. Dialogue, image, experience, and action are crucial if people are to have more than just words for words ("definitions")—if they are to be able to relate words to actual experiences, actions, functions, and problem solving. As they can do for more and more contexts of use, they generalize the meanings of the word more and more, but the words never lose their moorings in dialogue, embodied experience, action, and problem solving.

Video games are good at putting language into the context of dialogue, experience, images, and actions. They are not textbooks full of words and definitions. They allow language to be situated. Furthermore, good video games give verbal information "just in time"—near the time it can actually be used—or "on demand," when the player feels a need for it and is ready for it.[39] They don't give players lots and lots of words out of context before they can be used and experienced or before they are needed or useful. This would seem to be an ideal situation for acquiring new words and new forms of language for new types of activity, whether this takes the form of being a member of a SWAT team or a scientist of a certain sort.

Given the importance of oral and written language development (e.g., vocabulary) to school success, it is crucial that this assumption be tested both in terms of the complex specialist language players pick up from commercial games (e.g., young children playing *Yu-Gi-Oh*, a card and video game that contains very complex language, indeed) and in terms of how games can be made and used for the development of specifically school-based (or other institutional) language demands, such as the language of biology or history.

Conclusion

We started with an argument that people learn from experiences stored in long-term memory. We then stated the conditions experiences need to meet in order to enhance deep learning. Since video games are virtual experiences centered on problem solving, they recruit learning and mastery as a form of pleasure. The conditions experiences need to meet to enhance deep learning therefore translate into design principles for good games. We saw that these conditions go beyond the individual to include the individual's participation in social groups that supply meaning and purpose to goals, interpretations, practice, explanations, debriefing, and feedback, conditions necessary for deep learning from experience. This led us to make a distinction between a game (software) and the Game (social system in which the game is embedded) and to see both as crucial for good learning design and good game design.

The Situated Learning Matrix—which I illustrated through the game *SWAT4*—was one way in which good games work out learning based on the conditions necessary for experiences to be good for learning. In the Situated Learning Matrix, learning moves from identity to goals and norms, to tools and technologies, and only then to content. The notion of "identity" at play in the Situated Learning Matrix shows one way in which learning and playing games tie, in part, either to vicarious or to real participation in social groups and their values: SWAT teams in *SWAT4*, real members of professions in Shaffer's[40] "epistemic games," organically formed social groups in *World of Warcraft*. Here again the issue of the Game raises its head.

Beyond learning from problem-based, goal-driven experiences, I argued that some games stress models and modeling, not just as part of game play—as lots of games do—but as the very nature of their game play as a whole—for example, games like *SWAT4* or *Civilization*. Such games often dispense with avatars, allowing the microcontrol of many units. Models and modeling are inherently tied to learning and exploration, since they simplify complex phenomena in order to make those phenomena easier to deal with for the accomplishment of goals, problem solving, and action. They also allow for learning from experience—which is in danger sometimes of being too concrete—to be rendered more abstract and generalized.

I also discussed several things games do well that enhance learning—namely, recruiting distributed intelligence, collaboration, and cross-functional teams for problem solving; offering players "empathy for a system"; marrying emotion to cognition; being challenging while still keeping frustration below the level of the affective filter; giving players a sense of production and ownership; and situating the meanings of words and symbols in terms of actions, images, experiences, and dialogue, not just "definitions" and texts read outside of contexts of use. There are several other things, in this respect, I could have discussed had space allowed: for example, the ways in which games order their problems in effective ways so that earlier problems and levels lead to good hypotheses about how to approach later problems and levels.[41]

In the end, my "take home" message is, I admit, relatively abstract: the language of learning is one important way in which to talk about video games, and video games are one important way in which to talk about learning. Learning theory and game design may, in the future, enhance each other.

Notes

1. James Paul Gee, *What Video Games Have to Teach Us About Learning and Literacy* (New York: Palgrave Macmillan, 2003); and idem., *Why Video Games Are Good for Your Soul: Pleasure and Learning* (Melbourne: Common Ground, 2005).

2. John Bransford, Allen L. Brown, and Rodney R. Cocking, *How People Learn: Brain, Mind, Experience, and School*, expanded ed. (Washington, DC: National Academy Press, 2000); and R. Keith Sawyer,

Analyzing Collaborative Discourse, in *The Cambridge Handbook of the Learning Sciences*, ed. R. Keith Sawyer (Cambridge, UK: Cambridge University Press, 2006), 187–204.

3. Lawrence W. Barsalou, Language Comprehension: Archival Memory or Preparation for Situated Action, *Discourse Processes* 28 (1999): 61–80; idem., Perceptual Symbol Systems, *Behavioral and Brain Sciences* 22 (1999): 577–660; Patricia S. Churchland and Terence J. Sejnowski, *The Computational Brain* (Cambridge, MA: Bradford/The MIT Press, 1992); Andy Clark, *Associative Engines: Connectionism, Concepts, and Representational Change* (Cambridge, UK: Cambridge University Press, 1993); idem., *Being There: Putting Brain, Body, and World Together Again* (Cambridge, MA: The MIT Press, 1997); James Paul Gee, *The Social Mind: Language, Ideology, and Social Practice* (New York: Bergin & Garvey, 1992); idem., *Situated Language and Learning: A Critique of Traditional Schooling* (London: Routledge, 2004); J. Hawkins, *On Intelligence* (New York: Henry Holt, 2005); and Roger C. Schank, *Dynamic Memory Revisited* (New York: Cambridge University Press, 1999).

4. Andrea A. diSessa, *Changing Minds: Computers, Learning, and Literacy* (Cambridge, MA: The MIT Press, 2000); Gee, *Situated Language and Learning*; Janet L. Kolodner, *Case Based Reasoning* (San Mateo, CA: Morgan Kaufmann, 1993); idem., Educational Implications of Analogy: A View from Case-Based Reasoning, *American Psychologist* 52 (1997): 57–66; idem., Case-Based Reasoning, in *The Cambridge Handbook of the Learning Sciences*, ed. R. K. Sawyer (Cambridge, UK: Cambridge University Press, 2006), 225–42; Roger C. Schank, *Dynamic Memory* (New York: Cambridge University Press, 1982); idem., *Dynamic Memory Revisited*. See especially Kolodner, Case-Based Reasoning, 227.

5. Arthur M. Glenberg, What Is Memory For? *Behavioral and Brain Sciences* 20 (1997): 1–55; and Arthur M. Glenberg and David A. Robertson, Indexical Understanding of Instructions, *Discourse Processes* 28 (1999): 1–26.

6. Barsalou, Language Comprehension; idem., Perceptual Symbol Systems; Clark, *Associative Engines*; and Hawkins, *On Intelligence.*

7. Arthur M. Glenberg, Tiana Gutierrez, Joel R. Levin, Sandra Japuntich, and Michael P. Kaschak, Activity and Imagined Activity Can Enhance Young Children's Reading Comprehension, *Journal of Educational Psychology* 96 (2004): 424–36.

8. John S. Brown, Allan Collins, and Paul Duguid, Situated Cognition and the Culture of Learning, *Educational Researcher* 18 (1989): 32–42; Gee, *Situated Language and Learning*; Edward Hutchins, *Cognition in the Wild* (Cambridge, MA: The MIT Press, 1995); Jean Lave and Etienne Wenger, *Situated Learning: Legitimate Peripheral Participation* (New York: Cambridge University Press, 1991); and Michael Tomasello, *The Cultural Origins of Human Cognition* (Cambridge, MA: Harvard University Press, 1999).

9. Etienne Wenger, *Communities of Practice: Learning, Meaning, and Identity* (Cambridge, UK: Cambridge University Press, 1998); and Etienne Wenger, Richard McDermott, and William M. Snyder, *Cultivating Communities of Practice* (Cambridge, MA: Harvard Business School Press, 2002).

10. Gee, *What Video Games Have to Teach Us*; idem., *Situated Language and Learning.*

11. Gee, *Situated Language and Learning.*

12. James Paul Gee, *Social Linguistics and Literacies: Ideology in Discourses* (London: Taylor & Francis, 1996); idem., Situated Language and Learning; and David W. Shaffer, *How Computer Games Help Children Learn* (New York: Palgrave Macmillan, 2007).

13. Deborah Blum, *Love at Goon Park: Harry Harlow and the Science of Affection* (Cambridge, MA: Perseus, 2002).

14. Gee, *Situated Language and Learning*; and Shaffer, *How Computer Games Help Children Learn.*

15. See Shaffer, *How Computer Games Help Children Learn*, for specific examples.

16. Paul A. Kirschner, John Sweller, and Richard E. Clark, Why Minimal Guidance During Instruction Does Not Work: An Analysis of the Failure of Constructivist, Discovery, Problem-Based, Experiential, and Inquiry-Based Teaching, *Educational Psychologist* 41 (2006): 75–86.

17. Bruno Latour and Steve Woolgar, *Laboratory Life: The Social Construction of Scientific Fact* (Los Angeles, CA: Sage, 1979); and S. Traweek, *Beamtimes and Lifetimes: The World of High Energy Physicists* (Cambridge, MA: Harvard University Press, 1988).

18. Michelene Chi, Paul Feltovich, and Robert Glaser, Categorization and Representation of Physics Problems by Experts and Novices, *Cognitive Science* 5, no. 2 (1981): 121–52.

19. diSessa, *Changing Minds*; Richard Lehrer and Leona Schauble, Modeling in Mathematics and Science, in *Advances in Instructional Psychology: Educational Design and Cognitive Science*, Vol. 5, ed. R. Glaser (Mahwah, NJ: Lawrence Erlbaum, 2000), 101–59; idem., Developing Modeling and Argument in the Elementary Grades, in *Understanding Mathematics and Science Matters*, eds. Thomas Romberg, Thomas P. Carpenter, and Fae Dremock (Mahwah, NJ: Lawrence Erlbaum, 2005), 29–53; idem., Cultivating Model-Based Reasoning in Science Education, in *The Cambridge Handbook of the Learning Sciences*, ed. R. Keith Sawyer (Cambridge, UK: Cambridge University Press, 2006), 371–87; and Nancy J. Nersessian, The Cognitive Basis of Model-Based Reasoning in Science, in *The Cognitive Basis of Science*, eds. Peter Carruthers, Stephen Stich, and Michael Siegal (Cambridge, UK: Cambridge University Press, 2002), 133–55.

20. For citations and discussion, see Jasper Juul, *Half-Real: Video Games Between Real Rules and Fictional World* (Cambridge, MA: The MIT Press, 2005).

21. diSessa, *Changing Minds*; Lehrer and Schauble, Cultivating Model-Based Reasoning.

22. Clark, *Being There*; and Gee, *Why Video Games Are Good.*

23. Elinor Ochs, Patrick Gonzales, and Sally Jacoby, When I Come Down I'm in the Domain State, in *Interaction and Grammar*, eds. Elinor Ochs, Emanuel Schegloff, and Sandra A. Thompson (Cambridge, UK: Cambridge University Press, 1996), 328–69.

24. Ibid., 330–31.

25. Uri Wilensky and Kenneth Reisman, Thinking Like a Wolf, a Sheep or a Firefly: Learning Biology Through Constructing and Testing Computational Theories—An Embodied Modeling Approach, *Cognition and Instruction*, forthcoming.

26. Brown, Collins, and Duguid, Situated Cognition; and Hutchins, *Cognition in the Wild.*

27. Gee, *What Video Games Have to Teach Us*; and idem., *Why Video Games Are Good.*

28. David W. Shaffer, Pedagogical Praxis: The Professions as Models for Post-Industrial Education, *Teachers College Record* 10 (2004): 1401–21; idem., Epistemic Games, *Innovate* 1, no. 6 (2005). http://www.innovateonline.info/index.php?view=issue&id=9. Accessed June 20, 2007; and idem., *How Computer Games Help.*

29. John Hagel and John S. Brown, *The Only Sustainable Edge: Why Business Strategy Depends on Productive Friction and Dynamic Specialization* (Boston, MA: Harvard Business School Press, 2005); and James Paul Gee, Glynda Hull, and Colin Lankshear, *The New Work Order: Behind the Language of the New Capitalism* (Boulder, CO: Westview, 1996).

30. Gee, Hull, and Lankshear, *The New Work Order*; and G. M. Parker, *Cross-Functional Teams: Working with Allies, Enemies, and Other Strangers*, 2nd ed. (San Francisco, CA: Jossey-Bass, 2002).

31. John S. Brown and Douglas Thomas, You Play World of Warcraft? You're Hired! *Wired Magazine* 14 (April 4, 2006). http://www.wired.com/wired/archive/14.04/learn.html.

32. Constance A. Steinkuehler, Massively Multiplayer Online Videogaming as Participation in a Discourse, *Mind, Culture, and Activity* 13 (2006): 38–52; and T. L. Taylor, *Play Between Worlds: Exploring Online Game Culture* (Cambridge, MA: The MIT Press, 2006).

33. Gee, *Situated Language and Learning.*

34. Antonio Damasio, *Descartes' Error: Emotion, Reason, and the Human Brain* (New York: Penguin, 1994); idem., *The Feeling of What Happens: Body and Emotion in the Making of Consciousness* (Orlando, FL: Harvest Books, 1999); idem., *Looking for Spinoza: Joy, Sorrow, and the Feeling Brain* (Orlando, FL: Harvest Books, 2003).

35. Gee, *Social Linguistics and Literacies.*

36. Howard Gardner, *The Unschooled Mind: How Children Think and How Schools Should Teach* (New York: Basic Books, 1991).

37. Gee, *Situated Language and Learning.*

38. Tomasello, *The Cultural Origins of Human Cognition.*

39. Gee, *What Video Games Have to Teach Us.*

40. Shaffer, *How Computer Games Help.*

41. Gee, *What Video Games Have to Teach Us*; idem., *Situated Language and Learning.*

In-Game, In-Room, In-World: Reconnecting Video Game Play to the Rest of Kids' Lives

Reed Stevens

University of Washington, LIFE Center, College of Education

Tom Satwicz

University of Georgia, Learning and Performance Support Laboratory

Laurie McCarthy

University of Washington, LIFE Center, College of Education

Introduction

One of the burning questions that people ask about video games, including most parents we've told about our study of young people playing video games in their homes, is whether playing these games affects kids' lives when the machine is off. In particular, people want to understand what young people learn playing games that they use, or adapt, in the rest of their lives. This question is the focus of our chapter.

Learning scientists use the term *transfer* to refer to the phenomenon of taking what you have learned in one context and transferring it to another. Without getting into the technical details, we note that academic discussions about transfer are fraught with theoretical confusions and fierce debate. Not only do learning scientists disagree about what causes transfer or what prevents it from happening, they disagree even about what counts as transfer (i.e., knowing when they see it) and how to assess it when they think it might be taking place.

These questions are not merely academic pursuits, as our focus on video game play should make clear. We really do want to know whether playing first-person shooters actually teaches players how to use weapons in real life. Or whether playing simulation games that model flying jets increases the reliability and judgment pilots exercise in the cockpits of real planes. What about a young adult who has become an acknowledged leader of a successful clan in *World of Warcraft*; how would we know whether that success has an effect, and what kind of effect, on how that person leads others in collective action in her daily workplace? Does designing virtual cities in *SimCity* provide a starting point for a career designing real cities? Is that starting point different in any substantive way from building cities with wooden blocks?

Though we won't be directly addressing the complex arguments that animate the transfer debate in this chapter, we do see video games as an important type of human activity against which to pose the basic question of transfer, for at least two reasons. First, there are *widely* differing views on the positive, negative, and noneffects of video games on other aspects of life or learning. Second, video game play consumes an enormous amount of many young people's time and energy; this is time and energy that could be spent elsewhere, or—depending on the answer to the transfer question—spent playing *more* games. Consider the following thought experiment: imagine that a learning scientist definitely proved, all other things being the same, that a year spent immersed in a game-based curriculum better prepared a young person for a successful life and career than that same year spent in a traditional high school curriculum? What sort of changes might a finding like that suggest to the way we conceive of education and to the future of learning? It is clear that a lot hangs on the transfer question.

One of the limitations of the research tradition that has most closely concerned itself with transfer—academic psychology—is that its claims for transfer come out of experiments that researchers set up, usually around tasks that are not particularly consequential or common in people's lives. The tasks are selected, first and foremost, because they enable conclusions to be drawn within the logic and particular rigor of experimental research. Math, chess, and physics problems have been among the favorite tasks for transfer research in psychology.

An alternative approach to studying transfer is rooted in an ethnographic tradition that is sometimes called situated, everyday, or distributed cognition.[1] The work we report on in this chapter comes out of this tradition. Research in this tradition insists upon an "outdoor psychology"[2] in which researchers get out of the laboratories and into the fields of activity that people themselves, rather than psychologists, organize.[3] In taking this different approach from academic psychology, while sharing similar questions and concepts, researchers of everyday cognition give up the "control" of experimental research for "ecological validity."[4] Ecological validity is about having a basis to credibly claim that our research accounts are about how and what people do, learn, and think in daily life, and not simply about what they do within the context of contrived laboratory tasks.

Coming at our study from a different direction we are struck, as ethnographers of everyday cognition and informal learning, by the relative scarcity of empirical research on video game play. Why this surprises us is that video games have been called "a new medium,"[5] "a new form of art,"[6] a new educational approach,[7] and just about a new everything else. Sales of its products support a multibillion dollar industry that continues to grow. And while there is a good deal of innovative writing—both popular and academic—about video games, only a small percentage of this writing arises from ethnographic studies of game play.[8]

The research we describe in this chapter is ethnographic, based on a six-month-long study of young people in different families playing video games in their homes, using their own games and game systems. We video-recorded young people playing video games and interviewed them later when we had questions that our analyses of the recordings of game play could not answer. Our study involved eight focal kids and five friends, aged 9–15, and lasted approximately six months. We recruited the participants through advertisements on Craigslist, flyers in gaming stores, and word of mouth. We visited each focal participant approximately once a week and observed his or her play. Among our core participants we had four boys and four girls, including two sets of siblings. We purposefully selected participants in our study to maximize variation; this is a common strategy when pursuing a new research direction because it helps define an uncharted territory.

We came to this study with a primary interest in how children spend their time and what they learn in the process. Because children are interested in video games and devote energy and time to them, we have done so as researchers. This is part of a larger project to understand learning within and across informal and formal settings.[9] This focus distinguishes us from most others who write about video games from either side of a current flare-up in the Culture Wars. The two sides of this debate give us, on one hand, a view of video games as mind-numbing, antisocial, low culture activities or, on the other hand, as wellsprings of new cultural production, positive identity formation, and learning of all shapes and sizes. Our position in this—before we can decide what is and is not valuable about video games, we need to get much better descriptions of what people actually do and learn playing video games under as naturally occurring conditions as possible.

A steady theme in much writing about video games is what we will call the *separate worlds view* of video game play, a perspective that runs perhaps intentionally in exactly the opposite

Figure 1
An "in-room" and "in-game" recording. Brandon and Holly consult a strategy guide at a decision point in the game *Legend of Zelda—Ocarina of Time*.

direction than questions of transfer lead us. The *separate worlds view* holds, in different ways for different writers, that game play is a world apart of people's other activities in everyday life. Whether this separateness is framed in technocentric terms like "immersion in virtual worlds" or in academic terms that conceptualize video games as a "discourse" or "semiotic domain,"[10] we see a persistent bent that analyzes video game play as largely disconnected from the other moments and activities of people's lives.

Our goal in this chapter is not to dispute the separate worlds view directly, but to enlarge it by looking beyond the game space. What our study shares with the separate worlds view is its treatment of video game play as a cultural practice worthy of study in its own right. Such a view is a necessary antidote to taking account of popular cultural forms like video games and television *only* to the degree that they impact, either positively or negatively, other more normatively valued activities like school, work, and conventional definitions of family life. Where we seek to enlarge the separate worlds view is with an ethnographically grounded set of case materials that show that the culture of game play is one that is quite tangled up[11] with other cultural practices, which include relations with siblings and parents, patterns of learning at home and school, as well as imagined futures for oneself.

In this chapter our goal is *not* to provide causal explanations of transfer between video game play and other life activities, but rather to provide a set of careful descriptions of how "in-game" activity is tangled up with activity "in-room," and in the wider worlds of activity that young people inhabit. Our chapter will argue that "in-game," "in-room," and "in-world" are more permeable and blurred than the separate worlds view would suggest. And we mean "in-room" literally. Unlike empirical studies that implicitly take a separate worlds view,[12] we record not only a stream of in-game play (taken directly from the console or computer), but also what is going on in the living and family rooms where the players are sitting, crouching, or reclining. Phones ring, parents come in (or argue in the next room), and players interact in a variety of ways with friends, siblings, and material resources—other than the game—that are *in-room*.

Although we have collected various kinds of data, the primary form is audio-video recordings that synchronize the "in-game" and "in-room" recordings into a single image (figure 1). These recordings form the foundation of the analysis presented in this chapter. Our video-based ethnographic approach is similar conceptually and methodologically to studies of technology use in work settings.[13] Work of this kind draws its boundary around "functional systems" in ways that are sometimes willfully ambivalent toward received boundaries (either existing theoretical or commonsense ones), such as those between "in-game" and "in-room." We are after the ways that activity and meaning circulate; if these circulations take us across characters moving about in the game, to a conversation in a living room, to a relationship with a friend, that is where our analysis goes.

Overview of Our Case Material

In this section we present a collection of vignettes drawn from ethnographic field materials depicting how video game play is tangled up in other parts of kids' lives, including their relationships with siblings, parents, schools, and their own futures. We will show how actual game play is shaped, sometimes in very consequential ways, by people and material resources present in the room but invisible "in-game." For example, one of our participants, Tyler, frequently uses "cheats" during his game play. Tyler's use of cheats differs in intention and deployment depending on who he is playing with, what game he is playing, and how he has configured the game. We also describe trajectories of learning with video games and how in-room resources shape this learning. For example, Rachel often draws on her brother's expertise when playing games. Her questions are most often focused on specific aspects of the game, such as where in the game she can find the items she needs at that moment, rather than on general strategies for how to be successful. Rachel's brother functions for her as a just-in-time guide and instructor for a course of learning she herself is organizing in the moment.

Moving outward from how "in-game" is shaped by what and who are "in-room," we will also describe how game play seems to fit into the rest of kids' lives and how young people actively make connections between events in-game and events in their everyday lives (in-world). In order to better understand the question of how kids' video game play is tied up in their other activities, we also focused on one specific activity in the kids' daily round outside of game play—homework. We thought homework would make an interesting comparison for some of the following reasons: (a) like video game play, homework is something kids do at home in shared family spaces and their rooms (i.e., the same spaces games were played in), (b) homework, like games, is—in varying degrees—strategic, repetitive, scored, and designed to challenge, and (c) there are different moral stances about how homework, like games, *ought* to be played (i.e., should they be pursued collaboratively, should you cheat, etc.). Homework, therefore, provided us with a strategic context to compare with video game play.

Connections Between In-Game and In-Room: How Many Ways Can Kids Learn to Play Together—Let Us Count the Ways

In this first of two sections of vignettes drawn from our ethnographic case material, we present stories that, together, point to a remarkable variety of *learning arrangements* that young people create among themselves while playing video games. These vignettes clearly point to in-game and in-room connections, since it is through interactional activities in-room that most of the identifiable learning moments in our data were transacted. Also, in all cases presented here, and in most of those included in our wider data, these arrangements involve collaboration across young people rather than young people in solo interaction with a game system. Later in the chapter, we discuss the importance of both the diversity of learning arrangements and the fact that most of the learning happens in the context of varied arrangements of people working together.

Vignette 1—Cory the Expert as Just-in-Time Resource for Rachel the Novice

This is the first of five vignettes that show ways that young people learn and teach together while playing video games. In this vignette, we describe Rachel (age 15) and her younger brother Cory (age 12). Among all the participants in the study, Rachel spent the least amount of time each week playing video games; she was not an avid player. Not only did she spend little time playing (compared to other kids in our study) but also the games she played were not chosen; they were given to her as gifts or purchased by her younger brother, Cory, who was an avid game player. Cory also held the family memory of games; Rachel often deferred to him regarding how long they had owned a particular game or which version it was. Unlike in other families in our study, siblings Rachel and Cory seldom played together because, as reported by Rachel, they had very different ways of playing. However, Rachel relied heavily on her brother for help while she played. As she played or sought to begin playing, she often asked him very specific questions. Her questions were extremely focused, relating to particular game moves or to identifying unfamiliar icons on the screen. Cory was, to borrow a phrase from business jargon, a just-in-time resource for Rachel. The interaction in Segment 1 demonstrates how Rachel, while playing *Age of Empires II: Conquerors*, sought specific advice about killing boars from the younger sibling Cory. Once her brother provided the advice she needed (lines 2–4), Rachel immediately continued her hunting task. Cory continued to provide strategic information (line 7); however, it appeared Rachel was no longer paying attention, interrupting her brother to comment on her current activity (line 8).

Segment 1

1. *Rachel:* What about boars, bro. Would it be a good idea if my eagle warriors kill the boar?
2. *Cory:* No, then there would be no fruit—I mean no food. But if you get lots of villagers coming together=
3. *Rachel:* How many villagers do I have to have to do it?
4. *Cory:* Just have like three.
5. *Rachel:* Three?
6. [As Cory speaks, Rachel gathers two villagers. She scrolls through her village looking for a third.]
7. *Cory:* But if you're gonna actually start building up your economy, you should have like 8 on food. Like 8 on wood, like=
8. *Rachel:* =Oh! I'm gonna be so mad if I can't find that stupid person that got lost.

[Rachel 2005-11-12_00:04:30.05]

For Rachel, video game play seemed to be about having an experience of control. As she told us, "So you're in control and you have these different decisions that you have to make to um meet the goal" *[Rachel 2006-03-18_P1_00:12:33.21]*. She explained to us her preference for *Age of Empires II* over *Zoo Tycoon* in terms of control:

But the other game [*Age of Empires II*]? You have so much control over it? That it's more—like (.) I don't know. Like the other game? I like the control of having the whole—I can do what ever I want.
[Rachel 2006-03-18_00:11:12:20]

Rachel had available other ways of learning to play the game, including reading manuals and trial and error, but we observed her doing very little of either. In our view, her emphasis on control meant that she sought out the learning resource that allowed her the greatest control over the learning experience. In this case, the learning resource was her brother's knowledge, which she could draw on very selectively without having to bother with other material that she did not deem relevant to her immediate goals. Further support for this interpretation of the way Rachel organized learning for herself as a video game player can be found in the fact that she generally avoided in-game tutorials because "it's kind of annoying to have them like hanging over you and you have like no control over what you do" *[Rachel 2006-04-15_00:10:44:06]*. In other words, the tutorials, not Rachel, were in control of the timing and direction of the learning. The way that Rachel selectively drew upon her brother as a just-in-time resource and maintained focused control of her own learning poses some interesting questions for our general theme about the connection between in-game, in-room, and in-world activity. Does it suggest a person who maintains control in the rest of her life, with game play simply another expression of this control, or might games represent a unique context for its expression as compared, for example, with school, where she might have very limited control of her our learning paths? We cannot answer the question at this point, but will return to it later in the chapter.

Vignette 2—In the On Deck Circle: Apprenticing into Game Play

In this vignette, we describe another learning arrangement across a sister and brother. Our observations of Mikey (age 15) and Maddy (age 8) lead us to characterize their relationship around video games as an apprenticeship, something quite different from the arrangement that developed across Rachel and her brother Cory. In the instances presented here, Mikey helped his younger sister Maddy play her own games by advising her, in an ongoing way, on which game to play, and stepping in to assist when the system she was playing was not working.

Maddy's involvement in game play resembled other forms of apprenticeship in work settings.[14] It was Mikey (the older), not Johnny, who took on the exclusive role of master to Maddy's apprentice. This apprenticeship was not only a particular social arrangement (between Maddy and Mikey) but also a physical one in the room. Typically, in an inner circle in the room, Mikey and Johnny were at play, with Maddy at the periphery observing, often commenting, and sometimes entering play under the watchful eyes of her brother Mikey. Sometimes while the boys played, Maddy would sit behind them and play with other toys, or with an older portable *Gameboy*, almost as if in an "on deck" position. When the opportunity to play came, she would literally move up into the inner circle to play the game on the television screen with Johnny and Mikey. The physical positioning of the children in the room was such that Maddy was within an appropriate "horizon of observation"[15] and could act as a peripheral participant to Johnny and Mikey's play, before moving into position to actually join the play. When Maddy did play, a controller would have to be brought up from the basement (indicating further the atypicality of three-person play in this group of siblings) and there was a deliberate pause in the action.

An example of Mikey acting as guide for Maddy, a relative newcomer to video games, is represented in Segments 2 and 3 (below). These two instances, which took place within minutes of each other, show Mikey providing assistance to Maddy as she requests it, illustrating the working apprenticeship that formed between them.

Segment 2

1. [Maddy slides off a chair in the back of the room toward Mikey, who is sitting on the floor in front of the TV playing a video game with Johnny. Maddy asks Mikey for help with her Barbie game.]

2. *Mikey:* You really don't want to Maddy, you'll lose on every game because all of the games are color coded.
3. *Maddy:* [inaudible] color=
4. *Mikey:* Maddy you'll lose on every game cause when you've got to do a puzzle or you've gotta=
5. *Maddy:* I don't do puzzles.
6. *Mikey:* OK what do you do?
7. *Johnny:* Mikey look at my little PK thunder [referring to the video game on the TV which is now paused].
8. *Mikey:* Woah.
9. *Maddy:* I do:: shirts, I do:: lipstick=
10. *Mikey:* =right oh Maddy you'd never be able to tell especially with the lipstick. Cause they are all colors Maddy.
11. *Maddy:* It's really hard on the lipstick now because I've gotten far.
12. [As Maddy walks out of the room. Mikey and Johnny continuing playing the game on the TV. Maddy comes back into the room eighteen seconds later.]
13. *Maddy:* I'm just going to try it anyway.

[Johnny and Mikey 2005-09-16_00:27:38.04]

In this segment, the initial arrangement of their bodies in relation to the television screen was representative of the inner and outer circles of play described above; Johnny and Mikey sat close to the screen and Maddy observed from the periphery. At the beginning of Segment 2, Maddy slid off her chair toward the inner circle and asked Mikey for help with her Barbie game (see Segment 2, line 1). Mikey recommended that she not play the Barbie game, because it involved matching colors and the screen on their older *Gameboy* showed only gray scale: "You really don't want to Maddy, you'll lose on every game because all of the games are color coded." Maddy, however, did not put the game down, offering a reply that we interpreted to mean that she thought his commentary applied only to a single category of games on the handheld game device but not to the one she was playing (i.e., "I don't do puzzles," line 5). In the end, Maddy left the room and declared that she would "try it anyway" (line 13). This is an instance where Mikey attempted to guide his younger sister when she encountered some technical limitations of a particular video game display. It shows how Mikey acts as a guide by providing advice to Maddy as she plays a game; it shows also, in her not taking his advice, that Maddy is playing an active rather than a simply passive role in the apprenticeship and in her own learning.

In the next segment (Segment 3, below), which took place four minutes after Segment 2, Maddy again looked to Mikey for help in setting up the game. After a bit of disagreement about the problem Maddy was having (lines 3–8), Mikey took the game system from her (line 11). Notice that the game system, not Maddy, entered the inner circle of play. It suggests a typical arrangement for an apprenticeship; the work of the master (Mikey) is ongoing and is interrupted for a moment of instruction for or by the novice, but with an assumption embodied in the arrangement—that the master will quickly return to the activity at hand[16] while she remained at the periphery. After Maddy passed Mikey the game, he was able to get it started before passing it back to her (lines 15–17). Mikey then immediately returned to his play, without missing a beat. The apprenticeship's place in the room was reinforced by the fact that Johnny accepted the stoppage without comment; he was accustomed to this and impassively awaited Mikey's resumption of their play.

Segment 3

1. [Maddy is sitting on a chair in the back of the room facing the TV. Mikey and Johnny are in front of Maddy, also facing the TV playing a game.]
2. *Maddy:* Mikey how come it's not starting my game?
3. *Mikey:* What do you mean it's not starting your game?
4. *Maddy:* I'm pressing "b" but it won't go to the game?
5. *Mikey:* Why are you pressing "b"?
6. *Maddy:* It says, "press b to continue your game."
7. *Mikey:* No, it says "press start to continue your game."
8. *Maddy:* No, it says "press start to begin a new game."
9. [Game on TV is paused and Mikey turns around to look at Maddy.]
10. *Mikey:* Are you crying?
11. [Mikey reaches his hand out and Maddy passes him the *Gameboy*.]
12. *Maddy:* No.
13. *Mikey:* It sure sounded like it.
14. *Johnny:* Yeah. (quietly)
15. [Mikey looks at the *Gameboy* and pushes a few buttons.]
16. *Mikey:* You got your code wrong then, let me see it.
17. [Mikey reaches his hand out and takes a piece of paper from Maddy. He then reenters the code showing Maddy what parts she has entered wrong, passes the game back to Maddy, and continues playing the game on the TV with Johnny.]

[Johnny and Mikey 2005-09-16_00:33:09.11]

The content, as well as the apprenticeship-like form of this interactional moment, is of interest. Mikey instructed Maddy in a fairly arbitrary symbolic code of the kind that many theories of cognition crafted from studies in schools and laboratory studies would suggest should be beyond the capacity of an eight-year-old. Notably, Mikey's part in the interaction implicitly assumes just the opposite—that Maddy can understand and should do so *quickly*, so he can return to his play. Looking at Segment 3, we see that Mikey's guidance comes in many forms. And Mikey does not simply solve the problem for Maddy, which would suggest a mere helping orientation in the interaction; he instructs her on how to do it herself. This suggests one of the strongest themes in this study—young people organize themselves to teach and learn together, with adult intervention and as a taken for granted, as a natural part of playing video games together.

Vignette 3—Exchanging Knowledge and Shifting Roles Through Coordinated Talk and Embodied Display

This vignette describes two middle-school-aged boys, Johnny (age 13, brother of Maddy and Mikey) and his friend Evan,[17] working collaboratively through a two-player game. While playing this game (*Teenage Mutant Ninja Turtles*), a new one for both of them, they recurrently had difficulty with an important climbing task that they eventually mastered through a

Figure 2
An image from a *Teenage Mutant Ninja Turtles* segment, in which Johnny and Evan are attempting to get their characters to jump up the chimneylike cliffs. To do this, they need to discover a set of controller actions that will enable their characters to ascend the cliffs.

discovered innovation in their use of the controller. Their process of refinement involved interactions based in talk and gesture in-room, in coordination with action in-game. In essence, they managed to keep their play going while they demonstrated to each other successive attempts to create and solidify the climbing move with the controller, in a kind of "on the job" learning. Following the action as the boys produce the climbing move innovation, we see a shift in recognition and subtle renegotiation of who has the relevant knowledge. Unlike in the prior two vignettes, it is difficult to say here who is the more "expert" player. On the whole, we interpret the learning described here as a collaborative process between two players of relatively equal status.

Johnny and his friend Evan were playing a two-player round of *Teenage Mutant Ninja Turtles*, a video game the objective of which is to run through a course containing many obstacles that must be jumped over while simultaneously fighting other characters. They each controlled one character in the game and worked collaboratively toward shared goals negotiated in-room.

At several points during this game session, Johnny's and Evan's characters faced this new challenge: ascending chimneylike cliffs (figure 2). During one of their early encounters with the chimney-climbing challenge, Johnny's character made it to the top, but Evan's character had some difficulty. While Evan attempted the climb several times, Johnny's character fell from the top and had to redo the climb. Evan and Johnny handed the controller back and forth, and eventually Johnny got both of the characters to the top. After this early attempt, it seemed as though Johnny held the knowledge of the move, which they would need periodically throughout the game. Just over twenty minutes after the early encounter with the chimney, Evan stated that he had figured out a way to make climbing the chimney easier. He shared this with Johnny, saying "you just keep pressing jump" (see Segment 4, below).

Approximately seven and a half minutes later he demonstrated the move again. This time Evan produced an embodied display, holding the controller in such a way that the display was present in Johnny's field of vision as he continued playing (line 11).

Segment 4

1. [After the characters climb a chimney without any trouble.]
2. *Evan:* Oh, now I know how to do it without falling and stuff, you just keep pressing jump.

   [Seven minutes later.]
3. [The two characters run up to a chimney.]
4. *Evan:* Watch this Johnny watch this watch this don't look watch watch my controller.
5. [Johnny turns his head and briefly looks at Evan's controller, then turns toward the screen. Evan's character tries to jump up the chimney but is not able to get very far. Johnny's character stands back. Both boys are focused on the screen.]
6. *Evan:* Oh, hold on, there we go, dang it I can't get it started.
7. *Johnny:* Look.
8. [Johnny's character walks over to the chimney and begins to climb it. Evan's character begins climbing it as well.]
9. [Three seconds]
10. *Evan:* Johnny look Johnny look look.
11. [Evan holds out his controller with one hand toward Johnny. He is holding the "jump" button down, rather than pressing it repeatedly as the boys had been. Johnny glances at the controller, then turns to look back at the screen. Both characters make it to the top of the chimney.]
12. *Johnny:* Oh, once you get it started.
13. *Evan:* You have to get it started then you can do it for sure, but you have to get it started.

[Johnny and Mikey 2005-08-19_tape1_ 00:40:45.29]

In this vignette we see that interaction in-room directly shapes in-game action. More important for our general argument, we see another instance in which teaching is organized for learning during play (like the last vignette showing Mikey and sister Maddy). Here there is a plausible long-term rationale for the instruction that the boys may be oriented to, since having only one player able to achieve the move limits joint progress. Our interpretation is that the boys are oriented to this longer-term goal of both of them being able to make this climb, whereas a short-term perspective might entail Evan just taking Johnny's controller and doing it for him; but that is not what happens.

Vignette 4—Enrolling Unused Devices: How an Extra Controller Helped Two Boys Learn a New Skill

We use this vignette to expand on the image of collaboration described in Johnny's and Evan's attempt to learn the skills needed to climb the chimney cliffs. Here two different boys, Tyler (age 10) and Andrew (age 10), play, in single player mode, a game called *Dragon Ball Z: Budokai 3*. The interaction in Segment 5 resembles Johnny's and Evan's collaborative exchange but differs in interesting ways as well. First, the relationship between these boys is more asymmetric, with Tyler being the clear leader of game activity and talk in the room. It is a case where Andrew has an idea for Tyler, who was playing while Andrew watched. The idea involved helping Tyler defeat an opponent using a newly acquired in-game object called Hellzone Grenade. Immediately after getting the Hellzone Grenade, Andrew sought to give Tyler some advice on the button sequence for using the grenade against his opponent. The in-game activity of this nine-minute session, during which Tyler eventually defeated his opponent using the Hellzone Grenade, is a case of Tyler learning a new skill. But our interest here is not what was learned—in this case a basic in-game skill. Rather, our interest is in the way in which this learning occurred—through an evolving sequence of interactions between the boys and the spontaneous use of an unconnected controller as an instructional device. The first segment of this vignette begins with Andrew's initial enthusiastic bid to show Tyler how to do the move, punctuated with rhythmic sound effects accompanying an embodied display with the unconnected controller.

Segment 5, Moment 1

1. *Andrew:* Tyler! What you have to do is go du du du da da da da da da da da
2. [Andrew sits up and moves toward Tyler, then pushes buttons on a disconnected controller while making the sounds. Tyler turns his head toward Andrew and watches his friend's fingers move on the controller.]
3. *Tyler:* [Turns to look at the TV screen.] You're not—you're not even sure.
4. *Andrew:* Well just try it (.) when you get Hellzone Grenade.

In Moment 2 (below) the disconnected controller, previously useless in-game, was again used by Andrew, this time more demonstrably, as an instructional device. As in prior vignettes involving other children in other families, we see young people organizing themselves to teach and learn together—in ingenious ways.

Segment 5, Moment 2

1. [Tyler pauses the game to select the Hellzone Grenade. Tyler then unpauses the game and powers up the character, Piccolo, he is controlling in preparation for his next move.]
2. *Tyler:* OK!
3. [Tyler and Andrew sit up.]
4. [Andrew picks his controller up off the ground and brings it toward Tyler, while pushing buttons as though he is playing.]
5. *Andrew:* No! See?
6. *Tyler:* Oh you're right! You do have to hold it down!
7. [Tyler smiles; his character Piccolo has won.]
8. *Andrew:* You have to hold it down?
9. *Tyler:* Yes!
10. [A short movie plays on the screen indicating victory; Tyler mirrors the game character's celebratory gestures.]
11. *Andrew:* Nuh-uh!
12. [Andrew brings controller into view and pushes buttons as though he is playing. Tyler is looking at the screen.]
13. *Andrew:* It's this, this=
14. *Tyler:* =No, you were—you ARE right! [Three seconds] Yes you do have to hold it down Andrew! It was rumbling. [Three seconds] So that means [inaudible] I just have to know which one to hold.

Moment 2 ends with a debate between the two boys on how to execute the move. In this debate Andrew mimicked button pushes to make his point. In Moment 3 we see that Andrew continued to make a bid for his way of using the new skill by enrolling the unused controller, however Tyler ignored him.

Segment 5, Moment 3

1. [As in-game fighting continues, Tyler realizes that holding the buttons down is not working.]
2. *Tyler:* Come on!
3. *Andrew:* See it switches.
4. *Tyler:* You're right.
5. [Andrew holds the controller higher and pushes buttons as he talks. Tyler looks at the screen and plays the game.]
6. *Andrew:* See it switches and then you have to hold this and then you have to hold that.
7. *Tyler:* Say what?
8. *Andrew:* That's how you do it.
9. [Tyler eventually loses this round, ignoring Andrew's suggestions to implement the Hellzone Grenade. When Tyler does use the Hellzone Grenade, he is knocked out.]

Eventually, in Moment 4, Tyler took the advice, but did so as modeled by Andrew. Tyler looked toward Andrew and followed his moves on the unused controller.

Segment 5, Moment 4

1. [Andrew sits up and holds the controller out to demonstrate the move.]
2. *Andrew:* See hold. [Six seconds] See you gotta hold it until the arrow goes up. Hold it until the arrow goes up.
3. [Tyler is looking toward Andrew. Andrew pushes the buttons down when he says "hold it" and lets them up when he says "arrow goes up."]

[Tyler 2005_08-24_00:16:24.20]

Taken together, this vignette and the others in this section tell us something important about how kids learn to play video games and, perhaps, also a bit about why. Across four vignettes, we see real variation in the learning arrangements involved. Pure cases of clearly more expert players teaching more inexperienced players are not what we see; instead, we witness more complex situations in which less able players provide instruction to better players, in which a sister and brother establish a working apprenticeship into game play, and situations where friends collaborate with and cajole each other into learning relevant moves and skills. In general, these vignettes collectively show how important it is to understand what goes on in-room if we are to understand how young people come to learn and play in-game. These vignettes also suggest—in regard to the naturalness with which unprovoked teaching and learning occur among young people and their inventiveness in finding productive learning arrangements—that video games are indeed good learning environments, as others have argued. However, we believe games are good learning environments, not primarily because the game's design embodies good learning principles;[18] we see variation in game design quality and in ways that young people play as too great to draw this conclusion from the games themselves.[19] Rather we see the reason that games, or more specifically collaborative interactions around video game play, are good learning environments is that "in-room" interaction provides opportunities for sociality, joint projects, and empowerment through sharing one's knowledge and seeing it used for concrete success by others. Since this interaction occurs primarily without adult guidance or direction, it may be that the kid-organized and kid-managed aspects of these contexts—for kids of this preteen and early teen age—make them powerful learning contexts.

Connecting In-Game and In-Room to In-World

In this section, we move outward from in-game, beyond in-room, to connections we have found in our ethnographic data between in-game play and young people's wider fields of experience "in-world." In five vignettes, we establish a number of connections between in-game and in-world activity. Our primary argument shares with others a link between game play and identity formation,[20] but as we will argue, we see the link and the material games provide for identity formation differently from others who have written about video games. The connections we draw between in-game and in-world are less direct than those we drew between in-game and in-room, as those actions were concurrent and decisively linked. Yet we see the connections between in-game and in-world as important to establish, because they move us toward an understanding of the bidirectional continuities and discontinuities between game play and everyday life, this being a way that ethnographic research can approach the question of transfer we described in the introduction to our chapter.[21]

Vignette 5—Does Using "Cheats" Make a Player a Cheater?

Part of video game play involves using—or not using—cheat codes or cheats. These are, depending on your point of view, an example of the morally sanctionable behavior of "cheating," or an acceptable part of play. An example of a cheat code comes from the Web site Cheatcode Central, the subtitle of which is "Enhancing Game Experiences Around the World." Here we learn that a player of *Dragon Ball Z* can "[e]nter one of the following passwords under the 'Data Center' option to unlock the corresponding character: *Android 18 (Level 160)* NzEr vcJO)Jlv kW@N P@Wf hOIl $ABQ &@CG." There are hundreds of such pieces of information on this and Web sites like it.

In this vignette, we describe a set of situations in which the relationship between the use of cheat codes and the moral stain of cheating is being negotiated among two boys playing a game over multiple play sessions. Tyler (age 10) was a self-avowed user of cheats and would sometimes announce his intention to "cheat." At the same time, Tyler's use of cheats sometimes brought complaints and monitoring from his coparticipants, and it was clear from what we observed that some of his reputation as a player, and perhaps also as a person, was at stake in these moments.

An example of this occurred while Tyler played the car game *Burnout 3: Takedown* with friends; during play Tyler used a code that provided greater acceleration to his car for the upcoming race. After this, his competitors began monitoring his hands at the beginning of races, looking for evidence that he was entering a cheat code. This scrutiny—in turn—affected Tyler's play, as he would then hold the controller so his competition could watch his hand movements and see that he was not entering the codes. We do not know whether he actually had the sleight of hand to enter the codes and to falsify the demonstration, but we do not suspect this was the case.

At other moments during the game, Tyler made comments and acted in ways that intentionally led others to believe he was using cheat codes, which suggests that some aspect of his reputation as a user of cheats was of value to him. For example, during a *Dragon Ball Z: Budokai 3* fight with his friend Andrew, Tyler quit the match to research a particular skill (unfamiliar to him) that his character had acquired. Tyler opened the Edit Skill screen provided in the game, read the skill's description, then commented "Oh, okay. Now I know what to do." As he started up a new game, Tyler sang "I'm gonna cheat, I'm gonna cheat!" Although Andrew seemed undisturbed by the announcement, he was attending to it and seemingly put in motion a cheat of his own, setting his character's "health" to maximum, indicated by a full white (in contrast to the default half green) bar at the bottom of the screen.

Segment 6

1. *Tyler:* What the heck? Andrew, you're up to white?
2. *Andrew:* Tyler, you're cheating (.) too! You're cheatin' so I can cheat too.
3. *Tyler:* [smiling] How am I cheatin?
4. *Andrew:* Well you said you were gonna cheat!

[Tyler 2005-08-24_01:16:10.10]

While Tyler did nothing at this point, during battle he paused the game as his health was about to expire and used the same cheat code to reset his health to the maximum level. As he did so, Tyler announced, "If you're gonna go that far, I'm gonna go that far! I'm gonna cheat too! So there. And that will give me a giant advantage."

We find these moments of great interest, because in the variation of stances that Tyler takes, we see his working out among important consociates in his life a moral stance on cheating. He is both an unabashed user of cheats, sporting a somewhat transgressive personal reputation he values at times, and, at the same time, someone who does not want his play with friends interpreted as unfair—thus the overt display of his hands during the opening sequence to show his competitors that he is not entering cheat codes.

Tyler's reputation as a user of cheat codes seemed to set up further interpretation of his in-game actions as unfair. For example, he was accused of "cheating" when he modified his in-game play techniques—*without* the use of cheat codes—but in ways that were unexpected to his opponents. Taking these actions (called cheesing by some in game play discourse) was unexpected, because the actions diverged from courses of action perceived as normal in the real-world activity the game simulated. For example, during play of *Burnout 3: Takedown*, when Tyler saw that his friend's car was critically damaged, he pulled over to the side of the road and waited for a fatal crash. This allowed Tyler to win the race, not by having to run laps and risk taking more damage himself, but by default when his friend's car was inevitably destroyed. Andrew likened such behavior to Tyler's use of cheat codes. At one point during the game, he told Tyler "I hate it when you use cheat codes against me and a whole bunch of stuff," and then forcefully laid down a new rule: "No cheat codes. Just plain old running into the cars until you die" *[Tyler 2005-08-10_00:58:17.29]*. Tyler's reputation as a user of cheat codes had preceded him and affected how his friends interpreted his play, even when he was not using the codes. It seems that Tyler's use of cheats had become associated with his overall style of play.

Vignette 6—How Young People Customize the Same Game Differently Depending on What They Bring to Playing It From the Rest of Their Lives

This vignette describes how two girls in our study, Katarina and Rachel, played *Zoo Tycoon*, but in dramatically different ways. Our interpretation of these differences is that each tailored

Katarina's zoo: Statues included for aesthetic reasons but no economic benefit.

Rachel's zoo: All features have a function within the official economy of the game.

Figure 3
Katarina and Rachel arrive at zoos that look and function differently. Rachel's desire to build an efficient zoo led her to include only features that generated income. In contrast, Katarina designed features that added to the zoo's aesthetic feel but did not necessarily generate income.

her play to dispositions and interests in the girls' lives beyond the console. Broadly speaking, we found that Katarina cut her own path through the game, and Rachel played by the rules.

We found that Katarina played the game to "design" and reported that she learned what she called "design methods." Rachel played to efficiently beat scripted scenarios given by the game. Whereas Katarina sought to make her exhibits "pretty," Rachel arranged her exhibits for best functionality rather than aesthetic appeal (see figure 3).

Rachel also maximized her in-game funds by purchasing the minimum number of items necessary to keep her zoo's animals healthy and happy, whereas Katarina would add extra features to the exhibits, like trees and rocks, that did little for her in-game bottom line but improved the aesthetics of her zoo. Katarina was so unwavering in her focus on using the game as an aesthetic design medium that she actively occluded in-game instructions that recommended efficiency and point-maximizing behaviors, despite the chance this could lead to the failure of her zoo as a business. This, in turn, created the possibility that she'd no longer be able to extend her design, because if the business failed, her game would be over. She resolved this dilemma by using a cheat code that gave her extra money. Katarina showed no moral compunction whatsoever about using the code, indicating further that using the game as a context for design was her leading value.

Segment 7

1. *Katarina:* You know I have two million dollars.
2. *Tom Satwicz:* Is that how much it gives you when you start?
3. *Katarina:* No, it gives you like seventy-five thousand and then I cheated.
4. *Tom Satwicz:* Oh you cheated?
5. *Katarina:* Yes.
6. *Tom Satwicz:* Ohhh.
7. *Katarina:* Doesn't everyone? [laughs]

[Katarina 2005-08-30_00:12:31.23]

Katarina's design activities in-game had clear connections to other aspects of her life that she shared with us. She talked of designing her bedroom and showed us Japanese lamps she made. She told us that she enjoyed designing a Web page for a social studies project earlier in the school year, and was still proudly sharing the page months after the school project was completed. A school mandate limited subsequent presentations to PowerPoint, which Katarina described as boring and an unacceptable medium for her design interests. Similarly, Rachel's reported preference for efficiency was reflected in her approach to other everyday activities. She led a hectic life, carefully coordinating her sports, church, family, school, babysitting, and social activities on a calendar. Because she scheduled multiple activities in a single day, she efficiently allocated a specific amount of time to each activity. Rachel also had a different stance from Katarina regarding the use of cheat codes that we saw as reflecting her overall orientation to life and game play; she actively chose not to use cheat codes in the game *Zoo Tycoon,* choosing instead to play by the rules and observe the implicit moral order of getting ahead in the game by getting better through clearly sanctioned modes of improvement (e.g., controlled simulations and exploring strategies for maximizing profit).

> Before I did the scenarios I definitely used the cheats a lot . . . the money cheats . . . for the scenarios I feel like—I don't know. When I was doing the more free games . . . the thing that would get in your way of having a really nice zoo was not having enough money. So in the scenarios I try to—I don't know, work harder at being better.
>
> *[Rachel 2006-0318_00:02:45.18]*

While *Zoo Tycoon* incorporates many of the learning and teaching principles that have been attributed to other video games,[22] the realization/triggering of those mechanisms (as intended by the games designers) seems to presume some baseline commonality in the goals of all players and the designers. The cases of Rachel and Katarina illustrate otherwise—what individual players bring to the game shapes not only *how* they play, but *what* they play. Confronted with identical game packages, the girls had very different goals and expectations of what it meant to play *Zoo Tycoon.* In turn, these individualized endpoints influenced what parts of the game they attended to in learning how to play.

Vignette 7—Continuities in Sibling Relationships Across In-Game Play and (Home)Work

In this vignette, we bring together events from two situations involving Holly (age 14) and her brother Brandon (age 12) to show strong similarities and an important difference in the way they organize themselves collaboratively during game play and while doing homework. We observed that, in both activities, Holly often assumed a coaching or caretaker role, often without invitation to do so from Brandon. In these situations, she actively assessed his needs and attempted to provide a resolution to what she saw as *his* problem. Of interest here, especially in relation to our argument about the variation in learning arrangements described in earlier vignettes, is that Holly provided this support regardless of what she knew or thought she knew. In other words, she tried to help him even when she thought she knew very little about the topic at hand. Because of this, we see it quite clearly as a *role* she assumes with him. Furthering this interpretation, she was unlike other young people in our study temporarily sidelined while someone else played solo, since she did not try to join the play or become impatient waiting; she seemed comfortable in the role of coach. Brandon, in turn, assumed a role as a somewhat impassive but willing recipient of her coaching support.

With respect to video game play, both Holly and Brandon saw the younger sibling as the clearly more able player (again, not unlike an arrangement common in coaching scenarios). Both independently told us as much, and we saw Brandon consistently beat his sister during competitive play. Brandon occasionally enlisted Holly's help when he was playing solo; however, Holly more often provided unsolicited advice while Brandon played games with which she had only passing familiarity. We often observed Holly with a game's strategy guide in hand reading aloud sections she felt were relevant to Brandon's play. Even when Brandon went in search of a game guide, it would shortly end up in Holly's hands.

While Holly continuously dispensed advice and information, Brandon did not always follow or use it. This represents, then, yet another learning arrangement than those represented in our earlier vignettes. In this case, Holly played the role of running commentator, seemingly in hopes that some of her narration would prove useful to Brandon, but she showed little distress or frustration when he failed to follow her suggestions. The reciprocal impassivity that we observed across them in this arrangement was interesting; it may have been due to the fact that Brandon was the better player and both knew that he was assessing the value of her suggestions and deciding on the basis of the in-game situation whether it was sensible to act upon or disregard his sister's help. But this reciprocal impassivity also may have been a more durable feature of their relationship.

An example of the learning arrangement between them during game play comes from a time when Brandon began a new game (*Destroy All Humans*). As was typical, Holly made suggestions based on a reading of the game's instructions during his early play sessions. She suggested, for example, that he cross the street in a particular spot and look for the mayor in a specific area. The stream of suggestions came in, often through repetition and with reasons attached, but Brandon did not respond, nor did his play register the suggestions. Only after Brandon failed *repeatedly* to achieve his current in-game objective did he typically act on his sister's advice and then successfully completed a particular mission.

Their relationship during homework time bore marked similarities to the learning arrangement that existed between them during video game play. In both situations, Brandon faced a problem, Holly assessed the situation, and attempted to help him by making herself available as a resource, even though he had not explicitly invited her to do so. In the particular homework situation we describe here, Holly decided to move into the family room with Brandon to do her homework, just in case he needed help. One difference in the gaming and homework situations was that in the case of homework (in this instance math), both regarded Holly as the more expert. What was similar between the gaming and homework situations was the sense of Holly serving as something of an ambient resource for Brandon; she was just hanging around, waiting to be asked for help, and offering it even when he did not ask.

An exemplifying moment occurred when Brandon handed his math homework packet to Holly without saying a word, and she immediately set her own work aside to accept it—such was the tacitness of the arrangement between them. At one point, after she handed his textbook back to Brandon following a helping episode, he quickly handed her another math problem sheet. She responded with a tone of pleased and feigned exasperation, "*I'm never going to get out of here am I?*" She clearly had no real need, at that point, to "get out of [there]."

However, the problem that Holly was confronted with on this new worksheet involved the mathematical concept of functions, which she proceeded quickly to assert that she could not do.

Segment 8

1. *Holly:* Something tells me this is another thing that I didn't do [Holly takes textbook from Brandon's lap and Brandon turns his head toward the math packet that Holly had previously explained.] Maybe I'll learn something.
2. [Over the next six minutes, Holly reads the textbook aloud while Brandon works on his math packet. Still talking aloud, she tries to solve an example in the book. Brandon watches, then leans his head back and closes his eyes.]
3. *Holly:* I don't know Brandon, I never did functions. This is something that I didn't do and it's gonna screw me over when I go to math class next year. [Holly picks up the worksheet and looks at it.] So, I don't know. I guess ask mom or ask [Brandon's math teacher] tomorrow in class because I don't know functions. I've never done functions. I don't know anything about functions.
4. [Brandon turns and starts leafing through a stack of papers and hands a sheet to Holly.]

[Holly and Brandon 2006-05-31_00:52:45]

Here Holly's lack of knowledge about the content of *his* work changed the situation; she wanted to move someone else into the role of Brandon's helper and repeatedly asserted her lack of ability as reason to disengage from her role as helper. We find this a striking difference when compared with her helping during game play; in the gaming situation she knew equally little, and perhaps even less, about the content at hand, but in the case of the game, her own lack of ability was of no issue, while in the homework situation her lack of ability was a source of discomfort, self-negation, and disengagement, a point she made most emphatically, moments later, saying to Brandon with clear distress: "Oh. No no no. I don't know functions Brandon. [Raises left hand to rub eyes.] I've never done functions. I've never learned functions. No one ever taught me functions. Um I would only suggest asking Mom, wait until Dad gets home and ask him."

We find this comparison instructive in that it shows that while the basic learning arrangement between Holly and Brandon seems to travel across activities, it does so with an important difference that may tell us something about the differences between school and gaming as learning contexts. In this research, we have found that game play is a pretty productive learning context for young people; others, like Gee elsewhere in this volume, have reached a similar conclusion. Gee has argued that this is, in large part, because game designers have employed good learning principles, thus locating the locus of productive agency primarily in the games. Gee contrasts the "curricula" of games, designed with these good learning principles, against traditional school curricula, which, he argues, are designed under other, less productive, learning principles. Our data suggest a different account, at least in part. We locate the productive agency of game play as a learning environment in qualities of in-room collaboration—these being comfortable sociality, having one's knowledge valued and used by others and having the experience of being engaged in joint projects. From Holly's reaction, it seems also that less shame is attachable to not knowing how to play the game than not knowing how to do the homework, or at least that is secondary to helping her brother accomplish something. This is striking because game play, like school, is competitively structured as a social practice, but it seems perhaps gaming might be a more productively motivating competitive environment than school (except, of course, for some people). This is certainly a topic for further investigation.

Throughout this chapter we have argued that the productivity of these gaming environments for learning lies in the fact that kids among themselves are free to figure out and create learning and teaching arrangements that work for them. We might go so far as to say that young people across our study are presenting us with their implicit theory of learning in game play—their theory being that games are learnable and we (i.e., they) need only figure out how to learn them. The variations of learning arrangements across this and the earlier vignettes make this point.

This vignette involving Holly and Brandon also adds something to this account, through its comparison of a learning arrangement between two siblings that is durable in the gaming situation, and fragile—and a source of self-abnegation—in the homework situation. This contrast exists even though it was quite clear that Holly knew more than Brandon about mathematical functions than she did comparatively about *Destroy All Humans*. As such, we might expect her to feel more relationally confident with the math and likewise less fragile; but she didn't. In comparison to an implicit theory that games are learnable, Holly's comments about mathematical functions and her own lack of *knowledge* suggest her theory of learning in this case is more restrictive; that in fact, mathematical functions, and maybe all school knowledge, can only be known through the medium of adult instruction. Because she "missed" this in school, she can't really be expected to learn it now, despite being able to call on resources like her own background knowledge or the textbook she is reading from, resources as good or better than those that she has at hand for helping Brandon in the game situations.

Vignette 8—"I Wouldn't Really Do That" and "I Couldn't Get Away With That": Making Distinctions Between In-Game and In-World Consequences

At the beginning of the chapter, we referred to a perspective we called the *separate worlds view*—the idea that games are a world apart from the real world where players can take on new, and possibly transgressive, identities. Because games require players to control characters who explore imaginary worlds, build whole cities, and engage in battles with all manner of phantasmagorical creatures, there is a surface level at which we agree with the separate worlds view. But, at a deep level, are the selves that are engaged in game play truly remade, even in the moments of play? Are new identities of the people who are playing being remade, except, of course, as game players?

Our analysis suggests that identities are implicated in game play in a different way than the separate worlds view suggests. We, of course, see young people enjoying the imaginary worlds they are able to control and build during game play, and like other successful media (e.g., films and television), they display a sense of getting lost in the experience. But our study has taught us that the identities being crafted through game play are in fact real-world identities that are crafted as young people compare their actions in-game, and their consequences, with the consequences those same actions would have in the real world.

We had a number of situations in our data that led us to this interpretation. For example, Rachel (age 15) told us that she plays games because "it's kind of something different from the real world and it's entertaining because you have control over the little scenario and you can make them really good." During play, she often offered unsolicited comparisons of how her in-game behavior differed from her real-world behavior. While she played *Zoo Tycoon*—the simulation game in which players build and maintain zoos—this contrast was most striking. In her everyday life, Rachel and her family cared for stray and abandoned cats awaiting adoption through a local animal shelter. We often observed her readily pause her game play to monitor a cat's health or attend to its needs. In-game however, Rachel's decisions about the animals she was caring for as zookeeper were driven by monetary gain rather than the happiness or well-being of the animals. For example, while creating a zoo for different types of *cats* (e.g., tigers, lions, and leopards), Rachel learned of a new birth in her zoo and responded by selling the newborn animals immediately.

Segment 9

1. *Rachel:* Yeah, because the baby—um because there was a birth of an endangered animal? <...> that's really great. And it's especially great for me because I can sell the little baby for $1000. [Clicks button to sell baby.] That's a good deal.
2. [Rachel pauses, then explains herself.]
3. In real life? I would not own a zoo like—I would not, um, what would—what would you say, um, manage a zoo like this. I would be much more caring. But in this game, [smiles and nods her head] I'm more (.) greedy. But that's okay. Okay, so now that I have money, I actually can (.) that's really good. Except it will go very quickly.

[Rachel 2005-10-29_00:28:10.28]

Similarly, Rachel explained that she would never clear-cut the trees in real life, but she does so in-game because it makes her a lot of money. Rachel also commented that not only does the value of trees decrease as time goes by, but that there is no cost incurred to clear-cut, which didn't make sense to her. There should be a cost, she noted, "you know, kind of ecologically, but no, no cost."

For different purposes, Rachel also spent time highlighting alignments—rather than contrasts—between her real-world life and the in-game world of *Zoo Tycoon*. Her mother was a strong advocate and practitioner of ecologically sensitive business programs and, against that background, Rachel described a *Zoo Tycoon* composting program to her mother.

Segment 10

1. *Rachel:* Mom. In Zoo Tycoon? You have a- Part of your budget is the recycling benefit.
2. *Mom:* Oh go::d!
3. [Rachel turns her head toward her mother. She raises her right hand and moves it to emphasize her words.]
4. *Rachel:* That's part of the budget.
5. *Rachel [to researcher]:* My mom does recycling programs.
6. *Mom:* Goo::d! It needs to be calculated into more budgets.
7. [Rachel continues playing her game then continues explaining benefits.]
8. *Rachel:* Oh, and mom? You can buy a compost station? And you get $50 a month for composting? And there's NO upkeep cost. So, if you are making a zoo [Mom: wo::w!] it is beneficial to do the compost station. 'Cause then you get money.

[Rachel 2005-10-15_00:47:08.10]

In this instance, Rachel played up the positive features of *Zoo Tycoon* rather than the negative ones, but in both cases positive and negative accounts were clearly anchored to her perspectives and experiences in-world.

Another of our participants, Katarina, also made comparisons between in-game and in-world behaviors. For example, as she was bulldozing a forest of trees in the game, she stated that she would never behave that way in real life. Both girls were well aware of the differences between their in-game and out-of-game behaviors, which they sometimes felt compelled to explain. As Rachel put it:

[Games] are different [from the real world] because they don't have all the aspects and you're the only one controlling it and you can just click-out if you want and you don't really have to be involved in it. So it's just so much more like sheltered... [It's good] because then you can just do whatever you want in it.

[Rachel 2006-04-14_00:03:30.06]

Tyler and Andrew made similar comparisons of in-game and out-of-game events. While playing *Major League Baseball 2006*, for example, a pitcher–batter interaction provided an opportunity to talk about previous video game play, create "what if" real-life scenarios, and share their Little League baseball experiences. During one game session, Andrew was watching Tyler play as one team against the computer. After striking out a batter, Tyler brought up a contrast between Seattle Mariner Ichiro Suzuki's real-world demeanor and his in-game behavior. This lead to a recounting of play in a different baseball game called *Slug Fest*.

Segment 11

1. *Tyler:* You know how Ichiro never gets mad in real life? Well in the game he charged the mound. [smiles]
2. *Andrew:* Remember when um you got him mad? When I was playing with him?
3. *Tyler:* [Nods] I did- We just made that- He never gets mad but in the game he got all mad and he charged the plate.
4. *Andrew:* Notice how he throws the bat at someone? [laughs]
5. *Tyler:* *Slug Fest* is so funny! You know if you hit the batter good enough? He gets all mad? He gets really mad and uh-.
6. *Andrew:* Do *Slug Fest* after this. I want to see it.
7. *Tyler:* I don't have *Slug Fest.*
8. *Andrew:* Oh you don't?
9. *Tyler:* But he gets all mad, like if you beat the guy up really good? You'll get on fire and then you'll pitch really good? Then if you keep on beating up the batters? You'll pitch all- you'll pitch really good. It's funny.

[Tyler 2005-07-20_00:54:42.25]

This passage, taken in isolation, might support the separate worlds view; even worse, it might suggest that these boys are learning from the game the idea that it is both okay to beat someone up and it is a way to improve your pitching. Yet, following their conversation a bit further disabused us of this interpretation. In Segment 12, Tyler and Andrew continued the hitting batters discussion and talked about their actual and imagined reactions in similar Little League situations. Against the backdrop of Tyler controlling one team at bat, they laughed about beating up Little League pitchers whom they have imagined hit them with pitched balls. However, in contrast to the *Slug Fest* scenario, the boys recognized the consequences of bringing such behavior into their Little League play (lines 9–10), while at the same time had a safe space to imagine the dangerous actions.

Segment 12

1. *Tyler:* I'm about to get a rally. Watch this. [his batter hits the ball] Bam! [looks surprised as the ball goes over the fence] Told you I was about to start a rally. Only if it—too bad it wasn't a grand slam.

2. *Andrew:* Just two more people in there- I mean one more person in there. It would have been a grand slam.
3. *Tyler:* You know what really ticks me off when I'm batting? Like if I get hit by the pitch? Like if it's not—if somebody hits me in my leg, I'm, I'm not mad at the pitcher, but if someone hits me up in my helmet? That's when I get mad.
4. *Andrew:* MmHmm.
5. *Tyler:* But, I—I'd get in trouble if I charged the plate.[23] [smiles] I'd get in bi::g trouble. But I wouldn't think about charging the plate. I just give the pitcher a mean look.
6. *Andrew:* I'd throw the bat at someone. [both boys laugh] You know it's like, dude! could you please not do- [swings right arm up then downward across chest] Boom! Right in their face.
7. [Tyler's player in the game is running to second base.]
8. *Andrew:* Safe. If they hit me in my helmet I'm like (.) Hey ma::n. Like after the game I'm like, man could you not do that anymore? [swings arm up and then across chest] Boom! right with my bat!
9. *Tyler:* Yeah right man. You'd be in juvie.
10. *Andrew:* [laughs] I know. [leans back on sofa] That'd be messed up.

[Tyler 2005_07-20_01:02:08.12]

Taken together, these stories of Rachel, Katarina, Andrew, and Tyler suggest that young people are indeed forming identities in relation to video games. The idea that they can do things in the game that they cannot do in the real world is only part of the story; the other half is that they hold actions that they control in-game in regular comparative contact with the consequences, and morality, of those actions in the real world. Actions in games, then, are a resource for building identities in the real world, occurring through a reflective conversation that takes place in-room.

Conclusion

We began this study with questions about how and what young people learn playing video games—of their own choosing, in their own homes—and with questions about how they adapt to or use in the rest of their live what they learn playing games. Before collecting any data, we were familiar with the argument that games are remarkably good learning environments because they embody dozens of important learning principles.[24] As ethnographers and researchers of learning and cognition, we were struck by the lack of empirical backing for these claims, so that alone was sufficient reason for us to undertake the study.

But there were deeper reasons for doing this study, which became clear in hindsight. Regardless of the level of game play in our own lives, we identified with many of the kids at play in these living rooms and dens. Some of us may have watched broadcast television rather than played video games or played board-based strategy games rather than electronically programmed ones, but the consumption and repurposing of mass-produced media that we saw among these young people resonated deeply. Watching these kids lying around, talking, joking, and trying to figure things out in this ordinary way was very familiar. We suspect it strikes many readers of this volume, who've probably grown up in past two or three decades, in similarly resonant ways. So as people who were and are these kids, we wondered about the effects of our own media consumption at the same time as we wondered about theirs.

We will not indulge in the telling of these personal stories here, but we will say that what we hold true of ourselves we have rediscovered to be true across the participants in our study—that an "answer" to the question of how media consuming and repurposing has affected these young people is complicated and contingent; it depends on differing dispositions and purposes that people bring to play, who they play with, and perhaps more importantly what people *make of* these experiences in other times and places in their lives. By emphasizing this active role of making something of game playing experiences, we are stepping quite far away from any simple generalizations about effects of video game play. We are not here to deliver the news that playing games is a waste of people's time, nor are we here to say, "Yes it is the new wave that the next generation will ride to get smart and be more creative." But we do have a few general things to say.

The variety of ways that we saw young people arrange themselves to play games surprised us, especially since most of these ways were interpersonally and emergently organized by the young people themselves. One interpretation of why this happened would be to say that these kids were extremely "motivated" to learn to play video games, and so they learned however they could manage. If this were our conclusion, it would set up a research question that many are pursuing—what *properties* do games have that make them motivating? Watching the young people in our study, we did not see affective displays that led us toward the high motivation explanation. But there is a bigger lesson of our study that we think displaces the high motivation explanation, perhaps in principle. Video game play is too different in its purposes and uses across even our small number of cases to look for a property of it as an interactive medium.

For these reasons, we do not appeal to the games-are-highly-motivating explanation, but we do see a reason that young people play games and get them tangled up with the rest of their lives, and this reason is cultural. The phrase that best helps us explain it comes from one of our participants, Mikey, who in talking about games said, "It's what we do." The "we" he was referring to was kids these days, the young people of his generation. Video game play is now hunkered down in our culture. And "what we do" is something that gets learned somehow and someway.

There are things we expected to see, but did not. We expected to see, for example, kids taking on identities from the game; this sort of dramatic blurring of in-game and in-world did not occur in our study. We saw a few evocative moments with our more expressive participants when they borrowed a celebratory gesture or phrase from a game's character, but these moments were usually played for laughs and came directly after the in-game moment. They were more like echoes than borrowed durable elements for a real-world persona. Of course, we've had to consider that our ethnographic approach, studying observable behavior and exchanges between people and devices, has left too much unseen. It is certainly possible. And it is surely a claim that many psychologists would make, arguing that all the really important stuff was going on in their heads. This would include carrying or transferring traits from characters they have controlled in game situations into real-life situations. All we can say about this is that we did not see evidence for this in our study, nor did our participants tell us about this when interviewed. We leave it to other researchers to devise methods to discover what we might be missing.

What we did observe and have described in this chapter is a different kind of "transfer" between what we call in-game and in-world. It's a kind of transfer that the players are quite active in constructing themselves. We saw this in a number of the vignettes, as young people actively juxtaposed consequences for actions in-game and in-world. This study, therefore, supports a view of transfer that is best understood as an action that a person actively *does* rather than an automatic process that *happens to* a person's mind under appropriate conditions. This, in turn, has methodological implications in that if transfer is something someone does, actively using and repurposing learning from one setting to another, then we need to study these other settings. Setting up experiments in the laboratory won't help us much, because in laboratories we will almost certainly lack the very conditions that would allow us to see transfer as we are understanding it in this study—namely, a consequential context (i.e., consequential to the person) to which someone actively brings his or her gaming skills, dispositions, or learning arrangements.

Our study of kids playing games is part of a decade-long research program that seeks to look at people's activities, comparatively and across settings.[25] The theoretical idea that animates this program and related lines of work[26] is that practices—even practices like video game play that constitute a seemingly separate world—substantially acquire meanings for people not because they have this or that property (e.g., interactivity or narrative engagement), but by the ways that particular practices are in circulation with others. In our view, further productive research would extend the line of analysis we've pursued in this project, putting a spotlight on gaming, but also keeping a close eye on all the other activities in young people's lives that are tangled up with gaming. Further research also needs to look at gaming over time, taking seriously the idea that young people these days have *careers*—with all that this term implies—as gamers, and that these careers lead young people toward particular experiences, people, and identities, and away from others.[27]

Notes

1. Barbara Rogoff and Jean Lave, eds., *Everyday Cognition: Its Development in Social Context* (Cambridge, MA: Harvard University Press, 1984); Jean Lave and Etienne Wenger, *Situated Learning: Legitimate Peripheral Participation* (Cambridge, UK: Cambridge University Press, 1991); Edwin Hutchins, *Cognition in the Wild* (Cambridge, MA: The MIT Press, 1995); and John Seely Brown, Allan Collins, and Paul Duguid, Situated Cognition and the Culture of Learning, *Educational Researcher* 18, no. 1 (1989): 32–42.

2. Clifford Geertz, *Local Knowledge: Further Essays in Interpretive Anthropology* (New York: Basic Books, 1983).

3. Jean Lave, *Cognition in Practice: Mind, Mathematics, and Culture in Everyday Life* (Cambridge, UK: Cambridge University Press, 1988); and Hutchins, *Cognition in the World.*

4. Michael Cole, Ray P. McDermott, and Lois Hood, *Ecological Niche-Picking: Ecological Invalidity as an Axiom of Experimental Cognitive Psychology* (New York: Rockefeller University, Laboratory of Comparative Cognition, 1978).

5. Lev Grossman, The Art of the Virtual: Are Video Games Starting to—Gasp!—Mean Something? *Time Magazine* 164, no. 19 (2004).

6. James Paul Gee, *What Video Games Have to Teach Us About Learning and Literacy* (New York: Palgrave, 2003), 204.

7. Gee, *What Video Games Have to Teach Us*; Henry Jenkins, Game On! The Future of Literacy Education in a Participatory Media Culture, *Threshold,* Winter 2006. Reprinted on New Media Literacies Web site: http://www. projectnml.org/node/306/. Accessed June 20, 2007; Kurt Squire and Sasha Barab, Replaying History: Engaging Urban Underserved Students in Learning World History Through Computer Simulation Games, in *Embracing Diversity in the Learning Sciences: Proceedings of the Sixth International Conference of the Learning Sciences*, eds. Yasmin B. Kafai, William A. Sandoval, Noel Enyedy, Althea Scott Nixon, and Francisco Herrera (Mahwah, NJ: Lawrence Erlbaum Associates, 2004), 505–12 ; Michael Young, P. B. Schrader, and Dongping Zheng, MMOGs as Learning

Environments: An Ecological Journey into Quest Atlantis and The Sims Online, *Innovate* 2, no. 4 (2006). http://www.innovateonline.info/index.php?view=article&id=66. Accessed June 20, 2007; Marc Prensky, Computer Games and Learning: Digital Game-Based Learning, in *Handbook of Computer Game Studies*, eds. Joost Raessens and Jeffrey Goldstein (Cambridge, MA: The MIT Press, 2005), 97–122; and Chris Dede, Research on the Use of Games and Simulations in Education: What Are We Learning? Presented at the 2006 AERA Annual Meeting, San Francisco, April 2006.

8. For a notable and foundational exception, see Mizuko Ito, Engineering Play: Children's Software and the Productions of Everyday Life (PhD diss., Stanford University, 2002); and Mizuko Ito, Mobilizing Fun in the Production and Consumption of Children's Software, *The Annals of the American Academy of Political and Social Science* 597, no. 1 (2005): 82–102.

9. Cf., Reed Stevens and Rogers Hall, Disciplined Perception: Learning to See in Technoscience, in *Talking Mathematics in School: Studies of Teaching and Learning*, eds. Magdalene Lampert and Merrie L. Blunk (Cambridge, UK: Cambridge University Press, 1998), 107–49; Reed Stevens, Divisions of Labor in School and in the Workplace: Comparing Computer and Paper-Supported Activities Across Settings, *Journal of the Learning Sciences* 9, no. 4 (2000): 373–401; Reed Stevens, Sam Wineburg, Leslie Rupert Herrenkohl, and Philip Bell, The Comparative Understanding of School Subjects: Past, Present and Future, *Review of Educational Research* 75, no. 2 (2005): 125–57; John Bransford, Nancy Vye, Reed Stevens, Pat Kuhl, Dan Schwartz, Philip Bell, Andy Meltzoff, Brigid Barron, Roy Pea, Jeremy Roschelle, and Nora Sabelli, Learning Theories and Education: Toward a Decade of Synergy, in *Handbook of Educational Psychology*, 2nd ed., eds. Patricia Alexander and Philip Winne (Mahwah, NJ: Lawrence Erlbaum Associates, 2006).

10. Gee, *What Video Games Have to Teach Us*; Kurt Squire, From Content to Context: Videogames as Designed Experience, *Educational Researcher* 35, no. 8 (2006): 19–29; and Constance A. Steinkuehler, Massively Multiplayer Online Videogaming as Participation in a Discourse, *Mind, Culture, and Activity* 13, no. 1 (2006): 38–52.

11. For the evocative phrase "tangled up" that we borrow throughout the chapter and analyses of kids' lives that are sympathetic to our own, see Jan Nespor's *Tangled Up in School: Politics, Space, Bodies, and Signs in the Educational Process* (Mahwah, NJ: Lawrence Erlbaum Associates, 1997).

12. See, for example, Robert J. Moore, Nicolas Ducheneaut, and Eric Nickell, Doing Virtually Nothing: Awareness and Accountability in Massively Multiplayer Online Worlds, *Computer Supported Cooperative Work* 16, no. 3 (2007): 265–305; Tony Manninen and Tomi Kujanpää, The Hunt for Collaborative War Gaming—CASE: Battlefield 1942, *Game Studies* 5, no. 1 (2005). http://www.gamestudies.org/0501/manninen_kujanpaa. Accessed June 20, 2007; and Steinkuehler, Massively Multiplayer Online Videogaming.

13. Lucy Suchman, *Plans and Situated Actions: The Problem of Human-Machine Communication* (Cambridge, UK: Cambridge University Press, 1987); Charles Goodwin and Marjorie Goodwin, Formulating Planes: Seeing as a Situated Activity, in *Cognition and Communication at Work*, eds. David Middleton and Yrjö Engeström (Cambridge, UK: Cambridge University Press, 1996), 61–95; Stevens and Hall, Disciplined Perception; and Stevens, Divisions of Labor.

14. Hannah Meara Marshall, Structural Constraints on Learning: Butchers' Apprentices, in *Learning to Work*, ed. B. Geer (London: Sage, 1972); Hutchins, *Cognition in the Wild*; Lave and Wenger, *Situated Learning*; and Barbara Rogoff, *Apprenticeship in Thinking: Cognitive Development in Social Context* (New York: Oxford University Press, 1991).

15. Hutchins, *Cognition in the Wild.*

16. Marshall, Structural Constraints on Learning.

17. Evan was Johnny's schoolmate. We do not have Evan's actual age since he was not a primary participant in the study, but we infer his age to be 12–14 years because they are in the same grade in school.

18. Gee, *What Video Games Have to Teach Us.*

19. In the second collection of vignettes, we illustrate this general point with a comparative analysis of two girls playing the same game. They play the game *Zoo Tycoon* very differently and learn very different things from these different orientations to play. Though, arguably, this dramatic difference might be attributed to the game design itself, we see this as stretching the definition of design a bit too far, at least for purposes of attributing to the game's design the powerful learning effects we and others have observed.

20. Gee, *What Video Games Have to Teach Us*; and Constance A. Steinkuehler, Learning in Massively Multiplayer Online Games, in *Proceedings of the Sixth International Conference of the Learning Sciences*, eds. Yasmin B. Kafai, William A. Sandoval, Noel Enyedy, Althea Scott Nixon, and Francisco Herrera, 521–8 (Mahwah, NJ: Lawrence Erlbaum Associates, 2004).

21. For two efforts considering issues of continuity and transition outside the psychological approach to transfer consistent with ours, see Lave's *Cognition in Practice* and King Beach's Consequential Transitions: A Sociocultural Expedition Beyond Transfer in Education, *Review of Research in Education* 24 (1999): 101–39.

22. Gee, *What Video Games Have to Teach Us.*

23. Tyler seemingly means "charge the mound."

24. Gee, *What Video Games Have to Teach Us*; Marc Prensky, The Motivation of Game Play: The Real Twenty-First Century Learning Revolution, *On the Horizon* 10, no. 1 (2002): 5–11; Marc Prensky, Computer Games and Learning; and Kurt Squire, Educating the Fighter, *On the Horizon* 13, no. 2 (2005): 75–88.

25. Stevens, Divisions of Labor; Stevens and Hall, Disciplined Perception; and Rogers Hall and Reed Stevens, Making Space: A Comparison of Mathematical Work at School and in Professional Design Practice, in *Cultures of Computing*, ed. Susan L. Star (London: Basil Blackwell, 1995).

26. Bruno Latour, *Pandora's Hope: Essays on the Reality of Science Studies* (Cambridge, MA: Harvard University Press, 1999); idem., Reassembling the Social: An Introduction to Actor-Network-Theory (Oxford: Clarendon, 2005); Jan Nespor, *Tangled Up in School*; Kevin Leander and Jason Lovvorn, Literacy Networks: Following the Circulation of Text and Identities in the School-Related and Computer Gaming-Related Literacies of One Youth, Paper presented at the American Educational Association Annual Meeting, San Diego, CA, 2004; and Ron Scollon, *Mediated Discourse: The Nexus of Practice* (London: Routledge, 2001).

27. Reed Stevens, Tom Satwicz, and Laurie McCarthy, How Video Games Are Used in Heterogenous Ways to Build an Identity and a Future in the Real World, Forthcoming.

E Is for Everyone: The Case for Inclusive Game Design

Amit Pitaru

New York University, Intertelecommunications Program

Introduction: Mia

Mia is a lovely 10-year-old with a beautiful dark complexion and expressive brown eyes. She is warm, bright, friendly, and loves to laugh. Unfortunately, the average person would not notice initially these things about Mia, because she is also nonverbal and unable to ambulate. She spends the majority of her time in a manual wheelchair with her arms strapped to the armrests. This is necessary because Mia can uncontrollably injure her own lovely face.

Mia has Cerebral Palsy with athetosis and spasticity. This presents as continuous uncontrollable writhing movements in her extremities, head, neck, facial, and oral muscles. It can also cause fixing, which can "lock" her in uncomfortable postures. Mia expends a tremendous amount of energy due to the fact that her body is in constant motion. Volitional movements, changes in emotion, illness, and stress can all cause an increase in these extraneous movements. Mia knows what she wants to do, but is a prisoner in her own uncooperative body (Angela Passariello-Foray, Mia's therapist, "Mia case study," private online forum discussion with author, November 11, 2006).

The work described in this chapter is based on a truly collaborative effort, and would not have taken place without the support and guidance of the following individuals:

The Henry Viscardi School in Albertson, New York: I would like to thank the amazing students at HVS—your names have been modified for privacy considerations, but you know who you are. Learn your rights and advocate! In addition, this work would not have been possible without the guidance and support of the occupational therapists at HVS: Maureen Aliani, Jane Carvalho, Janet Gambitsky, Kelly Gannon, Ahmee Ko, Marlana Lipnick, Kate McGrath, Jennifer Noronha, Angela Passariello-Foray, and Chris Marotta. In the most humble manner, they are breaking new ground daily by using technology in a revolutionary, yet sensible and responsible, manner. Thank you for sharing your genius with me. I hope this chapter does it justice. On the executive end of HVS, I thank Patrice Kuntzler, Jeanette Glover, and Jill Carroll, as well as Alberto Bursztyn from the Global Institute at Abilities! for facilitating this most wonderful collaborative effort.

Interactive Telecommunications Program, Tisch School of the Arts, New York University:

My work at HVS, and particularly the *Tetris* case study emerged from a collaborative effort with two dear friends and colleagues, Jennifer Kirchherr and Hsiao-Ho Hsu, with the seminal guidance of Michael Schneider and Christine Brumback. I would also like to thank Marianne R. Petit and Anita Perr for their ongoing support and tutelage in the field of Assistive Technology. And to Nancy Hechinger, thank you dearly for your invaluable mentorship and guidance.

The MacArthur Foundation: Katie Salen, my editor, was entrusted with the task of molding coherent prose from within my rambling mind. I credit her with all that was made right in the chapter, and take full responsibility for that which is not. Thank you, Katie.

Because of her condition, Mia is dependent upon others for all activities of daily living. She requires assistance for all of the things most people take for granted, such as eating, drinking, dressing, hygiene, communication, mobility, as well as playing games.

Mia is a student at Henry Viscardi School (HVS)[1] in Albertson, New York. This remarkable school educates approximately 200 pre-K to twenty-one-year-old students with a variety of physical disabilities and medical needs. Some students are more physically able than Mia, while others are as medically fragile. It is important to note that despite these medical needs, the children at HVS are as academically able as other typical students their age.

In the winter of 2004, I was invited with a group of my NYU[2] colleagues—Jennifer Kirchherr and Hsiao-Ho Hsu—to visit HVS. Our goal was to observe the daily routine of the students to see if we could help devise hardware and/or software applications to assist them in their school activities. While not engineers, we are trained in the design and prototyping of computer software and hardware. My background is in new media art and game design. Therefore, I was particularly interested in learning about the gaming habits of the children at HVS. In order to facilitate the collaboration, several students were given the option to join us in the occupational therapy room for an hour of computer gaming. I was to bring the Playstation, Xbox, and computers, and children who wished to participate were asked to bring their favorite game titles. What an amazing opportunity to witness game play in the special need sector, I thought to myself.

We arrived at the school grounds during the lunch break. On our way in, we passed through the school's cafeteria, where we found children huddled in groups around tables, laughing and teasing each other. Some students were sitting in pairs, and some were being attended by a caregiver. Many sat in wheelchairs and some used respirators, but this did not stop the place from vibrating with the all-familiar energy of school cafeterias! I was happy that we got to see this spectacle, as it reminded us that above all, kids will be kids. When we entered the occupational therapy room at the school, it became apparent why it had been chosen as our playground for the day. The spacious room housed a wall closet filled with hundreds of games and crafts. Swings hung from the ceiling and colorful mats covered the floor. Interestingly, I noticed a row of laptop computers connected to a plethora of joysticks and other devices I'd never seen before.

Maureen Aliani, one of the school's nine occupational therapists (OTs), explained that lunch period had just ended and—any minute now—we should expect children to march in with their favorite games.

Five minutes passed, and no one showed. One child passed in the hall and Maureen ran out to meet him: "Hey Miles, are you here to play games?" Miles looked into the room, noticed me, looked back at Maureen and said, "No thank you, Miss Maureen, I have a history class right now." No one else appeared after that.

Needless to say, I was disappointed and bewildered by the apparent lack of interest. But mostly I was saddened. My own childhood was greatly enriched by computer games; my next-door neighbor was the first to have a computer on our street, and a group of four friends always played together at his house. When my parents also brought a computer home, I was the only one with enough "experience" to operate computers and so became the house expert. Whether it was playing alone or with friends, playing computer games was a highly imaginative, socially engaging, and overall empowering experience. But mostly—it was fun!

Twenty years laters, video games are one of the most coveted forms of play for our youth, so why didn't the children at HVS want to play?[3] Thinking this over, I realized that I had no idea how Mia could play video games when her two hands were secured to her chair. Were video games inaccessible to such a degree that some children at HVS simply avoided them? Was the problem related specifically to video games, or was it a subset of a larger phenomenon? If so, what kind of design intervention would be needed to accommodate Mia and children with similar restrictions? And once applied, how would it affect their lives?

In order to learn about the role of video games in the lives of children with disabilities, I would first need to understand the underlying play habits of children like Mia.

Lack of Play

Because of their disabilities, some of the children at HVS cannot play catch in the yard with their peers. A few are also not able to construct a Lego castle or even nudge a chess piece on their own. Instead they require an adult to carry out the physical aspects of these play activities for them. Jane, one of the OTs at HVS, explains that this lack of independent play starts at a very early age:

> We all start out by touching and putting things in our mouth and thus experiencing the world. This is our first form of play. So what happens when a child does not have all of these components, due to a disability? Can you imagine not having the opportunity to crawl on the rug, take your shoes off and run on the grass, or feel the water moving under your hand? These playful sensory motor experiences are the ones that shape our brains. But when they don't exist, the sensory-deprivation produces an inability both to explore, and later manipulate, the environment. (Jane Carvalho, Personal communication during Interview on October 31, 2006)

As a child matures, this lack of an opportunity to explore translates into deficiencies in the child's sensory-motor, cognitive-perceptual, and social-emotional abilities.[4] For example, not being able to run playfully in the yard, play catch, or toss things around produces difficulties in spatial relations, prediction, and directionality, which later affect the child's ability to navigate in space. At HVS, the therapists trace such perceptual deficits to the tremendous difficulties that some children have when learning to control their powered wheelchairs.

Lack of independent play also affects the child's self-image.[5] Typical children are bound to the rule sets that adults impose all day long—"finish your food," "brush your teeth," "time for bed," and so on. But moments of independent play allow them to disengage from these constraints, devise their own rules and use these rules as a framework for imaginative activities. However, for some of the children at HVS, attempting to play independently with traditional toys often yields frustrating results that only heighten an awareness of their disabilities. This leaves them with no choice but to concede to adult assistance (and thus supervision). In the long run, the children's inability to face challenges independently prevents them from learning resiliency, as well as from experiencing mastery. Instead, they get used to the caregivers' mediation and may, therefore, develop a sense of helplessness rather than control over their environment.

Ideally, a healthy child should have a balance between various play activities: mediated as well as independent, physical, and cerebral.[6] But a child with disabilities may require assistance to complete physical tasks, and therefore experience mostly mediated play, with little or no opportunity for independent play. This imbalance can affect the child emotionally, cognitively, and physically, and—as the next section illustrates—socially, as well.

Social Play

According to Chandler,[7] as typical children grow, they encounter and engage in several stages of play:

- *Solitary Play* is a form of play in which a child learns both to relate to and to manipulate his or her environment independently.
- *Onlooker Play* is the first form of Social Play, in which the child who is playing is observing the children around him or her.
- *Parallel Play* is a social activity in which several children are playing with the same materials, but not together.
- *Associative Play* is a social activity in which several children are playing together, but in a loosely organized fashion.
- *Cooperative Play* is the most developed form, in which children accept designated roles and are dependent on each other for achieving the goals of the play.

Although children encounter these stages of play within various sequences, children who experience problems with solitary play and sensory stimuli may not develop the appropriate self-esteem and confidence toward engaging in social play. This is one of several factors that can hinder the natural emergence of such social activities. For example, the extra time that some children with special needs spend completing simple activities of daily living (such as toileting, dressing, and eating) may come at the expense of the playtime that typical children enjoy. Furthermore, organizing social activities for children with disabilities may require a significant amount of effort and resources on the caretaker's behalf; such activities may not occur as often or as naturally as with typical children. The therapists at HVS find that when a peer-social setting eventually does become accessible, some may not know how to cope with it:

> Angela (OT): Even when our students are given the opportunity, as when the school organizes social events, some of them don't want to go. They come to therapy instead! We tell them 'Go Have Fun!' but they reply 'I have OT, I have OT' [trying to convince the therapists that it's time for their occupational therapy session]. They feel more comfortable with care-giving adults than peers of their own age. They simply don't know how to handle the social setting, and playtime is where they should have learned it.
>
> This has an enormous affect on their adult lives. When we start training them for job interviews, we find how hard it is for them to handle new challenges and new scenarios. Once again, they look for the familiar setting and wish to avoid the unknown. (Angela Passariello-Foray, Personal communication during Interview on November 7, 2006)

While listening to Angela's explanation, it became clear that I had made several mistakes in my initial visit to HVS. I'd invited the children to participate in an unknown social activity with a stranger, without providing any guarantees that they could actually engage in the proposed play activity. These factors placed the children in a vulnerable situation where *unmediated, independent* play was not likely to occur. It was not that the children at HVS did not like video games or did not want to play them. Rather, I had not provided the children with a comfortable social setting to engage in play. In fact, as the next section will illustrate, when therapists do provide the proper support, the children indeed happily engage in many forms of play, *especially* video games.

Pathways to Independent Gaming

Here lies the core difference in the manner that typical children and children with disabilities engage in play. While *all* children love to play games and crave these experiences, the *pathways* to these gaming experiences may be compromised, due to a disability. A typical pathway allows children to approach a play activity naturally with little risk of failure. But for some children with disabilities, there's no guarantee that the play activity is accessible to them. In other words, the pathway to the game or play experience is riddled with risks of failure and possible assertion of one's own disabilities. Such a pathway may deter the child from engaging in the activity to begin with. In addition, social settings provide witnesses to a potential failure, which further deters the spontaneous desire to engage.

As illustrated above, when a child with disabilities fails to engage in independent play activities, she does not gain the experience of play that typical children pick up during childhood. Instead, she learns how to depend on her caretaker and experiences highly mediated modes of play. In this sense, dependency and inexperience can be viewed as two sides of the same coin. Dependency on a caregiver causes inexperience in playing independently, and this inexperience creates further dependency on the caregiver. Hence, a vicious cycle commences, with each iteration of the cycle affecting development of self-esteem and confidence to engage in social settings.

To break this cycle, such children require better pathways to independent play, which can support the development of self-reliance and the confidence that leads to social aptitude. Many traditional play activities—such as playground sports and even board games—do not offer the necessary pathways, due to their constraining physical nature. Could digital games be any different?

Digital Technologies: New Pathways for Game Play

Digital technologies are allowing people with disabilities to do things that would have been considered science fiction in the past. Stephen Hawking's speech synthesizer (word-prediction device), for example, enables one of the most potent minds of our century to communicate his brilliance, despite an inability to talk or write. Like Hawking, many children at HVS also use regular desktop and laptop computers for communication. Some can control a mouse and keyboard, and only require that assistive software be installed on their computers. Others use a plethora of specially adapted hardware input devices, ranging from uniquely shaped joysticks to eye/face tracking camera systems (Eye Gaze and Head-Mouse). There's even a "Sip & Puff" straw that sends signals to a computer when the user inhales and exhales through it. These solutions all outfit a standard computer with assistive software and hardware, allowing users to operate typical applications such as Web browsers and word processing software. When more comprehensive solutions are required, Augmentative/Alternative Communication (AAC) devices are used. These are laptops that are dedicated to helping the user with communication tasks. Whether it's a simple $50 adaptive switch or an $8,000 AAC device, digital technologies allow millions of people to communicate and accomplish a myriad of everyday tasks, which can vastly improve their quality of life.

What is the "secret ingredient" that renders digital technologies so useful in this respect? Perhaps it is the manner in which they allow common tasks to be decoupled from their original physicality. For example, the "cut and paste" functions in a word processor do not actually require us to physically use scissors and glue, but rather *simulate* the act by using a keyboard/mouse interface. In this respect the software function offers an alternate (hopefully faster, more efficient, and easier) way to edit a document, such as the one you're reading now. This is particularly helpful to people with disabilities, as such solutions provide them with alternative and/or augmentative ways to accomplish tasks that would not have been possible to achieve in their original physical-operation form, including activities like typing, writing, vocalizing, operating household appliances, and also playing games.

Digital Play in the Therapy Room

At HVS, the OTs are no strangers to the importance of play and are well aware of the benefits that digital technologies provide. Traditionally, therapists have been using play as a motivational tool for children with disabilities to engage in therapeutic activities that are otherwise boring, repetitive, and even painful. For example, board games are used to practice hand–eye coordination, spatial relations, and other skills that children without such disabilities pick up as they play. Many different forms of traditional games are also used to assess the child's initial condition toward occupational treatment, as well as the child's progress over time.

But these traditional games also carry limitations. For children who cannot move the game pieces by themselves, the play activity is of a surrogate nature; the therapist conducts much/all of the game's physical actions in order to stimulate the child's cognitive processes.

However, using digital games that children can control independently enables them to act on their own and thus engage in a complete therapeutic experience that activates both motor and cognitive processes. These unmediated play activities are similar to a typical interaction between a caretaker and child during play: each party is *responsible for his or her own actions*. The children themselves find this play experience most invigorating, and are empowered by their accomplishments.

For example, some students at HVS cannot reach out and move chess pieces on their own. Instead, on every turn they must communicate their choice of move to an assistant, who then carries on the physical task for them. Playing the game in this manner develops valuable cognitive skills for the children, but it bears little value toward development of hand–eye coordination, muscular exercises, and other physical aspects. On an emotional level, not being able to control the play independently enforces the notion of helplessness that the child experiences on a daily basis.

In contrast, installing a digital chess game on an accessible computer may enable the child to move the simulated chess pieces on the screen *without assistance*. Here the child is in full control of the challenge by completing a cognitive desire with a physical act, which heightens the child's sense of accomplishment. From a therapeutic standpoint, the child improves hand–eye coordination, directionality, and visual perception. By practicing the operation of the computer on which the game is installed, the child also improves his or her overall literacy of using computers toward other nongame tasks.

In providing alternate means for children with disabilities to utilize their cognitive abilities, their pathway to the game mirrors that of a typical child. Aware of this fact, the children not only tap into the full learning potential of the game, but are also empowered by the fact that they can play the game in a "typical" manner. All of these factors render the digital game beneficial as a therapeutic tool, and an equally fun one for the children to play.

One other strength of digital games for children with disabilities is their ability to simulate physical space. Similar to the way a NASA pilot trains on a simulator for a real flight, therapists at HVS (and beyond) use 3D games to train the children to use their powered wheelchairs. Such activities help the children gain confidence as they make up for inexperience navigating in physical space.[8] The training also prevents many accidents from happening during the first few sessions with the real chair.

In fact, therapists at HVS use digital games for many training activities. I was surprised to learn that digital games are also used for helping children to do their homework. One of the *main* tasks of the OTs at HVS is to enable children to complete their school activities, be they reading class material or typing homework assignments. As mentioned above, students who cannot turn a page or use a pen often rely on computers as a means for reading and typing. But outfitting a computer for such a child is not an easy process; it first requires experimentation with various input devices and usage methods, as well as training in both cognitive and physical methods. The only way to achieve assessment and training is to have the child spend continual periods of time with the various devices. But like other therapeutic activities, this process is often boring, repetitive, and even painful for children. To solve this, therapists found that installing computer games on the children's computers can do much of the initial training. The children enthusiastically play the games using their adapted computer controllers (or keyboard/mouse in some cases), and inherently learn both general computer literacy skills and the unique aspects of their assistive technology systems. For occupational therapists interested in finding ways to engage kids in learning how to use the assistive devices they require, this kind of commitment to practice represents something of a holy grail. Consistent engagement with the assistive devices also enables the therapists to assess the systems and, over time, customize them to the child's particular needs. The therapists I worked with noticed that children who play computer games start using their devices at an earlier age and with greater success.

Overall the therapists at HVS are very excited about the benefits of digital games for therapeutic needs, and would like to see the benefits carry over from the therapy room to the living room, playground, and eventually workplace.

Beyond Therapy: Digital Games as Conduits for Social Belonging

When parents think of video games, they visualize a child sitting in a dark room shooting monsters. "Where are the good old days when children played with friends in a sunny backyard?" they ask. Such impressions can be disturbing to any parent who cares about the child's social activities, and this is doubly true for those who care for children who are already segregated by disabilities. If these children are already socially isolated, do we really want to place them in front of more isolating technologies? Shouldn't we be trying to get them to spend more time with their peers instead?

To better understand the potential of digital games as social conduits, we first need to dismiss the myth that *all* video game play is socially isolating. As Henry Jenkins explains:

> Almost 60 percent of frequent gamers play with friends. Thirty-three percent play with siblings and 25 percent play with spouses or parents. Even games designed for single players are often played socially, with one person giving advice to another holding a joystick. A growing number of games are designed for multiple players—for either cooperative play in the same space or online play with distributed players.[9]

In addition, Van Schie and Wiegman[10] found no evidence linking frequent game playing behavior with social isolation, while Colwell et al.[11] found that teenagers who reported frequent game playing are more likely to meet with friends after school.[12]

There are a number of mainstream games that capture the imagination of a large group of children across gender, race, age, and ability. In days past it was *Pong, Space Invaders, Tetris, Mario Brothers, The Sims,* and many more. These games often spark conversations and debate. Like a popular sport, video games provide a platform for competition and mentorship among peers and siblings. It is not uncommon to find children practicing a game at home, much like they would practice jump shots in the yard for tomorrow's big game. Here's one account of a child at HVS who uses video games as a way to connect with his brother:

Jack goes out with friends to play baseball and stuff but I can't join him. We almost never played together as kids. But now we have a PlayStation and play together when he's home. I'm better at *SmackDown*—it's the only place where I have a chance to beat him [He laughs]. Also when we play together [against the computer], I tell him "you got my back in real life, but I got your back in here."

Billy is lucky in the sense that he can control most video games. At HVS I only found a small number of students able to play mainstream video games in this manner. Interestingly enough, this group exhibits the same social interactions around games as those of typical children. For example, they meet up on Friday afternoons for competitions, arrange play-dates at each other's houses, and use their abilities to play these games in order to meet people outside of school. Of particular interest is Eric, who demonstrates remarkable skills when playing *Madden NFL 06 by EA Sports*—one of the most popular football video games of all times. Eric plays the game while sitting uncomfortably in his wheelchair, with limited motion in his arms and fingers. When competing against other typical players, he does not ask, or receive, any special treatment. Imagine the empowering feeling of a young man who can compete and win on equal terms as his nondisabled peers.

Breaking many of the stereotypes of a gamer, Eric is neither a "nerd" nor a recluse. He is one of the most social students at HVS. I asked Eric if there's a reason that he can play *Madden* so well. He explained that, although the game does not intentionally implement any accessibility features, it allows him to play in a way that emphasizes tactics over sheer speed. Eric stressed that he also plays many other games beyond *Madden.* I asked if he also plays *World of Warcraft.* He said that he does, but not nearly as much as *Madden.*

When I go to Giants stadium with my brother and say that I play *Madden,* everyone knows what I'm talking about. *Madden* is about football and everyone knows football. But if I say that I play *World of Warcraft* no one will have a clue what I'm talking about! ("Eric"—Student, Personal Communication during interview on November 14, 2006)

Eric's response epitomizes the full social potential of video games as conduits for social acceptance. For Eric, the added value of *Madden* is its wide social appeal—a game that carries social weight beyond the gaming world. As Eric points out, this particular game has embedded itself in football culture. Most of the other fans whom Eric meets at the stadium are either playing the game or know someone who does.

To get better at the game, Eric uses the XBoxLive feature which allows him to play with other players online. He also uses a headset microphone to talk with his opponents and discuss strategies. The person on the other end does not know that Eric has a disability. As far as that person is concerned, he's "just" a great player.

While playing online allows Eric to practice against hundreds of other players with unique strategies, he also loves to play face to face with his friends from HVS. Having a popular game become accessible and remain so over a long period of time can allow children like Eric to nurture their skills and prove their abilities in a medium that matters to their peers.

Unfortunately, Eric's ability to play Madden 2006 is mainly a happy accident rather than an educated design decision by the manufacturer. There's no guarantee that the features that make the game currently accessible to players like Eric and his friends will be carried over into the next versions of the game. Eric and his friends are constantly worried of how new "improvements" to the game or console will affect their abilities to play them.

Common sense would dictate that improvements to popular games, much like improvements to popular media, should include better accessibility to the general public. A good example would be the addition of closed caption for television. But, unfortunately, when it comes to the medium of games, this is yet to be the case.

Accessibility Barriers

Eric and his group of friends are the minority at HVS, as most kids cannot access the mainstream games that this group plays. Even the slightest impairments can severely compromise their ability to play mainstream video games. For example, color blindness may prevent some gamers from perceiving important details on the screen. This problem exists across game genres, whether it's the inability to distinguish between the puzzle pieces in casual games like *Luxor*, or to identify who's on your team and who's the enemy in games like *Halo* and *Counter-Strike*.[13] This problem could easily be remedied if game companies were to provide either better color schemes or more distinct patterns for game elements that share similar colors. Doing so could help several of the children at HVS, as well as about ten million potential players in the United States who exhibit symptoms of color blindness.[14] There's an avid community of independent game developers that is creating small audio games for the visually impaired,[15] proving that it is indeed possible to achieve this feat. Still, there are no attempts by mainstream game companies to attend to this large and currently untapped demographic.

Hearing impaired players often cannot follow the auditory portions of the game, be they spoken dialogue or other game events (like the roar of a spaceship approaching from behind). According to the National Institute on Deafness and Other Communication Disorders in the United States, some sort of hearing impairment affects 28 million people; 17 out of every 1,000 of them are children under the age of eighteen. These gamers could benefit greatly from closed captioning (CC), a system mandatory for television programming. Independent developers such as Reid Kimball,[16] a former member of LucasArts, are raising awareness around this issue by writing their own game mods to implement the CC system. Thanks to their work, several games—such as *Half-Life2* and *Doom3*—have been made accessible in this manner. Although these examples show that it is possible to implement CC in mainstream games successfully, most games still lack this simple and powerful accessibility feature.

Children with limited motor abilities may only be able to play with one hand, or to control the game with one type of device (keyboard/mouse/joystick). Unfortunately, most games do not allow these players to remap the controls of the game to these devices (despite the simplicity of doing so), leaving them unable to play. Furthermore, children with disabilities generally find it hard to play on standard game consoles such as the Playstation, Xbox, and Nintendo GameCube, because there are fewer adaptive and AAC devices that are compatible with these platforms, as compared to personal computers. Most adaptive gaming products are made by a handful of small companies that modify existing controllers or fabricate devices of their own. Modification is sometimes done by hand, one device at a time, or in low quantity production cycles, affecting the variety, availability, and price points of such devices. It is important to note that many of these hardware accessibility issues can be attended with software solutions, such as allowing users to remap the keys of a controller or using known techniques that allow players to control a menu with a single switch (called Scanning-Routines). Yet, despite the simplicity involved in doing so, most game companies do not provide an adequate level of customization for the hardware devices used to play their games.

These are just a few of the many problems that the children at HVS face when attempting to play video games. In fact, most games are so inaccessible that children with poor vision or mobility cannot even navigate to the menu button that starts the game! This leaves the children with a very small number of mainstream games that are playable in light of their limitations. Furthermore, a game that works for one child may not work for his or her friend, and thus social play is further compromised.

In the therapy room, the OTs work hard to cherry-pick the few games that are both accessible and age-appropriate for their students. Some of the games I observed in use are made specifically for educational and/or therapeutic use, such as *Fripple Town* by EdMark and *Roller Typing* by EdVenture Software. But many such "edutainment" games cater to ages K–3, and are therefore not age-appropriate for the majority of the students.

For the older students, the therapists search the Internet for casual and small online games that are simple to operate, yet still interesting. Although therapists would prefer games from educational sites like PBS and Scholastic, they rarely find accessible games there, as the designers of these sites do not have children with disabilities in mind when producing their content. This leads the therapists to other generic game-aggregating sites like lilgames.com, where the focus is on quantity rather than quality—the logic being that, out of the hundreds of small games available online, at least a few should be accessible to play.

While some of the games mentioned above are of good quality, they are rarely the default choices of the children themselves, who would much rather play the same mainstream games (*Tetris, Mario Brothers, The Sims*) that their siblings, peers, and even parents play at home. Interestingly, the therapists also prefer that the children play mainstream games instead of the smaller online games; while not explicitly educational, their complexity and depth could provide adequate motor and cognitive training that the children lack so much, and thus embed much-needed therapeutic value. Furthermore, mainstream games could allow children to engage in social activities and—like Eric and Billy—use video games as vehicles for peer learning and self-empowerment. Unfortunately, most mainstream games are simply not accessible to the children at HVS.

As seventeen-year-old Josh explains, the fact that mainstream video games are not accessible is especially disheartening:

> I'll never be able to run in the yard. Even when I play basketball in a wheelchair, I look weird and can only do it with other disabled children and a lowered basket. But I can play some video games like anyone else and it *looks* OK—no-one cares if I'm "crippled"—everyone is looking at the screen. It's annoying that so many games have stupid little things [access problems] so I can't play them. What the hell! Fix them already! How hard can it be to make the game work a bit slower or allow me to choose my own keys [to control the game]. They should amend the disability act that all video games include basic features like this. Don't even get me started! ("Josh"—Student, Personal Communication during interview on November 14, 2006)

Like Josh, many of the other children and therapists are deeply bothered that video games are not accessible, despite the fact that they bear a potential that traditional playgrounds never had. The potential stems from the fact that the children have better means of accessing computer software than they have for manipulating Lego sets, monopoly boards, and tennis rackets.

As a designer, I wanted to experience firsthand what it would require to make a *mainstream* game more accessible—a game that the children see others playing at home, and would also like to participate in. My main concern was that there are two hundred children at HVS, each with his or her own unique set of learning challenges. Was it even possible to develop a video game that could accommodate all of their individual requirements? And if such a feat could be achieved, would video games fulfill their full potential as conduits for both independence and social engagement?

Case Study: Adapting a Mainstream Game

Putting on my designer hat, I decided to learn about the design issues firsthand by attempting to adapt a mainstream game and make it accessible for as many children as possible at HVS. But which game to choose?

I knew that the game would be introduced during therapy sessions, but hoped the children would want to play it at home as well, with their siblings and parents. To allow the widest range of possible social connections to occur, it was important to find a game to which the therapists, parents, and siblings could relate positively. For example, I could not choose a violent game, as this could potentially alienate parents and therapists. Lastly, my resources were limited to a one-person programming team and a short production period, so I had to choose a game that I could produce on my own. One game that immediately came to mind was *Tetris*; I knew that the adults had probably enjoyed the game in the past, so familiarity with it was a bonus factor. I also wagered that the children would love the game once they got into it, despite the lack of fancy graphics and fireworks-style explosions.

Once I selected a commercial game to modify, I needed to figure out how to make it accessible to about 200 children with varying access circumstance and methods. Furthermore, making the game accessible would only be half of the task; I had to make sure that in modifying the game I retained its playability. What good is an accessible game that everyone *can* play if no one *wants* to play it?

Can They Play It?

A quick survey revealed that most of the school's children had either never played *Tetris* or tried the game once and did not enjoy it. To my surprise, there were quite a few children that had not even heard of the game.

I wanted to observe children in action, so I set up a regular *Tetris* game on one of the computers in the occupational therapy room. This computer was connected to a couple of assistive devices that cater to children who cannot operate a keyboard and/or a mouse. One of these devices was a switch interface—basically a number of large buttons that, when pressed upon, simulate designated keyboard keys. The computer was also connected to a special joystick device that simulates a mouse; moving the joystick on its axis operates the mouse cursor. To accommodate children who use these devices, I took four large buttons (switches) and I drew a big arrow on each of them. Using software that comes with the switch device, I mapped the buttons to the arrow keyboard keys, for example, pressing the large button with the left arrow is similar to pressing the left arrow key on a keyboard. I also changed the game's graphical interface to include four buttons with arrows on the screen.

Hovering or clicking on the buttons with the mouse/joystick would mirror the operation of pressing the keyboard keys. This allowed users to play the game even if they could not use a keyboard.

I expected most children to be able to operate the game using these adapted devices, but—to my surprise—this was not the case; some could not apply enough force to manipulate the controls in a timely manner. Some could not repeat the same motion more than a few times, due to fatigue and/or unwanted spastic movements. Some had to overcome tremors and did not have fine motor control over their fingers. On the cognitive end, some children had difficulties accomplishing hand–eye coordination between the physical device and the screen, asking "Which button do I press now?" Some children had difficulties with spatial relations, and could not figure out how to rotate the pieces into the desired slot. A few could not even perform left–right directionality, such as not moving a piece to the left even when it should have been an obvious move. Some children could not perceive the goal of the game ("Where did these blocks suddenly disappear to!?"), probably due, in part, to their overall lack of computer literacy. These were just a few of the many difficulties observed that day. Regardless of the particular difficulty, most children were easily frustrated and quickly gave up on the game's challenge after only a few minutes. While some children tried harder than others, it was apparent that the game was not enjoyable.

Returning from HVS that day, I was at a loss as to figure out how a game could be made to accommodate all of the difficulties that the children exhibited. Observing them at play was a sobering experience that made me realize how little knowledge I held in the field of assistive care. But although the particular circumstances I observed were foreign to me, I reminded myself that, at its core, this was still a game design problem; overall I'd observed over a hundred unique reasons that the children could not play the game. From a design standpoint, did each of these issues require a discrete solution, or did they stem from a larger design problem? If the former was true, I would have little chance to implement over 100 new features in the game in the time allotted (and no other designer could be expected to do it either). But if I could trace these issues back to a larger problem, there was a fair chance that I could implement the required changes to improve the game's accessibility for the children at HVS.

I began by considering the basic premises of game design: the craft of creating a game is based around the designer's ability to scaffold a series of challenges within the abilities of the player. The "trick" is to balance the difficulty of the challenge with the reward of conquering it. In practical terms, this means that a challenge that is *too easy* will result in a bland gaming experience, and one that is too hard will result in frustration. But what actually *happens* when the challenge is too difficult? Consider a marathon race. During the first few miles the runners are in good shape, but as the race continues, each runner reveals his or her weakness; some get dehydrated, others suffer muscle cramps, joint ache, low-blood pressure, and so on. Notice that all of these weaknesses can be traced back to the difficulty parameters of the race—its length, the terrain, the temperature, humidity, and so on. And it is only when these parameters create a challenge of great difficulty that these various weaknesses present themselves. This notion also carries over to video games. For example, if the parameters of a car racing game were made too difficult (via the speed of rivals, the force of the car's acceleration, etc.), some players would not be able to manage the controls physically, while others would have hand–eye coordination problems, lose focus, or simply tire out. By the same token, it was feasible that the children at HVS exhibited weaknesses that stem from game parameters that were too difficult. For a racing game, the solution would entail changing the parameters to slow down the rivaling cars, or increasing the capabilities of the player's car. What would the solution be for *Tetris*? How could the game play of *Tetris* fit within the ability range of children with disabilities? More precisely, what exact design factors were preventing the children from utilizing their *existing abilities* when playing *Tetris*?

By using this framework to analyze what I had observed with the initial *Tetris* sessions, I discovered that most of the symptoms exhibited by the children stemmed from two temporal aspects of the game: speed and pace.

1 *Speed:* In Level 1, a *Tetris* block takes roughly one to five seconds to reach the stack, depending on the board's configuration. This shape may require roughly one to ten interface operations (press and release actions via keyboard/mouse/joystick) to be manipulated into the desired position. This means the player may need to achieve operations at up to roughly one-tenth of a second (10 ms). Whether it's due to a cognitive, perceptual, motor, or other issues, some children at HVS simply cannot perform at this speed, even with assistive devices. Accuracy was also a problem, as some children couldn't release the block in time. This meant that the children required even more operations per second. For example, overrotating the piece (by not releasing the control in time) may require up to six extra operations to correct. Overall, even if a child knew exactly where the next *Tetris* shape should go, the game was simply too fast for the child to complete the action.

2 *Pace:* Some games like chess are turn-based, where the player performs an action and then waits for a response. But in *Tetris* the pace is constant, as the blocks just keep coming. Because of this, the children at HVS exhibited physical fatigue after only a few minutes. Furthermore, the game's ongoing pace did not allow intervention from the therapists, so there were almost no mediation opportunities to ease the initial frustrations of the children.

To rebalance the game to fit within the demonstrated abilities of the HVS players, I decided both to slow it down as well as to change its pace from that of a continual-action game to a puzzle game. I did so with one simple modification. In a typical *Tetris* game, blocks automatically fall downward toward the stack. I modified the game so the blocks "floated" in the air until the user explicitly dropped them with the down arrow key. This simple modification eliminated the temporal aspect of the game, allowing kids unlimited time to make a move, and also enabling mediation by therapists or peers to occur when needed.

Although, in theory, this should dramatically increase the accessibility of the game, it also presented a rather significant change to its core playability. I had concerns as to whether my changes would completely destroy the game and render it undesirable for the children at HVS. Would *Tetris* hold its timeless allure without its temporal challenge?

Will They Play It?

I brought the modified version of the game to HVS, and the OTs arranged for several students to try it out. Maya was the first to arrive: a sixteen-year-old with cerebral palsy (CP), a condition that affects her entire body. She's in a powered wheelchair, and her speech is hard to understand by those who do not know her well. Maya has little motor coordination with her hands, so pressing down on a keyboard key or a switch device requires her to exert effort equivalent to lifting a heavy box. While Maya had never played *Tetris* before, it took her less than a minute to figure it out, and she spent the next twenty minutes playing it. She used the four large buttons, and from the outside it looked more like she was exercising than playing a game.

The OTs explained to me that, despite her poor coordination and speech difficulties, Maya is planning to go to a typical college next year. She is one of the brightest children in the school, but her physical disability often blocks her from exercising and exhibiting her true talents. It is very hard for the OTs to find age-appropriate games for Maya, as most games with simple interfaces are made for younger children. This modified version of *Tetris* was one of the first games to provide an appropriate cognitive challenge for her. By removing the physical barrier, the modified game allowed Maya to enjoy and excel at its cognitive challenge. Lifting this barrier released a floodgate of excitement and joy, as Maya was definitely having a great time playing a game that she'd seen others play many times before but could never access herself. Witnessing Maya conquer the game so quickly was a powerful experience. I thought to myself, here is a girl that is obviously brighter and more will-powered than most typical children that I've met in the past.

The OTs next introduced me to Katerina, who—despite health issues—has full control of her hands. Due to visual deficits and perceptual issues, it takes Katerina a bit longer to process her physical surroundings. At first she did not fully grasp the game's goal and its operational aspect (such as using the top arrow to spin the shape, or why the rows disappear upon completion). But where play of the original *Tetris* game produced frustration, the modified version provoked discussion. Because there was no time limit (due to the floating blocks), Katerina and I were able to discuss strategies for solving the board and also to practice using the controls. In essence, the game allowed for a very important period of mediation to occur, which helped Katerina overcome her initial frustrations. After that, Katerina continued to play the game independently. Today, she plays the original version without adaptations.

As the day continued, it became apparent that most of the children successfully played the game. Over the next few weeks, the therapists continued to test it during therapy sessions. As time went by, we noticed that some children (like Katerina) started to improve to a point where the modified version became too easy. To remedy this, I added a feature to have the blocks either "float" (not fall down automatically) or fall regularly as in the original version of the game. I also added the ability to control the rate at which the blocks would fall, which allowed the therapists to adjust the challenge to an individual child's ability. Some of the children who started with floating blocks eventually tried to play with the shapes dropping at a slow speed, and then work their way up. This scaffolded feature was especially important to the children with cognitive issues, who were physically able to control the game but needed time to learn its basic rules. Many of these children just needed help overcoming their initial frustrations. Once they gained a bit of confidence, their abilities increased exponentially, and they eventually mastered the mechanics well enough to play the game as it was originally designed.

As a designer, I was amazed at how such a small change to a game's temporal aspect could have such a large impact on its accessibility. Notice that I did not directly attend to the multitude of child-specific symptoms. Doing so would have been impossible, even if I were an expert in the field of physical disabilities and child development. Instead, I identified the large design barriers from which the majority of these problems stemmed. By attending these barriers, I allowed the therapists and children themselves to fine-tune the game toward their own specific needs.

I realize that *Tetris* is a relatively simple game in comparison to many of today's mainstream game titles. Yet, by being attentive to the notion of designing inclusively for a wider range of abilities can vastly improve the accessibility of even the most complex games—perhaps not for everyone, but for many. At this chapter's end, I've provided a link to a Web site that includes a list of game-accessibility features (by several design experts, as well as by me) that could be implemented to any game with minimal resources, in order to increase its player audience.

Now that a pathway was cleared for the children to play with a video game on their own terms, I was curious to see if this pathway would also enhance social interaction through cooperative play.

Cooperative Play

I was, initially, not sure how to assess the social impact of the game. Fortunately, the first sign that my modified version of *Tetris* allowed for social interaction happened unintentionally. Due to a scheduling mix-up, two children showed up to play the game at the same time. (We initially had them separated into twenty-minute intervals). Both kids were around fifteen years old and used powered wheelchairs. Although they both have CP, Eric has fair control of his upper extremities and can communicate freely. An avid gamer, he had played *Tetris* before and masters almost any video game he picks up. Jonah, on the other hand, has a more severe condition that results in involuntary and coarse motion, greatly limiting his ability to communicate verbally. I expected Eric to take over the game immediately and leave Jonah in the background. But instead, Eric let Jonah sit at the controls. Jonah had never played the game before, and Eric started explaining it to him. We did not intervene. This mentorship went on for over thirty minutes, with a growing sense of excitement. With every shape that fell into place, Jonah became more visibly excited—occasionally turning around to us with a huge smile, but mostly laughing audibly at the screen, at times shouting—*"I love this!"* Eric, who picked up on Jonah's joy, became even more motivated to provide Jonah with strategies. Despite the fact that it took Jonah a considerable amount of effort and time to operate the buttons, not once did Eric take over the controls.

The game produced a tangible social relationship between two children that did not usually interact with each other. Eric happily surrendered his control over the game in favor of taking on a mentorship role. Jonah gladly accepted Eric's guidance and was uninhibited by the fact that he was the less skilled player. The therapists later explained that the two children do not usually hang out in school, primarily because they don't share common interests. Playing *Tetris* with Eric represented one of the few times that Jonah participated in this sort of spontaneous social interaction.

Beyond the Therapy Room

I had been able to make the game accessible to children in the therapy room. But to allow for a fully independent play experience by the children, the game needed to be accessible in the child's own environment. When playing a game in the therapy room, the therapist is there to help iron out any problems that may arise. This help ranges from making sure that the child has proper access to the controls to providing subtle suggestions and tips as the child plays the game. I was particularly worried about the latter, as I wanted the children to be able to conquer the challenges with absolutely no help from others. When typical children play alone in their rooms, they learn to rely on their own faculties. But some of the children at HVS are dependent upon their caregivers, and therefore exhibit low frustration levels and low confidence in their own abilities. To overcome this, I needed to scaffold a gaming experience that would encourage the children to remain engaged in the game even when difficulties arose.

As a first solution, I categorized the seven types of *Tetris* blocks according to their visual complexity. The square blocks and straight lines were categorized as the easiest; the *z*/*s* shapes were the most difficult. I modified the game to release the easy shapes first. Only once the player had completed a few full rows with simple shapes would the game introduce more complex ones. I added a menu-settings option to turn this feature on and off, for those children who wished to practice in this manner.

Another modification attended the fact that some children have conditions that flare-up or recede on a daily basis. Among other things, this fluctuation also influences their ability to play games. While a typical child can count on a constant improvement in playing the game, the lack of this sense of security in the quality of performance can be very frustrating. To address this, I used a traditional game design technique called Dynamic Difficulty Adjustment (DDA), where the game engine tracks player performance and adjusts itself accordingly. In a race game, for example, the lead car will slow down just enough to make sure that the player, who is running in second place has a chance to win the game. In *Tetris*, I created a system that tracked the player's ability over time, identified the current performance in the context of previous games, and modified the shape selection toward easier solutions when needed. To implement this feature, the player creates an anonymous user account that allows the game engine to store game play information. This online account also stores data of other game settings, including various controller settings, colors and sizes of the blocks, whether they should float or fall, and at what speed. These settings could be customized by the therapist during therapy and retrieved by the child when playing at home. Although not implemented due to privacy concerns, this user account could potentially be used to track the child's game play and to produce reports based on usage patterns.

Back at HVS, I presented the new version to the therapists and explained the customizable functionality. I also explained how the game could be downloaded from the Web and installed on the computer in the child's home. It was my hope that the above features would scaffold game challenge for the child in a way that would allow for truly independent play. The following interview with the OTs took place about a month later. I asked Jane to describe a memorable case study from the past month, and the conversation evolved from there.

Jane (OT):

Danielle is a sweet 15-year-old girl who is in the ninth grade at HVS. She is verbal and very eloquent, however she can't even breathe on her own. She is on a ventilator and requires nursing care 24/7.

The more I get to know Danielle, the more I realize that she lacks the fundamental social skills to interact with kids her age. Instead, she has gotten used to interacting with adults, because usually the attention is directed towards her. She constantly needs reassurance of how well she is doing and how smart she is. Her insecurity is probably rooted in her lack of essential life experiences—such as being able to play freely and easily. Because Danielle is a high achiever and seeks intense attention from her teachers, her classmates resent her. They often make remarks about her being a goody-goody, and how she is annoying.

With her, I particularly liked the idea of *Tetris* because I see the other students playing the game around her, and I think that this is something that—if she could do it—can help connect her with the other kids.

When I first asked her to play *Tetris* she said "I don't want to play because I'm awful in that game, I stink at that game!" She didn't even want to try because she had played the regular version before and had failed. I am sure Danielle has attempted to play other games in which she failed and eventually simply gave up.

I proceeded to explain to her about the adapted version created by Amit and insisted that she try. Reluctantly, she accepted and started to play, and she couldn't believe it. She said out loud, "I love this game! I'm really good at this game!"

As this was happening, there was another student playing at the same time, and he kept saying to her, "I'm so good at this game." She started accumulating points, and I could see that it was something that she could say, "Hey, you know I'm good at this game too—my classmate is doing well and so am I." It was clear that they where enjoying a good moment of parallel play.

How refreshing to see her so happy playing a game that most of her peers also enjoy! I think that she learned that there's a positive way to connect with the kids.

Kate (OT):

The boy that was playing on the other computer was my kid, and two weeks ago he was also saying, "I don't like this game I'm not going to play it. I'm no good at it." But the following week I set it up for him again, expecting the same response; but he said, "Oh yeah, I was doing it at home. I got an amazing score." Now he demands to play the game during therapy and write his high scores on the board for everyone to see.

Even when a kid is playing a game at home, he's actually participating indirectly with a social activity because that's what they'll be talking about tomorrow morning—eventually they will sit in front of the game together, eventually the kid will be able to show what he's achieved through practice. (Kate McGrath, Personal communication during Interview on November 7, 2006)

Ahmee (OT):

I agree. I was working with twin brothers who had just graduated. I put them right next to each other so they would play *Tetris,* and at the end of the period I would write their scores and keep a log. They wanted to beat each other, so I gave them the Web site for the new game, and they started practicing at home all the time, so that when they came in they'd be better than the other brother. These are two children that always shied away from challenges; but this sense of mastery provided them with confidence to challenge each other, and with the resiliency to try harder if they failed. I think that the social component of a mainstream game was crucial for this to happen. (Ahmee Ko, Personal communication during Interview on November 7, 2006)

Jane (OT):

It's interesting to see how the family members also play the game. One of my students uploaded the game at home, and both her parents ended up playing with her for the entire evening. When she went to sleep, her father wanted to play some more. Can you imagine her joy that she can play the same games as her parents? Can you imagine the parents' joy? (Jane Carvalho, Personal communication during Interview on November 7, 2006)

It was great to learn that the game allows children to exhibit mastery and connect among themselves, with their siblings, and even with their parents. There was one girl that I was particularly interested in learning about:

Angela (OT):

Doing "normal things" is mostly a far-fetched notion for a girl that communicates with the world by using a head-pointer—which is simple a stick attached to a visor on her forehead. To be honest, I did not expect Mia to be able to play *Tetris.* But that didn't stop us from trying. We set up four large switches on a slant-board and drew big arrows on them. The idea was to have Mia attempt to push the switches with the head-pointer by moving her head. Initially, Mia required maximum instruction and assistance to play the game, but was eventually able to play with minimal intervention from me. She was so pleased to be playing this game. She got so excited every time she heard the sound indicating that lines were disappearing and points were mounting. She indicated her score with her head pointer and tried to catch the eye of other therapists and students in the room as if to say, "Look what I did on my own." Who knew! Mia is playing a game with the other kids. (Angela Passariello-Foray, Personal communication during Interview on November 7, 2006)

In consequent weeks, Mia became very good at using her head-pointer device to play *Tetris*. Happily playing the game every day, she learned new techniques for controlling the four switches that Angela set up for her on a slanted board. At some time, Mia began demonstrating levels of control even beyond her ability to operate her communication device. Noticing this, Angela encouraged Mia to try to control her communication software using the *Tetris* method. It turned out to be a good idea. It allowed Mia to operate everyday computers and speech communication devices with more speed and accuracy than ever before.

I could not have wished for a better example of transfer from the therapy room into the real world. It's a nice example of how *just having fun* can have a serious impact on someone's life.

Conclusion

According to Fröbel, play is the work of children. From early childhood, play activities are a vehicle for the exploration of one's own abilities—to imagine, to win, to lose, to collaborate, to persist, and to master. As a child grows, the accumulation of these abilities contributes to a sense of self-identity. When a child cannot engage in play activities in a typical manner due to a disability, these aforementioned benefits are transformed into deficits: mastery turns into dependency, collaboration into isolation, and so forth. As the HVS therapists explained, because of this lack of play, some of their students do not know what to do when an opportunity for social play arises, affecting their ability later to engage in social activities such as those present in the workplace.

Aware of the dangers that lack of play poses, parents and therapists artificially re-create moments of play through supported activities both at home and in therapy sessions. Although vastly beneficial and always encouraged, these mediated activities intrinsically negate independent play, which naturally occurs for typical children. Granted, it is hard to create moments of independence for children with disabilities; leaving a fragile child alone on the playground with other children could be hazardous to the child's health. And how can a child with limited mobility build a Lego castle without assistance? It is, therefore, very challenging for a mediator to be supportive while allowing for situations of independence.

Enter digital games. By nature, digital games use technologies that many children with disabilities are already capable of operating, using adaptive input devices. As the chapter illustrates, while these technologies are used primarily to enable children to communicate, they can also be used to deliver play experiences of an independent nature, as well as to improve the nature of supported play. Allowing children to act on their own ideas (either independently or during mediated play) vastly improves their sense of self-reliance and self-esteem. Furthermore, games of a mainstream nature (like *Tetris*) bring added value to the play experience, as the child can participate in an activity that is also performed by typical peers, siblings, and parents. In that sense, the game becomes a conduit for social inclusion. As Josh explains: "Even when I play basketball in a wheelchair, I look weird . . . But I can play some video games like anyone else, and it *looks* OK."

While it is still too early to measure scientifically the impact of video games on the maturation of the child, the therapists at HVS have already established video gaming as a seminal therapeutic method in their sessions. At HVS, video games are used daily to produce tangible results; they are used for improving the student's fine-motor functions, hand–eye coordination, and other perceptual abilities, while also providing practice with cognitive skills. There's a clear carryover from the gaming environment to the real world, as children are motivated to practice with their communication devices by playing games using them. This has shown later to improve their abilities to use these devices for communication, as well as for standard school curriculum. In that sense, video games at HVS have revealed themselves to be valuable learning systems for problem solving, physical wellness, communication skills, formation of identity and sense of self, peer learning, and overall growth.

This chapter does not claim that video games are the *only* form of play for children with disabilities, but rather that they provide a viable complementary activity to existing mediated forms of play. As the chapter illustrated, digital gaming provides a new level of independence that may normalize overly adult-dependant play habits. In that sense, it enables children with disabilities to harvest the full benefit of a given play activity. If play is indeed the work of children, then video games provide new means of employment.

Next Steps

What can be done? And who should take on a leading role?

The initial change required is one of *attitude*. At a time when the overall effects of video games on typical youth are still being debated, we should acknowledge their unique benefits for children with disabilities. While some games are, indeed, overly violent for young children, this does not render the entire medium harmful. The real harm is done when we do not utilize the tools at our fingertips due to a lack of knowledge or imagination. With this in mind, caregivers and legislators should examine the medium without prejudice or moral panic. On the design front, game companies should become aware of the simple features that may make their products accessible to the millions who cannot access them (generating more money along the way). Perhaps most importantly, children themselves should know their rights and advocate for change.

Transforming this attitude into practical action requires various forms of engagement from the aforementioned groups, ranging from advocacy to collaboration. Whether you are a game designer, therapist, parent, policy maker, or a child that deserves better, please visit http://makebettergames.com for a pragmatic game plan for how *you* can help to make games more accessible.

There are no people with disabilities, just varying degrees of abilities.—Henry Viscardi Jr.

Notes

1. The Henry Viscardi School at Abilities. http://www.hvs.k12.ny.us/. Accessed June 20, 2007.

2. Interactive Telecommunications Program, Tisch School of the Arts, New York University http://itp.nyu.edu/. Accessed June 20, 2007.

3. George Carey, Wynne Tryee, Kristine Alexander, and Just Kids Inc., An Environmental Scan of Children's Interactive Media 2000–2002, *A Report to the Markle Foundation*, 2002.

4. Joe L. Prost, Neuroscience, Play and Child Development, Presented at the IPA/USA Triennial National Conference, Longmont, CO, 1998.

5. Carey et al., An Environmental Scan.

6. Elena Bodrova and Deborah J. Leong, The Importance of Being Playful: The First Years of School, *Educational Leadership* 60, no. 7 (April 2003): 50–3. http://pdonline.ascd.org/pd_online/substitute/el200304_bodrova.html

7. Barbara E. Chandler, ed., *The Essence of Play: A Child's Occupation* (Bethesda, MD: American Occupational Therapy Association, 1997).

8. P. N. Wilson, N. Foreman, and D. Stanton, Improving Spatial Awareness in Physically Disabled Children Using Virtual Environments, *Engineering Science and Education Journal* 8, no. 5 (October 1999): 196–200.

9. Henry Jenkins, Reality Bytes: Eight Myths About Video Games Debunked, 2003. http://www.pbs.org/kcts/videogamerevolution/impact/myths.html. Accessed June 20, 2007.

10. Oene Wiegman and Emil van Schie, Video Game Playing and Its Relations With Aggressive and Pro-social Behavior, *British Journal of Social Psychology*, 37 (1998): 367–78.

11. J. Colwell, C. Grady, and S. Rhaiti, Computer Games, Self Esteem, and Gratification of Needs in Adolescents, *Journal of Community and Applied Social Psychology* 5 (1995): 195–206.

12. Geoffrey Montgomery, Breaking the Code of Color: Color Blindness: More Prevalent Among Males. A Report from the Howard Hughes Medical Institute. http://www.hhmi.org/senses/b130.html. Accessed April 30, 2007.

13. Brannon Zahand, Making Video Games Accessible: Business Justifications and Design Considerations. Published by Microsoft, August 2006. http://msdn2.microsoft.com/en-us/library/bb172230.aspx. Accessed April 30, 2007.

14. Montgomery, Breaking the Code of Color.

15. See http://www.audiogames.net/. Accessed April 30, 2007.

16. See http://gamescc.rbkdesign.com/. Accessed April 30, 2007.

PART II: HIDDEN AGENDAS

Education vs. Entertainment: A Cultural History of Children's Software

Mizuko Ito

University of Southern California, School of Cinematic Arts

A few decades ago, the idea of consumer software designed for the education, entertainment, and empowerment of children was barely a glimmer in the eye of a few innovative educators and technologists. In the eighties and nineties, the United States saw the emergence of a new category of consumer software designed specifically for elementary-aged children, which blended different philosophies of education with genres and technologies drawn from interactive gaming and entertainment. Educators and technology designers experimented in creating a set of new media genres and a commercial sector that has variously been called children's software, learning games, or edutainment. Commercial children's software, designed to be both fun and enriching, lies at the boundary zone between the resilient structures of education and entertainment that structure contemporary childhoods in the United States. The history of how children's software emerged as an experimental media category, and its subsequent uptake by various social and political actors—including kids, parents, educators, and various commercial enterprises—is a microcosm for the social and cultural contestations surrounding new technology, children, and education. It describes efforts to incorporate gaming idioms into learning software, and the different understandings of play and learning that have motivated these efforts. It is also a story about the promise of technical and design innovation to transform the conditions of learning and play, as well as a cautionary tale about the difficulties of reforming existing social and cultural structures, even with the best of intentions and innovative new technologies.

This chapter draws on ethnographic material from my dissertation work[1] to consider the cultural politics and recent history of children's software and to reflect on how this past can inform our current efforts to mobilize games for learning. My focus is on describing the systemic and historical contexts in which children's software have been embedded in order to understand sites of conservatism and change. After first outlining my conceptual framework for analyzing the social and cultural contexts of new technologies, I describe three genres in children's software: academic, entertainment, and construction. The body of

---

The ethnographic research for this chapter was conducted as part of a project funded by the Mellon and Russell Sage Foundations and benefited from being part of the broader Fifth Dimension research effort. Writing was funded in part by a Spencer Dissertation Fellowship and the Annenberg Center for Communication at the University of Southern California. This chapter is excerpted from a dissertation for Stanford University's Department of Anthropology, entitled *Engineering Play*, which benefited from readings and comments by Carol Delaney, Joan Fujimura, Shelley Goldman, James Greeno, Purnima Mankekar, Ray McDermott, Susan Newman, Lucy Suchman, and Sylvia Yanagisako. The description of the history of the children's software industry was drawn from interviews with software developers.

the chapter describes how these three genres play out within a production and advertising context, in the design of particular software titles, and at sites of play in afterschool computer centers where I conducted my fieldwork. I conclude with an analysis of the dynamics that lead to genre hardening in learning games, and consider where there may be opportunities for social and cultural change.

Technology, Structure, and Genre

In examining new technology, it is a challenge to avoid the pitfalls of both hype and mistrust, or as Valentine and Holloway[2] have described it, the problem of polarization between the "boosters" and the "debunkers." New technologies tend to be accompanied by a set of heightened expectations, followed by a precipitous fall from grace after failing to deliver on an unrealistic billing. This was certainly the case with edutainment, which boosters hoped would transform learning for a generation of kids. While the boosters and debunkers may seem to be operating under completely different frames of reference, what they share is the tendency to fetishize technology as a force with its own internal logic standing outside of history, society, and culture. The problem with both of these stances is that they fail to recognize that technologies are in fact embodiments, stabilizations, and concretizations of existing social structure and cultural meanings. The promises and the pitfalls of certain technological forms are realized only through active and ongoing struggle over their creation, uptake, and revision. New technologies go through what sociologists of technology have called a period of "interpretive flexibility," where it is still not clear which social actors will have a role in stabilizing the meaning and form of the new technology. As time goes on and different social groups work to stabilize and contest the technology, we move into a period of closure and stabilization. Trevor F. Pinch and Wiebe E. Bijker[3] have described this process in the case of the bicycle in the late nineteenth century, which exhibited a wide range of design variation until it stabilized into the low-wheeled form with air tires, which we still see today. I consider this recognition of the socially embedded nature of technology one of the core theoretical axioms of contemporary technology studies, and it is foundational to the theoretical approach taken in this chapter. In this I draw from social studies of technology that see technology as growing out of existing social contexts as much as it is productive of new ones.[4]

It may seem self-evident that the representational content of media embodies a certain point of view and set of interests, but what is often less visible is how media is embedded in structures of everyday practice, particular technological forms, and institutional relations. We often see issues such as representations of gender or violence in games taking the fore in social controversies surrounding games, but in this chapter I argue that the broader institutional and business contexts of software production, distribution, and consumption are also important sites of contestation. To build an agenda for how games could contribute to systemic change in learning and education, it is necessary—but not sufficient—to analyze representational content and play mechanics. In addition, we need to understand the conditions under which the game has been produced, advertised, and distributed, as well as how it gets taken up and regulated in different contexts of play. In their textbook of cultural studies, Paul du Gay and his colleagues describe a "circuit of culture" that includes processes such as production and design, advertising, uptake, and regulation. In order to understand the meaning of a new technological artifact, they suggest that all nodes in this circuit, as well as the interaction between the nodes, need to be subject to analysis.[5] In other words, the design of a game has a structuring but not determining effect on how the game will be marketed or played, just as existing practices of gaming or education have a structuring but not determining effect on what kinds of games will get created. In the case of commercial media, although the representational content—such as characters and narrative—are constantly in flux, the industry relations, distribution infrastructure, patterns of player/viewer engagement, and genres of representation tend to be conservative and deeply engrained within existing social and cultural structures.

In this chapter I use the concepts of *media genres* and *participation genres* to read across the circuit of culture and to describe how culture gets embodied and "hardened" into certain conventionalized styles of representation, practice, and institutional structure that become difficult to dislodge. I draw from John Seely Brown and Paul Duguid's[6] notion of genre as something that crosscuts form and content in media artifacts. For example, in a book, genres involve things like typography, layout, paper weight, and binding, "the peripheral clues that crucially shape understanding and use." Participation genres similarly involve the explicit content or focus of an activity, as well as the subtle stylistic cues such as stance, gaze, and attitude that help us recognize a specific action as part of a category of practices. In this sense, participation genres do work similar to concepts such as habitus[7] or structuration,[8] linking specific activity to broader social and cultural structure. More closely allied with humanistic analysis, a notion of genre, however, foregrounds the interpretive dimensions of human orderliness. How we identify with, orient to, and engage with media and the imagination requires acts of reading and interpretation. We recognize certain patterns of representation (media genres), and in turn engage with them in routinized ways (participation genres). My argument is that we need to recognize the social and cultural patterns that keep repeating themselves in order to understand how things could be changed. I turn now to a discussion of the history of the industry and media genres before examining genres of participation drawn from my ethnographic observations of children's play.

Media and Industry Genres

The category of learning games for children is potentially a broad one, and one could imagine multiple origin stories and histories. Here I focus on a particular trajectory with origins in the late seventies and early eighties, where educators and technology makers built a new industry niche of software products for elementary-aged children. This period saw the founding of a category of software that came to be called "edutainment," or more broadly, "children's software." These titles were put forth as an alternative to the drill- and curriculum-based computer-aided instruction systems such as PLATO and Wicat that dominated the educational technology field from the sixties to the eighties. The new children's software titles instead drew from video game approaches being developed for arcades and game consoles, applying this thinking to educational technology. *Number Munchers, Oregon Trail, Reader Rabbit, KidPix,* and *Where in the World Is Carmen Sandiego?* are examples of the first major wave of software designed with learning goals in mind, and targeted toward the consumer market of elementary-aged children. In this, children's software drew from a longer history of educational reform efforts that looked to play as a site of learning. Although games were not the only way in which playful idioms were incorporated into these software titles, the centrality of gaming is in many ways what was distinctive about this particular historical moment in the evolution of the philosophies of "learning through play." In contrast to the prior history of educative playthings and media—typified by wooden blocks, puzzles, children's literature, and Sesame Street—educational software put gaming at the center of the enterprise. By focusing on software and games explicitly designed to mediate between educational and entertainment idioms, I do not mean to privilege the learning claims made by these titles. Clearly, there are many titles in the mainstream entertainment gaming market that embody important learning principles.[9] Rather, the importance of children's software is that it is part of the ongoing social agenda to bridge the cultural divide between education and entertainment. This history has three strands that correspond to different genres of children's software: academic, entertainment, and construction.

I use the term *children's software* to refer to a category of commercial software that is targeted toward elementary-aged children and embodies these general cultural commitments to learning and developmental goals. Educational or learning games could be considered a subset of this category, which also includes construction and simulation tools that don't have a strong gaming component. The three strands of academic, entertainment, and construction software are loosely tied to behaviorist, play-centered, and constructivist educational philosophies. This category of software emerged from my ethnographic record; choice of what constitutes the general category of "children's software" or "learning games" is remarkably consistent. The same types of games are identified as educational and prosocial types of software in publications aimed at teachers, educationally minded parents, as well as afterschool program staff. In the description to follow, I sharpen the difference between the three media genres of academic, entertainment, and construction in order to identify competing cultural codes and educational philosophies embodied in children's software. In the practices of play, and in the design of specific titles, however, these genres are often intermingled. A curricular title may embed elements from entertainment media or construction tools, just as an entertainment-oriented title may work to convey some curricular content. I will explore more of the messiness of these categories in my descriptions from the ethnographic record, but in this section I lay out the differences between the three genres and their relation to particular strands in software development.

Academic

The first strand was founded by educators who sought to embed traditional academic content within a gaming idiom. Anne McCormick, the founder of The Learning Company (TLC), described in an interview the excitement of the early years in the creation of the learning software industry. Developers shared a sense that they were creating possibilities for learning that freed it from the institutional constraints of schooling: "We created a new category by working with an Atari game designer and educators . . . I didn't want to call it educational because to me that meant schooling, dusty, institutional. That's why I called it The Learning Company not The Education Company." Through the eighties and nineties, titles created by companies like TLC captured the public imagination and became successful commercial ventures. At the same time that McCormick was producing software titles such as *Gertrude's Puzzles*, *Rocky's Boots*, and *Reader Rabbit* (see figure 1), other educational researchers at the University of Minnesota were beginning to commercialize products such as *Oregon Trail* and *Number Munchers*. The Minnesota Educational Computing Corporation (MECC) was originally funded by the State of Minnesota in 1973, and became a public corporation in 1985, riding the successes of these software titles. Jan Davidson, a former teacher, started her company Davidson & Associates in 1983, developing titles such as *Math Blaster*, which, in its various incarnations, has been the best-selling piece of math software through the years. While growing out of school-based uses of computers, these new products were designed for

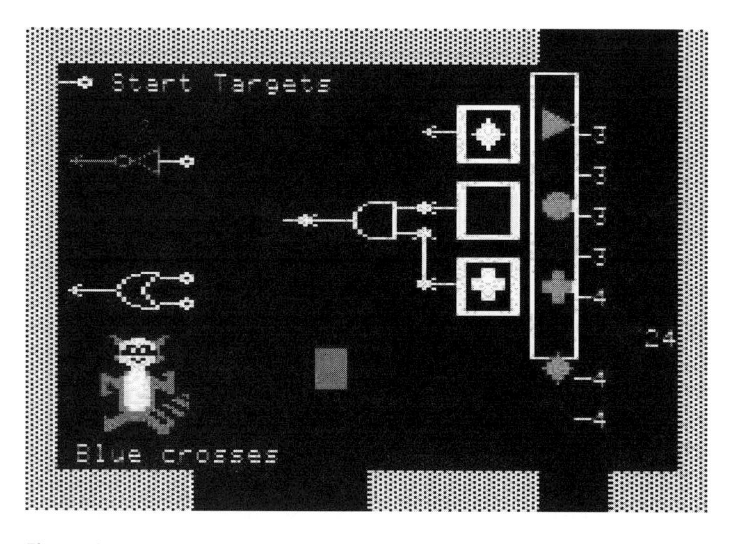

Figure 1
Screen shot from *Rocky's Boots.* (Reproduced with permission from The Learning Company.)

the consumer market. They departed from strictly curricular and instructional goals of the early generation of school-based software, incorporating visual and narrative elements from popular culture. For example, *Math Blaster* took a standard drill-and-practice-type instructional mechanism, but embedded it within a shooter game idiom.

The nineties saw the proliferation of PCs, the consolidation of software industries, and the emergence of a mass market in family-oriented software. Instead of being sold at specialty computer and hobby shops, by the nineties, most of the volume of children's software was being sold at superstores such as Costco, Wal-Mart, CompUSA, Toys "R" Us, and Office Depot. Career CEOs had pushed aside company founders, and by the end of the nineties, the children's software industry had largely consolidated under two conglomerates, one headed by Mattel and the other by media industry giant, Cendant. Eventually Mattel went on to sell its edutainment assets after incurring tremendous losses. Along the way to the mainstreaming of the industry, development shifted away from an experimental research mode that characterized the earlier ethos of companies like TLC, MECC, and Davidson & Associates toward a commercial model more focused on the bottom line. Most development budgets in this genre are currently spent upgrading graphics and sound and refining established formulas rather than on developing new models for interaction or game design. Products with innovative new designs or with more open-ended, complex, and multireferential goals are difficult to produce and disseminate in this current ecology. Easily represented marketing "hooks" like a licensed character, established brand, or the claim to transmit curricular knowledge are more central to a product's success than innovation.

This strand of software development increasingly came to focus on curricular content rather than innovative game play, and defined what I call the academic genre. The most typical design relies on academic minigames embedded in a role-playing scenario. Along the way to completing some kind of mission, the player encounters various problems or puzzles related to academic subject matter. This may be math problems, science questions, or reading games, but in general the content of the problems is unrelated to the role-playing fantasy narrative. Although not based in a narrow drill-and-practice approach, the educational philosophy might be broadly associated with a behaviorist approach, where children are given external rewards (action games, eye candy, points, etc.) for completion of academic tasks. Generally these games also keep close track of scores that are often tabulated in a passport- or report cardlike format. These games are often produced to correspond to specific subjects for particular grades (such as fourth-grade math, second-grade reading), and the packaging features checklists of particular curricular topics. This genre standardized around this form of game design primarily to streamline development around a successful formula. Companies committed to an underlying game engine that different forms of academic content and minigames could be plugged into, lowering the costs of development. Further, this formula meant that the relation between the more entertainment-oriented scenario and the academic minigames was incidental, so there didn't need to be a lot of intensive design or curricular work to make the meta-activity integrate with the drills. This is one example of a hybridization of educational and entertainment genres, but done in a way that kept them as essentially separate domains of activity.

Academic games are generally marketed directly to parents as tools for achievement. Thus the market is limited to children under the age of ten, where parents generally retain control of media purchasing. Grade-based educational software appeals to middle-class parents' desires for wholesome, creative, and interactive play for their children, which also gives them a leg up on subjects that will be covered in school. Unlike more entertainment-oriented games that are marketed directly to children on television and in gaming magazines, academic software runs ads in magazines such as *Family PC*. One ad for Knowledge Adventure's *JumpStart* software series (see figure 2), which ran in the December 2000 edition of *Family PC*, sets up an unambiguous relation between the products and academic achievement. A blond school-aged girl dressed neatly in white knee-high socks, Mary Janes, and a red skirt, still wearing her backpack, stands with her back to you (your child here), clutching a school worksheet. The sanitized space of the large kitchen and the girl's appearance code the home as white, suburban, conservative, and middle class. The girl faces a refrigerator already overflowing with assignments red-inked with gushing teacher notes: stars, "Good Work!" and "Excellent!" The backpack, the school assignments, and the voice of assessment are represented in a central role in the intimate sphere of the home. A drawing of mom, posted in the visually prominent area at the top left, hails the parent in charge of children-related purchases. She is a smiling blond mother with curly hair and rosy cheeks.

The software provides a jump start for stalled children in the academic rat race, mobilizing the metaphor of "education as a race," which dominates the culture of competition of elite schooling in the United States.[10] The ad campaign's tagline—"She's a JumpStart Kid, all right"—is subtly crafted to imply a status distinction with other kids, the perpetually stalled failures that don't use this software. In marketing, the pitch to the parents is not in the gaming and fun, but in addressing academic achievement goals. This shift in emphasis is an example of the genre hardening and the erasure of the hybrid cultural forms that were more evident in the early years of interpretive flexibility in children's software. Corporations market software as a vehicle for academic success to parents, who in turn market academics as an entertainment activity to their kids. The ads for the *Math Blaster* series feature children in moments of ecstatic play, swimming or playing superheroes, with thought balloons describing the mathematical significance of their play (see figure 3). A tiny caped crusader speculates, "If I fly 90 miles an hour and the earth is 24,902 miles around, can I still get back home for breakfast?" "Must be the Math Blaster®" suggests that ad copy below. "Software

Figure 2
Advertisement for *JumpStart 1st Grade.* (Reproduced with permission from Knowledge Adventure, Inc. JumpStart is a registered trademark of Knowledge Adventure, Inc.)

Figure 3
Advertisement for *Math Blaster*. (Reproduced with permission from Knowledge Adventure, Inc. Math Blaster is a registered trademark of Knowledge Adventure, Inc.)

that gets your kids into math. And math into them." This is the currently dominant logic of games following the academic genre:

The most effective forms of learning are fun. So let's package tasks that function to measure and sort children into something that is pleasurable. That way, the kids will have fun, they will also get ahead in life, and parents can feel they have fulfilled the impossible imperatives of contemporary middle-class parenting that say they must support competitive successes while also keeping their children happy and entertained.

As Loyd P. Rieber, Nancy Luke, and Jan Smith[11] argue in their review of learning game design philosophies, this is an approach that looks at "fun" as an extrinsic motivator of learning, rather working to support learning that is intrinsically motivated. The focus on entertainment as a motivator tends to "designate the role of games as a form of educational 'sugar-coating'—making the hard work of mathematics or language arts easier to 'swallow'."[12] These are the discourses that currently dominate the production and marketing of academically oriented commercial games.

Entertainment

The second strand of children's software development originated from the commercial software industry and the growing availability of multimedia personal computing, seeking to create products that were family friendly, pro-social, and appropriate for young children, but not necessarily academic in focus. While Ann McCormick was developing her first TLC titles for the Apple II in the eighties, Gary and Douglas Carlson were building a new business in selling computer games out of their apartment in Eugene, Oregon. In 1982 the Carlson brothers purchased the rights to *Bank Street Writer* and then went on to publish *Where in the World Is Carmen Sandiego?*, *Just Grandma and Me*, and *Myst*. In contrast to the educational goals of McCormick and Davidson, in my interview with him Douglas Carlson stresses childhood pleasure and wonder rather than academic content. "None of us had degrees in education. We didn't want to go out and make all these pedagogical claims.... Basically, our idea was to do products that we ourselves found interesting.... That's just kind of whatever seemed fun." In 1989 the Apple Multimedia Lab produced *The Visual Almanac* on laser disc. A few years later Voyager went on to publish titles such as *Countdown* and *Planetary Taxi* that took the content of the *Visual Almanac* and created the first full-color multimedia educational software titles with sophisticated sound, graphics, and animation. Companies such as Humongous Entertainment with their *Pajama Sam* series went on to create role-playing games for young children, and by the mid-nineties all the major children's toy and media companies had jumped on the bandwagon, making multimedia titles around popular licensed characters such as Barbie, Mickey, and Yoda.

Entertainment-oriented children's software is a comparatively broad genre. Although one can easily recognize the academic genre in series such as *JumpStart* or *Math Blaster*, entertainment titles could include software such as authoring tools, interactive storybooks, or simulations, and the box design and marketing pitches are less uniform. Most typically, titles that are specifically in the children's software category of entertainment feature an open-ended and exploratory online environment for players to explore. They may feature gamelike idioms, but are often more open-ended and toylike, and tend toward sandbox-style games rather than linear, goal-oriented ones. The classic entertainment genre for young children is "click and explore," where clicking on certain hot areas of a scene will trigger funny animations and sounds. Unlike academic genre games, however, these titles generally have a more unified fantasy scenario and do not embed academic minigames within the virtual world. Titles such as *A Silly Noisy House* and the early *Living Books* series set the standard for this kind of interaction modality. There is more likely to be some kind of building and construction or authoring component in entertainment titles, though it is not uniformly the case. Titles such as *Barbie Fashion Designer* or Tonka and Lego games are examples of entertainment titles with strong authoring components built into them. The ads for the more entertainment-oriented titles portray children as ecstatic and pleasure-seeking rather than reflective and brainy, and childhood as imaginative, pure, and joyous. The ethos is parent-friendly but child-centered, a formula established by children's entertainment companies ever since the Mickey Mouse Club aired on television.

Humongous Entertainment puts the child's pleasure close-up and front and center. "This is the review we value most" declares the ad copy above a large photograph of a beaming child (see figure 4). The ad mobilizes discourses from the established genre of film reviews by describing how "critics rave" over the software title. The endorsement from *PC Magazine* is particularly telling: "Nobody understands kids like Humongous Entertainment." The company is positioned as a channel to your children and their pleasures, the authentic voice of childhood. The box for *Pajama Sam*, one of Humongous's most popular titles (see figure 5), features the adorably caped hero, Sam, and describes the software as "an interactive animated adventure." The back of the box does list educational content, but in a small box that is not visually prominent. Although the title relies on a role-playing game format, the title is not labeled in that way. The list of "critical thinking, problem-solving skills, memory skills, mental mapping and spatial relations skills" does not make any curricular claims, and stresses the "creative and flexible" nature of the software and "the power of a child's imagination." "Feature-film quality animation" and "original music" are central selling points for the title. It can compete with television and videos for your child's attention, and it still has some educational value.

Entertainment titles use the same visual styles as education titles such as *Reader Rabbit* and *JumpStart*. They occupy the same shelves at retailers and are oriented to a similar demographic of middle and upper middle class families, but keyed somewhat toward the more progressive and permissive parent. What distinguishes the entertainment genre is the more open-ended structure. Educational titles, particularly those that make curricular claims, are generally linear and make much of achieving certain levels and scores. Unlike the *JumpStart* titles, where progress to new areas is contingent on solving problems in a linear trajectory, with *Pajama Sam*, the player can explore the world freely in order to collect the items associated with the quest. There are no embedded academic tasks or external markers of progress in *Pajama Sam*, *Myst*, or *Living Books*. With this entertainment genre, what gets packaged and marketed is not achievement, but fun, exploration, and imagination. These titles are also distinguished from entertainment titles such as first-person shooters, sports games, war games, and role-playing games marketed primarily toward teens and adults. In contrast to the darker hues and sometimes frightening characters adorning the boxes of these titles, entertainment software for younger children is clearly coded as a separate market with brighter colors and smiling, wide-eyed characters like *Pajama Sam*. The packaging and marketing of these titles gives clues as to the underlying cultural logics animating the software.

Construction

In parallel with these developments in entertainment software for children, another strand of software development was evolving that focused on construction and authoring. Seymour Papert, probably the best-known spokesperson for the use of computers in education,

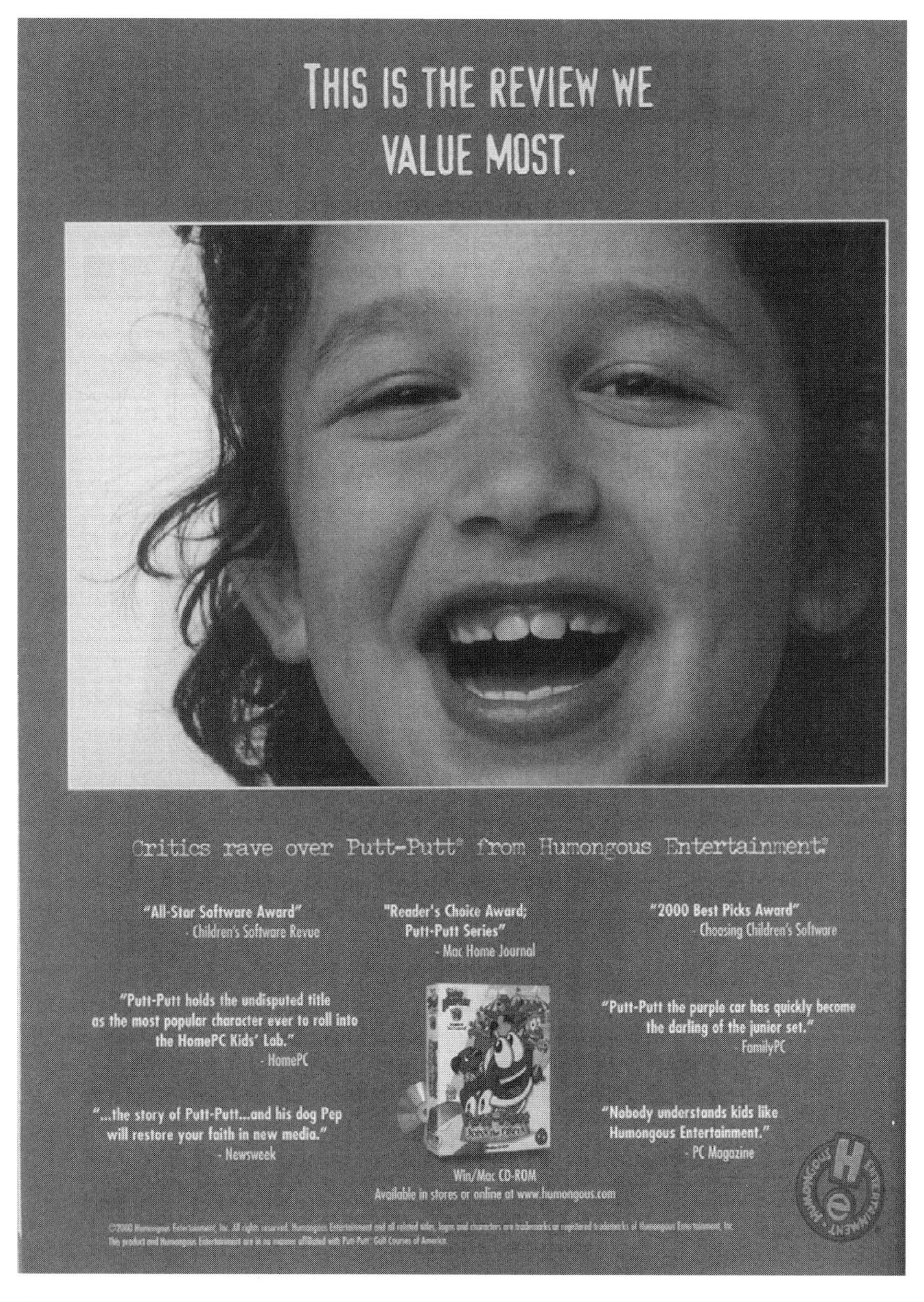

Figure 4
Advertisement for *Putt-Putt*. (Putt-Putt® Joins the Circus™ and Pajama Sam® artwork courtesy of Infogrames Interactive, Inc. © 2002 Humongous Entertainment, a division of Infogrames, Inc. All Rights Reserved. Used with Permission.)

Figure 5
Box art for *Pajama Sam 2*. (Putt-Putt® Joins the Circus™ and Pajama Sam® artwork courtesy of Infogrames Interactive, Inc. © 2002 Humongous Entertainment, a division of Infogrames, Inc. All Rights Reserved. Used with Permission.)

evangelized this construction sensibility, calling for the use of computer programming as an educational tool. Papert's efforts to promote programming in schools predate the period of children's software development I am focusing on here. However, the entry of the LOGO programming language and other child-oriented authoring tools into the consumer market happened during the same period that saw the rise of entertainment genre titles. Although part of a shared intellectual community as McCormick and others involved in children's software, Papert's position is distinctive in promoting programming as a key educational and developmental goal. Published in 1980, Papert's book *Mindstorms* describes the LOGO programming language for children, arguing against the drill-and-practice orientation of computer-based instruction dominant at the time.

> In most contemporary educational situations when children come into contact with computers the computer is used to put children through their paces, to provide feedback, and dispense information. The computer programming the child. In the LOGO environment the relationship is reversed: The child, even at preschool ages, is in control: The child programs the computer.[13]

This constructivist approach focuses less on conveying academic or cultural content and more on providing tools for construction and tinkering. Many titles in this category, such as *KidPix*, or Papert's own *Microworlds*, are closer to authoring tools than games, but simulation games such as *SimCity*, *SimTower*, *DinoPark Tycoon*, *Droidworks*, or *The Incredible Machine* also fall within this category. All of these titles provide kids with a toolkit to create computer-based programs or simulations.

The most successful titles in this genre are kid-oriented graphics programs such as *KidPix* and *Print Artist* and simulation games, most notably *SimCity*. Unlike the other genres of children's software, authoring and construction titles do not always posit a sharp break between the markets of adults and children. This can create problems in defining distribution and marketing channels. Although the Sim line of games has included major commercial successes, it has been more difficult to develop a sustainable market niche focused on authoring and construction games specifically for children. Licenses such as Barbie and Lego have had successes building on their existing brand and practices of open-ended and constructive play. *Barbie Fashion Designer* and *Lego Island* were both groundbreaking and successful titles that were based on design, construction, and open-ended play. Other entertainment companies, such as Lucas Learning, had a tougher time with titles oriented toward older kids but with an educational bent. Jon Blossom, who worked on *Droidworks* explained: "It's hard to convince parents that our games are educational and it's also generally hard to sell to a pre-teen, particularly someone who is ten or eleven, trying to be independent." The Lucas Learning products, almost all of which fell in the construction genre and were oriented to preteens, received a great deal of critical acclaim, but were not commercially successful, trapped in the shelf-space wars between the bright boxes of children's software and the dark boxes of mainstream games.

Authoring and construction titles generally package their appeal as technical empowerment, the ability to translate authorial agency into a media form. They draw less on explicit educational ideologies or images of play and more on images of mastery and control that reference creative or hackerlike subjectivities. "Create your own Star Wars world with fantastic 3D creatures" suggests the box of *The Gungan Frontier*. "Create anything imaginable in real-time 3D!" proclaims an ad for Disney's Magic Artist 3D, featuring a virtual Mickey stretching the surface of a shiny, 3D, textured Mickey logo. Like *SimCity 2000*, titles in this genre are often not age-specific and cross over between adult and kids markets. "The power to change history is in your hands" announces the ad copy for the game *Call to Power*, packaged in an adult entertainment genre but advertised in *Family PC*. Similarly, ads for *SimCity 3000* that ran in *PC Gamer* stress that radically different game outcomes can result from the player's actions (see figure 6). "Mr. Rogers or Mr. Hussein?" queries the ad copy over contrasting images of a peaceful town or a blown-out office building. "It's a beautiful day in the neighborhood when you've got the power to rule over *SimCity 3000*™." These titles all package their appeal on personal identification, customization, and

Figure 6
Advertisements for *SimCity 3000*. Reproduced with permission from Electronic Arts, Inc. (© 1998 Electronic Arts. SimCity 3000, SimCity, Maxis, and the Maxis logo are trademarks or registered trademarks of Electronic Arts in the United States and/or other countries. All rights reserved.)

Figure 6
(*Continued.*)

authoring, rather than claims that they will transmit specific bits of knowledge or spectacular pleasures.

Titles in this genre often fall outside of the bounds of what is considered "educational software" or "learning games," though the titles designed for children are still within the category of "children's software." Titles such as *KidPix* and *Magic Artist 3D* are considered more tools than software with an explicit learning agenda. Simulation games like *SimCity* or *Rollercoaster Tycoon* have been celebrated by educators, but the learning outcomes and fit with curricular goals are often not clearly defined. These titles also do not fit squarely within the categories of interactive entertainment and gaming. Titles with simulation elements are generally labeled as games, but often have little explicit game play. In fact, in my interview with Will Wright, he objected to the label of *SimCity* as a game, and preferred to call it a toy. As Papert has been arguing for many years, the educational value of these games lies less in their ability to convey academic content than in a certain stance toward technology, authoring, and creativity, a set of activities that is neither obviously "entertainment" nor "educational."

Genres of Participation

The different media genres and markets discussed have a complicated relationship to different modes of play. While the advertising of the products may suggest a clear mapping between software design and particular genres of learning and participation, in practice, the relation is highly contingent on situations of play.[14] Just as the children's software industry has been characterized by a struggle to define a space that is not absorbed into the dominant institutional structures of schooling and commercial entertainment, in contexts of play we see competing discourses and genres of participation jockeying for position in the micropolitics of kids' everyday lives. While parents and educators may be operating in an academic frame, kids may find ways of mobilizing more peer-oriented entertainment idioms. Kids and adults fluidly mobilize different genres or participation of educational achievement, fun entertainment, and creative construction, enlisting the genre structures that are embodied in the design in these performances of play. In this section, I turn to these complicated contexts of play, focused on fieldwork I conducted at afterschool computer clubs. The 5thD afterschool clubs are educational environments designed to mediate between home and school, education and entertainment. They rely on an activity system in which elementary-aged children and undergraduates from a local university come together to play with educational software. The clubs are located at community institutions such as Boys and Girls Clubs, schools, and libraries, and vary considerably depending on the local context and institution. What is common across the settings is a commitment to a collaborative and child-centered approach to learning, the nonhierarchical mixing of participants of different ages, and the use of personal computers running software designed for children.

My research was conducted as part of a three-year, collaborative ethnographic evaluation effort in the late nineties. Although the 5thD clubs are in many ways an idiosyncratic environment to observe play with computer games, they had the advantage of making visible the negotiations between kids and adults in defining the terms of play. They are also an example of a learning environment that was designed with a set of learning agendas roughly in line with much of the original impetus of children's software. The focus, with the 5thD, shifts in an important way, however, from the design of a specific artifact to the design of an overall learning environment that includes the software as an integral component.

Here I describe a few examples of play from our video record, exemplifying some of the negotiations between kids and adults, making visible genres of participation with learning games, and giving hints to the broader social and cultural structures that inform play. The three categories of practice I cover—achievement displays, spectacle, and building my own world—correspond roughly to the three software genres of academic, entertainment, and construction.

Achievement Displays

When engaging with software with clear markers of educational achievement, players often orient toward these recognitions of success at the expense of more constructivist or experimental modes of play. Children's software in the academic genre most often invites this achievement orientation. The following example is taken from a day when "Roger" completes the whole game sequence of *The Island of Dr. Brain* during one club period. Although not as sophisticated as current educational games, this game embodies the basic structure of educational children's software, engaging a player in academic minigames in the course of fantasy role playing. Although this game includes click and explore scenes, kids are quick to recognize the academic genre and tend to orient to the linear achievement stance of the game rather than pursuing exploratory play. Roger has played bits and pieces of the game previously with other kids, but this is the first day on which he gets sustained time with the game, and, with adult help, moves through puzzle after puzzle. In this first example, Roger has just begun to work on a puzzle that involves identifying the chemical code for elements in a set of objects, a tin cup, a zinc bar, and so forth. When the puzzle pops up, he reads the instructions, and then tries clicking around to determine the nature of the task.

A = Roger
Ad = Adult
SC = Site Coordinator

1 *R:* What am I supposed to do? I don't get this.

2 *SC:* OK did you analyze it? It says: "These chemical elements . . ."

3 *R:* [Pulls down another screen of directions and reads, moving pointer over lines.]

4 *SC:* Oh, you're doing trace elements OK, here.

5 *R:* Ahhh! I see. [Starts to read the description of the element to find. The object under question is a zinc bar.]

6 *Ad:* Oh, do you get the hints?

7 *SC:* "Blank"-oxide [referring to the description, which gives a hint that the answer is a "___ oxide"].

8 *R:* Carbon. Blank? Blank?

9 *Ad:* See the blank here? [Points to screen.] They're saying fill in the blank.

10 *R:* Yeah, I know.

11 *SC:* It's like the sunblock people put on their face . . . You know, people put it on their nose . . .

12 *R:* Yeah what is it?

13 *SC:* What is it called?

14 *R:* SPF.

15 *SC:* No. There's a thing that completely blocks it out.

16 *R:* What? Blank?

17 *SC:* Zinc-oxide, maybe?

18 *R:* Zi::nc...

19 *SC:* Have you ever heard of that?

20 *R:* [Nods.]

21 *SC:* It's the really white stuff. So you have to find that.

22 *R:* What's the *Z*? [Points to *Z* in table of elements.]

23 *SC:* Go up one. That's the zinc. See it up on top?

24 *R:* [Selects Z for zinc, and gets the first element identified correctly.] All right.

25 *SC:* OK. Now you're doing the next one. It's two percent. It says: "These chemicals are present only in minute amounts. The analyzer cannot trace them." So, that's the hint you got before, which is the trace element, which means there wasn't enough of them to pick up.

26 *R:* [Selects "Trace Element" and successfully completes analysis of the first object.] Al::right. Zinc Bar... [Places zinc bar to the side, and puts tin cup in the analyzer.] This is tin. I know it already. Tin...

In this sequence of activity, Roger orients quickly to the suggested task structure: read the directions, determine what the problem is, get the correct answer to the problem, and display knowledge. When Roger falters in determining the procedure, he enlists the help of the adults: "What am I supposed to do? I don't get this" (line 1). Roger and the site coordinator orient to the instructions, and then the initial recognition occurs, "Ahhh! I see" (line 5), as he is able to decode the instructions and recognize the call for action. Both Roger and the site coordinator then shift their orientation toward the content domain and solving the problem: What kind of oxide is it? (lines 7–10). The site coordinator then tries to get Roger to fill in the answer, by providing some hints, though she eventually must give him the answer: zinc (lines 11–17). Roger responds with another act of recognition: "Zi::nc," in an extended, low tone, and nodding to the site coordinator's confirmation that he understands the answer (lines 18, 20). For the remainder of the clip, she guides him in locating zinc on the list of elements, and he inputs the answer: "All right" (line 24). This mode of interaction with the puzzles—in which Roger decodes the instructions, executes them in solving the puzzle, completes the puzzle, and moves quickly on to the next—is typical of his engagement throughout most of the game. As he works through a puzzle, each successfully completed step is punctuated by an "All right," or "Ahhh!" of recognition. In this way, he repeatedly enacts the subjectivity of one whose knowledge and competence is being tested and assessed, orienting to a participation genre of academic performance. The point here is not exploratory play or authoring that we see in the entertainment or authoring genres of participation, but rather the orientation toward progress and achievement that characterizes an academic participation genre.

The next example is from one of the first instances of Roger's exposure to *Island of Dr. Brain*. Roger is working with another kid, Herbert, and they are just beginning "the rat-driven elevator" problem. The task is a complex one. They are asked to determine how many spokes on two different gears are required to balance a counterweight with the weight of the elevator. They spend quite some time keying in different answers and trying to figure out the nature of the problem, enlisting the site coordinator's help. They try various solutions, but the elevator continues to fly into either the ceiling or the floor, toppling the crash-test dummy inside. Eventually, they begin to enjoy simply watching the dummy crash time after time, moving for a moment away from an achievement orientation to pleasure in this spectacle, engaging in a more entertainment-oriented participation genre. After almost ten minutes, in which they continue their trial and error tactics, they finally happen on the correct answer. This excerpt is of this concluding sequence:

R = Roger
H = Herbert
SC = Site Coordinator

1 *R:* OK, fifty-six. Fifty-one and seventeen. You have seventeen and forty-eight. Forty-eight. OK let's try it.

2 *H:* Yeah.

3 *R:* I love doing this.

4 *H:* Yeah this is it. Yep. Nope. Nope.

[Elevator crashes.]

5 *R:* Ahhh!! I love that.

6 *H:* It must, it must be fifty-one. Oh, man.

7 *R:* This is so hard.

8 *H:* Eighteen teeth. Watch this, watch this. Watch this.

9 *R:* You think this is right? No, he got tired. [Elevator crashes.] Ahh!!! [Laughs.] I love this!!

10 *H:* Eight, twenty-one. Nooo!!!!

[Elevator crashes.]

11 *R:* I love doing this.

12 *H:* Thirteen. Yeah. [Elevator is lowered successfully.] Oh my gosh. We got it. We got it!!! Yeah, [site coordinator name]. We got it.

13 *SC:* All right!

14 *R:* And we did it by guessing too!

15 *H:* I know, huh!

16 *R:* We're so good. Yeah, we can ride it.

17 *H:* Yeah.

This clip records a gleeful moment, with Herbert calling out to the site coordinator about their accomplishment and the two boys mutually congratulating themselves (lines 12–16). They are particularly happy at having "tricked the system" by getting the right answer by guessing. Far from detracting from their sense of mastery, this accomplishment serves as a display of achievement. "We're so good. Yeah, we can ride it." In a subsequent day, Roger revisits the same problem and mobilizes the guessing tactic that he developed with Herbert, abandoning any attempts to decode the nature of the problem. Although the adult helper he is working with tries to get him to solve the problem by dividing the elevator weight by the counterweight, he insists on guessing instead, "I have no idea. I'm just guessing. It works!" These excerpts from the video record provide some hints as to how the genre of academic software plays out in the everyday play of kids. The focus on external assessment and the linear sequencing of the game encourages an orientation to accomplishing the technical conditions of success rather than deeper exploration of the problem domain. Even in the case of the 5thD, where adults try to push kids toward exploratory and imaginative play, the kids quickly recognize the genre expectations of educational achievement.

Spectacle

In contrast to a game like *Dr. Brain*, titles that have more open-ended and exploratory structures often elicit different genres of participation. Storybook games rely heavily on the uniquely spectacular features of interactive multimedia to draw children into engagement, and kids will often exhibit a more entertainment-oriented genre of participation as they play with these titles. During my period of observation at the 5thD, the club purchased *The Magic School Bus Explores the Human Body* (*MSBEHB*), which included multimedia sound and graphics that were state of the art for children's software at the time. Players randomly drive around the human body and click on objects to see what visual and auditory effect will result. Kids find these small animations highly amusing, particularly if they are accompanied by a gross noise or visual. One undergraduate describes how two girls working together wanted to click on every animated object in the classroom. One of the girls says she likes the game because of "the music and the weird sounds it makes and how you can go into the human body." In the tapes where kids are together at the game, observers will be constantly leaning in and pointing at things to click on. The kids rarely tire of this mode of clicking on animated objects, and will revisit areas to show particularly cool interactions to other kids and their undergraduate helpers. The animations that form the transitions between the different parts of the body often draw appreciative "EEEW"s from both undergraduate and kid viewers, as they watch the tiny bus drop into a puddle of stomach goo, or fly down a sticky esophagus. Kids identify these spectacles as "fun" elements of kid culture: "This is the fun part. This is fun. Watch," insists one kid as he initiates the opening animation.

One area of *MSBEHB*, involving a simple painting program, is particularly notable as an embodiment of the logic of the interactive special effect. Clicking on the drawing pad of one of the characters calls forth a screen with a canvas and various tools, shaped like body parts, along the side. After selecting a body part, the player can squirt, splat, or stamp blobs and shapes onto the canvas, accompanied by gross bodily noises appropriate to the body part. Often to the dismay of the accompanying undergraduate, kids will spend excruciatingly long minutes repeatedly squirting juices from the stomach or emitting a cacophony of farting noises from the tongue tool. One undergraduate notes, after playing with a group of girls: "Each different shape or design made it's own unique sound. I think the kids get a much better kick out of the sound than anything else. And they would laugh and laugh when they found the sound they liked best." Here is an example of another instance of play, which was captured in our video record.

R = Ralph
UG = Undergraduate

1 *R:* Look, I could pick any one of these. This one. [Selects an organ.]

2 *UG:* What's that stuff right there?

3 *R:* [Squirts juice out of an organ.] I don't know. Squeezing all the juice out of him.

4 *UG:* Lovely. Now what happens if you grab that one?

5 *R:* Big one, the big one. Blood, brain. [Continues to select organs and make blobs and squishing and squeaking noises.]

6 *UG:* Oh, you can do it on here? Oh, it does a print of what the brain looks like.

7 *R:* Oh man.

8 *UG:* You can do the mouth, you haven't done that one.

9 *R:* Spitting, it's spitting.

10 *UG:* I know there's more down this way too. Skin, oh that just changes the color of it.

11 *R:* Yup. Do you want to see the nose?

12 *UG:* Nose. I don't know.

13 *R:* Gross.

14 *UG:* Oh, gross.

15 *R:* Boogers, eww.

[Continues through each organ in a similar manner.]

16 *UG:* Your tongue. Oh wow.

17 *R:* [Creates long drawn out farting noises.] Ewww!!! [Pushes repeatedly on a squeaking, blapping organ.] OHHHHH!!

18 *UG:* Wow.

19 *UG:* What else is there that you could do?

20 *R:* Nothing.

21 *UG:* Is that the last one?

22 *R:* Yeah.

23 *UG:* Are you sure?

24 *R:* Yeah.

25 *UG:* How do you know that?

26 *R:* [Goes back to the farting noise, and hits it repeatedly.] It's my favorite. The tongue. Watch.

27 *UG:* Are there any more?

28 *R:* Oh yeah. The finger. [Clicks repeatedly, making more gross noises.]

29 *UG:* Eww.

30 *R:* Ewww. Look.

31 *UG:* Are there any more after the finger? Let's see. Muscles. Whoa.

32 *R:* I want to go to the finger again.

33 *UG:* Why don't we go back and explore the body.

34 *R:* Okay. I know why. I know why. Cause you didn't like the sounds.

35 *UG:* No, the sounds were great.

36 *R:* I don't want to play anymore.

This extended sequence of play with interactive special effects is gleefully engaged with by Ralph and tolerated by the undergraduate, but she eventually suggests that they return to the main areas of the game (line 33). Ralph then suggests that she is discouraging him from playing with gross sounds (line 34), and decides that he wants to stop playing (line 36). The undergraduate has actually been remarkably patient through a very extended sequence of play with each drawing tool, suggesting on various occasions that he try one or another tool. Yet the boy still insists that he knows why she suggests that he move on, "Cause you didn't like the sounds." In this case, the boy is more active than the undergraduate in constructing the opposition between the adult stance and kid stance with respect to the orientation to gross special effects.

All gaming titles in some way cater to a hankering for spectacle, which is a cornerstone of participation genres associated with entertainment media. Children are quick to recognize these forms of engagement as "fun" and part of their peer cultural exchange rather than the achievement economy of adults and education. In other sequences we have captured on tape, we have seen kids exploit cheat codes in *SimCity 2000* to build large structures for the purposes of creating spectacular explosions, much to the delight of kid onlookers and the chagrin of adult educators. These are not the dominant modes of engagement in play with children's software, but they are small, ongoing breaks in the narrative trajectories of multimedia titles. They are also sites of micropolitical resistance to the progress-oriented goals and adult values that seek to limit violent and grotesque spectacles in an educational setting like the 5thD. With titles that have multiple and open-ended goals, players are more able to define the genre of participation, sometimes even in cases when adults are trying to call them back to the educational goals of the game.

Building My Own World

Competitive and spectacular pleasures are present in simulation games like *SimCity* or *Dinopark Tycoon*, but differ from the pleasures involved in creating and authoring a unique virtual world. A game like *SimCity 2000* allows players to create their own spectacles, settings, characters, and interactive possibilities, constructing user subjectivity as a world-builder rather than world-explorer. Game play and mastery involves uncovering the technical functionality of the building tools and then executing a personalized vision of a city while managing the balance between different factors such as cash flow, population density, and aesthetics. The results of these construction endeavors are often highly invested with personal reference, style, and meaning, a sense of personal creative *accomplishment* that differs from a sense of *achievement* in meeting external goals. Kids will continuously debate which features and buildings are cool, and where they should be placed, and showing off their creations to one another. "My friend had one of those big shark-looking things up on a big hill that he had made!" "Look! Want to see my huge mountain? I made this huge mountain by hand and I covered it in water by hand. I did this all by hand." This sense of self-expression is characteristic of the participation genre of construction.

One way that *SimCity 2000* accomplishes a sense of identification is by suturing players into identification as the mayor of the city. Advisers from various city offices advise "you" on the state of transportation, education, and other city services. After achieving a certain population level, you are awarded a "mayor's house" that can be placed at will. Kids will often spend a great deal of time placing the house in a nice location—on top of a hill, overlooking a lake, distanced from the bustle of the city—and might add a private subway or park for the mayor's residence. The player with ownership of the city will without exception refer to the house as "my house," and the appearance of the house will generally initiate a sequence of imaginative projection, where interlocutors will talk about what it would be like to live in a particular location. "Girl you want to see it?" asks one of our teenage players to a new friend at the club. "Watch. That's my house girl." "Oh!" proclaims the friend, impressed. "I want to build. I'll make mine."

One instance of a boy (Jimmy) and an undergraduate (Holly) discussing the mayor's house is representative of these interactional moments.

J = Jimmy
Holly = Undergraduate
Italics signifies overlapping talk

1 *J:* I can make my house, the mayor's house [Clicks on rewards icon.] Where do I want to make my house?

2 *H:* [Laughs.] You want it overlooking everything? [Laughs.] Aaa... Do you want to have it overlooking the lake or something?

3 *J:* [Dismisses year-end dialog box.]

4 *H:* Yeah, you can have like those be the really nice houses or something. Like up in the hills?

5 *J:* Up here? [Moves cursor to flat area on ridge.]

6 *H:* Uuuu maybe over here [pointing] because this you'd be just overlooking over the power plant. That wouldn't be very nice. Maybe over by the lake or something?

7 *J:* How about, right here? [Positions cursor over flat ground by the lake.]

8 *H:* Sure, yeah, like right on the lake?

9 *J:* [Builds house on lake opposite city.] Yeah, I need power, *obviously* because it's my house.

10 *H:* [Laughs.]

11 *J:* [Builds power lines to mayor's house.]

12 *H:* You need water I would think.

13 *J:* Hate water! [Selects water pipe tool.]

14 *H:* [Reads from status bar.] Water shortage or something. Why would there be a water shortage? Something like a drought or something? You can't really . . . mmm . . .

15 *J:* [Builds pipes to mayor's house.] There! [Water keeps running out.] Better give me water! [The water doesn't flow to house.] I don't care though! [Dismisses budget window.] It's so hard . . .

16 *H:* What is?

17 *J:* Using this . . . [Selects hospital tool.] Hospital? Should I put in a hospital?

18 *H:* Another one?

19 *J:* Do I already have one?

20 *H:* Uh-huh. You have one by the college. You have another on . . . do you have a free clinic or something for the people *who can't afford it?–*

21 *J:* *How 'bout auuummm!* A prison.

22 *H:* You have a police station already, right?

23 *J:* Where should I have it, right here?

24 *H:* That's over by the hospital. You probably want it . . . how about over by the sewage, like the industrial area. So it's not, cause you don't, I mean, like, no one would want to live in that area.

25 *J:* [Tries to place prison on terraced ground.] I can't put it on the, like, it has to be on flat ground. How about right here? [Positions cursor by lake.]

26 *H:* Don't put it right by your house! You don't want to live by the prison do you!? [Laughs.]

27 *J:* [Laughs.] Right here? [Positions on opposite side of lake.]

29 *H:* Sure. That's right by the police station. You might as well.

30 *J:* More convenient.

Figure 7
Screen shot of Jimmy's mayor's house in *SimCity 2000*. (Reproduced with permission from Electronic Arts, Inc. © 1993–94 Electronic Arts Inc. SimCity 2000 and SimCity are trademarks or registered trademarks of Electronic Arts Inc. in the United States and/or other countries. All rights reserved.)

In this segment of activity, Jimmy begins by taking up the identification between him and the mayor: "I can make my house, the mayor's house," and then invites Holly into the decision of where to place it: "Where do I want to make my house?" (line 1). Holly's talk then draws in a series of connections from her knowledge about the world: what constitutes desirable real estate, a good view, and signifiers of power and wealth (lines 2, 4, 6). Jimmy takes up her first suggestion, to put it overlooking a lake, by trying to place it on a ridge overlooking an industrial area. She then offers an alternate suggestion, to place the house by the uninhabited region by the lake. Jimmy, with her agreement, places "his" house by the lake opposite the city (figure 7). They go on to lay down water to the mayor's house (despite the fact that is it difficult to do and Jimmy "hates" it), and then they consider the placement of a prison. Holly advises against placing it next to the mayor's house (lines 23–25). The placement of the mayor's house is inconsequential in terms of game outcomes, but functions as an effective hook for locating a subject position for the player within the game's mise-en-scène. While the tone of the talk is decidedly playful and peppered with laughter—it's just a game after all—Jimmy, Holly, and *SimCity 2000* have succeeded in organizing themselves around a series of identifications that link Jimmy, the mayor, "nice" parts of town, and a good view. In this case, the game, Jimmy, and Holly collaboratively perform the participation genre of construction.

On another day, two girls, Allie and Jean, are playing the game with an undergraduate. The undergraduate fieldnote describes how they engage in a series of imaginative projections in which they build a mansion for themselves, and then a home for others in their lives.

There is a young man named Seth whom Allie doesn't like, and she built him a house on the far corner of the city, and proceeded to surround his home with dense forest, far from civilization, roads, and water. Because neither girl likes Jean's four-year-old sister, Allie built her house in a deserted valley without water or electricity, to die in isolation. I said that it was mean, so Allie placed a teeny, tiny lake far away from the sister's home.

These are just a few examples of how kids use games to construct their unique viewpoints in a virtual world. This genre of participation tends to be tied to subjectivities of technical mastery and often a hackerlike ethos, as well as these more creative and personal projections of identities. It is a source of pleasure in harnessing the technical power of the computer, as well as forming a personal identification and sense of ownership of a unique creation. During the time that I was conducting my research, *SimCity 2000* was the state of the art in terms of software that enabled players to author within simulated worlds. Since then, this genre of software and participation has become much more central to the worlds of interactive entertainment and is being incorporated into a wider range of educational efforts. Now user-generated content and customization are buzzwords within the mainstream gaming industry, though a decade ago practices of game modding were still on the hacker fringe. In multiplayer online games, particularly worlds like *Second Life*,[15] user-generated content, modding, and customization are at the very center of game engagement. These trends have meant that even games without any clear educational value can become a focus for constructive play and hacking in the genre of authoring. *SimCity*, centered on player-generated goals, authoring components, and a wide array of cheats for easy hackability, foreshadowed the developments in gaming and learning that we see today.

Conclusions

The production, distribution, and play with children's software involve ongoing tension and intertwining of different genres, social agendas, and educational philosophies. These dynamics include the negotiation between adults and kids performing the genres of academic, entertainment, and construction; the ideals of learning, fun, and creativity; and the politics of enrichment, indulgence, and empowerment. These three genres are tied to different social investments. Academic genres became a vehicle for producing class and educational distinction. Entertainment produces age cohort identity by creating a space of childhood pleasures defined in opposition to adult disciplines. The participation genre of construction supports a subjectivity of creative self-actualization tied to technical mastery. These genres of media and participation all have much deeper historical roots than this apparently recent turn to learning games and children's software. They draw from long-standing discourses in education and middle-class parenting that attempt to transform play into a site of learning, either through behaviorist, play-oriented, or constructivist models of learning. Educational genres butt up against the entrenched idioms and institutions of commercial entertainment that have taken an increasingly stronger hold on childhood peer cultures in the post-TV era. The adult-oriented goals of progress and constructive play are defined in opposition to children's cultures of repetitive action, fun, and phantasmagoria.

Underlying my description has been a structural opposition between the cultural categories of education and entertainment. Contemporary childhoods in the United States are largely organized by the institutions of school and home, and each institutional setting has certain social imperatives and associated media products of educational and entertainment media. Well-established media industries and infrastructures insist on these distinctions, segment markets and advertising based on the opposition between play and learning, and build on established genre recognitions of kids and parents. While marketing education software to parents or entertainment to children falls into established genres, it is much more difficult to market and distribute genre-breaking titles. Although many of the early children's software titles such as *Oregon Trail*, *Carmen Sandiego*, and *SimCity* were not as genre-constrained in this way, genres hardened over time as the industry and market for children's software matured. As the development context shifted from a small, experimental research effort to a mainstream commercial enterprise, the founding impetus of educational and cultural reform shifted to one of catering to existing institutional and market demands. Children's software titles were increasingly polarized between those oriented toward academic goals and those that were meant to be fun and exciting and to compete with television for children's attentions.

The tendency for genres to harden over time indicates how media content is inseparable from the economic and structural conditions in which it is produced and circulates. Social change needs to be pursued at all levels of the circuit of production, distribution, and consumption,[16] a daunting task for anyone aiming to transform the relations between technology, social stratification, and learning. When new technologies go mainstream, they fall victim to their own success, shifting from experimental technologies controlled by innovative pioneers to conduits for existing social structures and norms. Early developers of children's software hoped to put accessible technical tools in the hands of the disenfranchised, alleviating the oppressiveness of narrow notions of education. Instead, children's software became another site for addressing achievement anxiety in parents and for instilling the habitus of upwardly mobile achievement for children who seem to have been born into success. Reform efforts that rely on educational media must produce innovative content as well as innovate in distribution mechanisms and contexts of reception to have systemic impact on issues such as educational equity. The problem of "using games to make learning fun" cannot be addressed simply as a research or software design problem. Although, as researchers, we may recognize the learning potential of games, this recognition alone does not change the structural conditions that insist on the bifurcation between entertainment and education and correlate only academic content with educational success.

Although I have stressed the conservative tendencies of genres, the circuit of culture I have described also suggests multiple points of negotiation, juncture, and disjuncture. The ongoing contestations between genres of participation and representation suggest ways of reshaping and appropriating the categories of education and entertainment that have been handed down to us. Titles in the construction genre create productive confusion in what we recognize as educational or entertainment. Just as the 5thD complicates our notions of what an educational institution is, games such as *SimCity* have challenged educators to consider alternative ways of recognizing learning. Educational institutions continue to have a determining effect on how childhood success and achievement is measured even outside the classroom; the history of children's software demonstrates the ways in which genres of education migrate and morph beyond the institutional boundary of school. Contexts of play and informal learning, while seemingly marginal to the high-stakes contestations over educational sorting and achievement, are sites that demonstrate the alignments and disjunctures between the cultural and social structures of children's lives. It is when these sites of reception can join hands with innovative software creators and distributors across the circuit of culture that we can begin to imagine alternative genres of media and participation that are both compelling and sustainable.

Local contexts of play are highly malleable and open to contestation. Kids are political actors mobilizing cultural, technical, and social resources in pursuing status negotiations and claiming agency, momentarily resisting the progress goals of adults, smuggling in forbidden idioms of action, entertainment, and spectacle, and using adults to support public knowledge and status displays. As technology and cultural trends increasingly support a malleable palette of styles and genres, these opportunities for creative mobilization are expanding for a media- and technology-savvy generation. In the micropolitics of everyday play, the balance of power between children, adults, and software is constantly shifting. A game like *SimCity 2000* can transform from a site of gleeful destruction and boyish status display to a contemplative site of conversation between an adult and a child about the relation between wealth and crime. One well-timed intervention can tip the scale toward a different genre, a different mode of engagement, a different power dynamic. The subtleties of software design are also highly significant in these micropolitics. Seemingly trivial design decisions, such as score-keeping mechanisms or a particular cheat code, can inflect play in substantive ways.

If I were to place my bet on a genre of gaming that has the potential to transform the systemic conditions of childhood learning, I would pick the construction genre. These forms of more geeky- and hacker-oriented play and software are moving from periphery to center; they hold out the promise of a more participatory form of learning and media engagement.[17] With the spread of the Internet and low-cost digital authoring tools, kids have a broader social and technological palette through with to engage in self-authoring and digital media production. With the growing popularity of online journaling, social network services, game modding, and remix cultures, we are in the midst of a much broader cultural shift that positions digital authoring and publication more centrally in the peer cultures of young people. These new practices challenge our research frameworks as well as the broader institutional structures of capitalism, entertainment, education, and the family. As the overall media ecology in which children are immersed shifts, construction-oriented learning games can more effectively function as a scaffold for activist genres of media engagement and learning that do not rely on an opposition between education and entertainment, learning and play.

Notes

1. Mizuko Ito, *Interactive Media for Play: Kids, Computer Games, and the Productions of Everyday Life* (PhD diss., Stanford University School of Education, 1998); and idem., *Engineering Play: Children's Software and the Productions of Everyday Life* (PhD diss., Stanford University Department of Anthropology, 2003).

2. Gill Valentine and Sarah L. Holloway, *Cyberkids: Children in the Information Age* (New York: Routledge, 2001).

3. Trevor J. Pinch and Wiebe E. Bijker, The Social Construction of Facts and Artifacts: Or How the Sociology of Science and the Sociology of Technology Might Benefit Each Other, in *The Social Construction of Technological Systems*, eds. Wiebe E. Bijker, Thomas P. Hughes, and Trevor J. Pinch (Cambridge, MA: The MIT Press, 1987), 17–50.

4. See, for example, Paul Edwards, From "Impact" to Social Process: Computers in Society and Culture, in *Handbook of Science and Technology Studies*, eds. Sheila Jasanoff, Gerald E. Markle, James C. Petersen, and Trevor Pinch (Thousand Oaks, CA: Sage, 1995), 257–85; Christine Hine, *Virtual Ethnography* (London: Sage, 2000); Lawrence Lessig, *Code and Other Laws of Cyberspace* (New York: Basic Books, 1999); and Daniel Miller and Don Slater, *The Internet: An Ethnographic Approach* (New York: Berg, 2000).

5. Paul du Gay, Stuart Hall, Linda Janes, Hugh Mackay, and Keith Negus, *Doing Cultural Studies: The Story of the Sony Walkman* (Thousand Oaks, CA: Sage, 1997).

6. John Seely Brown and Paul Duguid, *The Social Life of Information* (Cambridge, MA: Harvard Business School Press, 2002).

7. Pierre Bourdieu, *Outline of a Theory of Practice*, trans. Richard Nice (New York: Cambridge University Press, 1972).

8. Anthony Giddens, *The Constitution of Society: Outline of the Theory of Structuration* (Berkeley, CA: University of California Press, 1986).

9. James Paul Gee, *What Video Games Have to Teach Us About Learning and Literacy* (New York: Palgrave Macmillan, 2003); and Mizuko Ito, Japanese Media Mixes and Amateur Cultural Exchange, in *Digital Generations*, eds. David Buckingham and Rebekah Willett (Hillsdale, NJ: Lawrence Erlbaum, 2006).

10. Hervé Varenne, Shelley Goldman, and Ray McDermott, Racing in Place, in *Successful Failure: The School America Builds*, eds. Hervé Varenne and Ray McDermott (Boulder, CO: Westview, 1998), 106–15.

11. Lloyd P. Rieber, Nancy Luke, and Jan Smith, Project Kid Designer: Constructivism at Work Through Play, *Meridian: A Middle School Computer Technologies Journal* 1, no. 1 (1998): 1–19.

12. Ibid., 5.

13. Seymour Papert, *Mindstorms: Children, Computers, and Powerful Ideas* (New York: Basic Books, 1980).

14. See Reed Stevens, Tom Satwicz, and Laurie McCarthy, In-Game, In-Room, In-World: Reconnecting Video Game Play to the Rest of Kids' Lives, in *The Ecology of Games: Connecting Youth, Games, and Learning*, ed. Katie Salen (Cambridge, MA: The MIT Press, 2007), 41–66.

15. See Cory Ondrejka, Education Unleashed: Participatory Culture, Education, and Innovation in Second Life, in *The Ecology of Games: Connecting Youth, Games, and Learning*, ed. Katie Salen (Cambridge, MA: The MIT Press, 2007), 229–251.

16. du Gay et al., *Doing Cultural Studies.*

17. See the following: Ondrejka, Education Unleashed; Jane McGonigal, Why *I Love Bees:* A Case Study in Collective Intelligence Gaming, in *The Ecology of Games: Connecting Youth, Games, and Learning*, ed. Katie Salen (Cambridge, MA: The MIT Press, 2007), 199–227; Ito, Japanese Media Mixes; and Henry Jenkins, *Convergence Culture: Where Old and New Media Collide* (New York: NYU Press, 2006).

The Rhetoric of Video Games

Ian Bogost

The Georgia Institute of Technology, School of Literature, Communication, and Culture

Animal Crossing is an "animal village simulator" for the Nintendo GameCube and DS video game consoles.[1] As the game begins, the player has just left home to move to the game's small village. There he meets a host of cartoonish animal residents and settles into a new life. The player is penniless upon arrival, and the game quickly thrusts him into the reality of making ends meet. The village's resident real estate tycoon and shopkeeper, Tom Nook, helps the player out, offering him a small shack to live in and a job of planting trees, delivering goods, and creating marketing materials on the town notice board (see figure 1). After completing these chores, Nook releases the player to explore the town on his own. He may then work, trade, and personalize his environment. The game offers a series of innocuous, even mundane activities like bug catching, gardening, and wallpaper designing.

One of the more challenging projects in the game is paying off the mortgage on one's house. *Animal Crossing* allows players to upgrade their homes, but doing so requires paying off a large note the player must take out to start the game in the first place. The player must then pay down renovation mortgages for even larger sums.[2] While the game omits some of the more punitive intricacies of long-term debt, such as compounding interest, improving one's home does require consistent work in the game world. Catching fish, hunting for fossils, finding insects, and doing jobs for other townsfolk all produce income that can be used to pay off mortgage debt or to buy carpets, furniture, and objects to decorate one's house.

When my then five-year-old began playing the game seriously, he quickly recognized the dilemma he faced. On the one hand, he wanted to spend the money he had earned from collecting fruit and bugs on new furniture, carpets, and shirts. On the other hand, he wanted to pay off his house so he could get a bigger one like mine. Once he managed to amass enough savings to pay off his mortgage, Tom Nook offered to expand his house. While it is possible to refrain from upgrading, the unassuming raccoon continues to offer renovations as frequently as the player visits his store. My son began to realize the dilemma facing him: the more material possessions he took on, the more space he needed, and the more debt he had to assume to provide that space. And the additional space just fueled more material acquisitions, continuing the loop. This link between debt and acquisition gives form to a routine that many mortgage holders fail to recognize: buying more living space not only creates more debt, it also drives the impulse to acquire more goods. More goods demand even more space, creating a vicious cycle.

For a more detailed discussion of procedural rhetoric and persuasive games, see Bogost's book on the subject, *Persuasive Games: The Expressive Power of Videogames* (The MIT Press, 2007).

Figure 1
A player near her house in *Animal Crossing*. While it looks like just an idyllic cartoon world, the game also models commerce and debt.

In real life, when we pay our mortgage bill we don't see where that money ends up. But in *Animal Crossing*, the player experiences the way his debt makes bankers wealthy. After a player makes a major payment to his mortgage, Tom Nook closes his shop and upgrades it; the game starts with Nook's Cranny, a wooden shack general store, and ends with Nookington's, a two-story department store. Each upgrade allows Tom Nook to sell more goods. None of the townsfolk ever appear in Tom Nook's shop, although they occasionally refer to it somewhat disdainfully; the animals seem to have little drive to consume. *Animal Crossing*'s nonplayer characters (NPCs) are much less materialistic. The cute animals that occupy the village sternly berate the player if they haven't seen him around for many days, but they seem to have no concern for the quantity or type of material properties that the players possess. Occasionally, animals will express desire for a shirt or furniture item the player carries with him around the village, and they will offer to trade for it. But this type of transaction is both rare and charming; the animals frame their requests in terms of inveterate longing—"I've always wanted a Modern Lamp!"—quite a different refrain from the mallgoer's "one overriding interest, to spend money."[3]

In contrast, the player participates in a full consumer regimen: he pays off debt, buys and sells goods. Tom Nook buys the player's goods, which he converts to wealth. As the player pays off debt and upgrades his home to store more goods, he sees Tom Nook convert that wealth into increased commercial leverage—one's own debt makes the bank rich. Tom Nook then leverages that wealth to draw more capital out of the player, whose resources remain effectively constant. While the player spends more, Nook makes more. By condensing all of the environment's financial transactions into one flow between the player and Tom Nook, the game models the redistribution of wealth in a way even young children like my five-year-old can understand. Tom Nook is a condensation of the corporate bourgeoisie.

Animal Crossing simulates the social dynamics of a small town, complete with the material demands of keeping up with the Joneses. As such, the game serves as a sandbox for experimenting with the ways one can recombine personal wealth. While the player diligently works to pay off that new upstairs addition, the other animals retain their small shacks perpetually. They never sell old belongings or acquire new ones, seemingly unconcerned that their homes are filled only with fish, or rocks, or fruit furniture. *Animal Crossing*'s animals enjoy walks outdoors. They snooze on their porches at twilight. They stop to watch the player fish. They meander aimlessly and take great care to partake in the community events that transpire on holidays. They are not consumers but naturalists, more Henry David Thoreau than Paris Hilton.

Animal Crossing is a game about everyday life in a small town. It is a game about customizing and caring for an environment. It is a game about making friends and about collecting insects. But *Animal Crossing* is also a game about long-term debt. It is a game about the repetition of mundane work necessary to support contemporary material property ideals. It is a game about the bittersweet consequences of acquiring goods and keeping up with the Joneses. *Animal Crossing* accomplishes this feat not through moralistic regulation, but by creating a model of commerce and debt in which the player can experience and discover such consequences. In its model, the game simplifies the real world in order to draw attention to relevant aspects of that world.

We often think that video games have a unique ethos. Video game players have their own culture and values. Video game players often self-identify as "gamers" and devote a major part of their leisure time to video games. They discuss games online, follow new trends, and adopt new technology early. Video game play could be understood as a "community of practice," a name Jean Lave and Etienne Wenger have given to a common social situation around which people collaborate to develop ideas.[4] In this sense, the people who play video games develop values, strategies, and approaches to the practice of play itself. For example, a large group of *Animal Crossing* players contribute to an online community called Animal Crossing Community (ACC for short) to discuss the game, share things they've made, find strategies, or look up the value of different fish, insects, or furniture.[5] Within this community, as in all communities, cultural values develop, both by design and by evolution. For example, ACC offers players the option of "getting adopted." A veteran "Scout" is assigned to a new member as a "foster buddy" to help the newbie "learn the ropes of ACC . . . They'll also help you with any of your Animal Crossing questions, and may even give you a free item as a welcoming gift!"[6] Venues like ACC show that video game play is a cultural activity where values develop over time.

But the values of a video game community like ACC exist *outside* the game. While the neighborliness of the foster buddy program might suggest a carryover of values from the video game, the ACC is primarily focused on the social practices *of playing* the game, rather than the social practices *represented in* the game. This is an important distinction: video games are not just stages that facilitate cultural, social, or political practices; they are also media where cultural values themselves can be represented—for critique, satire, education, or commentary. When understood in this way, we can learn to read games as deliberate expressions of particular perspectives. In other words, video games make claims about the world, which players can understand, evaluate, and deliberate. Game developers can learn to create games that make deliberate expressions about the world. Players can learn to read and critique these models, deliberating the implications of such claims. Teachers can learn to help students address real-world issues by playing and critiquing the video games they play. And educators can also help students imagine and design games based on their own opinions of the world. When games are used in this fashion, they can become part of a whole range of subjects.

Play

One of the reasons we tend not to consider video games as legitimate venues for learning to take place is precisely because they are *games*, playthings. Play is often considered a children's activity, a trifle that occupies or distracts kids and which they eventually grow out of, turning to more serious pursuits. Play and learning have been segregated from one another in contemporary schooling, further cementing their perceived disparity. Children learn while seated in desks, listening attentively to a teacher or reading from a book. This sort of valid learning is interrupted by recess, where children are allowed to play. Understood in this way, play is a distraction useful only to let off the necessary steam to allow kids (or adults) to get back to the serious business of learning (or working).

Video games also subscribe to this value model. They are a part of the "entertainment software" industry, and they are generally considered a leisure practice by players and the general public alike. Video game play is considered an unproductive expenditure of time, time that fills the breaks between work. This goes for children playing games at home after school as well as adults playing games after work. Parents might worry about their children playing video games after school instead of doing their homework or playing outside. Video games are perceived to interrupt learning and social life, acting as a leech on normal childhood development. During the 1990s dot-com boom, many offices teeming with young workers took lunch or after-work breaks to play networked games on the office computers, taking respite from the "productive" practices of work. While it is rarely discussed directly, this conflation of work and play at the office serves as an archetype for the ill-founded business acumen of that era. These early Internet companies failed because they weren't serious; they were merely "playing" at business.

But this association of video games with leisure is not a necessary condition. It is, rather, a by-product of a misunderstanding of the nature of play. Instead of understanding play as child's activity, or as the means to consume games, or even as the shifting centers of meaning in poststructuralist thought, I suggest adopting Katie Salen and Eric Zimmerman's useful, abstract definition of the term: "play is the free space of movement within a more rigid structure."[7] Understood in this sense, play refers to the "possibility space" created by constraints of all kinds. Play activities are not rooted in one social practice, but in many social and material practices. For example, Salen and Zimmerman use the example of the play in a mechanism like a steering column, in which the meshing gears create "play" in the wheel before the turning gesture causes the gears to couple.

The possibility space of play includes all of the gestures made possible by a set of rules. As Salen and Zimmerman explain, imposing rules does not suffocate play, but makes it possible in the first place. On a playground, the possibility space refers to the physical properties of the play space, as well as the equipment, time allotted, and number and type of children. Kids are particularly adept at inventing new games based on the constraints of their environment; if one listens closely to children at play, one of the most common things to overhear is the establishment of new rules ("Now you be the monster," "This square is safe!"). When children play, they constantly renegotiate their relationship with a possibility space.

In more traditional media like poetry, the possibility space refers to the expressive opportunities afforded by rules of composition, form, or genre. For example, the poetic form of haiku enforces three lines of five, seven, and five syllables each.[8] The imposition of these restrictions constrains poetic authorship. To write haiku means exploring configurations of language that intersect with these rules of composition.

While possibility spaces like haiku develop over time (in this case, dating from a linked verse style of the fifteenth century), other literary practices have invented new possibility spaces with the specific purpose of creating new forms of expression. The artistic movement known as Oulipo (*Ouvroir de littérature potentielle*), founded in Paris in 1960, adopted precisely this practice. The group's members invented, revived, or adopted forms for literary expression, each of which changes the possibility space of literary expression. One familiar example is the palindrome, a word or phrase that reads the same forward and backward. Georges Perec wrote "Le Grand Palindrome" of roughly 1,500 words, although writers Nick Montfort and William Gillespie topped Perec's record with 2002, a palindromic novel of 2,002 words, authored in the year 2002.[9] Another Oulipian construct is the lipogram, a text in which use of a particular letter is forbidden. The most famous lipogrammatic text is Georges Perec's *La Disparition*, a lipogram in *E* (i.e., the letter *e* appears nowhere in the work).[10] The prisoner's constraint is a lipogram in ascenders and descenders; that is, letters that stick up or down from the line are forbidden (*b, d, f, g, h, j, k, l, p, q, t,* and *y*).

The constrained forms of Oulipo practitioners impose even more stringent restrictions than those of natural grammar and "ordinary" literary convention, but more importantly these artists deliberately *invented* new constraints, rather than adopting the forms provided by a particular historical and cultural moment. By designing the rules of literary composition, Oulipian writers share much in common with children on a playground: first they create a possibility space, then they fill that space with meaning by exploring the free movement within the rigid structure of literary rules. Likewise, readers of work like Perec's must take into account the rules of its composition, which tightly couple to the meaning of the work ("la disparition" means "the disappearance"; the novel follows a group of people who cannot find a hunting companion). Likewise, the rules children adopt in playground play alter the experience and meaning of the play. For example, consider a game of hide-and-seek in which an older player must count for a longer time to allow younger players a better chance to hide more cleverly. This rule is not merely instrumental; it suggests a value of equity in the game and its players.

In a video game, the possibility space refers to the myriad configurations the player might construct to see the ways the processes inscribed in the system work. This is really what we do when we *play* video games: we explore the possibility space its rules afford by manipulating the symbolic systems the game provides. The rules do not merely create the experience of play—they also construct the meaning of the game. That is to say, the gestures, experiences, and interactions a game's rules allow (and disallow) make up the game's significance. Video games represent processes in the material world—war, urban planning, sports, and so forth—and create new possibility spaces for exploring those topics. That representation is composed of the rules themselves. We encounter the meaning of games by exploring their possibility spaces. And we explore their possibility spaces through play.

Procedurality

We rely on the practice of *procedurality* to craft representations through rules, which in turn create possibility spaces that can be explored through play. Procedurality is a somewhat technical term that requires explanation. The term *procedure* itself does not usually give rise to positive reactions. We typically understand procedures as established, entrenched ways of doing things. *Procedure* often invokes notions of officialdom, even bureaucracy. In common parlance, a procedure is a static course of action, perhaps one established long ago and in need of revision. Often, we talk about procedures only when they go wrong: *after several complaints, we decided to review our procedures for creating new accounts*. But in fact, procedures in this sense of the word structure behavior of all types. Procedures (or processes) are sets of constraints that create possibility spaces, which can be explored through play.

In her influential book *Hamlet on the Holodeck*, Janet Murray defines four essential properties of digital artifacts: procedurality, participation, spatiality, and encyclopedic scope.[11] Murray uses the term *procedural* to refer to the computer's "defining ability to execute a series of rules."[12] Procedurality in this sense refers to the core practice of software authorship. Software is composed of algorithms that model the way things behave. To write procedurally, one authors code that enforces rules to generate some kind of representation, rather than authoring the representation itself. Procedural systems generate behaviors based on rule-based models; they are machines capable of producing many outcomes, each conforming to the same overall guidelines. The "brain" or "heart" of a computer is its *processor*, the chip that executes instructions. *Procedurality* gets its name from the function of the processor—procedurality is the principal value of the computer, which creates meaning through the interaction of algorithms. While Murray places procedurality alongside three other properties, these properties are not equivalent. The computer, she writes, "was designed . . . to embody complex, contingent behaviors. To be a computer scientist is to think in terms of algorithms and heuristics, that is, to be constantly identifying the exact or general rules of behavior that describe any process, from running a payroll to flying an airplane."[13] This ability to execute computationally a series of rules fundamentally separates computers from other media.

Among computer-based media, video games tend to emphasize procedurality more than other types of software programs. Chris Crawford has used the term *process intensity* to refer to the "degree to which a program emphasizes processes instead of data."[14] Higher process intensity—or in Crawford's words a higher "crunch per bit ratio"—suggests that a program has greater potential for meaningful expression. That is to say, video games more frequently and more deeply exploit the property of the computer that creates the kind of possibility spaces that we can explore through play. Furthermore, unlike productivity software such as word processors and spreadsheets, video games are usually created with some expressive purpose in mind; they represent models of systems or spaces that players can inhabit, rather than serving as mere tools.

Video games depict real and imagined systems by creating procedural models of those systems, that is, by imposing sets of rules that create particular possibility spaces for play. Often, when we think of video games we think of the themes of fantasy and power, like the space marine of *Doom* who must combat demons to save the world.[15] But these themes represent only part of the expressive capacity of games. Other games go beyond models of fantasy worlds, creating representations of the ordinary world that might give players new perspectives on the world they inhabit. For example, *Animal Crossing* creates a representation of everyday life in which labor and debt are a part. When video games represent things—anything from space demons to long-term debt—they do so through procedurality, by constructing rule-based models of their chosen topics. In *Doom*'s model of the world, emphasis is placed on the trajectory and power of weaponry. In *Animal Crossing*'s model of the world, emphasis is placed on work, trade, and arrangement of the environment.

In the context of digital media and learning, video games offer two overlapping opportunities. In one, players can learn about aspects of the world that particular games model, such as consumption in *Animal Crossing* or urban planning in *Sim City*.[16] This is a kind of subject-centered literacy focused on examples of human practice. In the other, players can learn about procedurality itself, an inscriptive practice that will become more important only as computers continue to expand their role in society.

Rhetoric

Some games' procedural representations serve mostly to create an entertainment experience, a fantastic situation that transports the player to another world. But other games use procedurality to make claims about the cultural, social, or material aspects of human experience. Some do this deliberately, while others do it inadvertently. When we talk about making claims or arguments about things, we enter the domain of *rhetoric*, the field of communication that deals with persuasive speech. I would like to take a brief historical detour through the field of rhetoric in order to connect it to procedurality, learning, and to video games in turn.

Like procedurality, rhetoric is not an esteemed term. Despite its two-and-a-half-millennia-long history, today rhetoric invokes largely negative connotations. We often speak of "empty rhetoric," elaborate and well-crafted speech that is nevertheless devoid of actual meaning. Rhetoric might conjure the impression of *hot* air, as in the case of a fast-talking con who crafts pretentious language to hide barren or deceitful intentions. Academics and politicians are particularly susceptible to this sort of criticism, perhaps because we (and they) tend to use flourish and lexis when coherence runs thin, as in this very sentence. Rhetoric is often equated with a type of smoke screen; it is language used to occlude, confuse, or manipulate the listener.

However, turgidity and extravagance are relatively recent inflections to this term, which originally referred only to persuasive speech, or oratory. The term rhetoric (ῥήτωρικη) first appears in Plato's *Gorgias*, written some 2,500 years ago, in reference to the art of persuasion. The term itself derives from the rhetor (ῥήτωρ), or orator, and his practice, oratory (ῥήτωρεύω).[17] Rhetoric in ancient Greece meant public speaking for civic purposes.

Because of the importance of public speech in Golden Age Athens, rhetorical training became a promising business opportunity. Technical rhetoric, as this type is sometimes called, is useful for the everyman but perhaps too simplistic for the professional orator. Skilled orators developed numerous other techniques in much the same way as motivational business speakers do today. These experts charged for their services, and were called *sophists*. The popularity of books and sophistry bred critique. Such approaches motivated the work of Socrates and Plato, who rejected the social and political contingency of the court and the assembly in favor of more lasting philosophical truths.

Responding to Plato, Aristotle attempts a systematic, philosophical approach to the art of persuasive oratory; he argues that rhetorical practice has the final cause of persuasion to correct judgment. For Aristotle, rhetoric is "the faculty of observing in any given case the available means of persuasion."[18] The adept rhetorician does not merely follow a list of instructions for composing an oratory (technical rhetoric), nor does he merely parrot the style or words of an expert (sophistic rhetoric), but rather he musters reason to discover the available means of persuasion in any particular case. This variety of rhetoric implies an understanding of both the reasons to persuade and the tools available to achieve that end.

Classical rhetoric passed into the Middle Ages and modern times with considerable alteration. Civil rhetoric never disappeared entirely, and indeed it remains a common form of rhetoric today. But the concept of rhetoric expanded to account for new modes of inscription—especially literary and artistic modes. Writers and artists have expressive goals, and they deploy techniques to accomplish those goals. Here, persuasion shifts from the simple achievement of desired ends to the effective arrangement of a work so as to create a desirable possibility space for interpretation. In contemporary rhetoric, the goal of persuasion is largely underplayed or even omitted as a defining feature of the field, replaced by the more general notion of elegance, clarity, and creativity in communication. In this sense, rhetoric "provides ways of emphasizing ideas or making them vivid."[19] Success means effective expression, not necessarily effective influence.

Twentieth-century rhetorician Kenneth Burke identifies the need to identify with others as the ancestor of the practice of rhetoric. He extends rhetoric beyond persuasion, instead suggesting "identification" as a key term for the practice.[20] We use symbolic systems like language, says Burke, as a way to achieve this identification. While rhetoric still entails persuasion for Burke, he greatly expands its purview, arguing that it facilitates human action in general. In addition to expanding the conception of rhetoric, Burke expands its domain. In the tradition of oral and written rhetoric, language remains central. But Burke's understanding of humans as creators and consumers of symbolic systems expands rhetoric to include nonverbal domains known and yet to be invented or discovered.

The wide latitude Burke affords to rhetoric won him both champions and critics, but his expansion of the concept is particularly useful for our interest in video game rhetoric.[21] Thanks to the influence of Burke, and amplified by the increasingly inescapable presence of nonoral, nonverbal media, increasing interest has mounted around efforts to understand these other, newer modes of inscription that also appear to serve rhetorical ends. In particular, the emergence of photographic and cinematic expression in the nineteenth and twentieth centuries suggested a need to understand how those new, nonverbal media mount arguments. This subfield is called *visual rhetoric*. Visual communication cannot simply adopt the figures and forms of oral and written expression, so a new form of rhetoric must be created to accommodate these media forms.

Visual rhetoric offers a useful lesson in the creation of new forms of rhetoric in the general sense. One would be hard pressed to deny that advertisements, photographs, illustrations, and other optical phenomena have no effect on their viewers. To be sure, visual rhetoric is often at work in video games, a medium that deploys both still and moving images. But visual rhetoric does not account for procedural representation. This is not a flaw in the subfield of visual rhetoric; in procedural media like video games, images are frequently constructed, selected, or sequenced in code, making the stock tools of visual rhetoric inadequate. Image is subordinate to process.

Other efforts to unite computers and rhetoric do not make appeals even to visual rhetoric, instead remaining firmly planted in the traditional frame of verbal and written rhetoric. *Digital rhetoric* often abstracts the computer as a consideration, focusing on the text and image content a machine might host and the communities of practice in which that content is created and used. E-mail, Web sites, message boards, blogs, and wikis are examples of these targets. To be sure, all of these digital forms can function rhetorically, and they are worthy of study. James P. Zappen begins his integrated theory of digital rhetoric on this very note: "Studies of digital rhetoric," he writes, "help to explain how traditional rhetorical strategies of persuasion function and are being reconfigured in digital spaces."[22] But for scholars of digital rhetoric, to "function in digital spaces" often means mistaking subordinate properties of the computer for primary ones. Other digital rhetoricians likewise focus on the use of digital computers to carry out culturally modified versions of existing oral and written discourse; letters become e-mails, conversations become instant message sessions.

Procedural Rhetoric

I suggest the name *procedural rhetoric* for the practice of using processes persuasively, just as verbal rhetoric is the practice of using oratory persuasively and visual rhetoric is the practice of using images persuasively.[23] Procedural rhetoric is a general name for the practice of authoring arguments through processes. Following the classical model, procedural rhetoric entails persuasion—to change opinion or action. Following the contemporary model, procedural rhetoric entails expression—to convey ideas effectively. Procedural rhetoric is a subdomain of procedural authorship; its arguments are made not through the construction of words or images, but through the authorship of rules of behavior, the construction of dynamic models. In computation, those rules are authored in code, through the practice of programming.

My rationale for suggesting a new rhetorical domain is very similar to the one that motivates visual rhetoricians. Just as photography, motion graphics, moving images, and illustrations have become pervasive in contemporary society, so have computer hardware, software, and video games. Just as visual rhetoricians argue that verbal and written rhetorics inadequately account for the unique properties of the visual expression, so I argue that verbal, written, and visual rhetorics inadequately account for the unique properties of procedural expression. A theory of procedural rhetoric is needed to make commensurate judgments about the software systems we encounter everyday and to allow a more sophisticated procedural authorship with both persuasion and expression as its goal. As a high process intensity medium, video games can benefit significantly from a study of procedural rhetoric.

Procedural rhetoric affords a new and promising way to make claims about *how things work*. As I argued earlier, video games do not simply distract or entertain with empty, meaningless content. Rather, video games can make claims about the world. But when they do so, they do it not with oral speech, nor in writing, nor even with images. Rather, video games make argument with *processes*. Procedural rhetoric is the practice of effective persuasion and expression using processes. Since assembling rules together to describe the function of systems produces procedural representation, assembling particular rules that suggest a particular function of a particular system characterizes procedural rhetoric.

Another way to understand procedural representation is in terms of *models*. When we build models, we normally attempt to describe the function of some material system accurately—for example, in this volume James Paul Gee offers a number of ways one might create a model of a plane, from child's toy to engineer's wind tunnel stress test.[24] Models of all kinds can be thought of as examples of procedural rhetoric; they are devices that attempt to persuade their creators or users that a machine works in a certain way. Video games too can adopt this type of goal; for example, a flight simulator program attempts to model how

Figure 2
Molleindustria's *McDonald's Videogame* makes a procedural argument about the business ethics of fast food. Here, the player manages corporate communications.

the mechanical and professional rules of aviation work. But since procedurality is a symbolic medium rather than a material one, procedural rhetorics can also make arguments about conceptual systems, like the model of consumer capitalism in *Animal Crossing*. Gee argues that modeling allows "specific aspects of experience to be interrogated and used for problem solving in ways that lead from concreteness to abstraction."[25] Games like *Animal Crossing* demonstrate that such models include, but extend far beyond physical and formal models to include, arguments about how social, cultural, and political processes work as well.

Artifacts that deploy procedural rhetoric can also make arguments about how things *don't* work just as easily as they can make arguments about how they do. Consider a particularly sophisticated example, *The McDonald's Videogame*. The game is a critique of McDonalds's business practices by Italian art collective Molleindustria, an example of a genre I call anti-advergames, games created to censure or disparage a company rather than support it. The player controls four separate aspects of the McDonald's production environment, each of which he has to manage simultaneously: the third-world pasture where cattle are raised as cheaply as possible; the slaughterhouse where cattle are fattened for slaughter; the restaurant where burgers are sold; and the corporate offices where lobbying, PR, and marketing are managed (see figure 2). In each sector, the player must make difficult business choices, but more importantly he must make difficult moral choices. In the pasture, the player must create enough cattle grazing land and soy crops to produce the meat required to run the business. But only a limited number of fields are available; to acquire more land, the player must bribe the local governor for rights to convert his people's crops into corporate ones (see figure 3). More extreme tactics are also available: the player can bulldoze rain forest or

Figure 3
The player of the *McDonald's Videogame* makes ethical and material choices about third-world farming and governance.

dismantle indigenous settlements to clear space for grazing. These tactics correspond with the questionable business practices the developers want to critique.

To enforce the corrupt nature of these tactics, public interest groups can censure or sue the player for violations. For example, bulldozing indigenous rainforest settlements yields complaints from antiglobalization groups. Overusing fields reduces their effectiveness as soil or pasture; too much use without crop cycling creates dead earth, which angers environmentalists. However, those groups can be managed through PR and lobbying in the corporate sector. Corrupting a climatologist may dig into profits, but it ensures fewer complaints in the future. Regular corruption of this kind is required to maintain allegiance. Likewise, in the slaughterhouse players can use growth hormones to fatten cows faster, and they can choose whether to kill diseased cows or let them go through the slaughter process. Removing cattle from the production process reduces material product, thereby reducing supply and thereby again reducing profit. Growth hormones offend health critics, but they also allow the rapid production necessary to meet demand in the restaurant sector. Feeding cattle animal by-products cheapens the fattening process, but is more likely to cause disease. Allowing diseased meat to be made into burgers may spawn complaints and fines from health officers, but those groups too can be bribed through lobbying. The restaurant sector demands similar trade-offs, including balancing a need to fire incorrigible employees with local politician's complaints about labor practices.

The McDonald's Videogame mounts a procedural rhetoric about the necessity of corruption in the global fast food business, and the overwhelming temptation of greed, which leads to more corruption. In order to succeed in the long-term, the player must use growth hormones, he must coerce banana republics, and he must mount PR and lobbying campaigns.

Furthermore, the temptation to destroy indigenous villages, launch bribery campaigns, recycle animal parts, and cover-up health risks is tremendous, although the financial benefit from doing so is only marginal. As Patrick Dugan explains, the game imposes "constraints simulating necessary evils on one hand, and on the other hand . . . business practices that are self-defeating and, really just stupid."[26] Players learn to "read" this argument in the system of play and can interpret the relevance of the argument in the context of their own lives.

Ways of Using Procedural Rhetoric: Interrogating Ideology

I have argued for procedural rhetoric as a representational form, and as the specific communication practice at work in games like *Animal Crossing* and *The McDonald's Videogame.* But to use games for learning purposes requires general approaches that might be applied to many games and many subjects. As such, it is worth sketching a few of the different ways video games can be used rhetorically, whether for design, critique, or learning.

One use of procedural rhetoric is to expose and explain the hidden ways of thinking that often drive social, political, or cultural behavior. We often call such logics *ideology,* a term with a long and conflicted intellectual history. In Plato's famous parable of the cave in the *Republic,* humans' understanding of the world is likened to prisoners watching shadows cast on the wall of a cave by objects and agents passing above. The prisoners see only a flawed shadow of the ideal form (ειδος) of the object.[27] For Plato, the disparity between the ideal and material realms can only be reconciled through a recollection of the forms, a claim that assumes that our souls were once connected to these forms and, therefore, are also immortal. The term *ideology* itself can be traced to eighteenth-century French revolutionary Antoine Destutt de Tracy, who conceived of it as a science of the origin of ideas, that is, of how humans access the ideal realm from the material.[28] As Raymond Boudon clarifies, it was Napoleon's response to de Tracy that gave ideology its more familiar meaning:

> When Destutt de Tracy and Volney tried to thwart Napoleon's imperial ambitions, he scornfully called them *ideologues,* meaning people who wanted to substitute abstract considerations for *real* politics, as it was later called. From that time on, ideology signified those abstract (and rather dubious) theories allegedly based on reason or science, which tried to map out the social order and guide political action.[29]

Karl Marx understood the concept this way, and gave it perhaps its most famous characterization, "they aren't aware of it, but they do it [*Sie wissen das nicht, aber sie tun es*]."[30] Ideology thus lost the sense of a weapon against entrenched ideas and gained a decidedly negative connotation, as the very entrenchment of those ideas.

Like all cultural artifacts, no video game is produced in a cultural vacuum. All bear the biases of their creators. Video games can help shed light on these ideological biases. Sometimes these biases are inadvertent and deeply hidden. Other times, the artifacts themselves hope to expose their creators' biases as positive ones, but which of course can then be read in support or opposition.

In 2002, the U.S. Army released an unprecedented government-funded first-person shooter (FPS) game. *America's Army: Operations*[31] was conceived and openly publicized as an Army recruiting and communications tool, one crafted "to recreate the US Army for the benefit of young civilians."[32] The game represented a major step for the military-entertainment complex; it was created on the then-current Unreal 2 engine, a costly professional-grade game engine, and released for free on the Army's Web site (see figure 4). Within the first six months, over a million users had registered, of which over 600,000 had completed the

Figure 4
America's Army, a high production value simulation of life in the U.S. Army, meant for recruiting and public relations.

game's basic rifle marksmanship and combat training (BCT), a necessary step before gaining access to combat missions.[33]

While *America's Army* shares a genre with other popular multiplayer FPS games, the Army's desire to offer "a realistic look at army personal and career opportunities via sophisticated role-playing" altered or eliminated many of the conventions of movement in both conventional and tactical first-person shooters.[34] But the game's political simulation is more interesting than its mechanical and physical simulation. *America's Army* enforces strict Army Rules of Engagement (ROE), preventing the brouhaha of typical squad-based fighting games. Whereas *Counter-Strike* encourages the player to log as many kills as possible, *America's Army* players collaborate in short missions, such as rescuing a prisoner of war, capturing an enemy building, or assaulting an enemy installation. The ROE guides play with an iron fist. Writing about the game, designers Michael Zyda et al. explain:

> All players abide by rules of warfare. If a player violates the Uniform Code of Military Justice, rules of engagement, or laws of land warfare, reprisal is instant. He will find himself in a cell at Fort Leavenworth, accompanied by a mournful harmonica playing the blues. Continued violation of the rules may cause a player to be eliminated from the game. To rejoin, he must create a new ID and restart.[35]

Many players discover this constraint in basic training; turning a weapon on one's drill sergeant immediately lands the player in the brig. The direct mapping of in-game behavior to the very ability to continue playing serves as a convincing procedural rhetoric for the chain of command, the principle structure new recruits must understand immediately. Even the use of foul language is grounds for in-game discipline.

But the game also ties ROE and chain of command directly to the moral imperative of the U.S. Army. As in many similar games, when players successfully complete levels, they earn points that persist on Web-based global statistics boards. At specified point targets, a player character's Honor statistic increases. Since Honor telegraphs commitment and expertise, disincentives to violate the ROE and chain of command become especially strong; losing a character through violation would require considerable effort to rebuild.

The correlation of honor with the performance of arbitrary and politically decontextualized missions offers particular insight into the social reality of the U.S. Army. While the use of arbitrary honor points may seem contrived at first, the system bears much in common with the practice of military decoration. Ribbons, medals, and other designations reward successful completion of military objectives. Training, professional development, wounds, completion of missions, and many other events earn soldiers decorations, which when worn on a dress uniform speak to the honor and nobility of the bearer. The average citizen's lack of familiarity with the specific actions that warrant a ribbon or medal ensure that these designations signify the soldier's abstract worth rather than his individual achievements. *America's Army*'s Honor mechanic successfully proceduralizes this value system. As Zyda et al. summarize, "The game insists on the mission orientation of the US Army. Above all, soldiers must be team players, following army values and rules."[36]

This approach is similar to, but different from, the idea of epistemic games advanced by David Williamson Shaffer.[37] Shaffer argues that games can model how professions work, offering an incomplete, yet embodied experience of real-world jobs. As Gee explains in this volume, these types of games "already give us a good indication that even young learners, through video games embedded inside a well-organized curriculum, can be inducted into professional practices as a form of value-laden deep learning that transfers to school-based skills and conceptual understandings."[38] On first blush, *America's Army* would appear to be a superb example of epistemic games: the game models the values and practices of the army, giving the player an embodied experience of the recruit. However, *America's Army* also shows that epistemic games bear a risk: sometimes, we may want to question the values of professional practices rather than assume those values blindly. Procedural rhetoric offers an approach to do so.

Ways of Using Procedural Rhetoric: Making and Unpacking an Argument

Video games that expose ideology may or may not do so intentionally. But video games can also be created to make explicit claims about the way a material or conceptual system works. *The McDonald's Videogame* is an example of such a one, albeit a satire and a political commentary meant to critique the processes employed in the fast food business. Other games strive to explain and support a particular method for accomplishing a political or social goal; these games use procedural rhetoric to make an argument, and players unpack that argument through play.

In the early fall 2004, the Illinois House Republicans commissioned a game I designed to represent their positions on several public policy issues at the center of their 2004 state legislative election. These issues—medical malpractice tort reform, education standards policy,

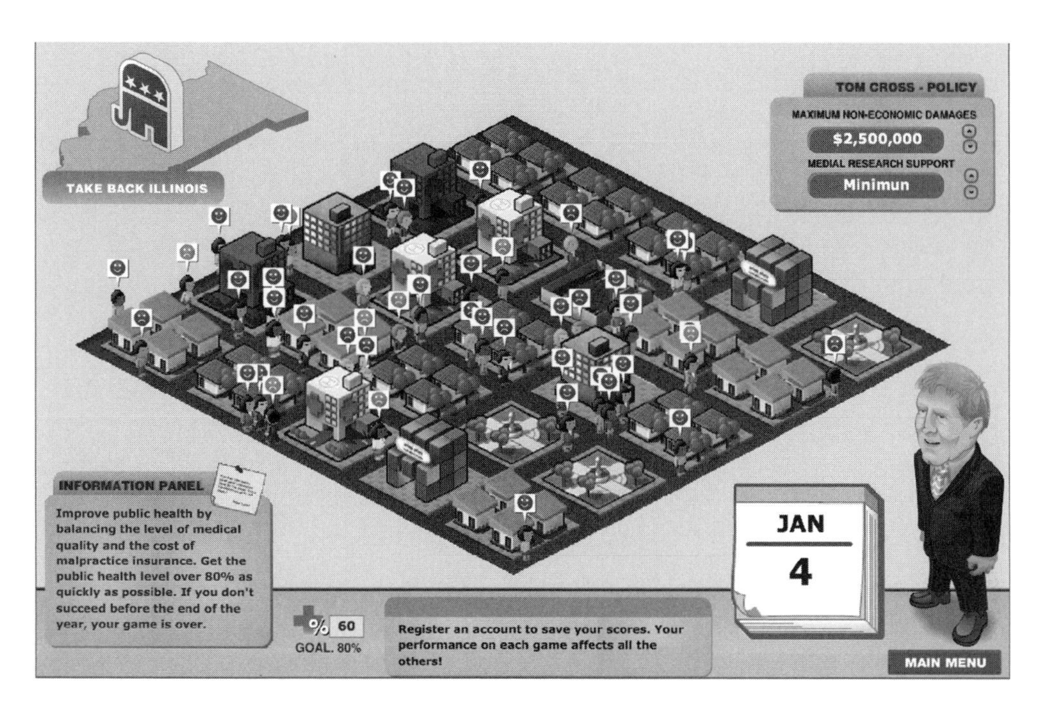

Figure 5
A public policy game in *Take Back Illinois*, this one about tort reform.

and local economic development—are abstract and dry at best. As such, citizens were even less likely to engage with them in the public or private forum, which provided only soapbox sound bites or lengthy, unreadable policy documentation. Moreover these topics, like most public policy issues, are tightly interwoven. Educational quality affects job qualification, which in turn affects economic welfare. *Take Back Illinois* attempts to create a complex, interrelated procedural rhetoric that communicated the candidates' positions on these topics.[39]

Four subgames comprise the game, three for each of the policy issues and one game about citizen participation. These subgames interrelate; play in one affects performance in the others. Each subgame provides a goal for the player to reach. For example, in the medical malpractice reform subgame, the player must raise the public health level to a predefined target. The subgame goal and the player's progress toward it are displayed directly under the game field. A small calendar serves as a timer for the game, starting at January 1, and counts up one day for every few seconds of game time. To win, the player must reach the goal before the calendar reaches the end of the year. Faster success yields a lower, and therefore better, score (see figure 5).

The procedural rhetoric for each policy issue was designed to compress as much detail into the smallest possible rule-set. For example, in the medical malpractice reform subgame, a representation of a city was filled with citizens of varying health—healthy, ill, gravely ill. Unwell citizens were contagious, and healthy citizens nearby them would eventually become ill themselves. If left untreated, gravely ill citizens would die. The city contained several medical offices, and the player could send sick citizens to those offices for treatment. However, Illinois suffered higher medical malpractice insurance rates than its neighboring states. The

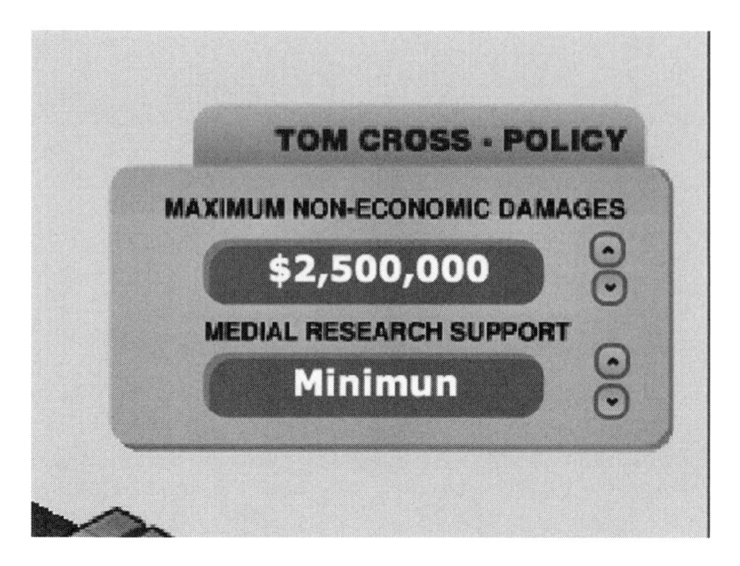

Figure 6
Levers allow the player to make simple policy.

candidates' positions on tort reform were partially motivated by the potential reduction in insurance rates such changes would encourage. The game provides a "policy panel" that allows the player to change simple public policy settings for the game environment (see figure 6). In this case, the player could alter maximum noneconomic damages awarded in medical malpractice lawsuits as well as investment in medical research to prevent repeat tragedies. In the medical malpractice subgame, maintaining a high threshold on noneconomic damages keeps insurance rates high, which is likely to cause doctors to leave the state. Once this happens, the medical office dims and the player can no longer treat citizens there.

The other policy subgames created similar procedural rhetorics for each of the issues. In the education reform subgame, players simultaneously manage a handful of school districts across the state. Some districts start out with different educational standards in place, while other districts enjoy disproportionate funding and teacher-to-student ratios. To play the game, the player has to "teach" in each district by keying in a Simon-like memory sequence that corresponds with the educational standard in each district (see figure 7). This procedural rhetoric embodies the candidate's policy position: maintaining multiple standards across the state made the educational system on the whole difficult to manage. Players would quickly understand this position upon being forced to remember four or five different memory sequences for all the schools. To play more efficiently, the player could reassign standards on a district-by-district basis by changing policy. The player could also reassign funding to needy schools in order to raise their educational output.

In public forums, policy issues are often discussed independently, even though most are bound to one another in significant ways. To communicate the rhetoric of interrelations, *Take Back Illinois* maintained a set of scores for each subgame and used those scores as inputs for settings in other games. For example, higher performance in the educational reform subgame increased the efficiency of job training centers in the economic development game. The parameterized interaction between simulation models serves as a rudimentary

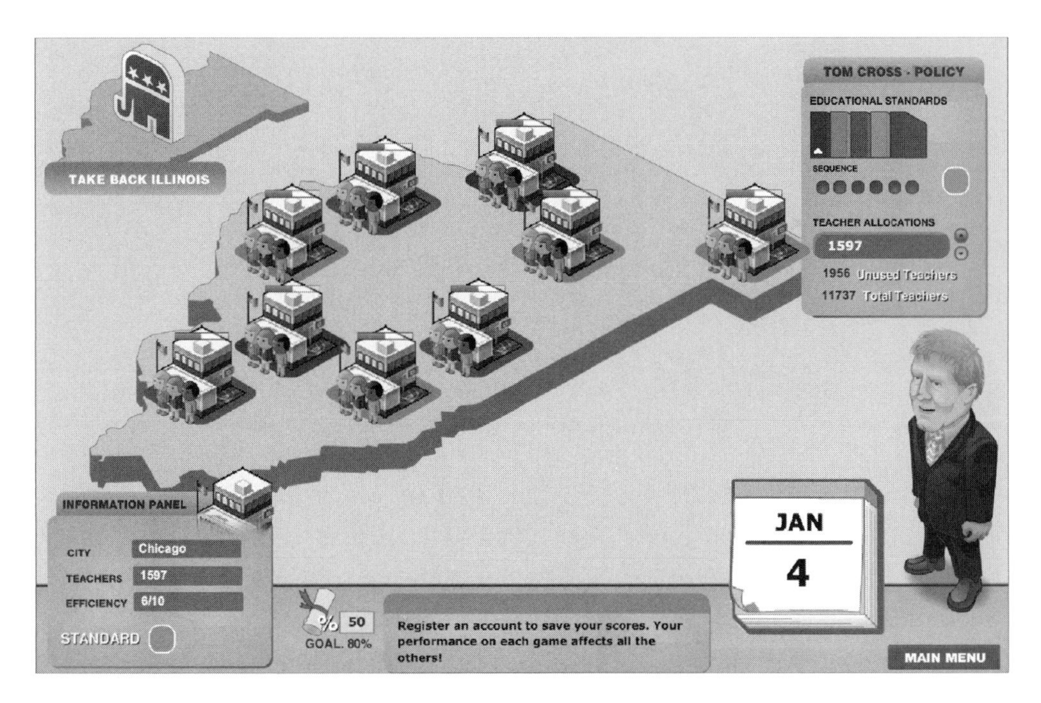

Figure 7
A *Simon*-like matching game operationalizes a public policy position on educational reform.

procedural rhetoric for the interrelationship of these issues in particular, and other issues by extension.

To play the game successfully, the player is forced to acknowledge the campaign's position on the issues it represents—for example, it is impossible to win the medical malpractice reform subgame without reducing maximum noneconomic damages for malpractice lawsuits (although reducing them beyond reason decreases the likelihood of faults). The game's procedural rhetoric is a compressed version of the campaign's policy position. In playing the game, the player is not "brainwashed" or otherwise fooled into adopting the candidates' policy position. Rather he is afforded an understanding of that position for further inquiry, agreement, or disapproval. However, none of the subgames argue that policy change alone is sufficient to create social change. In each of the games, the player must perform nontrivial actions to accomplish goals like improved health care and education. These actions trace the interconnectedness of political conditions.

Take Back Illinois and *The McDonald's Game* are specialty titles, created for specific purposes in which their persuasion outweighs entertainment. But procedural rhetoric is not limited to the narrow domain of educational or political games; the same properties can be found in commercial titles as well.

Consider *Bully*, from Rockstar Games, the creators of the *Grand Theft Auto* series.[40] In *Bully*, the player takes the role of Jimmy Hopkins, an adolescent just dropped off at Bullworth Academy by his disinterested mother and stepfather, who are on the way to their lavish honeymoon. The school is riddled with bullies and troublemakers, and Jimmy struggles to get by amidst the conflicted social situation of high school politics. The game has been reviled for supposedly glorifying bullying, but the experience it creates is anything but celebratory.

Figure 8
Although many critics though *Bully* was a celebration of schoolyard harassment, it is a model of the social politics of high school more than a hazing sim.

Even if the player struggles to steer Jimmy away from trouble, it catches up to him thanks to the petty malevolence of his peers. Students mill in the quad and buildings, either verbally and physically abusing each other or receding from verbal and physical attacks. Staying out of the way of the bullies (bullies in the game conveniently have their own clique, and all wear the same clothes) allows a player to avoid tussles. If a player stands in front of the wrong locker, he or she should expect to get shoved out of the way (see figure 8). *Bully* models the social environment of high school through an expressive system of rules, and makes a procedural argument for the necessity of confrontation. Confronting bullies is not a desirable or noble action in the game, but it is necessary if one wants to restore justice. The game privileges the underdogs—nerds and girls—and the player spends most of his time undermining the bullies and the jocks in order to even the social pecking order.

Bully is part social commentary, part satire. But it also bears the usual features of an entertainment title. While games like *The McDonald's Game* are more didactic, games like *Bully* are more subtly expressive. Neither technique is inherently more or less valid than the other, but each accomplishes a different kind of video-game-based speech, each of which might be more or less appropriate in different circumstances.

Rockstar does not generally discuss or acknowledge the procedural rhetorics they build into games like *Bully*. But other designers make more deliberate efforts to frame the ideas they put forward in their games. Consider the Will Wright/Maxis game *Spore*.[41] In *Spore*, the player starts with a microorganism and grows it into a complex sentient creature, then

Figure 9
Spore advances a perspective on the development of planetary life by simulating a theory from astrobiology.

a civilization, then a military power, and finally a space-traveling superrace. The game is a rich and complex one that clearly addresses a number of topics, most notably the tension between evolution and natural selection (creatures evolve, but the player carefully designs their attributes). But in a discussion of the game at the annual Game Developers Conference, Wright explained that the real topic he hoped to address in the game was astrobiology, the study of life throughout the cosmos.[42] Often when we wonder if there is intelligent alien life in the universe, we assume that life arises naturally and evolves slowly. Thus the chance of finding intelligent life seems remarkably small; to do so would require the greatest of coincidences in a place as large as the (ever expanding) universe. In the theory Wright hopes to advance in his video game, intelligent life does not occur and grow naturally, but is cultured and transported from planet to planet by other, more advanced civilizations. The perspective on astrobiology Wright advocates borrows the concept of seed spread by wind or other environmental factors; these reproductive structures are called *spores*. *Spore* adopts the logic of this particular view on astrobiology, subtly arguing through its game play that the spread of life in the universe is most likely caused by sentient beings transporting other creatures from star to star (see figure 9). While a book might make this argument by explaining the process, in *Spore* the player discovers the argument by playing in the possibility space the game's rules create. This act of discovering a procedural argument through play is endemic to procedural rhetoric.

Learning From Procedural Rhetoric

Video games are models of real and imagined systems. We always *play* when we use video games, but the sort of play that we perform is not always the stuff of leisure. Rather, when we play, we explore the possibility space of a set of rules—we learn to understand and evaluate a game's meaning. Video games make arguments about how social or cultural systems work in the world—or how they could work, or don't work. Video games like *Spore* and *Take Back Illinois* make arguments about abstract, conceptual systems the way mechanical models make them about material ones. When we play video games, we can interpret these arguments and consider their place in our lives.

In this way, playing video games is a kind of literacy. Not the literacy that helps us read books or write term papers, but the kind of literacy that helps us make or critique the systems we live in. By "system," I don't just mean large-scale, impersonal things like political systems. Any social or cultural practice can be understood as a set of processes, and our understanding of each of them can be taught, supported, or challenged through video games. *Animal Crossing* presents a model of consumer capitalism that players might embrace, reinforcing their interest in property in the material world. Or, through their experience of the game, players might question the goals they set for themselves, particularly the often endless feedback loop between the desire for material goods and the work needed to support it. When we learn to play games with an eye toward uncovering their procedural rhetorics, we learn to ask questions about the models such games present.

The kind of technology literacy that procedural rhetoric offers is becoming increasingly necessary for kids and adults alike. As more of our cultural attention moves from linear media like books and film to procedural, random-access media like software and video games, we need to become better critics of the latter kind. This process starts at home where parents can help their kids play games critically, just as they might help their kids understand novels or films by virtue of their own familiarity with those media. Of course, such a future requires parents who are themselves literate in the medium of video games. Parents of all kinds can learn to play video games, but those who grew up with video games themselves are already raising the next generation of children—a six-year-old who played the Atari VCS in 1978 was thirty-five years old in 2007. These parents must play games with their kids just as a previous generation watched westerns or read comic books with them. And before they do so, they must begin playing games critically themselves, perhaps unlearning decades of treating video games as mere distraction.

Educators also have a role to play. When video games are used in schools, we often think that they should be used pedagogically. That is, if video games have any purpose in schools, it is for supplementing or replacing lesson plans for concrete, factual learning, such as principles of chemistry. But once we understand video games as procedural representations that make arguments about systems in the world, they resemble creative artifacts as much as—and perhaps more so—than they do pedagogical tools. Educators should consider adopting video games as artifacts to be discussed alongside traditional media in subjects like literature, language arts, history, and art, teaching game playing as an argumentative and expressive practice alongside reading, writing, and debating.

Finally, procedural rhetoric has a role to play in the way we teach programming and video game development. As interest in games as a cultural activity increases, and as the importance of computing itself has increased, some educators have hoped to teach game development as an entry point into computer science.[43] Video games are appealing, kids want to play them, and they also want to make them. By luring kids into computer science through video game development, we can attempt to increase dwindling interest in math, science, and technology.

This is not a bad approach to programming education. But unfortunately, such approaches risk assuming that creating any kind of video game offers the same pedagogical value. Programming education must take care to ensure that it supports sophisticated responses to the medium, rather than reinforcing the idea that play is equivalent to leisure, and that video games are intended to produce fun and distraction rather than critical response. In addition to using video games to teach kids how to write computer programs (procedural literacy), we can use them to teach kids how to write computer arguments (procedural rhetoric). When kids program, just as when they write, they can learn to make their own claims about the world in the form of processes. Such a practice reframes video game development as a rhetorical practice, not just a craft practice or a technical practice. By actively teaching kids to mount arguments in procedural form—even simple ones like models of their everyday life—video games can become a carrot medium for both programming and expression. Work in teaching kids to program games has already begun (examples include MIT's Scratch,[44] the MacArthur-funded University of Wisconsin/Gamelab Game Designer project,[45] the London Knowledge Lab's Making Games Project,[46] Carnegie Mellon University's Alice,[47] among others). Efforts like these can be used as the basis for a combined program in procedural literacy and rhetoric.

Video games are not mere trifles, artifacts created only to distract or to amuse. But they are also not *automatically* rich, sophisticated statements about the world around us. Video games have the power to make arguments, to persuade, to express ideas. But they do not do so inevitably. As we evolve our relationship with video games, one of the most important steps we can take is to learn to play them critically, to suss out the meaning they carry, both on and under the surface. To do this requires a fluency in procedurality, the core representational form of computing. But programming or using computers is not the sole answer to such a charge. Rather, we need to play video games in order to understand the possibility spaces their rules create, and then to explore those possibility spaces and accept, challenge, or reject them in our daily lives.

Notes

1. Nintendo, *Animal Crossing* (Kyoto, Japan: Nintendo, 2002); and idem., *Animal Crossing: Wild World* (Kyoto, Japan: Nintendo, 2005).

2. Just to give the reader a sense of the magnitude of work that faces players of *Animal Crossing*, the final renovation mortgage is over 700,000 "bells" (the currency unit in the game). The most lucrative fish and insects one can catch in the game sell for 10,000 bells, but they are quite rare. More typical items sell for 300–1,000 bells.

3. John de Graaff, David Wann, and Thomas H. Naylor, *Affluenza: The All-Consuming Epidemic* (San Francisco: Berrett Koehler, 2005).

4. Jean Lave and Etienne Wenger, *Situated Learning: Legitimate Peripheral Participation* (Cambridge, UK: Cambridge University Press, 1991).

5. See http://www.animalcrossingcommunity.com/. Accessed June 1, 2006.

6. See http://www.animalcrossingcommunity.com/getting_started.asp. Accessed June 1, 2006.

7. Katie Salen and Eric Zimmerman, *Rules of Play: Game Design Fundamentals* (Cambridge, MA: The MIT Press, 2004).

8. In Japanese, the divisions are not precisely commensurate with English syllables, although this is usually the way we adapt haiku for Western languages.

9. Georges Perec, Le Grand Palindrome, in *La clôture et autres poèmes* (Paris: Hachette/Collection POL, 1980).

10. Idem., *La disparition*, trans. Georges Perec (Paris: Gallimard, 1990); and idem., *La disparition*, trans. Gilbert Adair (Boston: Verba Mundi, 2005).

11. Janet Murray, *Hamlet on the Holodeck* (New York: Free Press, 1997), 71.

12. Ibid.

13. Ibid., 72.

14. Chris Crawford, Process Intensity, *The Journal of Computer Game Development* 1, no. 5 (1987). http://www.erasmatazz.com/library/JCGD_Volume_1/Process_Intensity.html.

15. iD Software, *Doom* (Mesquite, TX: iD Software, 1993).

16. Maxis, *Sim City* (Alameda, CA: Brøderbund, 1989).

17. Plato, *Plato: Complete Works* (New York: Hackett, 1997), 453a.

18. Aristotle, *The Rhetoric and Poetics of Aristotle* (New York: McGraw Hill, 1984), 24, see I.2, 1355b26.

19. George A. Kennedy, *Classical Rhetoric and Its Christian and Secular Tradition* (Chapel Hill, NC: University of North Carolina Press, 1999), 3.

20. Kenneth Burke, *A Rhetoric of Motives* (Berkeley and Los Angeles, CA: University of California Press, 1969), 19.

21. Sonja K. Foss, Karen A. Foss, and Robert Trapp, *Contemporary Perspectives on Rhetoric* (Prospect Heights, IL: Waveland Press, 1985), 214.

22. James P. Zappen, Digital Rhetoric: Toward an Integrated Theory, *Technical Communication Quarterly* 14, no. 3 (2005): 319.

23. A much more detailed version of this argument, with additional examples from the domains of politics, advertising, and education, can be found in my book on the subject, Ian Bogost, *Persuasive Games* (Cambridge, MA: The MIT Press, 2007).

24. James Paul Gee, Learning and Games, in *The Ecology of Games: Connecting Youth, Games, and Learning*, ed. Katie Salen (Cambridge, MA: The MIT Press, 2007), 21–40.

25. Ibid.

26. Patrick Dugan, Hot Off the Grill: La Molleindustria's Paolo Pedercini on the McDonald's Video Game, *Gamasutra* February 27, 2006. http://www.gamasutra.com/features/20060227/dugan_pfv.htm.

27. Plato, 515a–16a.

28. Raymond Boudon, *The Analysis of Ideology* (Chicago: University of Chicago Press, 1989), 25.

29. Ibid.

30. Karl Marx, *Capital: Vol. 1, A Critique of Political Economy*, trans. Ben Fowkes (New York: Penguin, 1992), 166–67. The translation here has been modified.

31. Modeling, Simulation, and Virtual Environments Institute (MOVES), *America's Army: Operations* (Washington, DC: U.S. Army, 2002).

32. Michael Zyda, John Hiles, Alex Mayberry, Casey Wardynski, Michael V. Capps, Brian Osborn, Russell Shilling, Martin Robaszewski, and Margaret J. Davis, Entertainment R&D for Defense, *IEEE Computer Graphics and Applications* 23, no. 1 (2003): 28–36.

33. Ibid., 34.

34. Ibid., 28.

35. Ibid., 30.

36. Ibid.

37. David Williamson Shaffer, Epistemic Games, *Innovate* 1, no. 6 (2005); and idem., *How Computer Games Help Children Learn* (New York: Palgrave/MacMillan, 2007).

38. Gee, Learning and Games.

39. Persuasive Games, *Take Back Illinois* (Atlanta, GA: Persuasive Games/Illinois House Republicans, 2004).

40. Rockstar Games, *Grand Theft Auto III* (New York: Take Two Interactive, 2001); idem., *Grand Theft Auto: Vice City* (New York: Take Two Interactive, 2003); idem., *Grand Theft Auto: San Andreas* (New York: Take Two Interactive, 2004); and Rockstar Vancouver, *Bully* (New York: Take Two, 2006).

41. Maxis, *Spore* (Redwood Shores, CA: Electronic Arts, Forthcoming). As of this writing, *Spore* is expected to be released in 2009.

42. Will Wright, What's Next in Content? Paper presented at the Game Developers Conference, San Jose, CA, 2006.

43. For examples, cf. Brenda Cantwell Wilson and Sharon Shrock, Contributing to Success in an Introductory Computer Science Course: A Study of Twelve Factors, *ACM SIGCSE Bulletin* 33, no. 1 (2001): 184–88; and Randolph M. Jones, Design and Implementation of Computer Games: A Capstone Course for Undergraduate Computer Science Education, *ACM SIGCSE Bulletin* 32, no. 1 (2000): 260–64.

44. See http://scratch.mit.edu/. Accessed March 1, 2007.

45. As of this writing, the Game Designer project is still in the early stages of development. An overview of the project can be found at http://website.education.wisc.edu/gls/research_gamedesigner.htm. Accessed March 1, 2007.

46. See http://www.lkl.ac.uk/research/pelletier.html. Accessed March 1, 2007.

47. See http://www.alice.org/. Accessed March 1, 2007.

The Power of Play: The Portrayal and Performance of Race in Video Games

Anna Everett

University of California, Santa Barbara, Department of Film Studies

S. Craig Watkins

The University of Texas at Austin, Department of Radio-Television-Film

Introduction: Young People, Games, and Learning

The growing presence of games in the lives of young people creates perils and possibilities. Games have been a constant source of criticism and alarm among parents, researchers, child advocacy groups, and elected officials. The potential harmful effects of gaming have been linked to society's understandable concerns about the increasingly sedentary lifestyles of youth and childhood obesity, addiction, gender socialization, poor academic performance, and aggressive behavior.[1] An area of growing concern is the role of games in the learning experiences and environments of youth.[2]

While there is growing consensus that learning takes place in games, the question we ask is: "What kinds of learning?" In this chapter we shift the focus on youth, learning, and video games generally to consider the extremely significant but often overlooked matter of race. Specifically, we address the following question: In what ways do young people's interactions with video games influence how and what they learn about race? We present a critical framework for thinking about how popular game titles and the professionals who design them reflect, influence, reproduce, and thereby teach dominant ideas about race in America. Engaging with an assortment of media—books, animation, television, home video, video games, and the Internet—children as young as three years old develop schemas and scripts for negotiating perceived racial differences.[3] Research suggests that by the time children are five years old they have already started to develop strong ideas about race and difference. Historically, the popular media examined in this context have been television.[4]

In their discussion of the role television plays in the multicultural awareness and racial attitudes of children and adolescents, Gordon L. Berry and Joy Keiko Asamen write that "fact or fiction, real or unreal, television programs create cognitive and affective environments that describe and portray people, places, and things that carry profound general and specific cross-cultural learning experiences" for young people growing up in a media-saturated culture.[5] As digital media forms like video games compete with television for the time and attention of young media users, researchers must examine rigorously how the shift to digital and more interactive forms of media influences how and what young people learn about race.

We, therefore, direct these questions and issues toward video games to increase our understanding of the rapidly evolving ways in which young people are exposed to and learn

---

The authors would like to thank Katie Salen for carefully reading earlier drafts of this chapter and offering both her academic expertise and generous thoughts that helped to refine the structure of the chapter and our argument.

racial narratives, representations, and belief systems. Parents and critics readily discuss the potential negative social outcomes associated with exposing young people to violent or sexual content in video games. But, as Anna Everett has asked elsewhere, "'When and where does the racial problematic enter in contemporary culture's moral panics about gaming's potential dangers?' Society's moral outrage over video game culture's gender troubles (to borrow Judith Butler's fecund phrase), especially its sexist and misogynistic constructs of women and girls, has not found a parallel in terms of race." This leads us to ask, "What are the consequences of exposing youth to content that renders racist representations, beliefs, and attitudes playable and pleasurable?"[6]

The chapter sets out to demarcate some of the specific ways in which race resonates throughout the culture and industry of video games. We begin by examining the design of one of the most heavily marketed categories in the video games marketplace, what we call "urban/street" games. Specifically, we consider how these games, and the richly detailed and textured urban landscapes they present, establish powerful learning environments that help situate how young gamers understand, perform, and reproduce race and ethnicity. Next, we focus on the aesthetic and narrative properties of one of the most controversial yet successful video games franchises in America, *Grand Theft Auto* (*GTA*). More precisely, we consider how *GTA* teaches dominant attitudes and assumptions about race and racial otherness through what we term "racialized pedagogical zones" (RPZs). In other words, these games draw heavily from racist discourses already circulating in popular and mainstream culture and arguably intensify these messages and lessons of racial difference through the power and allure of interactive gameplay. Essentially, we argue that by striving to locate players in what are often promoted as graphically real and culturally "authentic" environments, urban/street games produce some of the most powerful, persistent, and problematic lessons about race in American culture.

In the final section of the chapter, we shift from discussing race as representation, simulation, and pedagogy to considering race as an important dimension in the ongoing but steadily evolving public conversation regarding the digital divide. Here, we advocate expanding the discussion of race and video games to include concerns about access to and participation in digital media culture, communities, and user-generated content.

Learning Race

Recent theories on digital games and learning argue that games represent a dynamic learning environment.[7] Marc Prensky has argued that games encourage learning and challenge the established conventions in more formal spaces of learning, such as in schools. He notes, for instance, that games demand parallel versus linear processing. Additionally, Prensky maintains that games promote problem solving in the form of play versus work.

Similarly, James Paul Gee believes that games offer good learning principles. For Gee the genius of games is their ability to balance the delivery of overt information and guidance (think of the manual that offers instructions for a game) with "immersion in actual context of practice" (think of the process of trial and error that is involved in mastering a game). Games, unlike conventional schooling, effectively combine "telling and doing." Good video games, Gee notes, require gamers to "learn from the bottom up" and master the technical and logical aspects of games.[8] This, he argues, is accomplished via experimentation, exploration, and engagement. What games ultimately accomplish, according to both Prensky and Gee, is the creation of environments in which active (doing) rather than passive (telling) learning takes place. It is this aspect of video gaming—the act of doing—and its implication for both learning and performing race that we address here.

Still, while advocates of video games as learning spaces argue that they provide a new means to engage young people by producing rich educational experiences, we would like to caution that not all forms of learning that take place in the immersive world of video and computer games are socially productive. Thus, we ask a slightly different set of questions regarding video games as learning tools, namely, "Can video games facilitate learning that is anti-social?" Put another way, "Do the entertainment and interactive aspects of video gaming reproduce common-sense ideas about race and gender?" Ideas, that is, which can enliven long-standing and problematic notions of racial difference and deviance.

Portraying Race

At least some of the absence of discussions of race in public and policy dialogues about video games can be attributed to the fact that the use of racially marked characters, themes, and environments, historically speaking, is a relatively recent development in video games. That is not to say that video games, even during the earliest periods of development, were necessarily race neutral but rather that efforts to build explicitly raced characters and worlds were limited by the styles of games being produced, screen resolution (4-, 8-, and 16-bit), and processing speeds. Indeed, as Steven Poole maintains, the early attempt to design characters for video games was limited by technology.[9] "In the early days of video games," Poole writes, "technological considerations more or less forced designers into exactly the same style."[10] That style typically led to one-dimensional blocky characters such as *PacMan* that lacked few, if any, truly distinguishing features or marks.

The first, and most famous, humanoid character in a video game was the moustached hero, Mario. Poole notes that because of the low resolution offered at the time, character designers had a limited number of pixels to play with. That period, described by Japanese game designer Shigeru Miyamoto as the days of "immature technology," imposed certain technological constraints on both game design and representation.[11] But as the rendering power of video game engines evolved, artists and designers benefited from the ability to produce characters who were more lifelike in appearance and motion. Whereas the ethnically marked features of Mario, the Italian plumber, were limited primarily to relatively innocuous phrases like, "it's-a me, Mario" or, later, his love of pasta and pizza, games like *GTA: Vice City,* and *Godfather: The Game* benefit from enhanced technology and software that portrays the markers of race and ethnicity—skin color, gestures, voice, music, and setting—in a much more explicit and powerful manner.

Though technological changes have opened the way for upgraded representational depictions, and a more diverse range of themes and characters, the portrayal of race in video games remains remarkably narrow. In an examination of racial diversity in the top-selling console and computer games, an important study by the Children Now organization concluded that black and Latino characters were often restricted to athletic, violent, and victim roles, or rendered entirely invisible.[12] Since that report, the state of race in games has, paradoxically, changed and stayed the same due, in part, to the rise of "urban/street" games. The arrival of this generic category has led to a discernible growth in the number of black and Latino-based characters and themes in some of the most heavily marketed games. But urban/street games also reproduce many of the representational problems identified by Children Now.

Games within the urban/street category cut across a variety of genres: for example, third-person action/shooter games like hip-hop star *50 Cent's Bulletproof*, action/adventure titles like *Saints Row*, sports games like *NFL Street* 3 and *NBA Ballers: Phenom*, fighter games like *Def Jam: The Fight for NY*, and racing games like *Midnight Club 3: Dub Edition Remix*. Despite the range of genres represented, the games tend to share similar types of characters, narratives, environments, and gameplay elements. For instance, earning street credibility or respect is a recurrent theme across these games as is the emphasis on building and playing hyper-masculine characters who use street slang and aggressive behavior to navigate the urban world boldly and effectively. More importantly, they demonstrate the degree to which game developers are moving toward recreating culturally specific and racialized environments that are packaged and marketed as authentic expressions of the social world. Significantly, these games, and particularly their questionable claims of authenticity, establish compelling learning environments that help facilitate how young gamers develop their knowledge of and familiarity with popular views of race and urban culture.

Can You Feel It? Simulating Blackness

The successful development and marketing of urban/street games is based on the idea that these titles represent culturally authentic spaces. Claims of authenticity in the sphere of cultural production are, of course, always fraught with tensions. As we explain in great detail below, the aspects of urban/street gaming that are often presented as authentic—the characters, environments, music, and language, just to name a few—are, in reality, deliberately selected symbolic materials that draw much of their appeal and believability from representations of urban life in other popular media cultures.

Like the gaming landscape in general, the evolution of urban/street games is shaped by an increasing emphasis on photorealistic environmental designs, recognizable stories/plots, compelling character ensembles, and dramatic action sequences that work to achieve greater verisimilitude in overall gameplay design and presentation. Geoff King and Tanya Krzywinska maintain that "the history of video games is one that has been dominated, on one level, by investments in increasing realism, at the level of graphical representation and allied effects."[13]

But the commitment to designing games that are more realistic points to the need not only to capture more honest character portrayals, human motion, and environments, but also and perhaps more importantly, to capture the cultural sensibilities of a particular racial or ethnic group's world experience. This aspect of a video game's design is a constant selling point in the marketing positions staked out by some of the video game industry's most prominent players. For instance, in its promise to offer sports game enthusiasts a powerful and engaging gameplay experience, Electronic Arts' (EA) tagline asks, "Can You Feel It?" Likewise, Microsoft's Xbox 360 invites gamers to "jump in" to their online gaming world. And Sony PlayStation encourages gamers to "live in your world, play in ours." In games studies, the idea of creating a world that feels real is referred to as "presence" or a "sense of being there."[14] This represents the degree to which developers strive to create gaming environments that deepen the sense of engagement in the game world through simulation, leading to what some argue is a richer sensory experience.

Part of achieving a believable simulation includes maintaining fidelity to what we already know or expect from a specific world and those who are likely to people it. Consequently, the design of gaming environments that look, sound, and feel real is critical in order to achieve high degrees of "perceptual" and "social" realism. The former refers to how closely the characters, environments, objects, and other in-game elements match popular perceptions of urban street life and culture. The latter refers to the extent to which the events and activities in a video game resonate with those in the real world. The quest by the designers of urban/street games to immerse gamers in culturally specific or authentic spaces also offers insight into the ways in which these games become powerful learning environments that construct informal yet effective spaces for teaching, or in many instances, reproducing particular ideas about race, ethnicity, and difference. More significantly, if video games portraying urban life and culture are perceived as authentic, then they become effective and, in many cases, uncontested devices for transmitting certain kinds of ideas about race, geography, and culture. For example, Children Now asks game developers to "think about the messages they deliver to youth when characters of color often are found at the business end of a fist, club, or gun or competing in a sports arena."[15]

What makes urban/street games feel "authentic?" More precisely, what is it about these titles that enables gamers to experience presence, a sense of urban culture? First, many of the titles in this category feature a rarity in entertainment games: visually recognizable black lead characters. Children Now's analysis of the ten top-selling games for each of the six video game consoles available in the United States found that the characters populating the virtual world of video games at the time were predominantly white.[16] White males, for example, represented 52 percent of the male player-controlled characters compared to 37 percent for black males and 5 percent and 3 percent, respectively, for Latinos and Asians. According to the report, when black and Latino characters did appear in video games, it was often as supporting rather than lead characters and oftentimes in stereotypical roles (i.e., athletes, urban outlaws, violent offenders, etc.). Unlike the bulk of commercial video games, black and Latino characters appear throughout urban/street games both as primary and secondary characters, thus establishing the genre as a gaming space distinct in its representational focus.

In his discussion of *True Crime: Streets of LA*, Chan notes that while the game offers a first in a North American designed game—a Chinese antagonist—the game's digital cast of characters and setting reinscribe popular notions of racial otherness and exotica.[17] In addition to the representation of racially marked spaces like Chinatown, Chan notes that the game's Asian American central character and the use of neo-Orientalist motifs demonstrate "how racial difference may be simultaneously fetishized and demonized, and how hegemonic whiteness is positioned as the taken for granted racial norm in game-world environments."[18]

In addition to the hypervisibility of black and Latino characters, the environments in urban/street games are marked as racially specific story-worlds. Above, we suggested that the first humanoid character, Mario, did not bear many explicitly recognizable racial markers besides white skin. This also holds true for the game environment in the first game in which Mario appeared, *Donkey Kong*. Gameplay typically took place in brightly lit fun spaces, or an occasional dimly lit place that signified heightened danger. Rarely, however, did these game environments evoke racial and/or culturally specific spaces like an urban ghetto *Saint's Row* or an elite boarding school as in *Bully*. As designers strive for greater cultural authenticity, the spatial environment itself, where the characters live, play, fight, and compete, also becomes a culturally specific location that animates ideas about race, class, and gender.

The elaborately textured environments in urban/street games feature a wide range of objects associated with socially and economically marginalized communities. *NBA Street Volume 2*, for example, uses digitized photos from many urban playgrounds around the country, including Harlem's legendary Rucker Park and Oakland's Mosswood. In Mark Ecko's

Getting Up: Contents Under Pressure, several of the game's key action sequences take place in dark underground subways where graffiti artists once "tagged" their way to local fame. Other objects typically appearing in these video games include graffiti-covered buildings, dilapidated housing, trash-filled streets, candy-painted low riders (customized cars), and background characters engaged in petty crimes, drug deals, and prostitution. The selection of these objects works ideologically to invigorate dominant ideas that construct poor urban communities as deviant, different, and dangerous.

EA hired urban street artist Bua as a consultant and artist for *NFL Street*. His work, along with the work of other hand-selected street artists, was incorporated not only to give the game an "urban feel," but also to provide credibility among young gamers as an authentic engagement with urban culture. The environments in urban/street games are not only racially coded as black and brown spaces, they are also built to simulate dangerous and exotic spaces. Many of these video games take players into the center of illegal street activities, drug-infested neighborhoods, street gangs, and rampant gun violence. In instances like these, game design labors to simulate an authentic environment in order to deliver a more compelling gaming experience.

Along with immersing players in a world that *looks* urban, designers of urban/street games also strive to immerse players in a world that *sounds* urban. In many urban/street action and shooter games, police and emergency vehicle sirens, rounds of gunfire, and screeching tires from drive-by shootings, and other ambient noises, establish—via sound design—a place and mood. As the games have grown more cinematic in tone and style, developers have also employed carefully selected voice actors. The makers of *Saint's Row* worked with street gang members to help script dialogue and gang-related slang. Hip-hop-based sound tracks are pervasive, and it has become common practice among developers to hire hip-hop producers and performers to select music that evokes the ethos and energy of urban ghetto life. In many ways, the rise of urban/street games illustrates how hip-hop has influenced young people's media and cultural environment by projecting meticulously packaged images of "urban realism" into a media mix that includes video games, film, music, and other sources of entertainment.

The design of urban/games is a vital aspect of how learning takes place. But equally important are the repertoires of cultural knowledge that players bring to their gaming experiences. In other words, whatever forms of learning that take place in video games happens not only because of meticulous game design elements, but also because of the social schemas, scripts, and beliefs players develop from the larger cultural and ideological environment.

Learning to Reproduce Race

Learning in urban/street games is based on multiple competencies—technical and cultural. In his argument explaining what games can teach us about learning, Gee emphasizes the technical aspects of the learning process in games. The technical aspects involve learning how to navigate and, eventually, master the challenges and obstacles that structure the gameplay experience. Indeed, the open mode design of many urban/street games demands that players progressively build their technical mastery by "adapting and transferring earlier experiences to solve new problems."[19] But mastery of urban/street games also requires a great degree of cultural competency and knowledge. In this case, we are referring to the familiarity with certain racial themes, logics, and commonsense ideologies that make urban/street gaming a resonant, entertaining, and, ultimately, powerful learning experience. Part of the payoff in urban/street gaming, that sense of accomplishment and immediate reward gaming provides, is understanding, though not necessarily subscribing to, the racial cues, assumptions, and sensibilities embedded in these games. For instance, if urban/street gamers are already predisposed to believe that "authentic" poor urban neighborhoods are violent and drug-infested, then these games go a long way in confirming those views.

The selling and marketing of urban culture is premised on notions of difference that, ultimately, reproduce rather than contest racial hierarchies. Discussing this very fact, S. Craig Watkins writes that "certain types of representations of blackness are more likely to be merchandised, not because they are necessarily real but rather because they fit neatly with the prevailing commonsense characterizations of black life."[20] Thus, hip-hop–oriented video games, like other hip-hop–oriented media, establish the ideas, values, and behavioral scripts that facilitate how young media users make sense of blackness.

Urban/street games rely on subject matter and gameplay elements that construct authentic urban culture as ultraviolent, hypersexual, exotic, and a repository of dangerous and illegal activity. The content descriptors for urban/street games support this representation. *Def Jam: Fight for NY* and *True Crime: New York City* carry descriptors like "blood and gore," "realistic violence," and "suggestive themes." *Def Jam Vendetta*, a game rated T for teenagers, contains "strong language," "strong lyrics," and "suggestive themes." Mature (M) rated titles, *GTA: San Andreas* and *Saint's Row*, add descriptors like "strong sexual content" and "use of drugs and alcohol." These descriptors not only describe games; they also illuminate the narrative and thematic conditions under which black and brown bodies, cultures, spaces, and styles are simulated and rendered visible in the world of video games.

These narrative and thematic conditions are visible in sports-themed video games that also simulate black urban bodies, culture, spaces, and styles. Titles like *NFL Street 3* and *NBA Ballers Phenom* bring urban/street gaming to the sports category in video games. According to the Entertainment Software Association (ESA), sports titles (17 percent) were second only to action games (30 percent) in terms of market share in 2005. Overall, seven of the twenty top-selling games belonged in the sports genre. In 2000, a new generation of sports games entered this highly competitive niche with EA release of *NBA Street*. The publishing giant marketed *NBA Street* as an extreme sports game complete with state-of-the-art graphics, over-the-top character animation, and street-tough attitude. Shortly after developing *NBA Street*, EA released *NFL Street*, a football video game that looked to create characters, sounds, and environments that simulated an urban culture that was familiar to young media audiences.

Unlike previous sports titles, however, this new generation of video games had little interest in simulating the strategic and tactical aspects of basketball and football. Rather, like many of the urban/street games discussed previously, the cultural and lifestyle aspects of the modern sports world came to the fore. *NBA Ballers*, for example, represents a digital articulation of the classic "hoop dream" phenomenon that teaches many poor and working-class black boys that athletic celebrity, despite impossible odds, is an attainable goal.[21] One of the primary incentives for mastering the different challenges and sequences in *NBA Ballers* is to acquire status conferring symbols that include, among other things, palatial homes, luxurious cars, expensive jewelry, designer clothing, and, most problematically, women. The pursuit of these goals establishes a seductive learning environment, one that enlivens hegemonic notions of black masculinity and urban social mobility. For many young black males the power and pervasiveness of these representations can often skew their values and thus profoundly influence the lifestyle choices and behaviors that impact their life chances.

In addition to privileging hegemonic ideas about race, urban/street games privilege hegemonic ideas about gender. In their analysis of the top-sixty selling console and computer games, Children Now's gender results are instructive. Not surprisingly, they found that video games are an overwhelmingly male-dominated universe. Of the 1,716 characters identified in the study, 64 percent were male, 19 percent nonhuman, and 17 percent female. The racial dimensions of the gender patterns are equally revealing. More than two-thirds of the female player-controlled characters, 78 percent, were white. African Americans made up 10 percent of the female player-controlled characters, whereas Asian and Native American women constituted 7 percent and 1 percent, respectively. Not one of the 874 player-controlled characters in the study was identified as Latina. The characterization of women in urban/street games is also consistent with another Children Now's finding. "African American females," Children Now reports "were far more likely than any other group to be victims of violence."[22] Many titles from the urban/street category resist some of the notable changes that have labored to make the video games industry more receptive to women.

Whereas the industry, historically, has relegated women to the periphery, there has been a movement to make games much more gender-inclusive.[23] But whereas recent game protagonists like Lara Croft and Jade (*Beyond Good and Evil*) break away from some of the strict gender norms of games, the heavily marketed urban/street games in which black women and Latinas are likely to appear are much more restrictive.

In games like *GTA: San Andreas*, *Def Jam Vendetta*, and *Saint's Row*, women remain marginal and generally figure as props, bystanders, eye candy, and prizes to be won by the male protagonists. Like other background visual elements—street signs, graffiti art, cars, buildings—women are presented as accessories and used to enhance the presentation of the environment, not the core action. The fact that black women and Latinas are also portrayed quite casually as sexually available bystanders in fighter games like *Def Jam Vendetta* and as streetwalking prostitutes in action/adventure/shooter games like *GTA: Vice City* reinforces lessons about race and sexuality, especially the sexual mores, appetites, and behaviors of women marginalized by race and ethnicity.

What makes these elements in urban/street games prominent sites and sources of learning? First, urban/street games represent the first concerted effort by developers of entertainment-based video games to create characters and worlds that presumably draw from black American life. Moreover, the developers of these games hire artists, music producers and performers, voice actors, and highly skilled designers to build worlds that resonate with popular perceptions of urban culture. Ultimately, these video games bring the popular notions of blackness circulating in the cultural environment to the world of video games and interactive media. This enables young game players not only to experience powerfully rendered representations of urban culture but also to immerse themselves in environments that encourage active ways of playing with and learning about race. Urban/street gaming does more than present urban life in photorealistic ways or immerse gamers in racially designed environments. These titles also establish dynamic environments for performing race and gender.

Digital Minstrelsy: Doing and Learning Race in the Urban Game World

In his assessment of urban/street games, Adam Clayton Powell III characterizes them as "high-tech blackface."[24] David J. Leonard has also explored the notion of digital minstrelsy in games.[25] The idea that games constitute a form of minstrelsy compels us to think carefully about how learning about race takes place in video games. Powell and Leonard note that the articulation of the minstrel tradition, for example, is visible in the digitally manipulated black caricatures that populate urban/street themed games—distorted body types and facial features, clothing, voice acting, and over-the-top behaviors and movements that reflect a design ethos that mobilizes certain notions of blackness for popular consumption.

As we have seen, in the action/shooter variety of urban/street gaming, blacks and Latinos are portrayed as brutally violent, casually criminal, and sexually promiscuous. Blacks are typically characterized as verbally aggressive[26] and extraordinarily muscular and athletic[27] in sports action games. Minstrelsy, from this perspective, refers to how blackness is configured as a racialized body (albeit virtual) and commodity. Our focus, however, is on gameplay and what we believe is another manifestation of minstrelsy in gaming—performance. How, we ask, do urban/street games establish a powerful learning environment for not only *portraying* but also *performing* race in the form of blackface?

Many historians of minstrelsy allude to the complex social and psychological aspects of the tradition, the fact that it embodied whites' fear of and fascination with black bodies, what Eric Lott calls racial insult and racial envy.[28] At its most basic level, historians note, minstrelsy became a means for white men to occupy and play out fantasized notions of black masculinity, but in ways that were entertaining, nonthreatening, and committed to sustaining racial hierarchies. The same dynamics, in many respects, are at play in the case of urban/street gaming.

In this context of play and entertainment, distorted notions of blackness are rendered consumable and desirable, playable and accessible for young gamers. Referring to the growing inventory of urban/street-based sports titles, Leonard writes, "the desire to 'be black' because of the stereotypical visions of strength, athleticism, power and sexual potency all play out within the virtual reality of sports games."[29] In the immersive environment of urban/street gaming, young people not only interact with photorealistic environments, they also have the opportunity to interact with and perform fantasy-driven notions of black masculinity. Hence, when we talk about young people and video games marketed as authentic depictions of urban culture, the performative and interactive aspects of video games facilitate learning race by "doing" race. Video games represent another distinct development in young people's rapidly evolving media environment: the movement of racial image production into the terrain of "new media."

While the term *new media* should be used cautiously, it is often deployed to refer to technologically mediated conditions like interactivity, convergence, genre hybridity, and nonlinearity.[30] Take, for example, the shift from portraying blackness on television (the equivalent of telling about race) to performing blackness in video games (the equivalent of doing race). Historically, critical media scholars have examined how television projects racial imagery and narratives. In one of the most productive analyses of race, representation, and television, Herman Gray carefully explores how the textual, narrative, and aesthetic properties of television facilitate how we "watch race."[31]

Video games, however, have a way of allowing players not only to watch the action, but to participate in and drive the action. Consequently, in the context of video games, players are not only watching race; they are also performing and, as a result, (re)producing socially prescribed and technologically mediated notions of race. The rise of digital media culture demands that we modify "old media" derived terms like audience and text.[32] Audience, for instance, conjures up the image of someone who is positioned primarily to receive a one-way source of narrative/information transmission passively. But in video games, *players* supplant audiences and imply a much more dynamic engagement with media. Similarly, text can suggest that narrative and representational forms are static, fixed, and redundant. The scenes in a favorite television program or classic film never change. But in video games, the process of narration and representation is dynamic, contingent, and variable. Video games respond to player choice; as a result, it is possible—and even likely—to have a different experience with a game each time you play it.

No title epitomizes urban/street gaming more spectacularly or problematically than the *GTA* franchise. Like many of the urban/street games, this franchise is populated by a host of black and Latino characters, located in culturally specific and photorealistic environments, and purports to immerse gamers in authentic black and brown urban spaces. The bold and imaginative gameplay elements in *GTA: San Andreas*, for example, greatly expanded the technical and representational parameters for urban/street gaming, as well as the means by which blackness and Latinoness are rendered playable, pleasurable, and knowable in the burgeoning world of video games.

Understanding Race and Ethnicity in Games' Racialized Pedagogical Zones (RPZs)

Haitians have been protesting *GTA*, calling it racist. Funny, but I thought Haitians were a nationality, not a race. Besides, the game portrays everyone negatively regardless of race, ethnicity, and so forth. I mean, "HELLO, ITS CALLED GRAND THEFT AUTO!!!" —Paul Gonza

Please bear in mind that I'm a huge fan . . . Sure the game portrays everyone negatively. But Haitians are the only nationality being explicitly referred to in the game . . . The statement . . . "Kill all the Haitians"—could be replaced with, say the name of that Haitian gang, in which case probably no one would have raised an eyebrow . . . There is a big difference between reading about killing members of a group or culture, or watching a movie portraying slaughter of said group, and actually doing the slaughtering in a game. —Nickelplate

To explore the racial discourse in the *GTA* game franchise, we want to propose a consideration of what we term the games' racialized pedagogical zones. RPZs refer to the way that video games *teach* not only entrenched ideologies of race and racism, but also how gameplay's pleasure principles of mastery, winning, and skills development are often inextricably tied to and defined by familiar racial and ethnic stereotypes. In working through these ideas, Katie Salen and Eric Zimmerman's[33] influential work on the rules and subsequent meanings of gameplay is quite instructive, especially their fitting return to Johan Huizinga's[34] key metaphors of childhood play: the "playground" and the "magic circle." Following Salen and Zimmerman, we see Huizinga's powerful metaphors of childhood play and rules as productive for analyzing ways that contemporary game designers and players/users often reflect, rehearse, reenact, and reaffirm culturally familiar and highly problematic discourses of race in gaming space. It is Salen and Zimmerman's own articulation of games' "framing systems" that addresses more precisely the present discussion. On the matter of games' cultural connotations, and formal systems of play, and utilizing the game of *Chess* as one exemplar, they write:

[T]he system of play is embedded in the cultural framing of the game. . . . For example, answering a cultural question, regarding the politics of racial representation would have to include an understanding of the formal way the core rules of the game reference color. What does it mean that white always moves first? Similarly, when you are designing a game you are not designing just a set of rules, but a set of rules that will *always* be experienced as play within a cultural context. As a result, you will *never* have the luxury of completely forgetting about context when you are focusing on experience, or on experience and culture when you're focusing on the game's formal structure. . . . it is important to remember that a game's formal, experiential, and cultural qualities *always* exist as integrated phenomena [emphasis added].[35]

The cultural framing of the *GTA* games within hegemonic or dominant structures of race and class systems is exactly what this study evaluates through a formulation of the *GTA* trilogy's RPZs. More specifically, *GTA* game designers and players understand, expect, and desire these games' formal structures to participate in our culture's "integrated phenomena" of urban crime literature, films, and TV shows, hip-hop and other musical idioms, street fashion/costuming, slang and profane speech/dialogue, and hyperviolent as well as hypersexual activities. Rather than bracketing the real world's racist logics or subverting them through the artificial construct of the game world, "[for] better or for worse, kids use video and computer games as a filter through which to understand their lives" and the role of race therein.[36]

Mapping RPZs in *GTA* Games

This interrogation of race in the production and consumption of gaming poses a challenge to our collective understanding of video games as powerful, next-generation learning tools increasingly celebrated for being easy and pleasurable lead-ins to computer literacy and advanced placement in colleges and universities.[37] This analysis is about seeing how they also can be equally pleasurable tools for teaching racism and other modes of social intolerance. In mapping some pertinent contours of RPZs in the *GTA* games, we easily recognize familiar discourses of race and racial stereotypes from print, film, TV, radio, music, and other cultural productions at play within *GTA*'s video game spaces.

We have seen that the portrayal of race is embodied in many aspects of a video game's design, from its visual and audio stylings to the world space, narrative context, and play mechanics. Similarly, RPZs emerge from a range of intersecting features. In the *GTA* series, for example, RPZs are established through (a) its hyperviolent genre norms—a hybrid first-person shooter and adventure game; (b) its aesthetics and formal structures—realism, cinematic look, and function (especially the cut scenes)—and its hip-hop music and other youth culture influences; (c) its narrative structures: open-ended and mission driven; (d) its settings: urban locales, ghetto environments; (e) its dialogue: street and ethnic slang, thug and gangster-speak; (f) its star discourses: racially and ethnically diverse celebrities from the film, TV, and music industries; and (g) its marketing iconographies online and in print.

The significance of this tentative schematic is to locate precisely where we can expect to encounter, interact with, and indeed learn the RPZs in the *GTA* trilogy's carefully crafted and "incredibly immersive" game worlds. As Marc Prensky points out, a most effective game technique for transmitting contextual information is immersion. "It seems that the more one feels one is actually 'in' a culture," he elaborates further, "the more one learns from it—especially non-consciously . . . Kids will learn whatever messages are in the game."[38] The veracity of this observation will be supported by some gamers' postings to online game fora, excerpted below.

We should note briefly several obvious film and TV crime genre markers that contextualize and render race in the series meaningful and intelligible: for example, the 1970s and 1980s Italian mafia films—*Scarface*, *Goodfellas*, and the *Godfather* series; the 1990s black 'hood films—*Menace II Society*, *Straight Out of Brooklyn*, *New Jack City*, among others; and the 1980s-era procedural crime dramas par excellence the *Miami Vice* TV series. Each became the standard after which the *GTA* games were modeled. In terms of aesthetics, we call attention to the games' interactive functions that mimic cinema's moving camera perspectives, mise-en-scène constructions, gangster and other underworld costumes, pervasive semiautomatic assault weapons, drug and alcohol paraphernalia, and voyeuristic strip club settings. All this is coupled with the games' reliance on recognizable celebrities who are cast as the central character voices in the *GTA* games. Indeed, the actual voices of film and music stars Ray Liotta, Samuel Jackson, Dennis Hopper, Burt Reynolds, Phillip Michael Thomas, Deborah Harry, James Woods, Ice-T, George Clinton, Louis Guzman, and others enliven the dialogue in the games' crucial mini-filmlike scripted sections or "cut scenes" as they are more familiarly known. It is within the games' effective and affective remediation of these already meaningful cinematic and televisual conventions that we find *GTA*'s RPZs.[39]

RPZs in *GTA: San Andreas* and *Bully*, Toward a Discourse Analysis

It is telling that as the controversy surrounding Rockstar Games' "Hot Coffee" bonus segment (an encrypted pornographic cut scene in the *GTA: San Andreas* game) waned, the company released a sort of mea-culpa game entitled *Bully* in late October 2006. *New York Times* columnist Seth Schiesel described the game as "a whimsical boarding-school romp."[40] Based on screen grabs from Rockstar Games' *Bully* Web site (in advance of the game's release), the game trailers, the preliminary game description, and other information provided by Schiesel, and gameplay observations prior to and shortly after the game's release, this game represents an important corollary to our consideration of RPZs in the *GTA* series.[41] As a result of *Bully*'s setting in an upscale environment denoting white privilege and nonlethal juvenile pranks, the game arguably provides certain counternarratives and iconic visuals representing racial difference and otherness unavailable in the highly controversial *GTA* games. For example, *GTA* games seem to reproduce dominant messages about the rampant dangers of black urban/street life, and *Bully* simultaneously contests and affirms social ideas about race and ethnicity through its rendering of abusive teen life in an affluent school not restricted to an urban setting. Although it is interesting that some of *Bully*'s outdoor settings suggest an urban feel, its sprinkling of black and white athlete characters, who are bullies, complicate somewhat notions of the two games' essential racial discourses (figures 1 and 2).

Comparing the representational economies of race and difference in *GTA: San Andreas* and in *Bully*, it becomes clear that meaningful play in these games is predicated on Rockstar Games' appropriation of mainstream cinematic and televisual taxonomies of contemporary youth cultures and their specific environmental dangers. The urban 'hood versus the upscale prep school setting clearly demarcates relative zones of danger triggered by gamers' racialized points of reference, real-life experiences, peer group composition, and degrees of actual interracial contact and interaction on all sides of the racial–ethnic divides. Coupled with these powerful, photorealistic digital renderings of socially constructed environmental spaces and neighborhood dangers are equally compelling representations of dangerous game characters, and racially situated narratives or gameplay missions.

While a one-to-one comparison of RPZs in *Bully* and *GTA* games is beyond the scope of this study, several screen shots provide useful—if limited—points of contrast between the varied depictions of violence in black and white contexts as imaged by the company's game designers. Regardless of the company's rationale and timing for introducing *Bully* (on the heels of the June 14, 2006, Senate hearings on sexuality and violence in *GTA: San Andreas*), the fact remains that these comparable constructions of masculine power and action convey

Figure 1
Screen shot from *GTA: San Andreas*—Digital Boyz-N-the San Andreas Hood.

Figure 2
Screen shot from *Bully*—Menacing Digital Bullies in the Bully Schoolroom.

Figure 3
CJ, the *GTA: San Andreas* game's star avatar.

Figure 4
Jimmy Hopkins, star of *Bully*.

incomparable messages about the game characters' use of their powerful actions. Both games present an antihero lead character playing through a series of missions. For gamers playing as Carl "CJ" Johnson (figure 4),

GTA: San Andreas provides big guns and bigger firepower to effect drive-bys and targeted shootings in the 'hood. Conversely, for gamers playing as Jimmy Hopkins (figure 5), *Bully* provides big CO_2 canisters to extinguish even bigger fires in the school. Nothing about these two RPZs contests dominant culture's socially constructed messages/lessons about race, masculinity, and class in America. Instead, everything about CJ, *GTA*'s black protagonist, conforms to America's hyperviolent and superpredator black male stereotypes, and the racially codified violence that defines success in the gameplay missions undertaken throughout the virtual ghetto environment. Similarly, Jimmy Hopkins, *Bully*'s white protagonist, comports with our stereotypical expectations about white males' moral superiority and demonstrations of social responsibility even though "he's been expelled from every school he's ever attended, left to fend for himself after his mother abandons him at Bullworth to go on her fifth honeymoon."[42]

One professional review of *Bully* posted on YouTube characterizes the game's narrative departure from the *GTA* games rather adeptly. According to RockstarAl:

> The story is nowhere near as raunchy as any of the *Grand Theft Auto* games and ends up playing out like a slightly scandalous Nickelodeon cartoon. There is little to no swearing and the violence only adds up to a few black eyes here and there. But there's still plenty of laughs to be had from the conniving and emotionally imbalanced characters Rockstar writes so well.[43]

Contrast *Bully*'s rather benign story description to its *GTA* counterpart, also on YouTube. In a review entitled "The History of *Grand Theft Auto*," the game world and gameplay are defined as amoral and forbidden digital spaces of danger and hyperviolent performance:

> These missions would take you all over the city and varied from simple taxi jobs to assassinations and even car theft rings. A big part of the fun was exploring each city and finding the secret missions to do, or just causing general mayhem while eluding the police and using weapons like machine guns, rocket launchers, and flame throwers ("The History of Grand Theft Auto").[44]

As these game reviews make clear, on the one hand, *GTA: San Andreas* positions CJ as a digital simulation trading on the cinematic tropes of the endangered, as well as dangerous, black male protagonists delineated in John Singleton's 1991 film *Boyz N the Hood* and the 1993 Hughes brothers' film *Menace II Society* (outlined above), or the *de rigueur* menacing black youths who dominate newspaper headlines, TV and radio news shows, and other mainstream media texts. On the other hand, Jimmy Hopkins is Rockstar Games' innovative digital persona simulating a troubled-yet-heroic white teenager verging on juvenile delinquency, whose cinematic alter ego could easily have been expelled from the privileged schoolyard of the wildly popular *Harry Potter* films, or TV's charmingly angst-driven coming-of-age narratives found in *The Wonder Years* and *Boy Meets World* shows, for example.

What many video game theorists and critics agree upon, and what matters most to our inquiry, is the fact that video games teach—they are pedagogical—and that "what we're learning from them bears no resemblance whatsoever to what we think we're learning."[45] It is precisely the learning "about life" in America with its entrenched racial problems that is at issue here. As the foregoing examples demonstrate, and as Ian Bogost points out elsewhere in this volume, it is difficult, if not impossible, for games not to have a pedagogical function. Given the increasing number of hours youths today spend playing—fourth-grade boys spend about nine hours per week playing and eighth-grade boys log nearly five hours per week at play[46]—young people are spending a great deal of time immersed in the kinds of RPZs discussed here (figure 6).

Reception and Fandom Contexts

Any foray into the online fan culture of the *GTA* games quickly reveals an alarming reality: the video game playground on- and offline too often replicates racist attitudes, values, and assumptions found in larger social structures. As contested a site as actual children's playgrounds often are, some online fora are notorious zones of contestation and violent speech acts when race and issues of diversity surface.[47] In evidence was the racial diversity of the online gamers, whose debates about race often bordered on flame wars. The majority of gamer-respondents freely self-identified along racial lines. They were African American, Asian, Arab, black, Mexican, Jewish, white, or racially mixed. Overwhelmingly male, these

Figure 5
Screen shot from *GTA: San Andreas* illustrates familiar criminalized image of black male youths with guns.

gamers used screen names and expressed sentiments, which ranged from racial inclusion (or color blindness) to outright racist rants, with some featuring both. Exchanges also ranged from a sort-of free-speech, Habermassian public sphere ideal to condemnations of the system administrator for permitting such a topic to appear on the forum at all. In some instances, posts to the threads were censored or replaced with a note that read, "This message was deleted at the request of a moderator or administrator."[48]

The rhetorical rough-and-tumble in these discussion threads began largely with assertions that many white gamers boycotted *GTA: San Andreas* because the lead character, CJ, was black and the game protagonist's digital skin could not be modified to present as a white avatar. Reviewing the emotional content on various user fora dedicated to the *GTA* games and their fan bases reveals much about the complexity of gamers' racial attitudes and belief systems, at least those posting to the sites under consideration here. While these sites are worthy of more detailed analysis than time or space permits here, a few select quotes can illustrate quite convincingly the need to think seriously about the lessons video games teach and how we can fairly, honestly, and effectively address and assess games' potentially harmful—as well as beneficial—RPZs.

In his recent historical analysis of modern boy culture in formation, E. Anthony Rotundo's insights are useful for framing the selected quotes. According to Rotundo, "Rivalry, division, and conflict were vital elements in the structure of boy culture." He added that "the boys world was endlessly divided and subdivided" and split into groups by residence, ethnicity, and social status, with daring and bravado as a "ritual expression in boy's games."[49] We culled the following quotes from three separate discussion threads. The first set of quotes are direct responses to a discussion entitled "What the hell is everyones [*sic*] problem?" The fracas in this discussion concerns a new video game (not identified in this thread, but likely the game is *GTA4*). The postings concern gamers' attitudes about the possibility of another black protagonist in this next *GTA* game.

#1: The thing is that in *SA* [*GTA: San Andreas*] you played someone who dealt drugs and is in a gang . . . you know your average black guy. Now you have someone who upholds the law and is black???? People need to realize that this game is in no way trying to emulate reality like *SA* was. I believe it is cel-shaded so people won't lose themselves in it and believe it's happening in the real world."[50]

#2: ∧ ∧ ∧ ∧ ∧ Oh ****!!!! Wait. Your average black guy???? Okay, obviously you live under a rock in a small hik [*sic*] town because the average black in Houston, TX or at least my friends are in college. I have braids but I've never been in a gang and neither has my family or friends. Just because 50 Cent raps about detailed stories that he fabricates, America thinks ALL black guys are gangsters. Your ignorance is hilarious because 50 used his proceeds from his album to make a sports mineral water and cheaper version of Apple computers. People like you should not be allowed to reproduce.[51]

#3: Well one of my big gripes with *GTA* and one of the main reasons why I don't [*sic*] play the francise, except at friends houses is because they don't let you customize your character. Im mexican and I have yet to see a mexican protagonist in a game, except that stereotypical under the border game. I just want to be able to make the character look like me, or how I want.[52]

Discussion thread number two is entitled "Is the main character black again?"

1: BobbyQt [a pseudonym] is right!!! I don't wanna play as a black character. Ever since the 8 bit era, the characters have been white, why change all that. I'm pretty sure black people don't mind playing as white characters. There are already enough games with black characters, NBA live, Madden, Fifa and San Andreas of course isn't that enough?!?![53]

#2: Well that was pretty interesting why aren't you ok with playing as A character (oh and by the way I am capitalized [*sic*] 'A' because that is exactly what game characters are, simple, not specifically white, male, american, 18–34). It does matter what they look like they are a character I think its great that there are different ethnicities in games but I think that shouldn't turn a logical person away from a game because of an individuals race or gender. If you have a problem playing with an african american character then you have a problem with people in general not just video game persona's. END[54]

The third and final discussion topic is "So, what minority character should the new character be?"

#1: I don't care what the character is, but I wouldn't mind a Hispanic character or another White character. Maybe a Jew. Like me

#2: with the current situation in the states [*sic*] Im leaning towards the mestizo character also, granted I am a White bigot but I wouldn't mind playing as a salvadoran or mexican killer, those dudes are ruthless, plus they sound cooler than ol cj

#3: Are you for real?

#2: Me? Yeh im "for real" flame me all you like I really don't care if your gonna say something homophobic its your own problem

#4: I'd like a white or Italian guy. I'm black but for some reason, I don't like playing video games as black people. Playing as a white guy makes the game feel more normal. And Italian guy makes it more mafia like and mafia=good.

#5: asian. so I can finally connect with a character in *GTA*.[55]

The expressions here range from blatant racism to racial tolerance or inclusion, and provide an interesting feedback loop for some of the concerns outlined above. We wanted to juxtapose some feedback from *GTA* gamers themselves to comments of these games' designers and industry critics, to balance out our own considerations of industry practices and player response. While this study is not arguing that *GTA* fandom represents a racist community, it does suggest, however, that there is much food for thought here.

It is our aim to explore and better understand how usefully and effectively to study young people's increasing interaction with discourses of race in video gaming culture. This formulation of RPZs sketches out directly, if not fully, gamers' readings and likely enactments of game scenarios such as those found in *GTA*. These are scenarios told in racial terms and in alluring role-playing game structures, where gamers are said to have more choice and freedom in producing, as well as consuming, the video games' narratives or story lines.[56] Our inclusion of such frameworks is intended to encourage the monitoring of how these games' various missions depend upon the mastery of established mainstream codes of meaningful play bound by racially suspect cultural scripts.[57]

The significance of this project is contextualized quite convincingly by Salen and Zimmerman's reminder of Huizinga's truism, that "all play means something."[58] It is also important to recognize one of gaming's welcome unintended consequences—how it alters the familiar descriptive trifecta of nonwhite youths as poor, minority, and illiterate. For one thing, as the above quotes from *GTA* gamers bear out, these video games require a certain amount of computer and other cultural literacies simply to play the games well. After all, there are manuals, onscreen instructions, and community fora devoted to improved gameplay and social networking that require basic-to-exceptional literacy competencies.

Want to Play? Some Final Thoughts on Race and Games

Our focus in this chapter on the simulation and representation of urban culture in video games, and the consequences for learning, does not intend to be exhaustive in the effort to illuminate the rising significance of race and ethnicity in the ecology of games. In the final section of this chapter, we move away from discussions of representation, game design, and pedagogical zones to identify and cautiously map what we believe are additional, yet underexplored matters related to race, video games, learning, and young people. As we stated in the opening, public dialogue about race and video games has been marginal at best. In addition to the issues addressed above, we want to identify some other ways in which race matters in the video game world. Specifically, we consider video games in the context of a rapidly evolving digital media environment.

Any analysis of the relationship between video games, young people, and learning must also seek to understand the larger context in which these issues began to take on their complex shape. One of the more notable transformations taking place in the rapidly evolving digital media landscape is the extent to which young people have gained access to tools and skills that enable them to produce as well as consume cultural content. According to the Pew Internet & American Life Project (2005), more than half, 57 percent, of the teens aged 12–15 create and share content online.[59] Many scholars celebrate the sense of freedom and empowerment that young people gain from "participatory culture."[60] Salen and Zimmerman argue that a Do-It-Yourself (DIY) approach to cultural resistance, most notably reskinning and modding, has made video games a form of culturally transformative play.[61] Moreover, the brave new world of digital media culture—modding, world-building, user-generated content, and file sharing—has the potential not only to build new learning environments and modes of digital literacy, but equally importantly to empower young people to cultivate actively practices that resist the once-taken-for-granted hegemony of corporate produced and preprogrammed media into their lives.

Young people are not passive consumers of media and cultural content. Increasingly, they are producing and sharing content with their peers, thus altering their media and cultural environment in unprecedented ways.[62] Video games, for example, can no longer be viewed as merely a source of leisure and entertainment, but also as a site of cultural resistance and empowerment.[63]

However, as we begin to understand more thoroughly the lively ways in which digital media enables young people to assert greater control over their cultural environments, we must also be mindful of the fact that this does not hold true for all young people. We ask then, what are the consequences for young people whose access to digital technology is either limited (i.e., accessed at school or the local library) or essentially nonexistent? As video games evolve into a dynamic form of cultural production, personal expression, and social capital, we see, once again, how the divide between the "technology haves" and "technology have-nots" continues to matter. Elite gaming communities usually, though not always, involve a high degree of involvement in online digital publics that cultivate very specialized bodies of knowledge and expertise. Deep participation in elite video gaming also demands more than casual or occasional access to digital media, that is, the ability to access gaming environments from wired homes, offices, college dormitories, and public spaces—environments that are not universally available to all. In this case, we draw attention to multiple forms of access—physical access to the hardware and broadband connections, as well as access to the mentors and learning environments that cultivate digital forms of literacy, skills, and social capital.

Poor and working-class youth play video games, but primarily on consoles rather than on the personal computers, that foster more transformative gaming practices like modding and world-building. According to Roberts et al. black and Latino youth are *more likely* than their white counterparts to live in homes that own a television or video game console.[64] Additionally, black and Latino youth are *less likely* than their white counterparts to live in a household with a personal computer. And while computer ownership among the poor and working class continues to increase, these households are still unlikely to have access to high-speed Internet connections.[65] Young people who have limited access to advanced computing technology are less likely than their more affluent counterparts to participate in digital media culture as producers and distributors of content.

In addition, overcoming the barriers regarding content creation in games poses tough challenges. In his analysis of how Asian Americans are portrayed in games, Dean Chan urges scholars and cultural critics to "remain steadfast in the call for more diverse and equitable representations in commercial games."[66] However, before game content becomes more diverse, the industry will have to cultivate greater racial and cultural diversity in its workforce. This is especially important given that video games which simulate culturally specific environments require designers to be not only technically literate, but socially and culturally literate as well.

So, what do we know about the makeup of the video game development community? In a 2005 published report titled "Game Developer Demographics: An Exploration of Workforce Diversity," the International Game Developers Association (IGDA) set out to answer one question: "who makes games?" Whereas the Children Now report found that the overwhelming majority of player-controlled characters in games are white, the IGDA found that an overwhelming majority of the personnel creating games is also white. According to the IGDA, the "typical" game development professional can be described as white, male, young (median age 31), and college educated. If high degrees of learning and education are essential for gaining meaningful employment in the video games industry, the future prospects of black and Latino talent finding a secure place among programmers, design artists, writers, and designers seem limited.

One interesting avenue of intervention involves the creation of digital learning environments that work to close the participation gap. As debates about the digital divide have been refined, technology activists note that successful intervention requires more than providing the technology-poor access to hardware. The technology-poor also need access to mentors and environments that enable them to cultivate the skills that lead to greater forms of agency. Addressing the participation gap, researchers claim, is the next great challenge in closing the digital divide. Nichole Pinkard, principal investigator of the Center for Urban School Improvement, writes, "the new divide will not be caused by access to technology but rather by lack of access to mentors, environments, and activities where the use of digital media is the language of communication."[67] Community technology centers like this one are not only making technology accessible to poor and working class youth but also, as Pinkard notes, developing programs that "enable urban youth to become discerning new media consumers and fluent media producers."

In short, we believe that future discussions about race and games should be twofold. First, we must continue to document and analyze what the racial content, themes, and design elements in video games teach young people about race. Second, we believe that future discussions about race and video games should engage broader debates about the rise and diffusion of digital media technologies and the educational pathways that lead to greater forms of new media literacy and participation in the digital media sphere, particularly as they pertain to race and ethnicity. Empowering young people on the social and economic margins to create content not only diversifies what content they consume; it also holds the promise of expanding how they learn and reproduce race for public consumption for generations to come.

Notes

1. Elizabeth A. Vandewater, Shim Mi-Suk, and Allison G. Caplovitz, Linking Obesity and Activity Level with Children's Television and Video Game Use, *Journal of Adolescence* 27 (2004): 71–85; Carol A. Phillips, Susan Rolls, Andrew Rouse, and Mark D. Griffiths, Home Video Game Playing in School Children: A Study of Incidence and Patterns of Play, *Journal of Adolescence* 18 (1995): 687–91; K. Roe and D. Muijs, Children and Computer Games: A Profile of Heavy Users, *European Journal of Communication* 13 (1998): 181–200; and Jeanne B. Funk and Debra D. Bachman, Playing Violent Video and Computer Games and Adolescent Self-Concept, *Journal of Communication* 46 (1996): 19–32.

2. James Paul Gee, *What Video Games Have to Teach Us About Learning and Literacy* (New York: Palgrave Macmillan, 2003).

3. Gordon L. Berry and C. Mitchell-Kernan, eds., *Television and the Socialization of the Minority Child* (New York: Academic, 1982).

4. Gordon L. Berry and Joy Keiko Asamen, Television, Children, and Multicultural Awareness: Comprehending the Medium in a Complex Multimedia Society, in *Handbook of Children and the Media*, eds. Dorothy G. Singer and Jerome L. Singer (London: Sage, 2001).

5. Ibid.

6. Anna Everett, Serious Play: Playing with Race in Contemporary Gaming Culture, in *Handbook of Computer Game Studies*, eds. Joost Raessens and Jeffrey Goldstein (Cambridge, MA: The MIT Press, 2005), 311–26.

7. Marc Prensky, *Digital Game-Based Learning* (New York: McGraw-Hill, 2001); and Gee, *What Video Games Have to Teach Us*, 136–37.

8. Gee, *What Video Games Have to Teach Us.*

9. Steven Poole, *Trigger Happy: The Inner Life of Video Games* (London: Fourth Estate, 2000).

10. Ibid, 152.

11. Poole, *Trigger Happy.*

12. Children Now, *Fair Play? Violence, Gender and Race in Video Games* (Oakland, CA: Children Now, 2001).

13. Geoff King and Tanya Krzywinska, *Tomb Raiders and Space Invaders: Video Game Forms and Contexts* (New York: I. B. Palgrave Macmillan, 2006).

14. Alison McMahan, Immersion, Engagement, and Presence: A Method for Analyzing 3-D Video Games, in *The Video Game Theory Reader*, eds. Mark J. P. Wolf and Bernard Perron (New York: Routledge, 2003).

15. Children Now, *Fair Play*, 23.

16. The six consoles included in the study were Dreamcast, Game Boy Advance, Game Boy Color, Nintendo 64, PlayStation, and PlayStation 2.

17. Dean Chan, Playing with Race: The Ethics of Racialized Representations in E-Games, *International Review of Information Ethics* 4 (2005): 24–30.

18. Ibid.

19. Gee, *What Video Games Have to Teach Us*, 127.

20. S. Craig Watkins, *Representing: Hip Hop Culture and the Production of Black Cinema* (Chicago: The University of Chicago Press, 1998), 228; see also S. Craig Watkins, *Hip Hop Matters: Politics, Pop Culture and the Struggle for the Soul of a Movement* (Boston: Beacon Press, 2005).

21. Richard Lapchick, *Five Minutes to Midnight: Race and Sport in the 1990s* (Lanham, MD: Madison Books, 1991).

22. Children Now, *Fair Play*, 23.

23. Justine Cassell and Henry Jenkins, eds., *From Barbie to Mortal Kombat: Gender and Computer Games* (Cambridge, MA: The MIT Press, 2000); and Diane Carr, Games and Gender, in *Computer Games: Text, Narrative and Play*, eds. Diane Carr, David Buckingham, Andrew Burn, and Gareth Schott (London: Polity, 2006).

24. Michel Marriott, The Color of Mayhem in a Wave of "Urban" Games, *New York Times*, August 12, 2004.

25. David J. Leonard, High Tech Blackface: Race, Sports Video Games and Becoming the Other, *Intelligent Agent* 4 (2004): 1–5.

26. Children Now, *Fair Play.*

27. Leonard, High Tech Blackface.

28. Eric Lott, *Love and Theft: Blackface Minstrelsy and the American Working Class* (New York: Oxford University Press, 1993).

29. Leonard, High Tech Blackface, 2.

30. Sonia M. Livingstone, *Young People and New Media: Childhood and the Changing Media Environment* (London: Sage, 2002).

31. Herman Gray, *Watching Race: Television and the Struggle for Blackness* (Minneapolis, MN: University of Minnesota Press, 1995).

32. Martin Lister, Jon Dovey, Seth Giddings, Iain Grant, and Kieran Kelly, *New Media: A Critical Introduction* (New York: Routledge, 2003).

33. Katie Salen and Eric Zimmerman, Game Design and Meaningful Play, in *Handbook of Computer Game Studies*, eds. Joost Raessens and Jeffrey Goldstein (Cambridge, MA: The MIT Press, 2005), 59–80.

34. Johan Huizinga, *Homo Ludens: A Study of the Play Element in Culture* (Boston: Beacon Press, 1955).

35. Ibid., 68–9.

36. Marc Prensky, Computer Games and Learning: Digital Game-Based Learning, in *Handbook of Computer Game Studies*, eds. Joost Raessens and Jeffrey Goldstein (Cambridge, MA: The MIT Press, 2005), 106.

37. Henry Jenkins, "Complete Freedom of Movement": Video Games as Gendered Play Spaces, in *From Barbie to Mortal Kombat: Gender and Computer Games*, eds. Justine Cassell and Henry Jenkins (Cambridge, MA: The MIT Press, 1998), 262–97; and Aphra Kerr, Non-Entertainment Uses of Digital Games, in *The Business and Culture of Digital Games* (London: Sage, 2006).

38. Prensky, Computer Games and Learning, 107.

39. While this comparative media framework does provide useful parallels to understanding and mastering gaming's racialized *meaningful play*, to borrow Katie Salen and Eric Zimmerman's term, it is not a reductive exercise that fails to recognize the raging debate in game studies between theories of narratology and ludology, with other emergent critical paradigms in the offing. Narratologist Janet Murray correctly cautions that "one cannot use old standards to judge the new formats," while acknowledging that "games are always stories," with a specific type of interactivity unique to games' cyber-dramas (Janet Murray quoted in Kerr, Non-Entertainment Uses of Video Games, 24). Ludologists, mainly building upon the seminal works of Johan Huizinga and Espen Aarseth, to name two, posit the necessity for moving games studies "away from representation towards simulation semiotics or 'simiotics.'" Moreover, their largely formalist critiques pivot on the "shift from narrative to ludic engagement with texts and from interpretation to configuration," as Stuart Moulthrop sees it (quoted in Kerr, Non-Entertainment Uses of Video Games, 33–4). And while such ground-clearing critical approaches to game studies constitute a necessary move forward for the nascent field, they do recall the infamous realism versus formalism debates of classical film theory that remain generative and productive to established cinema and TV studies even today. And for our purposes, Aphra Kerr is on target with the observation that "[g]iven both the diversity of narrative theories and the diversity of games, some of which are clearly more narrative driven than others, it would be unwise to dismiss narrative theory outright" (ibid., 26). When we contextualize the RPZ idea within the *GTA* metanarratives and interactive modes of engagement, we feel the need to retain narratology and embrace ludology, though not always in equal measure. After all, game theorists correctly emphasize that games position players as the spectator and protagonist simultaneously (Kerr, Non-Entertainment Uses of Video Games, 38; and Mark J. P. Wolf, Genre and the Video Game, in *Handbook of Computer Games Studies*, eds. Joost Raessens and Jeffrey Goldstein

[Cambridge, MA: The MIT Press, 2005], 193). Thus, it seems that we can benefit from both critical approaches.

40. Seth Schiesel, Welcome to the New Dollhouse, *New York Times*, May 7, 2006, Sec. 2: 1f.

41. Anna Everett acknowledges the superb assistance she received from her graduate students at UCSB, Noah Lopez and Dan Reynolds, especially, and the entire group of students enrolled in her New Media Theory seminar in 2006. Noah Lopez was her summer research assistant with whom she spent numerous thrilling hours playing *GTA: Vice City* and *GTA: San Andreas*, and the *Sims 2* games. They embarked upon an odyssey of exploration into these games' depictions of race, gender, and class politics, and specific treatments of the game genres and other aesthetic features. She thanks Lopez for helping to lower the learning curve of *GTA*'s mission structures and logics. Dan Reynolds was instrumental in presenting some of *Bully*'s game details immediately after that game's release. Reynolds played (actually finished) the game within a few weeks and discussed many of its racial dimensions with her during the course of their New Media Theory seminar that focused particularly on games theory and practice. She hopes to revisit the wealth of information they provided as avid gamers and critically aware graduate students of film and media study.

42. Rockstar Games, *Bully*: "Overview." http://www.rockstargames.com/bully/home. Accessed October 20, 2006.

43. Rockstar Al, "*Bully* Gametrailers Review." YouTube. http://www.youtube.com/watch?v=9ioKpSb6AEO. Accessed October 20, 2006.

44. While the production date of this video review of *GTA* ran initially on GameSpot.com, a user posted the review to YouTube on May 6, 2006.

45. Ralph Koster, quoted in Jane Avrich, Steven Johnson, Ralph Koster, and Thomas de Zengotita, Grand Theft Education: Literacy in the Age of Video Games, *Harper's Magazine* 313 (2006): 31–40.

46. Sandra Calvert, Cognitive Effects of Video Games, in *Handbook of Computer Game Studies*, eds. Joost Raessens and Jeffrey Goldstein (Cambridge, MA: The MIT Press, 2005), 125–32.

47. In a sampling of representative gamers' thoughts on race in the gaming firmament, the forum at GameSpot.com proved to be one of the most popular, prolific, and useful, followed by the user fora at the IGDA Web site and at Gameology.org.

48. Is the Main Character Black Again? *Gamespot.com*, Forums, 2006. http://www.gamespot.com/ebox360/action/crackdown/show_msgs.php?topic_id=1-31063566&pid=930144&page=0. Accessed October 20, 2006.

49. E. Anthony Rotundo, Boy Culture, in *The Children's Culture Reader*, ed. Henry Jenkins (New York: New York University Press, 1998), 337–62.

50. "What the hell is everyones [*sic*] problem?" http://www.gamespot.com/xbox360/action/crackdown/show_msgs.php?topic_id=m-1-31063566&pid=930144&page=0.

51. Ibid.

52. Ibid.

53. Is the Main Character Black Again?

54. Ibid.

55. So What Minority Should the New Character Be? *Gamespot.com*, Forums, May 18, 2006. http:www.gamespot.com/pse/action/grandtheftauto4/show_msgs.php. Accessed May 18, 2006.

56. Avrich, Grand Theft Education, 31–40.

57. Anna Everett, P.C. Youth Violence: What's the Internet or Video Gaming Got to Do with It? *Denver University Law Review* 77, no. 4 (2000): 689–698.

58. Katie Salen and Eric Zimmerman, Game Design and Meaningful Play, in *Handbook of Computer Game Studies*, eds. Joost Raessens and Jeffrey Goldstein (Cambridge, MA: The MIT Press, 2005), 59–80.

59. Pew Internet & American Life Project, *Teen Content Creators and Consumers* (Washington, DC: Pew Research Center, 2005).

60. Henry Jenkins, *Fans, Bloggers, and Gamers: Exploring Participatory Culture* (New York: New York University Press, 2006).

61. Salen and Zimmerman, Game Design and Meaningful Play.

62. Pew Internet & American Life Project, *Teen Content Creators and Consumers.*

63. Salen and Zimmerman, Game Design and Meaningful Play.

64. Donald Roberts, Ulla G. Foehr, Victoria J. Rideout, and Mollyanne Brodie, *Kids and Media in America* (Cambridge, UK: Cambridge University Press, 2004).

65. U.S. Department of Commerce, *Computer and Internet Use in the United States: October* (Washington, DC: U.S. Census Bureau, 2003).

66. Chan, Playing with Race.

67. Nichole Pinkard, Developing Opportunities for Urban Youth to Become Digital, 2006. http://spotlight.macfound.org/main/entry/nichole_pinkard_developing_opportunities_for_urban_youth_to_become_digital/. Accessed June 16, 2007.

PART III: GAMING LITERACIES

Open-Ended Video Games: A Model for Developing Learning for the Interactive Age

Kurt Squire

The University of Wisconsin–Madison, Curriculum and Instruction, Academic ADL Colab

With *Grand Theft Education: Literacy in the Age of Video Games* gracing the cover of *Harper's* September 2006 magazine, video games and education, once the quirky interest of a few rogue educational technologists and literacy scholars, reached broader public awareness. The idea of combining video games and education is not new; twenty years ago, Ronald Reagan praised video games for their potential to train "a new generation of warriors." Meanwhile, Surgeon General C. Everett Koop declared video games among the top health risks facing Americans.[1] Video games, like any emerging medium, are disruptive, challenging existing social practices, while capturing our dreams and triggering our fears.

Today's gaming technologies, which allow for unprecedented player exploration and expression, suggest new models of what educational gaming can be.[2] As educational games leave the realm of abstraction and become a reality, the field needs to move beyond rhetoric and toward grounded examples not just of good educational games, but effective game-based learning environments that leverage the critical aspects of the medium as they apply to the needs of a twenty-first-century educational system. We need rigorous research into what players do with games (particularly those that don't claim explicit status as educational), and a better understanding of the thinking that is involved in playing them.[3] We need precise language for what we mean by "video games," and better understandings of how specific design features and patterns operate,[4] and compelling evidence of game-based learning environments. In short, the study of games and learning is ready to come of age. Researchers have convinced the academy that games are worthy of study, and that games hold potential for learning. The task now is to provide effective models of how they operate.[5]

This chapter offers a theoretical model for video game-based learning environments as *designed experiences*. To be more specific, it suggests that we can take one particular type of video game—open-ended simulation, or "sandbox" games—and use its capacity to recruit diverse interests, creative problem solving, and productive acts (e.g., creating artwork, game

The author would like to thank Ben Devane, Levi Giovanetto, and Shree Durga for their help and insights in conducting the research on which much of this chapter is based. Further, the author thanks editor Katie Salen for her many insightful comments, suggestions, and improvements on this text. Finally, he thanks the faculty and students of Madison Wisconsin's Games, Learning, and Society Group, as well as James Paul Gee and Ed Meachen, for their support in conducting this research. Portions of this Research were funded by the Academic ADL Colab, the Wisconsin Alumni Research Fund, and the MacArthur Foundation. I would like to acknowledge Henry Jenkins, PI of the MIT Games-to-Teach Project, and Philip Tan, Tim Heidel, Tom Wilson, Robert Figueiredo, and Megan Ginter, for their work on *Supercharged!*

mods, or using games as tools for modeling, i.e., for building digital models of phenomena, such as world civilizations). It ties together studies of gamers "in the wild," within school, and in afterschool programs designed specifically for learning. It concludes with an investigation of how we might use such games to develop players' *productive* literacies, their ability to use digital technologies to produce both meanings and tangible artifacts.[6]

Earlier research has shown how *targeted* games (i.e., games focused around particular concepts) might be used to create conceptual change.[7] With *Supercharged!*, for example, working with Physicists at MIT, a team of MIT researchers and I created a simulation game in which players "entered" a world of electromagnetism. Based on our studies of how physicists thought about electrostatic forces (and similar to more detailed studies by Eleanor Ochs and colleagues), we developed a game that modeled a key aspect of how experts think about physics, specifically how they adopt the perspective of charged particles in thinking through problems. The game allowed students to also "think like a particle" by traveling through mazelike spaces where they had to place charged particles strategically in order to propel themselves through the space (using real-time strategy-type mechanics). Our studies of students playing *Supercharged!* revealed that they developed more robust conceptual understandings of physics.[8]

More importantly, they developed a better understanding of *why* scientists use visualizations to describe forces. As one student commented, "before they were just lines in a book, but now I understand why that they are there . . . to help you see the forces."

Over the course of a year, we piloted the game in a variety of contexts, ranging from middle schools to high schools to MIT courses.[9] We found that the game was most successful for two types of students: MIT students who were struggling to understand the concepts behind the ideas they were learning in their textbooks (which were typically represented through physics formulas), and secondary school students who were struggling readers disaffiliated with school. High-achieving MIT students resisted the game somewhat, suggesting that it was a "crutch" of sorts for those who could not "hack" harder problems. Secondary school students generally responded favorably, and in our tests, on average, did better than those learning via traditional means (including experiments and visualizations). We saw the highest gains, however, with those students who were struggling readers, and who traditionally reacted negatively to the experiments (e.g., they saw experiments as a chance to goof off in class, and were usually off task).

The data from these studies suggested to us that *Supercharged!* was successful in helping students build more robust conceptual models of physics, but left few directions for players to go after playing the game. The game did little (outside the cut scene) to suggest to students how these concepts related to electricity or magnetic phenomena seen in the world around them. Similarly, the game did little to suggest what a successful player might do to extend this interest *beyond* the game, such as in science career. We felt that, although successful, at its core *Supercharged!* was still a targeted conceptual game, designed to teach students a very specific way of thinking about physics. It was less effective at reaching other domains (much like a puzzle game—such as *Bejeweled*—involves patterns, but doesn't necessarily push one to pursue a career in Mathematics). Of course, the game was designed to be aesthetically pleasing, to enthrall students with some of the interesting and nonintuitive aspects of physics, and generally to raise students' interest in physics, which—by all accounts—it did. Still, at its core, we saw the game as having relatively little potential for leading players not already interested in science into life trajectories in which they would become affiliated with science, without significant out-of-game curricular materials.

In addition to targeted games are professional role-playing games—games that situate learners in the roles of engineers, biologists, or forensic scientists in the process of solving complex scientific problems. These games offer an intriguing mix of sociocultural and constructivist learning theory. As a sociocultural learning theorist might want to see, they set up roles for players to inhabit, and all problem solving, game play, and argumentation take place within the service of those roles. Within commercial entertainment games, *Full Spectrum Warrior* is an excellent example of such a game, as players lead a squad of soldiers who behave according to army doctrine.[10] The nonplayer characters and narrators all speak to the player as if he or she is the character in the world, allowing the player to become initiated into the discourse of the military. For many educators, role-playing games—especially the more open-ended, simulation variety (such as games produced by Irrational, e.g., *SWAT4*, and Looking Glass Studios, e.g., the *Thief* series)—serve as excellent models for how we might build learning games.[11]

Epistemic games[12] are still another example of games that situate players in professional roles. Shaffer argues that, through closely studying the professions (urban planners, science journalists), we can create gamelike experiences that re-create the practicum. We can use games as a way to provide simulated field experiences, experiences that eliminate some of the less efficient, or exploitive elements of apprenticeships and focus, instead, on practices most central to the domain. Building on Schon's work[13] on reflective practitioners, Shaffer argues that we can develop generative ways of thinking through these games, ways of thinking that transfer into other domains.

Augmented reality role-playing games—such as *Pirates* (a game played on cell phones in which players seek to raid one another's ships by positioning themselves effectively in space)[14] and *MAD Countdown* (a game created by Steffen Walz and colleagues in which players try to locate a bomb hidden in London)—offer an additional spin on the professional role-playing games developed at MIT and the University of Wisconsin–Madison. Like epistemic games, these games seek to use digital gaming technologies to re-create field experiences for participants. However, these games are less concerned with re-creating the *epistemic frame* of the professional practice and more concerned with using gaming devices, mechanics, and modes of interaction to situate the learners in meaningful learning experiences that prepare them for participating in twenty-first-century society. Specifically, they seek to immerse players in complex problem-solving spaces in which they must think creatively and collaboratively with a suite of digital tools.

The MIT/Madison team (led by Eric Klopfer and me) has produced several iterations of alternate reality role-playing games, using them to teach high school earth sciences, undergraduate environmental engineering, undergraduate scientific writing, and various middle school topics. These games seek to place learners in roles in which they confront authentic challenges central to the domain, providing them access to authentic resources and tools that extend their cognition. All tools and resources are situated within game-play mechanics designed to produce collaboration that scaffolds and supports scientific thinking. In these games, for example, players might try to ascertain the cause of a mysterious death of a friend thought to be caused by environmental health problems, or try to solve a contemporary fictional urban planning dilemma by traveling back in time to interview residents of a neighborhood (see Squire et al.).[15]

These games employ several game-play mechanisms to support learning. One such mechanism is *differentiated roles*, which has kids playing different roles, all with differentiated access to information. While one student may play as a water chemist (gaining access to the data, tools, and resources that a chemist might have), another might be a governmental official (with access to special documents and other data not available to the public). Another mechanism relies on the concept of *contested spaces*, the idea that games are (in part) spatial mediz, and good game contexts can be created by finding spaces that are under contestation (such as places that have experienced urban renewal).

One of the questions driving this line of research is: Can quasi-fictional contexts relating to one's physical place create the kind of engagement one finds in fictional games? In other words, could asking "What would be the health effects of a TCE spill on one's college campus?" create an emotionally compelling, educationally productive learning context? Emerging research suggests that these quasi-fictional contexts can be emotionally engaging.[16] Although these pilot tests are still relatively limited, lasting two to four hours in duration, evidence gathered in game play and shared in postinterviews suggests that players willingly adopt the roles of water chemists, environmental scientists, or investigators in game play. None of the players expressed any hesitancy in adopting fictional roles, or in entering the fictional context, and indeed reported that they enjoyed doing so. As one student commented, the learning experience was actually *more* authentic than school, as it allowed him to get a semirealistic view of the profession. Much like entertainment RPGs, players found the opportunity to enter roles where they participated in interactive narratives composed of sequences of problem-solving tasks fun and challenging. In particular, these games seemed to offer productive contexts for engaging students in scientific argumentation. Just as *World of Warcraft* players debate the merits of particular character builds and strategies as a part of their game play, players in our games debate problems of a scientific nature, arguing over the causes of problems introduced in the game, weighing theory and evidence, and judging the merits of counterarguments. These early studies suggest that such narratively driven games can engage kids in problem solving that overlaps with academic content in a productive manner. Of course, there are other factors involved (in particular, the fun of leaving the classroom or making cognitive connections between academic content and local place).

Open-Ended Simulation Games

The previous examples suggest the potential of targeted and role-playing game formats to support learning. We might also consider two other relatively unexplored genres: (1) massively multiplayer online (MMO)—or persistent world—games and (2) open-ended simulation games. Neither genre has been particularly explored for use in education, even though several educational projects—typically billed as multiuser virtual environments (MUVEs)—use some of the key features of MMOs. Virtual worlds, such as *River City*,[17] include fully 3D worlds with multiple avatars copresent, along with the ability to communicate via text-based chat. *Quest Atlantis*[18] uses similar technologies, although *Quest Atlantis* is designed explicitly as a *transmedia* property, using playing cards, novels, and various other digital and nondigital media to present the world. Further, *Quest Atlantis* attempts to tie in-game challenges to out-of-game experiences and—critically—is available 24/7 so that players can log on from anytime, anywhere, making it closer to a true "persistent" world than any other system discussed so far.

Rather than focus on MMOs, this chapter tackles the second category mentioned: open-ended simulation games (or sandbox games)—games that have open-ended worlds, through which there is no one single, correct pathway. Sandbox games are known for their status as contexts for creative player expression, with multiple solution paths (their quality is judged according to their ability to deliver such an experience) as opposed to their ability to create a more-or-less common experience. As a rule of thumb, if a game has many spots where a player can say to another, "remember where you did *x*," then the game is a role-playing game, not a sandbox game. Many targeted games, such as abstract puzzle games with a high degree of emergence, also have this particular quality.

In this chapter, I will consider two games, *Civilization III* and *Grand Theft Auto: San Andreas* (hereafter called *GTA* when referring to a game in the series generically, and *GTA: SA* when referring to the *San Andreas* title specifically). Admittedly, these games are typically classified in different genres (perhaps the action/adventure and turn-based strategy categories). However, from a design-for-learning standpoint, they share several critical qualities. Both require over one hundred hours for anything close to "completion." Structurally, completion isn't an operative term in *Civilization*, as most players continue playing and replaying the game until they get bored. Similarly, one can finish a *GTA* game, but few actually do. And when they do, picking the game up to run races, orchestrate chase scenes, or generally muck about town are commonplace events.

Open-ended games typically place one in a role of sorts (such as the leader of a civilization). Despite this, the game is less about assuming a particular type of identity (say a SWAT team member, or a science journalist in an epistemic role-playing game), and more about inhabiting a world from a general perspective, which the player can play out in whatever manner suits his or her taste. In these games, learning resembles a process of coming to understand a system, experimenting with multiple ways of being within that system, and then using that system for creative expression, usually enacted within communities of other players. The game structure is less about reproducing a particular way of thinking and more about creating spaces for knowledge creation and discovery. This chapter seeks first to understand how open-ended games work, in order then to design learning spaces based on their qualities and characteristics.

Secondly, this chapter seeks to link research and theory on how open-ended games operate (taking the *Civilization* series and *GTA: SA* as its starting points) and then works to build theories of game-based learning environments on them. This is not, nor should it be, the only theory of game-based learning. In particular, I will argue for similar theories for targeted (or conceptual) games, role-playing games, and persistent world games (see table 1). Key variables differentiating these genres might include time to completion, replayability, and degrees of open-ended problem solving (i.e., is there one right solution or are there multiple acceptable solution paths?). Notice that this is not a traditional genre grouping in that it does not distinguish by content (science fiction vs. elves and orcs, for example).[19] This framework tries to sidestep many of the debates in game studies by acknowledging that there are substantial differences between and across game genres (as depicted in table 1), and that different theories may be required to explain how learning operates in each domain.

Several aspects of this framework are worth noting. First, it seeks to outline the typical *timescale* in which a player plays the game. Targeted games typically are played for one to eight hours, consuming a week or so of game time (with *Tetris* or *Bejeweled* being perhaps exceptions in that many players have spent hours upon hours with them). In contrast, a sandbox game such as *Civilization* operates more like a hobby (to borrow from Will Wright's excellent taxonomy), in that players invest hundreds of hours in them and come back to them over the years, playing them multiple times, using them as content creation tools or as spaces to revise continually.

As a result, this chapter argues that open-ended simulation games function as *possibility spaces* for their players to try on, inhabit, and ultimately develop new identities with

Table 1
Framework for examining different games

Game genre	Time to completion	Timescale	Open-endedness	Modes of creative expression	Educational examples
Targeted games (puzzles, minigames)	1–4 hours	Weeks	Low	Style of completion; level creation	*Supercharged*
Linear games (*Viewtiful Joe, Ninja Gaiden*)	20–40 hours	Month	Low	Style of completion, machinema	*Full Spectrum Warrior*; epistemic games
Open-ended, sandbox games	100–200 hours played over multiple months	2–24 months	High	Style of completion, multiple solution paths, modding	*Civ, Sim City*
Persistent worlds (*WoW, Everquest*)	500+ hours	6–48 months	High	Modding, social engineering, game play	*Quest Atlantis*

trajectories for participation that extend out of the game world and into new spaces. The games themselves are not stories, nor just abstract rule systems, but *worlds* built according to (implicit or explicit) values, visions, and ideas, which I call *ideological worlds*. Players develop knowledge through performances in them, the meanings of which are then reflected upon, negotiated, and given legitimacy through participation in *interpretive communities*. These interpretive communities range from the small and informal (like families and friends) to large and highly structured (like Apolyton University, which will be discussed later in this chapter). As learning contexts, these sandbox games function as design *possibility spaces* for people, spaces wherein they can develop along trajectories of experience into new ways of knowing, learning, and being in the world. Critically, they contain multiple trajectories of experiences, offering multiple trajectories into the space, multiple modes of interaction within the space, and multiple trajectories outward (see figure 1).

In order to understand more fully the details of this model, a general theory of learning for sandbox games must be put forth, which also suggests a model of instruction. That is a primary goal of this chapter, one I will meet by first examining the meanings that groups of game players make around one sandbox game (*GTA: SA*), specifically by investigating how players make meanings around depictions and race in the game. This analysis suggests how differences in play style, prior experience, and participation in interpretive communities function to legitimize and support interpretations of play, and how game experiences become models-to-think-within players' lives. Second, I will review early attempts to build a game-based learning program around *Civilization III* in school-based settings, emphasizing both how sandbox games can function as a model-to-think-with in academic domains and how these learning experiences are mediated by social norms (perhaps for the worst as school cultures intervene in learning). Third, I will describe a cognitive ethnography of Apolyton University, an online community of game players dedicated to furthering their knowledge

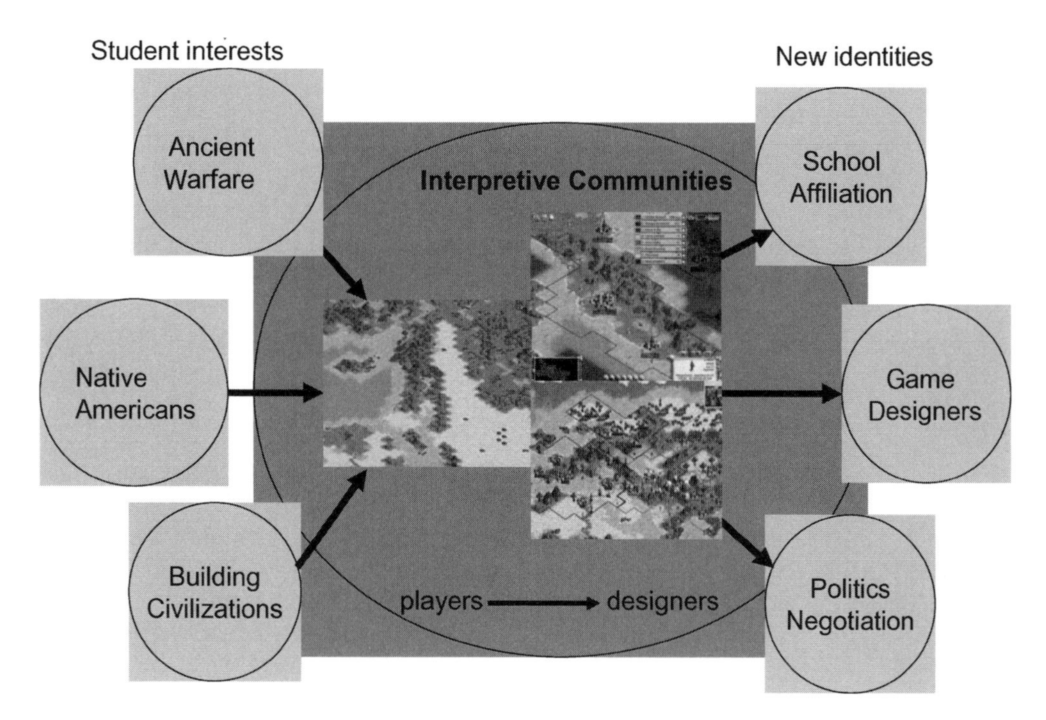

Figure 1
Depiction of students' movement into and through "Centers of expertise." The first phase involves the game activating an interest in players/students. The three interests included here are typical, although other common ones include caring for people, competitive gaming, and geography. We have adopted a model in which all students begin with the same initial scenarios, mapped to traditional academic standards (e.g., early civilizations), designed to appeal to broad interests. As players progress through our program, they encounter any number of games. (Students who enter the program "mid-semester" typically start by playing with friends or just joining whatever game is in progress.) Often, the game scenarios are designed by the students themselves, either to try out ahypothetical concepts ("What if I give the Scandinavians iron and horses?") or just to entertain their friends ("I thought Levi would like playing as the Russians in this one"). Interpretations of game events happen in situ, within the community, both during game play (e.g., "You don't want to give the Egyptians horses because of their war chariots") and afterward (e.g., "You should have never given up Europe to the Romans"). Because these interpretations are built on histories and ideas that have a "life" of their own (e.g., everyone in this program knows that Roman legionaries will dominate the middle part of the ancient scenario), this is referred to as an interpretive *community*. The process results in kids filtering out of the program with new identities, which include school affiliations and interest in advanced game design.

of *Civilization III*, emphasizing the underlying mechanisms that drive this community and suggesting particular models for how online communities might function in the future. Last, I will examine my current work designing afterschool programs for *Civilization*-playing students, seeking to tie together these themes into an integrated model of instruction appropriate for the digital age. Underlying this approach is an attempt to tie together studies of gamers and gaming culture, game design work modifying commercial computer games, and educational design research orchestrating social events around them.

Playing Race, Gender, and Class in *GTA: SA*

I want those diamonds. My people need the bling!

—Honovi, a twelve-year-old African American youth describing his efforts to obtain gems while playing *Civilization*.[20]

After hearing Honovi describe his efforts to obtain diamonds for his people, I realized he and I were not playing the same game of *Civilization*. Whereas I saw such luxuries as tools for appeasing my people, Honovi's language reflected a vivid visualization of material wealth. Perhaps Honovi's interest in "bling" even reflected the role of jewelery in his African American community in communicating wealth and status. Either way, this exchange and others like it suggested important differences in the kinds of experiences that Honovi and I might find compelling in a video game. Our research team became interested in what games he played outside of school. As with most of the poor, African American kids with whom I have worked, *Civilization* is not something that they typically have at home (although many have *Age of Empires*). When asked what he played, Honovi enthusiastically responded, *GTA: SA*. We asked what Honovi liked about *GTA: SA* and his response surprised us. Honovi didn't mention the ability to steal cars or commit crimes, but rather the way he could design cars and race them throughout the streets (perhaps a power fantasy relating to his personal lifeworld). To find out just what kinds of game experiences Honovi enjoyed, and what kind of meanings he took away from them, particularly as they relate to controversies surrounding violent game play, we decided to interview Honovi and his friends about their game experiences with *GTA: SA*.

GTA: SA is the fifth game in the *GTA* series. The game is set in the 1990s, in three regions mapping roughly to Los Angeles, San Francisco, and Las Vegas. The player inhabits the character of Carl Johnson, a black man who is returning to *San Andreas* to attend his slain mother's funeral. The player is handed a bicycle, which he is told to ride home. After the first mission, however, the players are more-or-less free to do as they please (although most of the verbs available involve shooting or driving). To be sure, there is a particular version of LA depicted in *San Andreas*; the streets of *San Andreas* are violent places ripe with gang warfare. Certain actions—for instance, hitting a drug dealer—are rewarded with money, while others—such as having a conversation with him—are not. One is generally safe in his or her own territory—on home turf in the hood. But as the game progresses and one develops a reputation, other factions become violent toward the player. To survive in *GTA: SA*, players need to learn to read these elements and their interactions as part of the underlying rule systems that make up the game.

Whose Game Are We Playing? Open-Endedness and Multiple Modes of Game Play

Over the next year, Ben Devane and I[21] interviewed Honovi, several of his friends, and other groups of *GTA: SA* players about their experiences with the game. We were particularly interested in how they would respond to recent political controversies surrounding the game. In interviews with us, Honovi described his game play as extending his interests in hip-hop culture and automotive design—a practice he valued both socially (he had friends who had pimped-out cars) and economically (as a future profession). Honovi made extensive use of the car customization features in the game, and for Honovi, *GTA: SA* was a space where he could pursue an interest, develop expertise, and show off his skills to his friends. Honovi also made wide-ranging use of cheats, as they enabled him to pursue these interests without the "artificial" limitations of the game design rules (i.e., you need complete missions to earn money to buy car parts). For Honovi, the game was as much a "car detailing simulation" as anything.

But when grouped with friends, Honovi's responses to our question differed. Honovi talked about the game as a space for performing impressive (often violent) feats, pulling off stunts, driving erratically, or "capping" people, which he did while playing with his friends. When surrounded by older males, Honovi's retelling of his game play was a performance of American urban masculinity. In the telling, Honovi showed relatively little interest in the missions or storyline, but rather seemed to use the game as a way of participating in a discourse of masculinity. Honovi and his friends enjoyed swapping tales of daring do, whether it be pulling off a difficult driving stunt or completing a difficult mission. When queried, Honovi and friends had little concern for questions about race or violence, and little interest in discussing it. Retelling game exploits within the company of friends and adults generated a discourse of adolescent male gaming performance.

For Honovi, the game was a sandbox, a set of representations and behaviors with which he could play and which he could use to express himself. Game play itself was a performance, one that arose in context, shaped—in part—by the other participants in the gaming experience (such as those who might be huddled around the television watching). When played alone, the iconography and experiences presented allowed Honovi to perform an identity of an automobile designer, an identity that affords status within his community and ties to identities to which he aspires. When played socially, the same iconography was leveraged to display other aspects of his identity. These experiences suggest that, for players, there is no *one* game that is played. Different game-play models and experiences are activated by play in different contexts. Similarly, discussions of game play are activated by different discourses. As researchers, parents, political leaders, and journalists attempt to study games, it is critical that we remember that games are not texts, but contexts that emerge from the intersection of representations in the game, players' goals, and the social contexts in which they are embedded. Significantly, *how* people talk about their game play depends on these variables as well.

Games as Competitive Spaces: The Differing Cultural Models of Games

To better understand how different groups of players make sense of their game play, we conducted a series of interviews with fourteen- to fifteen-year-old avid *GTA: SA* players (all of whom were white) from a working class neighborhood located a few miles away from where Honovi lives. Inspired by how Honovi played *GTA: SA*, our goal was to learn how different kids from different social groups thought about race, class, and violence in their game play. All of the players were serious fans of the series, with each having spent at least one hundred hours playing the game. Like Honovi, play of the game was used as an opportunity for performance and expertise; unlike Honovi, their performance privileged gaming skill, particularly as manifested through an ability to complete missions by driving and shooting with accuracy. They also valued encyclopedic knowledge of various locations, names, and features in *GTA: SA*. In short, this was a gaming culture of *expertise*.

We asked these gamers about their impressions of race and violence to see if they were any more concerned about violence than Honovi and his friends had been, looking to see if perhaps their particular backgrounds affected their read of the game space. When asked about the violence in the game, these players responded that they were a little concerned that other "crazy kids" may play the game and become violent, although they were personally unaware of anyone who would be at risk. They were more concerned about racial depictions in the game, particularly around stereotypes. The following exchange typifies their discourse.

Gamer 1: Your main character just got out of jail, a black dude in LA joining back up with a gang. All the gang members the skinny guy and the fat guy smoking bowls and passing shit. It's so stereotypical.

Gamer 2: Dude all the other *GTAs* are stereotypical. They're about Italian Americans and stuff. I heard that *Vice City* had one line that was really controversial. Kill all the Haitians. He was being like "genocide." It wasn't bullshit that they threw in there. There was controversy between those two groups in New York. When I played *Vice City*, it was like being in the movie *Scarface*. Same movie, same city. They are all the same ones in *Scarface*. You pretty much live in the same house it's all down to the detail. When I played *SA*, the first movie I thought of was *Menace to Society*. All their names are all brought from those characters.

Here we see a relatively sophisticated discourse surrounding racial representations. They see and identify stereotypes in the game borrowed from media, and perhaps even enjoy finding them. They read the game off of previous films in a similar genre, and—in short—enjoy their role as sophisticated media consumers.

As the conversation continues, the players talk about the game, this time in regard to design issues, within the context of the game as a competitive space:

Gamer 3: They've taken the storyline, characters, the way they act and the surrounding area and made it into a game. They're trying to sell games. . . . Each gang person has, they have their own colors so that you can see a group of people. Like, if I run over there, I can kill those people but not another. Gangs are more represented by the colors than race.

Gamer 2: They do it more so it's obvious to the player. They're not sneaking things in.

For these players, interpretations of representations of race and violence were ultimately filtered through their understanding of the game *as a competitive space*. Gangs, colors, and ethnicities were largely "window dressing" (cf., Koster)[22] designed to facilitate game play. From a game design perspective, one might say that they saw racial representations serving as mechanisms providing clear feedback on the state of the system to players. Through these passages, we see how their interpretations of the game experience are rooted in the design of the game as a rule system, designed to provide feedback to players about their actions. We can also see how these meanings are interpreted and negotiated through social interaction, as the players' experiences are colored by participation in an interpretive community of gamers.

Identity, Experience, and Interpretation in Game Play

We interviewed a third group of high school gamers, all African American working poor, and all dedicated *GTA: SA* players. These players played in a variety of ways, unlocking missions, using cheats, and discussing specific points in the game. They were somewhat reluctant to talk with us, and would do so only after we demonstrated (through talk) that we had played hundreds of hours of *GTA* ourselves. There are many reasons this could be, but we believe that this may be because playing games, particularly *GTA: SA*, is usually looked down upon by adults and the politically contentious. As other games researchers have reported,[23] revealing one's gaming experience seems like an important step in gaining trust with gamers around games that are socially marginalized. Race and class differences between us—as researchers and participants—only exacerbate these issues. Having knowledge of the game gave us a context for understanding comments, and allowed us to follow up with participants to probe areas, such as asking them if they got to the "model airplane" mission that occurs late in the game. Although these guidelines are typical for participant observers in qualitative research while doing ethnography, they may extend to interview-type studies with gamers.[24]

The third group of players expressed even less concern than the other groups about the game violence, and—in fact—were more concerned about the "real" violence in their neighborhoods. For them, *GTA* was "realistic" in mapping ethnic, economic and social segregation onto space, and they were happy to see a game speaking to their cultural landscape. In particular, these gamers enjoyed the references to hip-hop music and fashion. The gamers spoke favorably about the game's choices in radio stations, cars, and characters. As one player commented, "It's got great radio stations and awesome cars." Interestingly, the early 1990s hip-hop that forms *GTA: SA*'s core culture is as much the music of their parents as it is theirs.

Unlike Honovi or the second group of gamers interviewed, this group was particularly attentive to the *structural* forms of racism in the game, raising critical questions about how easily one could become economically mobile in the game, buying a house and moving out of the ghetto. When asked what was unrealistic about the game, they responded that the way that blacks could save to buy a house and eventually move to the suburbs was the "most unrealistic." They were particularly concerned that white kids might develop false impressions about economic mobility for African Americans in the United States. As one participant said, "A black man can't just save a few dollars and go buy a house in a white neighborhood." They did appreciate how the game modeled racial and ethnic tensions by neighborhood. "You drive your car in the wrong neighborhood, like in Sherwood Hills [an affluent suburb near them], and you're going to get pulled over or in trouble," one reported. To what extent these assertions are true in Madison, Wisconsin (or anywhere), is beside the issue; for these kids, a game about race, violence, and car culture was tremendously exciting and provided an interesting framework for talking about very real social issues.

These same kids were very *uninterested* in talking about violence in the game. They perceived game violence as unrealistic, at least compared to the violence they experience in their neighborhoods. As one said, "Stuff like that happens, you know. The game isn't going to make you do anything like that." These kids knew of both youth and adults engaged in various forms of violent crime, and to them, it was almost insulting to suggest that access to a video game about violence, race, class, and material goods (i.e., cars), rather than *actual* ethnic tensions, widespread access to guns, and segregation and poverty, was causative of violence in their real lives. In other words, these kids found it somewhat bizarre that we would ask them about violent video games (and their parents' attitudes toward them) when there were clearly many more tangible causes of and forms of violence in their lives (i.e. poverty, drugs, lack of economic mobility). Part of what we found fascinating about *GTA: SA* is that these players seemed able to construct a fairly serious critique of the current socioeconomic order in the United States, developing *through play* seedlings of a structural theory of how race and class are reproduced in contemporary America (tied to property values) that could be explored further.

These three groups of gamers illustrate how interactions among players' identity, expertise, desires, and game play manifest themselves in game experience. *GTA: SA* spoke to gamers' desires for achievement, game experiences in their cultural landscape, pursuit of hobbies and interests (e.g., car customization), and display of masculinity. Each of these desires contributes to the emergent meaning of the game experience, making the player himself, in a very real sense, a part of the game experience and the resultant meanings. Examining them, it's evident that with a game like *GTA: SA*, there is no *one* game out there that anyone plays; in fact, even within groups, participants reported finding new things to do with the game and new ways to play it. This notion—that there is no "one" game out there to be played in open-ended sandbox games like *GTA*—presents both opportunities and challenges for educators seeking to use such games for learning.

Open-Ended Games Functioning as Possibility Spaces

Following this model, games can be thought of as possibility spaces, spaces in which we can live, experiment, and play for different reasons and with different outcomes. Even the most "open-ended" of games are imbued with potential meanings instantiated in rule systems and representations. Players learn the rules of the system, using them as a backdrop to play off of, a context to perform within, rather than as a stable system of meaning that they're "inculcated" with. The specific meanings of any play experience are negotiated within interpretive communities, which overlap and extend into broader cultural discourses. To understand the meanings of game play, within both open-ended and other forms of games, we can't just look at the rules; we need to look at players' performances and understand *their* understandings of them. This suggests that a mature theory of communication and media in gaming will draw on performance theories as much as on traditional media theory. From these players, we can see how meaning making occurs in relation to their experiences and lifeworlds; interpretations build off and extend their own concerns.

For those with an interest in educational experiences via games, we see that educators and game designers share some common characteristics. Both are tasked with an interesting second-order design problem: How to create spaces that ultimately exist for people to do interesting things?[25] Good games are vehicles for player expression. From this perspective, designers face the task of choreographing the rules, representations, and roles for players—in other words, the contexts in which players can generate meaning.[26] Educators attempt to establish worldviews that we want students to understand, be they those of a scientist, Maori tribe member, or ancient Roman. But if much of the interpretive work occurs within interpretive communities, then a challenge for educators is how to design social structures that effectively support students' learning, in much the same way that many game developers design in features that produce socializing. A potential paradox arises as educators seek to reconcile game players' multiple ways of and reasons for being engaged in games, with the divergent learning outcomes that are likely to occur as a result.

Thus, an interesting set of opportunities and tensions emerges. On the one hand, open-ended sandbox games appear to be a productive space for studying and designing game-based learning environments. On the other hand, the particular learning outcomes that result seem to rely heavily on players' experiences. We might consider *why* they're playing and what kinds of interests they bring into the game world color their experiences of it, along with the particular kinds of interpretations they draw. The *GTA* example showed how working-class white students focused on racial representations, while a group of working poor African American students focused on structural issues of race. Drawing on the example of Honovi, we see these interpretations not necessarily as the only ones to be drawn from the game, but ones that were activated through social interactions with researchers and peers. Imagine what kinds of productive dialogue might result from a dialogue across these groups.

The next section of this chapter focuses on efforts to design learning systems around such open-ended games, particularly the *Civilization* series. It focuses on what kinds of interpretations players make from the game, and the use of the game as a model to think about history *and* the design of social systems around the gaming experience. In both cases, games function as possibility spaces for students. We can think of these possibility spaces in at least two ways: (1) as *intellectual* play spaces where players can explore the interplay of historical ideas, much as the *GTA* players used *GTA* as a way of thinking through race and class, and (2) as *identity* play spaces where players develop new identities as game players. These identities may include status as expert players, competitive players, members of guilds, teams, and other social roles, such as modders or machinema directors. The section closes by arguing for open-ended game-based learning environments as productive for deeply transformative learning, learning where one develops a new identity that can impact one's identities in school and in the home as well.

Designing Gaming Communities for Learning

Over the past five years, several colleagues at the University of Wisconsin–Madison and I have been investigating the potential of the *Civilization* series to support learning in social studies (particularly geography, politics, and history). In *Civilization*, players lead a civilization from 4000 BC to the present. Players utilize natural resources, build cities, trade, and—of course—wage war, giving rise to situations such as civilizations negotiating (and perhaps warring) over scarce resources such as oil. As such, the central features of the game system present an argument for the fates of civilizations as largely governed by geographical and materialist processes, an argument also made by Jared Diamond[27] in his Pulitzer Prize–winning *Guns, Germs, and Steel*, but perhaps with a greater emphasis on political negotiation.

Pedagogically, the game offers an interesting reframing of history from one organized around "grand narratives" to one marked by themes and patterns, a method of teaching world history advocated by an increasing number of educators.[28] In fact, the geographical and materialist underpinnings to the model serve as a healthy contrast to those made available at school, where most students are presented a story of the steady march of Western liberty, democracy, and rationality.[29] In contrast, *Civilization III* can offer a story of advantageous geographical conditions that provide access to global trade networks, resources, technologies, and limited opportunities for population expansion. The game also offers opportunities to think about broad domestic decisions (e.g., guns vs. butter) and foreign policy decisions (e.g., isolationism vs. trade).

A number of educators and critics have raised valid concerns that what players learn from games is not the properties of complex systems, but simple heuristics, such as always keep two spearmen in every city. The fear is that, without access to the underlying model, students will fail to recognize simulation bias or the "hidden curriculum" of what is left out.[30] Which biases, or aspects of the game's ideological system, do players interpret, and which parts do they fail to notice? In *GTA: SA,* we saw that players' different experiences of race and class influenced how they interpreted the game systems. What basis do players use to make these distinctions? These concerns point to theoretical questions core to learning sciences and game studies, in terms of how players interpret game experiences, what they might learn from these experiences, and how they make judgments in applying them back to the world.

Multiple Forms of Engagement and Diverse Practices in Open-Ended Games in School Settings

In my dissertation, *Replaying History*, I used *Civilization III* both in a high school class and in an afterschool setting to investigate these questions. The goal of the project was to help students use game experiences to think about why civilizations grow, flourish, and fade, and how wars, revolutions, and civilizations' evolution are the products of interweaving geographical, social, economic, and political forces. Ross Dunn[31] has called this approach to world history the "patterns of change" model, whereby world history is presented as patterns of human activity across broad timescales, as opposed to traditional national or "western civilization" history.

How students became drawn into the game space was a complex phenomenon, occurring at the intersection of personal goals and fantasies, the possibility space of *Civilization III* as a simulation, a desire to learn world history through the game, and at times, the social pressure to complete the presentation for the other classes. Whereas some players readily took to the game as a fun and interesting way of learning world history, others were motivated by a desire to compete with others or impress friends, while others simply wanted to do whatever it took to get good grades. Most of the players *did* become engaged with the game at some point. Different "hooks" worked with different players, including a desire to explore, to build, to maximize the game rules, to nurture their civilizations (much like pets), and to transgress the rules of history and school, in part by playing in antisocial ways.

Specific game practices differed among these players as well. Some players spent hours opening maps and exploring new territories; others were in constant negotiation with other civilizations. Some students turned the game into a colonial simulation, investigating the forces contributing to cross-Atlantic colonization. Others used the game as a global historical simulation, enjoying playing events and then comparing them against historical accounts. And as we saw in the play of *GTA: SA*, these different play styles seemed to emerge from the players themselves, as they played the game. One girl, for example, was primarily interested in protecting her people, the Egyptians. When the Greeks settled in Northern Africa, she was forced to learn more about the military aspects of the game, which led her to learn about economics (she needed to research new technologies to stay ahead), and eventually geography, as she realized that she needed to locate Greece on the map, create a military force to enter its borders, and negotiate from a stronger position. Perhaps ironically, this self-avowed pacifist ended up mostly engaging in war. Another student took great interest in the colonization of Australia, and enjoyed examining how well the game did or did not simulate European–indigenous interactions. Most of the students approached the game with vague goals and interests, and then developed deeper interest in particular areas. For example, another student became interested in the geography of Alaska as a result of emergent phenomena in game play.

For other players, game play was largely a social experience, and they explained the pleasure of gaming as largely one of socializing with friends. Other groups (particularly middle-school girls) used the game as a context for competition, comparing which player had the most money, allies, cities, or percent of the globe explored. These girls became expert political negotiators, understanding aspects of the political system unknown to the teachers and researchers. (As an example, they realized that one could determine the relative advancement of a civilization by seeing its clothing.) Cedric, a talkative, easily distracted student, was an excellent example of this style of play. He spent much of his time walking about the room, examining different students' games. When asked what he was doing, he usually framed his answer in terms of another student's game, saying things like, "trying to keep up with Dwayne" or "trying to get cavalry like Tony." Much like Bartle's (1996) socializers, Cedric was frequently a conduit for information, sharing knowledge about Dwayne's game (such as effective military strategies) with students like Tony. Much as other game theorists have argued that game play is social, for each of these kids, their game-play practices could only be understood as socially situated practices, being affected and constituted by their local contexts.[32]

The fact that any player's particular interest in a game often emerges once play begins raises important questions for educators, as it suggests that a core value of open-ended games for learning could be their capacity to open up *new* academic interests, rather than relying on prespecified, standardized teaching objectives. Although most of these *Civ* players could now pass a test on basic geography (especially the "explorers"), not all could. Some students engaged in intricate diplomatic maneuvering, luring allies into war and manipulating historical enemies for their own gain. These students developed strong understandings of political negotiations, which might serve as excellent preparation for a political science course, but not every student investigated these aspects of the game.[33] If open-ended games like *Civilization* open many new academic interests for their players, part of this success is due to the fact that they enable players to explore different aspects of the simulation game according to their own interests. While this can be seen as a strength, it also creates problems for learning contexts requiring fixed objectives.

Identity, Experience, and Interpretations of World History

Many students ultimately turned *Civilization III* into a colonial simulation, which affected the kinds of questions students asked of the civilization (e.g., could Native Americans have "discovered" China, changing global politics?), thereby affecting their observations and interpretations of history. Students interpreted from the game model that civilizations conquered others due to particular geographic properties yielding military advantage, access to global trade networks, access to key natural resources, and particular diplomatic strategies (e.g., trading is generally better than isolationism), not due to specific cultural or genetic traits. As people marginalized within the narrative of Western progress typically taught in schools, this interpretation certainly spoke to them.

Surprising to the researchers, these students already held fairly materialist views of world history. In preinterviews, they were asked to read critiques of U.S. foreign policy arguing that it was historically motivated by a desire to secure natural resources and create alliances to protect these interests, rather than any interest in spreading democracy. Every student who participated in interviews agreed with these statements, with most citing the conquest of Native Americans and the war in Iraq as examples of American imperialism. Playing *Civilization III* gave them a better sense of how, where, and why these resources gained importance throughout history. As an example, students were surprised to learn about the historical importance of rubber. A few enjoyed "replaying" American imperialism as they sought to colonize South America for access to rubber. For these students, all of whom identified themselves as marginalized by traditional historical narratives, there was a transgressive pleasure in reenacting imperialist American foreign policy under the guise of "spreading democracy." As one student commented, "I *owe* it to these savages to conquer them. Think how happier they'll be in my civilization." The class laughed aloud at the obvious satire, particularly in light of current events with the Iraq War.

There was no evidence, however, that these game experiences *changed* students' ethical beliefs about war. In postinterviews, some stated that the game taught them that war was always futile. A majority of students held onto prior beliefs about the ethics of war and colonization. For example, most maintained that the Europeans were basically "evil," and—in contrast—Native Americans were essentially pacifists. Notably, the game does nothing to confront these naive beliefs about civilizations, nor particular historical events (although in class, we did discuss the atrocities committed by the Spanish conquistadors, which perhaps underscored these sentiments).

Indeed, many students who rejected traditional school-based curricula as "heritage" or cultural myths of "western progress" found that *Civilization* allowed them to "replay history" and learn history through geographical materialist lenses rather than the ideology of Western progress. In one discussion, students reported what it is they learned through playing *Civilization III*:

Dwayne: Unifying Africa made us powerful. . . . Politics and geography. I got all of these resources then I could trade them with other countries. So it made my politics stronger.

Tony: It makes more production. Everyone can work faster and more efficiently.

Teacher: [Leading the organization activity] Where should we put that; In what pile?

Tony: Well, in some ways, they're all related to each other. [General nodding]

Teacher: That could be one thing we learned. How would you write that?

Tony: Well, money is the key . . . money is the root to everything. With money you can save yourself from war, and that also means that politics . . . with money, that ties everything together. Luxuries buy you money and money buys you everything. The right location gives you luxuries, gives you income. More income gives you technology, which affects your politics. It all connects.

Kent: Geography affects your diplomacy because it gets your more resources and affects how they treat you.

Tony: Geography can affect the growth of your civilization.

Dwayne: It affects your war.

As students played the game and discussed it in class, they began to recognize its underlying ideological framework—one that privileges geographic location, access to trade networks, technology, and negotiation. (One might also argue efficient management. See Friedman, 1999 for a good analysis of *Civilization* as a designed artifact and game experience.) For Tony, the model proffered by the game offered a good explanation of why Native American civilizations were conquered by Europeans, rather than vice versa.

Open-Ended Games Remediating Historical Understandings

However, open-ended games also remediate games in ways that educators ought to consider more deeply. When asked to describe what he learned from this unit, Tony commented, "I learned that, no matter how it plays out, history plays by the same set of rules." To paraphrase McLuhan, if the medium is the message, then the message for Tony was that history could be treated as the results of a rule-based simulation—the rules of which are the underlying "content" of history, not the subsequent events. This idea, while foreign to most historians, is actually the core intellectual enterprise of world historians, who seek to identify broad patterns across thousands of years of history.[34] Other students said that ultimately they were learning about management. "We're learning about managing civilizations... You worry about how much you spend on science compared to how much on money."

For these students, it was impossible to achieve any success in the game without learning some basic relationships between politics, economics, and geography. Tony described the interactive nature of *Civilization* as a game. (The fact that it pushes back on their understandings through consequences tied to their actions was central.) "Playing the game forces you to learn about the material. It actually forces you to learn about other civilizations in order to survive." Tony explains his impression of what he learned from the game:

Interviewer: Do you think that playing *Civilization* taught you anything about social studies?

Tony: I think it did. I always knew that certain locations helped certain people; but with this, I have a better understanding of it. In some ways, I have a better idea of, like, if you're in the middle of a forest. Sure there's a lot of things there, but your civilization doesn't grow that quickly and money is hard to come by. That affects population, the mood of your civilization, and food...

Interviewer: In class, you said that geography affects politics, which affects history. Could you talk more about that?

Tony: Well, if you're next to the ocean, that's a good place for any city to be: It has food, water, the climate would be moderate, and that's a good place for a city to flourish. If you have luxuries around water, that brings in trade—brings in money, so that you can talk with other Civilizations. If you have enough money, you can buy a lot of things and you can sell a lot of things.

Tony: Geography is the main game. Because if you're in the mountains... In my other game I started next to the mountains and next to the water as well, and the water was the only thing sustaining me was in the water. I'm secluded from everything else, but the barbarians snuck in, and everyone else sort of hates us because we're weak people and they won't share whatever they have. They only come in when I find something good. Then they start calling me. Do you want to trade this?

Tony: When you're isolated, it's good and bad. In some ways it's good because you don't really have any enemies; you flourish. It's kind of bad because you develop at a slower pace.

As players experienced events in-game, they developed narrative accounts of events (e.g., "My cities died because I didn't have access to enough food"). Through extended play across several games, coupled with debriefing, these narratives became more like theories of the game system (e.g., cities flourish near water resources). Players were later able to discuss the utility of this theoretical model in more abstract situations and apply it to thinking about historical situations and current events—such as the Iraq War—but time limitations prevented querying these understandings further. As such, a key cognitive value of such open-ended games may be in giving players models with which to think.

Civilization III suggests how an open-ended game designed according to particular ideas—in this case a geographic materialist view of history—can function as a model that players use to think with. Because they are performing within that system, actively building and testing ideas about its nature, players are able to build robust theories of how it behaves—theories far more sophisticated than the sorts of simplistic understandings characterized by others in the literature.[35] As students build and discuss these interpretations in social contexts, they reflect on their understandings and mobilize them as tools with which to think. In much the same way that the meanings ascribed to *GTA: SA* by players were transformed by the context of play, the meaning of *Civilization* for players was shaped through its play. It is important to note that this was a designed context, one in which students were encouraged to ask particular questions to their games, compare results, and build theories of game play.

However, students' desire to share stories about their games seemed almost innate. Whereas video games have the reputation of being socially isolating, it is worth noting that, in these cases at least, students were incredibly social, sharing stories about their games; they were also eager to learn from one another's play.

Part of what makes *Civilization* a *game* (rather than a traditional simulation) is that it recruits their interests, passions, and identities as participants, doing so within a context in which they develop expertise at manipulating the forces of history. In short, they were engaged emotionally and experienced success in manipulating complex variables. *Civilization III* gives players concepts with which to think, while also offering them a very real, tangible sense that they could be *good* at something related to school-based history. In our study, disengaged students failing in school were successful at mastering a complex game, developing historical understandings in the process. In postplay interviews, the participating teachers stressed the importance of this outcome for students like Dwayne, who refused to participate in most school-based activities. As one teacher commented, "Dwayne shows up for less than half of his classes, and even when he does, he doesn't do much. This gave him and a few others like him the chance to shine. It might be the only thing he looks forward to all day." *Civilization III* recruited his identity as a hardcore PC gamer (he played a lot of *Diablo II* and *Age of Empires*), allowing him to channel expertise developed in gaming into a productive school-based identity. In this way, games could be an excellent bridging mechanism for disengaged students, particularly adolescent boys, many of whom are labeled ADHD and causing many problems in schools.[36]

Despite these successes, our research revealed several (perhaps predictable) challenges to implementing *Civilization* in school-based scenarios. First, with the time necessary for setup and debrief, the game is difficult to run in forty-five- (or even seventy-five-) minute time blocks. Second, different students had different interest levels in *Civilization*, and the game takes dozens of hours to learn. Third, the divergent play styles and divergent learning outcomes were not necessarily congruent with the demands of school. Finally, learning through game play involves learning through failure (i.e., learning when one loses), a condition that was not always motivating to students.

Finally, the biggest limitation may have been simply that learning history through *Civilization* in this context may have missed the biggest educational potential associated with the game. As I left the study, a number of students seemed to be just scratching the surface of what the game could do. Tony was developing an interest in geography. Wade was interested in designing his own games with the editor. Dwayne was beginning to attend camp regularly, showing his first interest in an academic subject area all year. The teachers commented that, in general, a small group of students was beginning to develop deep, specialized knowledge that they hoped could continue throughout the year.

If we think of games as designed experiences, experiences that are constructed out of performances within ideological worlds interpreted within communities, we have to also acknowledge the *social systems* encompassing game experiences that constrain and shape them. In essence, the designed experience of school—which mandates that students all work at the same pace, where learning is organized by topic area occurring in forty-five-minute blocks along uniform learning outcomes, and where breadth of "exposure" to content is privileged over depth of understanding—greatly shapes the learning that ultimately takes place. Reflecting on the expertise that Tony, Dwayne, Norman, and their classmates were developing with *Civilization III*, it became apparent that perhaps a learning program that offered even more powerful learning trajectories would be valuable. What if Tony were given opportunities to play (and create) different historical scenarios in and out of school? What if he could play games in conjunction with other history assignments? In essence, how might the model of "open-ended" game play be used to design a learning system for an interactive age?

Learning Systems for the Interactive Age

I began looking for new models of what a *Civilization*-based learning program might look like, and soon found it in Apolyton University, a community of *Civilization* players based at Apolyton.net. Formed about a year after the release of *Civilization III*, Apolyton is an informal community of players—not an accredited university—founded to extend players' interest and learning while playing *Civilization III*. While many Apolyton students have met one another offline, all official "university" business is conducted online.

Apolyton University seeks to help players to become more expert *Civilization* players, while also serving to develop in them a sort of *design expertise* whereby players understand how changing particular elements of the game has an impact on other components of the system. Here players are parsing not only the underlying rule system of the game, but the complex set of interrelationships which make up this rule system. Players dissect the game system, modify the underlying rule set for various purposes (usually to improve the game balancing), design their own scenarios to communicate particular ideas, and run their own courses on specific ideas. Given work in literacy studies that argues that the chief goal of education ought to be to create learners with a *design orientation* toward reading, writing, texts, learning, and technology, Apolyton University seemed like a fruitful site for extended study.

In 2004, Levi Giovanetto and I began a year-long ethnography of Apolyton University, in order to understand how it worked formally and socially, so that we could design afterschool programs based on its underlying logic. Specifically, we sought to understand how expert players used *Civilization III*, how interpretive gaming communities functioned within it, and the potential use of its model for learning in educational settings.

Apolyton University: Participatory Education

Apolyton University is run entirely by students and for students, making it even more intriguing. After only two years, Apolyton had generated roughly 23 courses, supported by approximately 100 core members, with an estimated 1,500 lurkers. The core mode of participation took place in forum discussions: Players played a series of collective games of *Civ* at the same time, and posted reflections as they played. This process quickly evolved into the During Action Report (DAR), a mechanism for formally reporting and reflecting on game progress. This format enabled players to reflect while engaging in joint activity with experts, a form of apprenticeship that is known to be especially effective. Players not only gained access to expert cognition, but gained it just in time and when needed on the same tasks.[37] The DAR generated 19,000 posts and boasted a median response time of two to five hours between posts.

The following exchange, occurring in the middle of a discussion about a game scenario, typifies a typical DAR exchange. Earlier in the exchange, Newbie posted a screenshot of his game, qualitative and quantitative descriptions of his game scenario, and a synopsis of how he interprets the current state of his game. He left with a seemingly simple question, asking if he should upgrade his units from knights to cavalry so that he will have an attack strength of "5" compared to "4." (The community had previously identified an "exploit" in the game with knights, which—in the original "stock" game—had a strength of "6," making them overpowered.)

Newbie: (Should I upgrade knights to cavalry) 5/3/3 versus 4/3/2??

Theseus: I'd upgrade in a New York minute. I would upgrade, the question is would I want to research the tech. Remember you will soon be in the next age and have the better units. Especially if you are a scientific civ. Largely the AI will not be a big problem for you at this point with the knight type unit. Of course you will have some games that make that strategy wrong, that is what is good about civ, you cannot do the same thing in all cases. Anyway, I am not presenting this as a sure thing, only as a food for thought, a consideration.

Stuie I think the a-5 still makes the beeline an option, it just won't be as attractive an option, thus opening up other possible avenues for approaching the Middle Era tech tree. As is, I *always* do the beeline to Military Tradition. Reducing the attack by one will force me to consider other options depending on circumstances in my game.

Theseus responded that "yes," of course one would want to upgrade. However, the deeper question is whether it is worth investing the resources in researching the technology required to do so. He contextualized the decision in terms of the broader flow of the game, and then acknowledged some contingencies to be considered, promoting flexible knowledge about the system. Stuie then interjected that upgrading is still a legitimate strategy, and suggested how making this change now simply balances the choices in the Middle Era.

Many students of Apolyton University entered as competent players with advanced understandings of the game system, and left with a design understanding of the underlying rules (see figure 2). The process roughly works as follows: Players enter as advanced (some would say expert), with knowledge of the basic game concepts, terms, and strategies. As advanced players go through the community, they begin identifying exploits, such as the cavalry upgrade. They experiment with various changes to the official stock game rules, such as using the game editing tools to lower the advantages of cavalry, identifying superior strategies. As a community, they formalized these strategies, developing names for particular approaches, like "Alex's archer rush." Next, players mod game play by changing entire rule systems, which takes place in particular courses. Within a course players would remove entire systems, such as the military combat system, or create other rule systems designed to change the game experience radically. For example, in the "Give Peace a Chance" course, players are prohibited from starting wars or going to wars—including committing acts of aggression designed to "irk" the computer-controlled civilizations so that they attack.

If the "designed experience" of school is one built around mass-producing students with "mastery" over a uniform curriculum (or set of standards), the learning system exemplified by Apolyton University is one designed to produce independent, creative problem solvers with an ability (and expectation) of developing new knowledge. In short, as learners, participants of Apolyton's "curriculum" are not just consumers of information, but knowledge producers as well. Further, the university is open to anyone, regardless of age or credentialing. Advanced learners and newcomers learn side by side. The learning space is organized not just around transmitting information, but also around discovering *new* information. Everyday, participants have opportunities for taking responsibility for the learning of the group, in the form of proposing changes to the stock game rules (or curriculum), or even entire courses.

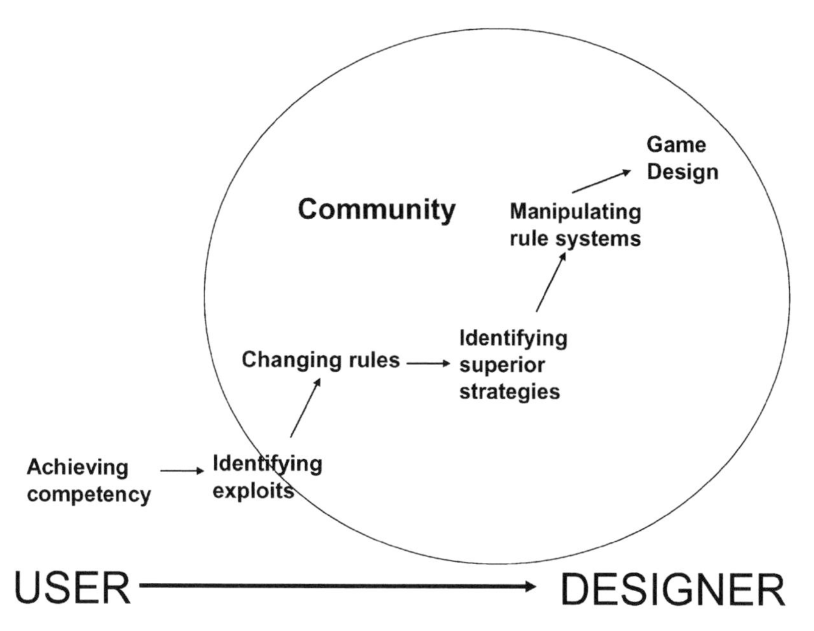

Figure 2
Trajectories of player experience. This diagram represents the process that we have seen occurring both within Apolyton University and within our *Civilization* programs. It stresses the gradual shift from player to designer, blurring distinctions between the two. Much like Salen (Salen and Zimmerman, 2003) we find that players frequently change the rules for their own enjoyment, a process that for some gradually evolves into creating mods, scenarios, or even new games.

Developing a Productive Orientation to Knowledge and Media

One can tease from this process an interesting approach to developing players with a *productive* or *design* orientation toward games. First, it is critical to acknowledge the importance of developing a mastery over a game system—understanding the interrelationships among its rules and their consequences before one ever attempts to design. This may seem simple, and perhaps even obvious: How many people would set out to write a song without having listened to a few, and hopefully, enjoyed some to the point of dissecting their composition to understand song composition? Whereas many approaches to game-based learning have emphasized design, perhaps it has been at the expense of understanding the value of *playing*.[38] Presented here is a gradual continuum whereby one enters as a player, begins identifying and exploiting rules, and graduates having participated in a redesign of the system. Here, designing is a natural outgrowth of playing, with one's desire to create emerging from experiences (satisfactory or otherwise) of play. A parallel can be made with the way players of *GTA: SA* (discussed earlier) moved from *players* to *producers* of their own meanings within the game system. Honovi and the other boys studied developed rich and rigorous interpretations of the game as it related to their own lived experiences only after they had entered the game as players. Each exited after having designed his own experience of play, and leveraged the meanings of this design within an interpretive community.

Design is also a deeply social experience. Members of Apolyton University are designing their "courses" for specific audiences and for specific purposes. Each design has a specific objective, including testing particular ideas or getting the player to experience particular things. This model offers an intriguing approach to game design in that one might compare these design challenges to specific design exercises one might do in a class. Perhaps most importantly, all of these activities are situated within a culture of inquiry, whereby the goal is for both the participants and the community to improve their skills and knowledge.

After roughly two years of activity, the community died off. In interviews, participants attributed this death to an exhaustion of the number of possible topics; the game was tested and perfected to the point where there was little need to continue. Most players were taking a break, waiting for the release of *Civilization IV*. The Apolyton community itself developed a wish list/alternative design document—hundreds of pages long—for the developers of *Civilization*. In fact, the most active of members of the community were recruited by the lead designer of *Civilization IV*, Soren Johnson, to participate in the *Civilization IV* design process. Roughly, 200 participants from Apolyton and other rival sites spent nearly two years testing ideas and making mods to the game, in effect running their university before the game came out. Eventually, a few participants were even hired by Firaxis to work as scenario designers. In effect, the community provided a trajectory of experience for these participants that literally resulted in them becoming professional designers.

Designing Learning Systems for the Interactive Age

In the summer of 2005, Levi Giovanetto, Shree Durga, Ben Devane, and I[39] began designing afterschool world civilization clubs based on the design principles of Apolyton University. The goal of the program was to create a modding community of practice around *Civilization III*. We sought to give students the experience of participating in and designing their own site of collective intelligence, which would hopefully result in them developing a design orientation to media that would also open trajectories to other valued practices. Specifically, we wanted to facilitate the formation of a learning community like Apolyton University, but one that allowed them to learn academic content of world history through a thematic series of historical scenarios. Perhaps more importantly, participation in this community of practice would also allow them to develop problem solving and creative thinking skills with technology, such as model building, game design, and community organization. Indeed, one of the theses that we are investigating is that core to meaningful participation in the twenty-first century is the ability to seek out, create, and participate in affinity spaces that further one's interests.

We began work with twelve fifth and sixth graders, mostly African American, all of whom were from lower socioeconomic backgrounds. The following exchange with two students typifies their orientation toward media at the beginning of the program:

Interviewer: Would you like to learn how to do game design?

Malcolm: No, it's too hard.

Monroe: No, that's not something I could do.

Most of the students had little technological background and very low self-efficacy toward technology. None of them could navigate a Windows PC file structure. In fact, on one occasion the most technologically savvy student took home a CD ROM to play at home and was surprised that his games were not saved to the CD ROM when he returned to school. They were all far from having any design knowledge of games.

Most of the students also had little interest in school, as typified by this exchange.

Interviewer: Do you like school?

Jason: I don't really like school, unless there's something fun going on, that's the only time there's actually something to do. You just sit there going [puts hand on head as if to sleep]. That's all you ever do really.

Interviewer: How do you feel about social studies?

Jason: Umm social studies can be fun depending on what you're doing. Last year we made a mountain out of graham crackers and we made it stuck together out of frosting and in the end we got to eat it.

Throughout the year, we regularly asked students what they were studying in school. Most reported that they were studying "culture." In the initial months of the project, few could locate the ancient civilizations on a map or identify many countries outside of the United States on a world map.

Creating an Academic/Gaming Culture

Over the next year, we designed and implemented an afterschool program for kids designed to initiate them into a gaming community of practice, that is, a community organized around a key practice (e.g., becoming good *Civ* players).[40] We designed a series of custom scenarios making the game easier to learn and easier to play. These custom games were designed to speed game play, allowing players to have the kind of rapid game-play analysis/replaying of games that was core to the Apolyton community. Students were encouraged to play with partners, and most players kept close ties to friends' games throughout the first week. Finally, we decided to have adult gamers play alongside the students, in order to better model the kind of thinking in which we wanted students to engage, such as modeling advanced game play or using maps and other resources as tools for game play. As the adults achieved successes (and losses), they shared their strategies with students, in part in an effort to emulate the kinds of thinking occurring at Apolyton University.

By the third week of camp, we introduced the possibility of playing multiplayer games to the kids, and they responded positively. These gaming sessions had a profound impact on the culture of the lab, transforming the space from a collection of single-player experiences to that of a shared, collaborative space focused learning, much as the shared games—games where community members would download and play a common saved game file—transformed the Apolyton community. Players began using game terms with each other while negotiating game vocabulary. For example, during negotiations over control of southern Europe, the Persians, Greeks, and Romans almost *always* engaged in debate over the control of iron and the impending military of Romans legionaries. In another example, players also claimed, "You should be worried about Egypt attacking you so they can get your horses so that they can build war chariots." Specialized language (legionaries, war chariots) flowed naturally in this context and became useful tools for communicating among players. Here, having adults playing alongside (and in teams with) kids also allowed for more cognitive apprenticeship opportunities as they shared and debated strategies in context.

These mentoring interactions took any number of forms, but generally stemmed out of having adults playing alongside students, with the adult, expert players unabashedly playing as experts. The adult players modeled how to negotiate with younger players, asking them what technologies they had, what they needed, and so on. They also "read aloud" the game screen for kids, examining the status of the game board (where key resources were, where strategic military points were, and predicting how the game might play out), essentially providing access to an expert view of the game system.

The second way that experts mentored students was by opening trajectories of experiences to students. For example, when a player liked a particular scenario, mentors asked him if he wanted to know how it was made, and explained to him how it was designed, effectively "lifting the hood" of the simulation. If a student wanted access to horses, the mentor might open the editor to show him how extra resources could be added to the game board. On almost a daily basis, mentors attempted to open new trajectories for students, showing them how to change their saved games, create new maps, change underlying game rules, or—in an extreme case—even show them how to do a total conversion mod, using the game tools to create a *Lord of the Rings* game.

Over the summer, these students developed a level of game play in *Civilization IV* similar to that of the students reported earlier. All could locate the major ancient civilizations on a map, could name key historical military units, and could make arguments about the growth of cities in particular geographic areas. Students were routinely succeeding in the game on more difficult levels, and a few began playing against other kids and adults online. The program culminated with a multiplayer game in which the students attempted to devise a takeover of the adults. One of the kids explains:

> We (Korea and Japan) saw how close Greece was and figured that Australia had to be closer, so we got out maps. I have this big map, and we built a galley with settlers, and were going to create a civilization and research to sail to Greece to make a secret attack on Levi.

The idea, while interesting, was ultimately ineffective as, by the time they developed the requisite sailing technologies, the game was largely lost. The group discussed the strengths and weaknesses of this strategy, a type of debriefing that typically resulted from the summer's multiplayer game sessions. Immediately following big events in the game (such as someone losing a city), players would jump out of their seats, run to one another's computers, and start constructing narratives of what happened and why. They would retell their strategies (e.g., researching sailing-oriented technologies to launch a secret attack on a distant civilization), and then argue over which strategies might have countered this strategy.

From Game Players to Creators

By the Fall, each student had developed a particular interest in history and gaming strategy, as the following quotation illustrates:

> *Interviewer:* Who are you playing as today?
>
> *Jason:* Scandinavia like always . . . Because I get berserkers . . . I put them on the galleys and any cities close to the shore, I can just go off and use them to attack whoever is in the city . . . .
>
> *Interviewer:* So do you think that is like the real Vikings?
>
> *Jason:* Actually it is, because the berserks would take this stuff which they made called wolf-bane . . . . like with Ivan the Boneless, which is my name in the game.
>
> *Interviewer:* Where did you learn this?
>
> *Jason:* It's from a book I'm reading. It's a fantasy, but all the land and stuff is just like real Europe. They have Iceland on the map, and the long ships.

Interviewer: So have you read about this at school at all?

Jason: No . . .

Jason, like every student who participated in the camp, began reading books on his favorite civilizations, checking books out from the library related to his game play, and doing extra background research related to his game. Jason was also an early adopter of the scenario design software, which he used as a tool to explore his interest in Scandinavian history.

Interviewer: So what is the scenario you made?

Jason: Well, I am Scandanavia, and I have the island that I really wanted, or that I had to get to if I wanted to win the game because it has every resource. Every island has horses and iron and the basic stuff . . .

Like most students, Jason was initially attracted to the scenario tool to experiment with exploits. In this case, he gave his civilization horses (which they did not have) as well as extra supplies of iron. We queried Jason on the historical accuracy of this hypothetical scenario.

Interviewer: So what do you think about that historically? Were the Vikings sort of isolated, were they on an island?

Jason: Well, Vikings were up in the Netherlands, but then they also controlled Iceland and the northern tip of the United Kingdom. They were kind of isolated, and if you saw them in battle or if they came to your town you were very unlucky because—well you were kind of lucky and kind of unlucky because they don't really attack a lot. If they are sailing, they go to different islands, and if there are no people there, they will leave guys there to start building up cities. Then they'll just have more people come to the city. They'll just keep on taking over the land. If there is a village in their way, they will destroy the village.

Here we begin to see a stark contrast between Jason at the beginning of the camp, when he was uninterested in game design and largely disaffiliated from school, and Jason now, where he is checking books out from the library, reading about history, and designing games for his own play. He is learning geography and historical terminology far beyond what is expected in school, and is even beginning to build micronarratives of historical events. This background knowledge is just the sort that has been shown to be critically important for academic success, as students attempt to make sense of more complex history texts that assume a basic background knowledge most students lack.[41] By the spring of 2006, these same kids were now regularly creating their own game files for camp. They experimented with different starting points for civilizations, different rates of game play, and the allocation of resources. Students would hold sleepovers in order to create new scenarios, and held informal competitions with one another to see who could create the best games. Researchers began fielding calls at home asking about the intricacies of the editor, or answering requests to play competitive games over the Internet. For these students, the desire to modify games was not an abstract goal, but arose as a natural outgrowth of their gaming practices, especially, a desire to entertain their friends, a desire to express themselves, and a desire to achieve status in their community.

By the end of the year, each student had undergone easily identifiable transformations, taking on new roles in the community and developing new identities. The following conversation, initiated by Monroe, suggests these changes:

Monroe: This whole game has changed my life. Yep.

Facilitator: This Rome scenario or CIV?

Monroe: I mean like the game, ever since I played it.

Facilitator: How has it changed your life?

Monroe: Well like, most of the other videos games are boring, but this isn't.

Facilitator: And this one isn't?

Monroe: Yeah, and my family plays it.

Sid (brother): No they don't.

Monroe: Mom and dad want to, my mom does.

Around this time, Monroe began seriously pursuing the game editor. As a part of a *Civilization* camp competition, he created a scenario depicting the Gulf War. Monroe started with a realistic map he downloaded from the Internet, and began extensive research (about forty hours) identifying important countries, their positions on the Iraq war, struggling with how to model the complex global events given the constraints of the editor. Around this time, Monroe shared that he "wants to become a senator some day" as a result of playing *Civilization.* As a school project, Monroe created a model of the American Revolution, which he was expanding and completing at the time of this writing.

Naturally, a causal claim that "playing *Civilization* will make a child want to become a senator" based on this (or any other data) is impossible to make. However, this kind of transformation is the sort that we believe is possible as the result of a comprehensive program designed to leverage students' interest in gaming toward other ends. For educators, one key outcome may be that, rather than shunning their students' interest in games, perhaps a more productive route would be to capitalize on the transformative power of the games to engage students in new experiences. Across all of our participants, we identified trajectories whereby students entered as novices and developed interest, knowledge, and skills related to world history and/or game design. Nearly all of them developed models of history with which they can think. From here, they naturally gravitated toward identifying and leveraging exploits, which we have been able to transition into a natural desire to modify games. In the context of our program, those who enjoy playing *Civilization* naturally seem to progress to a desire to create their own scenarios as well.

Conclusions

We are still in the early stages of creating theories of game-based learning environments, but I believe that open-ended, sandbox-type environments (exemplified here by *GTA: SA* and *Civilization*) are excellent places to start. The style of play afforded appeals to a broad range of students, provides opportunities for creative performance in game play, and offers multiple trajectories of participation. Here, I have attempted to outline an approach to designing game-based environments for learning, based on opening trajectories of experience for students. I have called these environments "designed experiences," in an attempt to capture a sense that the environment itself is designed to give players a series of experiences that they can take with them into new endeavors. The idea is to develop worlds that are worth understanding, which support multiple readings mediated by interpretive communities of practice, developing multiple compelling trajectories through the space, and supporting students in identifying new kinds of experiences in which to take part (see figure 1). As educators, we can nurture, develop, and extend students' participation within the game environment beyond the specific context of play.

Figure 1 depicts this process, and shows how students enter these designed worlds with divergent knowledge, interests, and skills. As they become "players," they develop new and divergent knowledge, interests, and skills, moving along a continuum toward becoming experts, wherein they develop a design-type understanding of the game space. As players gain expertise, their experience of the game space becomes more unique; they begin exploring different aspects of the game system, playing different game scenarios, and experiencing more and more diverse aspects of the game system. Players may begin at a relatively common starting place (similar tutorials, missions), but then diverge further in their interests. Unlike schools, within the type of learning system discussed here, players are encouraged to develop specific areas of expertise, separate from one another and perhaps even from the adults/facilitators. As students progress, they develop new interests, which then propel them out of the community of practice toward new areas of interest, such as game design or ancient history.

Figures 2 and 3 highlight two key processes: Induction into the community and propulsion out of the community. At first glance, one would think that induction into communities would be simple: Which media has a stronger attractor than video games? However, we have found that this is not always the case. Students do not always "see" (or even value) the roles available to them, such as becoming an expert *Civilization* player. In our early studies, it was not uncommon to have a student question whether participation in a game-based learning program would help them in school or on standardized tests. Identifying and promoting examples of expert gaming identities, ideally in the form of advanced participants who already embody them, may be an important step in induction. This point also highlights the importance of such communities being multiaged, fostering significant opportunities for interaction between novices and experts—something rare in most schools but common to learning outside of schools.[42] The second process is that of propulsion out of the community toward new communities of practice. Although mentoring is critical in all phases of this process, we see mentoring as especially critical during this last phase. As Jason and Monroe began developing an interest in new activities, facilitators (expert players, teachers, and parents) helped nurture these emerging passions to open new paths for participation in new kinds of practices. Sometimes creating such a pathway was as simple as opening up the editor and suggesting that a student take a look at a new feature; at other times, it meant encouraging Monroe to investigate politics further through reading books. One pathway that we made available to students is helping the adults run the camp. Monroe, in particular, has shown great interest in recruiting and teaching other kids to play. Jason, however, is less interested, and would probably rather pursue a more competitive type of gaming environment. As participants begin developing interests and expertise, it is critical that new pathways be opened for them. We also hope to be reflective about *this* process, helping kids understand that they can "teach themselves to learn" via the formation of learning communities, once the camp is over.

Part of what makes open-ended games intriguing for educators is their ability to nurture, sustain, and develop participants' interests for years (much like a spiraling curriculum might). At the time of this writing, we see participants periodically "checking out" and coming back to our program, as they develop new academic interests. Monroe, for example, renewed his interest in *Civilization III* while reading about European colonization in school. Over the

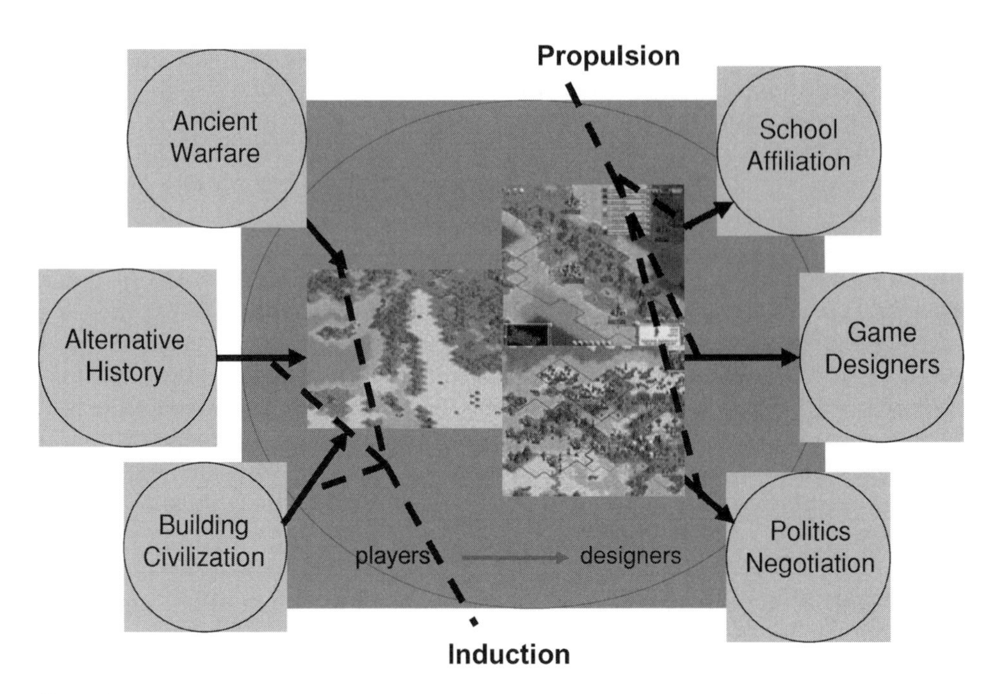

Figure 3

Induction and propulsion. This figure shows induction, the process by which players "get turned on" to *Civilization*, usually as something in the game captures their imagination. Like many games, this often represents a failure of some sort, as students want to achieve particular goals but perceive obstacles (like wanting to expand Egypt across Northern Africa, but Greece settling the shores of Egypt). We use the term *propulsion* to describe how playing *Civilization* serves as a propelling mechanism out of the community into new practices, although students frequently come back with renewed interests in new aspects of the game and new game-play/design practices.

last few weeks, he has taken to "replaying" specific historical moves in an effort to simulate historical events (even going as far as to having his textbook out while he plays). Much as expert *Civilization* players report *Civ* playing as feeding into a lifelong interest in History,[43] perhaps other open-ended games could give players experiences from which they draw from throughout their lives.

This model around the learning potential of open-ended sandbox games attempts to link sociocultural approaches to learning with more traditional constructivist/constructionist game-based approaches by suggesting how learning occurs through both individual and social game play. Certainly, interactions with the game are crucial to learning. At the same time, game play in these contexts is unequivocally a social experience wherein the desires to play and to produce both stem from social experiences. Players' desire to game, becoming experts or game producers, was thoroughly social. Unlike what we see in some social learning theory models, this model instead emphasizes that players do learn important skills, knowledge, and attitudes from open-ended sandbox games. Specifically, they develop models of the game system, which include basic facts, concepts, and relationships among them. Good players develop systemic knowledge of how changes in one factor (say the economics of a civilization) will affect its political negotiations.

At the same time, open-ended sandbox games may result in a more diverse range of learning outcomes than targeted or professional role-playing games. Certainly, these game-based learning models also have the potential to turn learners on to a range of different areas.[44] However, whereas one would normally describe *Supercharged!*, *Mad City 2020*, or *Full Spectrum Warrior* players as more or less playing the same game, advanced *Civilization* or *Grand Theft Auto* players engage in activities that other players—even after hundreds or thousands of hours of play—will never experience. With open-ended sandbox games, players enter the game with divergent interests, take divergent approaches and pathways through the game experience, have interpretations mediated by different interpretive communities, and embark on different trajectories out of the game space.

I argue that the interpretive community is the site wherein people develop even deeper meanings—including design-based understandings and understandings of how and when these are applied to other phenomena. In the *Grand Theft Auto* example, we saw how different interpretive communities make sense of issues such as race and violence, although further ethnographic work examining how these processes unfold is needed.[45] There are surprisingly few studies of how such social interactions function within single-player games. (With multiplayer games, we know that much of this apprenticeship and learning to "value" the world in particular ways occurs through joint collaborative activity such as group hunts.)[46]

One hypothesis emanating from the model proposed here is that "single-player" game play at any deep level is significantly mediated by interpretive communities as well; our interviews with *Civilization* and *GTA* players show that most kids and adults learned to play their first games in a genre from a friend and still regularly game with friends.[47] Indeed, players see gaming as a fundamentally social phenomenon. However, consistent with Gee,[48] I would argue that such social configurations probably function as *affinity spaces* as often as they do *communities*. Affinity spaces, such as Apolyton.net (not Apolyton University), feature less rigid participation structures, more transient relationships, and freer access to information. Consistent with Gee, I believe that such spaces may also hold important clues for developing learning, although for the purposes here, I have chosen to pursue communities as a framework of analysis.

Our next steps are to begin supporting distributed communities of practice of game players over the Web. Can we create distributed centers so that kids can play with and against other students from around the world, much like Apolyton University? How will making our *Civ* Clubs part of an International effort affect how kids use and make sense of the game? We hope that having more diverse play styles and interests will deepen players' experiences of the game and open entirely new avenues for participation. Having the chance to interact with expert *Civilization* players from different socioeconomic classes could open these students to practices unavailable in their local settings.

Notes

1. Walter Holland, Henry Jenkins, and Kurt Squire, Theory by Design, in *Video Game Theory Reader*, eds. Bernard Perron and Mark Wolf (London: Routledge, 2003), 25–46.

2. Ibid.; David Shaffer, Kurt Squire, Richard Halverson, and Jim Gee, Video Games and the Future of Learning, *Phi Delta Kappan* 87, no. 2 (2005): 104–11.

3. Constance Steinkuehler and Marjee Chmiel, Fostering Scientific Habits of Mind in the Context of Online Play, Paper presented at the 7th International Conference of the Learning Sciences, Bloomington, IN, 2006.

4. Doug Church, Abdicating Authorship, Presentation made at the Annual Meeting of the Game Developer's Conference, San Jose, CA, March 2000; Games-to-Teach Team, Design Principles of Next-Generation Digital Gaming for Education, *Educational Technology* 43, no. 5 (2003): 17–33; and Staffan Björk and Jussi Holopainen, Games and Design Patterns, in *The Game Design Reader: A Rules of Play Anthology*, eds. Katie Salen and Eric Zimmerman (Cambridge, MA: The MIT Press, 2005).

5. Jim Gee, *What Video Games Have to Teach Us About Learning and Literacy* (New York: Palgrave/St. Martin's, 2003); and Henry Jenkins and Kurt Squire, Harnessing the Power of Games in Education, *Insight* 1, no. 3 (2004): 5–33.

6. Games, Learning, and Society, *Games, Learning, and Society*, in *Report to the Spencer Foundation*, ed. James Paul Gee (Chicago: Spencer Foundation, 2006).

7. Kurt Squire, Michael Barnett, Thomas Higgenbotham, and Jamillah Grant, Electromagnetism Supercharged! Paper published in *The Proceedings of the 2004 International Conference on the Learning Sciences* (Los Angeles: UCLA Press, 2004).

8. Ibid.

9. Henry Jenkins, Kurt Squire, and Philip Tan, You Can't Bring That Game to School! Designing *Supercharged!* in *Design Research*, ed. B. Laurel (Cambridge, MA: The MIT Press, 2003), 244–52.

10. Jim Gee, *Language, Learning, and Gaming: A Critique of Traditional Schooling* (New York: Routledge, 2004).

11. Kurt Squire, Cultural Framing of Computer/Video Games, *Game Studies: The International Journal of Computer Game Research* 1, no. 2 (2002). http://www.gamestudies.org/0102/squire/. Accessed January 15, 2007.

12. David W. Shaffer (2005). Epistemic Games. *Innovate* 1(6). Reprinted in *Computer Education* (in press). http://www.innovateonline.info/index.php?view=article&id=79.

13. D. A. Schon, *The Reflective Practitioner: How Professionals Think in Action* (London: Temple Smith, 1983).

14. Jennica Falk, Peter Ljungstrand, Staffan Björk, and Rebecca Hansson, Pirates: Proximity-Triggered Interaction in a Multi-Player Game, *Extended Abstracts of Computer–Human Interaction (CHI)* (Seattle: ACM Press, 2001).

15. Kurt Squire, Mingfong Jan, James Matthews, Mark Wagler, John Martin, Ben DeVane, and Chris Holden, Wherever You Go, There You Are: Place-Based Augmented Reality Games for Learning, in *The Educational Design and Use of Computer Simulation Games*, eds. B. E. Shelton and D. A. Wiley (Rotterdam, The Netherlands: Sense Press, Forthcoming).

16. See, for example, E. Klopfer & K. Squire (in press). Developing a platform for augmented reality gaming. To appear in *Educational Technology Research and Development.*

17. B. Nelson, D. J. Ketelhut, J. Clarke, E. Dieterle, C. Dede, and B. Erlandson, Robust Design Strategies for Scaling Educational Innovations: The River City MUVE Case Study, in *The Educational Design and Use of Computer Simulation Games*, eds. B. E. Shelton and D. A. Wiley (Rotterdam, The Netherlands: Sense Press, Forthcoming).

18. Sasha A. Barab, Miriam Cherkes-Julkowski, Rod Swenson, Steve Garrett, Robert E. Shaw, and Michael Young, Principles of Self-Organization: Ecologizing the Learner-Facilitator System, *The Journal of the Learning Sciences* 8, nos. 3 and 4 (1999): 349–90.

19. It could be argued that this "open-ended" category is similar to Will Wright's "hobby" category, which is probably correct. Although we have examples of players using these games competitively and

enjoying the story (in the case of *GTA*), the game itself would fall somewhere closer to the hobby end of Wright's continuum.

20. In this chapter, I use the term *Civilization* to refer to Sid Meier's *Civilization* series, and unless noted otherwise, specifically his *Civilization III* (the third installment of the franchise). *Civilization* is a strategy game in which the player rules a civilization sometime between 4000 BC and the present, or perhaps in a different time frame, depending upon the scenario. The game is based on a geographical-materialist game system in which players build cities to gather natural resources (food, natural resources, and commerce). Depending on how one plays, there is a robust political negotiation system as well.

21. B. DeVane and K. D. Squire, Pimp My Ride: Analysis of Grand Theft Auto: San Andreas Playstyles. Keynote presentation delivered to the Media, Cultures, and Communications Special Interest Group at the Annual Meeting of the American Educational Research Association, San Francisco, CA, April 2006.

22. R. Koster, *A Theory of Fun* (Scottsdale, CA: Paraglyph, 2005).

23. Constance Steinkuehler, R. W. Black, and K. A. Clinton, Researching Literacy as Tool, Place, and Way of Being, *Reading Research Quarterly* 40, no. 1 (2005): 7–12.

24. Sherry Turkle, From Powerful Ideas to PowerPoint, *Convergence: The Journal of Research into New Media Technologies* 9, no. 2 (2003): 19–28.

25. Alice Robison, The "Internal Design Grammar" of Video Games, Paper delivered at the 2004 Annual Meeting of the American Educational Research Association, San Diego, CA, April 2004.

26. Marc LeBlanc, Tools for Creating Dramatic Game Dynamics, in *The Rules of Play*, eds. Katie Salen and Eric Zimmerman (Cambridge, MA: The MIT Press, 2004); Alice Robison, The Internal Design Grammar of Games. Unpublished doctoral dissertation (Madison, WI: University of Wisconsin, 2005); Salen and Zimmerman, *The Rules of Play*.

27. Jared Diamond, *Guns, Germs, and Steel: The Fates of Human Societies* (New York: Norton, 1999).

28. Ross E. Dunn, Constructing World History in the Classroom? In *Knowing, Teaching and Learning History*, eds. P. N. Stearns, P. Seixas, and S. Wineburg (New York: New York University Press, 2000).

29. Ibid.; and Patrick Manning, *Navigating World History: Historians Create a Global Past* (New York: Palgrave MacMillan, 2003).

30. Paul Starr, Seductions of Sim, *The American Prospect* 5, no. 17 (1994); and Sherry Turkle, From Powerful Ideas.

31. Ross Dunn, Constructing World History.

32. See Katie Salen and Eric Zimmerman, *The Rules of Play*, for an excellent discussion of games as social and cultural phenomena.

33. For a good, critical discussion of the politics embodied in the game, see David Epstein, Not Just Child's Play, *Inside Higher Ed.*, November 2005. http://www.insidehighered.com/news/2005/11/28/civ. Accessed January 15, 2007.

34. For an excellent discussion of this, see Ross Dunn, Constructing World History.

35. E.g., Sherry Turkle, From Powerful Ideas.

36. Joseph Tobin, *Good Guys Don't Wear Hats: Children's Talk About the Media* (New York: Teachers College Press, 2000).

37. A. Collins, J. S. Brown, and S. E. Newman, Cognitive Apprenticeship: Teaching the Crafts of Reading, Writing, and Mathematics, in *Knowing, Learning, and Instruction: Essays in Honor of Robert Glaser*, ed. L. B. Resnick (Hillsdale, NJ: Lawrence Erlbaum Associates, 1989), 453–94.

38. As an example of this, see Mitchel Resnick, Amy Bruckman, and Fred Martin, Pianos, Not Stereos: Creating Computational Construction Kits, *Interactions* 3, no. 5 (September/October 1996): 40–50.

39. Kurt Squire, Levi Giovanetto, Ben Devane, and Shree Durga, From Users to Designers: Building a Self-Organizing Game-Based Learning Environment, *Technology Trends* 49, no. 5 (2005): 34–42.

40. Jean Lave and Etienne Wenger, *Situated Learning: Legitimate Peripheral Participation* (New York: Cambridge University Press, 1991). I use the term *communities of practice* here to emphasize the relatively close-knit nature of this group, and to contrast this with Gee's notion of affinity spaces (Jim Gee, *Situated Language and Learning: A Critique of Traditional Schooling* [London: Routledge, 2004]).

41. Isabel L. Beck, Margaret G. McKeown, and Erika W. Gromoll, Learning from Social Studies Texts, *Cognition and Instruction* 6, no. 2 (1989): 99–158.

42. Jean Lave and Etienne Wenger, *Situated Learning*.

43. Kurt Squire and Levi Giovanetto, The Higher Education of Gaming, *E-Learning*, forthcoming.

44. For an excellent description of this within epistemic role-playing games, see David Shaffer, Epistemic Games. *Innovative* 1, no. 6 (2005). Reprinted in *Computer Education* (forthcoming). http://www.innovateonline.info/index.php?view=article&id=79. Accessed August 23, 2007.

45. See Anna Everett and S. Craig Watkins, The Power of Play: The Portrayal and Performance of Race in Video Games, in *The Ecology of Games: Connecting Youth, Games, and Learning*, ed. Katie Salen (Cambridge, MA: The MIT Press, 2007).

46. See Constance Steinkuehler, *Cognition and Learning in Massively Multiplayer Online Games: A Critical Approach*, Unpublished dissertation (Madison, WI: University of Wisconsin-Madison, 2005); and T. L. Taylor, *Play Between Worlds: Exploring Online Game Culture* (Cambridge, MA: The MIT Press, 2006.)

47. See Reed Stevens, Tom Satwicz, and Laurie McCarthy, In-Game, In-Room, In-World: Reconnecting Video Game Play to the Rest of Kids' Lives, in *The Ecology of Games: Connecting Youth, Games, and Learning*, ed. Katie Salen (Cambridge, MA: The MIT Press, 2007).

48. Jim P. Gee, *Why Video Games Are Good for Your Soul: Pleasure and Learning* (Melbourne: Common Ground, 2005).

Why *I Love Bees*: A Case Study in Collective Intelligence Gaming

Jane McGonigal

Institute for the Future

How can people and computers be connected so that—collectively—they act more intelligently than any individuals, groups, or computers have ever done before?

—Thomas W. Malone, Director, MIT Center for Collective Intelligence[1]

We experienced being part of a collective intelligence . . . participating in a search for, or perhaps creation of, a greater, shared meaning.

—Phaedra, *I Love Bees* player[2]

Can a Computer Game Teach Collective Intelligence?

The term *collective intelligence*, or CI for short, was originally coined by French philosopher Pierre Levy in 1994 to describe the impact of Internet technologies on the cultural production and consumption of knowledge. Levy argued that, because the Internet facilitates a rapid, open, and global exchange of data and ideas, over time the network should "mobilize and coordinate the intelligence, experience, skills, wisdom, and imagination of humanity" in new and unexpected ways.[3] As part of his utopian vision for a more collaborative knowledge culture, he predicted: "We are passing from the Cartesian *cogito*"—I think, therefore I am—"to *cogitamus*"—*we* think, therefore we are.[4]

The result of this new "we," Levy argued, would be a more complex, flexible, and dynamic knowledge base. In a CI culture, he wrote, knowledge "ceases to be the object of established fact and becomes a project."[5] Members of a CI would not simply gather, master, and deploy preexisting information and concepts. Instead, they would work with the collected facts and viewpoints to actively author, discover, and invent new, computer-fueled ways of thinking, strategizing, and coordinating.

Whereas Levy was making predictions about a collaborative culture to come, real-world examples of early forms of CI today proliferate. Perhaps the most well-known CI experiment is Wikipedia,[6] the free online encyclopedia written and edited by the public, using the collaborative writing software known as a Wiki. Yahoo! Answers[7] allows users to pose any question, on any topic, to the online public; amateurs and experts alike offer their best answers, which are rated by other users so that those deemed most helpful or insightful rise to the top. Google Image Labeler,[8] originally developed by Carnegie Mellon University researchers as the ESP Game, invites the public to improve its image search engine by working collaboratively to categorize online pictures by agreeing on specific, descriptive tags. MapHub[9] enables users to upload personal stories and experiences of specific geographic locations to online maps, so that they become rich with site-specific data that paint a picture of collective experience. SFZero,[10] an online role-playing game, describes itself as a "collaborative productive game," relying on its players to generate and to score virtually all of its missions. And multiple online prediction markets, from the Hollywood Stock Exchange[11] to the World Economic Forums' Global Risks Prediction Market,[12] allow individuals to wager on the likelihood of future events, from entertainment awards to terrorist attacks—typically with a startling degree of success.

What do these myriad CI projects share in common? They all use digital networks to connect *massively multi*-human users in a persistent process of social data gathering, analysis, and application. Their goal: to produce a kind of collectively generated knowledge that is different not just quantitatively, but also *qualitatively*, in both its formation and its uses.

As more and more popular examples of CI have emerged, institutional interest in understanding and cultivating CI has grown steadily. Most notably, in the fall of 2006, the Massachusetts Institute of Technology (MIT) launched a dedicated Center for Collective Intelligence. The Center, which brings together faculty from the fields of computer science, artificial intelligence (AI), cognitive psychology, business management, and the digital media arts, describes its central research problem as this: "How can people and computers be connected so that—collectively—they act more intelligently than any individuals, groups, or computers have ever done before?"[13] According to Professor Thomas J. Malone, director of the Center, the stakes of this question are high. "New technologies are now making it possible to organize groups in very new ways, in ways that have never been possible before in the history of humanity . . . better ways to organize businesses, to conduct science, to run governments, and—perhaps most importantly—to help solve the problems we face as society and as a planet."[14]

To explore these possibilities, cutting-edge CI research at MIT and elsewhere is just now beginning to generate theories about what kind of interactive design and technological infrastructure will be necessary for a CI to emerge consistently from the global digital network.[15] But while the design and development of digital systems that support CI is a significant problem that deserves our immediate attention, it is not the only major challenge that faces proponents of a more open and participatory knowledge culture.

There is no guarantee that everyone with access to computer network technologies will be automatically absorbed into this culture of CI. Indeed, in *Convergence Culture*, media theorist Henry Jenkins reminds us that as we embark on an age of powerful, networked collaboration, "We are just learning how to exercise that power—individually and collectively—and fighting to define the terms under which we will be allowed to participate."[16]

Once CI systems are in place, how do we ensure widespread entry for today's youth into the collective? To engage as many and as diverse young people as possible in the new knowledge network, specific CI skills, such as the ability to parse complicated problems into distinct parts and a facility for real-time virtual coordination, will need to be taught. Indeed, as CI increasingly becomes a vital component of our social, political, and creative lives, it seems ever more likely that our formal education system will need to include both instruction and practice in how to construct and contribute to a CI. A CI curriculum would provide students with the opportunity to develop a new kind of digital network literacy, one specifically tuned to the techniques, challenges, and rewards of massively scaled collaboration.

In *Rainbows End*, award-winning science fiction author Vernor Vinge gives us a tantalizing glimpse of what such a CI curriculum might look like in the near future. Set in the year 2025, Vinge's novel describes a world in which globally distributed, intergenerational teams of amateurs and experts collaborate by the thousands, the hundreds of thousands, and even the millions to make political decisions, to solve mysteries, to create art, and to predict and forestall health pandemics, terrorist attacks, and economic crises. Acknowledging that myriad forms of collective network participation already are beginning to occur across a wide swath of emergent technological cultures, Vinge subtitles his book: "A novel with one foot in the future"—implying that the foundation for its fiction is already being laid by CI experiments in the present. But Vinge is interested in outlining the possibilities for a more formal foundation. In his novel, young students are prepared to be effective CI members through rigorous in-class instruction. Specifically, Vinge's imagined educational system requires high school students to take a course called Search and Analysis, in which they learn both practical technological skills and social strategies for how to participate in a CI network.

Vinge dedicates only a couple of pages to describing this fictional class; it serves primarily as texture for his science fiction landscape. But the following passage stands out as a provocative illustration of how CI might be taught and inspired in young students:

> "I have a theory of life," said [the teacher] Chumlig, "and it is straight out of gaming: *There is always an angle.* You, each of you, have some special wild cards. Play with them. Find out what makes you different and better. Because it is there, if only you can find it. And once you do, you'll be able to contribute answers to others and others will be willing to contribute back to you. In short, synthetic serendipity doesn't just happen. By golly, you must create it."[17]

The fictional students are informed that they will have to take an active role in securing a place for themselves in the CI. Individual relevance and participation in a CI culture is not guaranteed, the teacher Chumlig insists, and therefore each student must cultivate unique interests, talents, and core knowledge sets. As Levy observed in his early treatise on *Collective Intelligence*: "No one knows everything, everyone knows something."[18] Vinge's futuristic class, therefore, offers the students *differentiation* as a practical strategy for developing individual relevance and power in a CI culture. Specialized, distinctive capabilities and resources will later serve as their personal currency in the intelligence market.

Perhaps more important than these practical strategies, though, are the social and psychological aspects to Vinge's fictional course work. Levy's original treatise on CI stressed that the individual thinker must not be lost in this new and more powerful "we." To the contrary, Levy wrote, "The basis and goal of CI is the mutual recognition and enrichment of *individuals.*"[19] And so, by promising that there is something that makes each student "different and better," Chumlig encourages her students to be secure in their individual identities. She urges them not to be overwhelmed by the daunting size of the CI community or made to feel insignificant by the seemingly infinite scope of its efforts. Instead, she prepares each student to see him- or herself as playing a singular, meaningful role in the network, with valuable individual microcontributions to make to the massively scaled effort.

Vinge's fictional teacher offers her year-2025 advice by talking metaphorically about the culture of CI as a kind of game. But in our present-day society, real "search and analysis" computer games are already taking up the task of teaching young people a basic literacy in CI. How can massively multiplayer games function as immersive tutorials in network collaboration and coordination? This case study is an exploration of one such game.

The Rise of Collective Intelligence in Digital Gaming Culture

In the summer of 2004, the commercial game design company 42 Entertainment launched *I Love Bees*, a Web-based interactive fiction that used Web sites, blogs, e-mails, JPEGs, MP3 recordings, and other digital artifacts to create an immersive backstory for Microsoft's sci-fi shooter video game *Halo 2*. I was the lead community designer of *I Love Bees* and, in this role, my primarily responsibility was to oversee the emerging CI of its players. In this case study, I will explore the design and deployment of *I Love Bees* as an experiment in constructing a game-based digital learning environment, in which players can experience firsthand in a low-risk setting the challenges and pleasures of becoming part of a massively collaborative knowledge network.

The distributed fiction of *I Love Bees* was designed as a kind of investigative playground, in which players could collect, assemble, and interpret thousands of different story pieces related to the *Halo* universe. By reconstructing and making sense of the fragmented fiction, the fans would collaboratively author a narrative bridge between the first *Halo* video game and its sequel. As the project's lead writer Sean Stewart explains: "Instead of telling a story, we would present the evidence of that story, and let the players tell it to themselves."[20]

At the outset of *I Love Bees*, however, we explained none of this to the players. We kept secret the project's intentions to serve as an interactive backstory, and we did not disclose the search and analysis mechanics we had designed. In fact, we never officially announced the launch of a new *Halo*-related online game—instead, we simply hid the game in plain sight on the World Wide Web. We hoped the mystery would generate buzz about the project. And by requiring the players to discover by themselves the existence, secret purpose, and patterns of the game, we also took the first step toward gaining the players' constructive participation in the project. The only clue we gave that a strange, new game was afoot came in the form of an unassuming URL, which flickered briefly across the screen in the final frames of a theatrical trailer for *Halo 2* (see figure 1). The hidden URL pointed sharp-eyed viewers to www.ilovebees.com, the real, working Web site of a fictional character—an amateur beekeeper named Margaret, who seemed completely unrelated to the *Halo* mythology. As *Halo* fans wondered what on earth beekeeping had to do with *Halo*'s futuristic alien wars, they were drawn into a mystery: *I Love Bees* clearly was no ordinary Web site. It had been hacked, and its webmaster desperately needed help figuring out why—and what to do about it.

The hacked home page blasted visitors with cryptic warnings of "system peril" and "network throttling."[21] It promised: "This medium will metastasize," and displayed an ominous looking timer marked "Countdown to Wide Awake and Physical" (see figure 2). Players quickly performed calculations and realized that the timer was counting down the hours, minutes, and seconds to a specific date four weeks in the future: August 24, 2004. They immediately began a massively multiplayer investigation: What would happen on August 24?

The players soon discovered another clue: on the same Web site, the hacker had replaced the beekeepers' favorite honey-based recipes with 210 unique pairs of Global Positioning System (GPS) coordinates (see figure 3). Each pair of coordinates—such as a latitude of 38.891883 and a longitude of –077.026117—appeared directly above a matching time code—such as 06:07 PDT.[22] The 210 time codes were precisely spaced apart three or four minutes each, so that they stretched across a twelve-hour period: from sunrise to sundown in the Pacific Daylight Savings Time zone. A smaller countdown on the recipe page, marked "Axons Go Hot," was counting down to the same date as the home page.

Amidst all of this confounding content, a single FAQ at the bottom of the hacked home page posed an explicit opening challenge to the *Halo* fans: "Q: What happened to this site? A: Help me find out here." Players who clicked on the Web link "here" found the blog of a young

Figure 1
Screen shot of *Halo 2* trailer. A hidden URL, www.ilovebees.com, signals fans that a strange new game is afoot (42 Entertainment, 2004).

woman named Dana, the beekeeper's niece and Web site administrator, who was soliciting the public's help with fixing www.ilovebees.com. But in a frantic post titled "emergency exit," Dana told players that she was contemplating going into hiding.[23] Indeed, after exchanging nearly one hundred personal e-mails with the players, she disappeared, leaving them to deal with the countdown and its looming threats on their own.

The players received no further instructions. The *I Love Bees* game did not articulate a specific goal, a win condition, rules, or any of the other formal guidelines traditionally associated with games. Nor did it offer any obvious choices to make, or sequences of buttons to press, or virtual objects to collect. Instead, the players had only a call to action, a very complex data set, a few seemingly random threads of story—and the freedom to respond to them however they wanted. In the end, this single core mystery of the hacker and its GPS coordinates took more than 600,000 collaborating players—largely high school and college students—nearly four months to solve.[24]

42 Entertainment's main goal in producing the project as a commercial game was, of course, exciting entertainment through immersive storytelling. But we also built *I Love Bees* as a tutorial in CI. Elan Lee, the director of *I Love Bees*, has famously described the core mandate of his game design philosophy: "To create puzzles and challenges that no single person could solve on their own."[25] And in a postgame online chat with *I Love Bees* players, lead writer Sean Stewart wrote: "The game isn't the art, or the puzzles, or the story. They are designed to precipitate, to catalyze the actual work of art. Which is you."[26] In other words, the massively collaborative, search and analysis game play of *I Love Bees* was a means to an end beyond

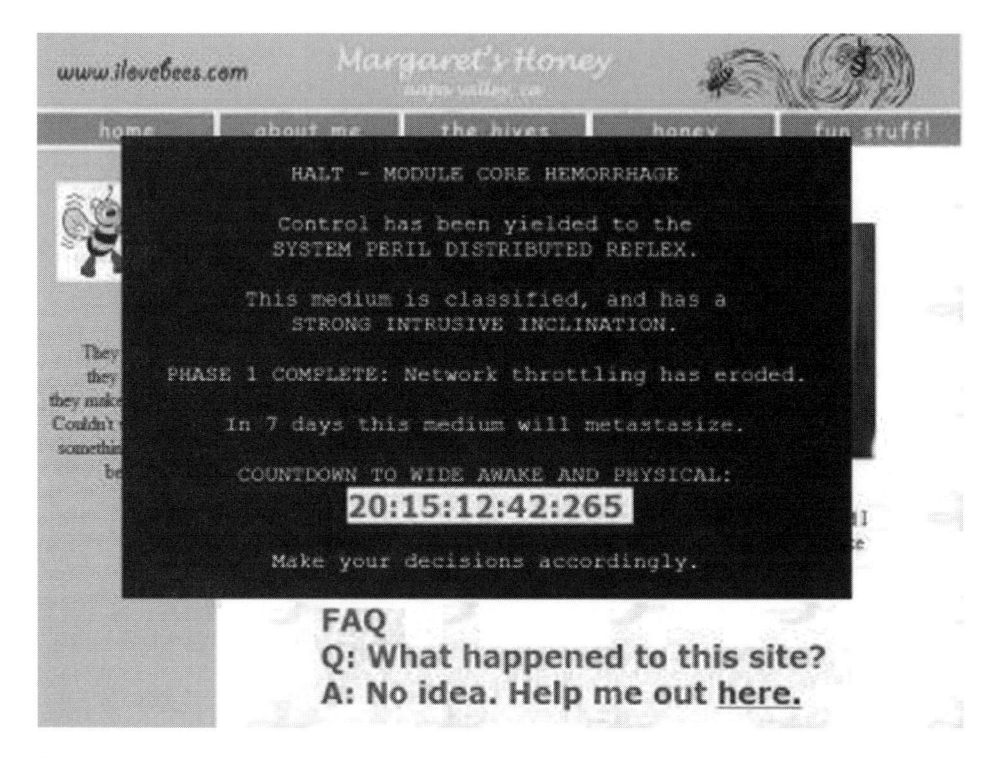

Figure 2
Screen shot of *I Love Bees* home page. Cryptic warnings and an ominous countdown on an amateur beekeeper's hacked Web site are the first clues encountered by players (42 Entertainment, 2004).

innovative entertainment. It sought to create a highly connected player base dedicated to, and impressively capable of, defining and solving large-scale problems together. Lee and Stewart describe the players of 42 Entertainment games as "a collective intelligence that is unparalleled in entertainment history."[27] Why create a CI around the *Halo* video game series? Digital gaming culture is already moving swiftly in the direction of networked collaboration. *Halo 2*, specifically, was produced by Microsoft Game Studios (MGS) for Xbox Live, an online service enabling players worldwide to connect their Xbox consoles to a global game-play network. To this end, MGS designed *Halo* 2 as a highly and unusually collaborative video game experience. It described the game's innovative "cooperative play mode" in promotional materials: "New technology lets groups of friends stick together . . . Team up with a friend and save humankind together."[28] *I Love Bees* presented this same challenge on a more ambitious scale. By extending the platform of play into the entire ubiquitous computing network, the cooperative sixteen-player *Halo* networks enabled by Xbox Live became a massively collaborative *Halo* network.

In this case study, I explore the three stages of *I Love Bees* game play that ultimately produced a game-based CI. They are (1) *collective cognition*, (2) *cooperation*, and (3) *coordination*. These three stages encompass, respectively, the initial formation of community, the development of distributed skill sets, and the scaffolding of group challenge that are essential elements of both massively multiplayer game systems and the new CI knowledge networks. I also identify the three aspects of *I Love Bees'* game design that resulted

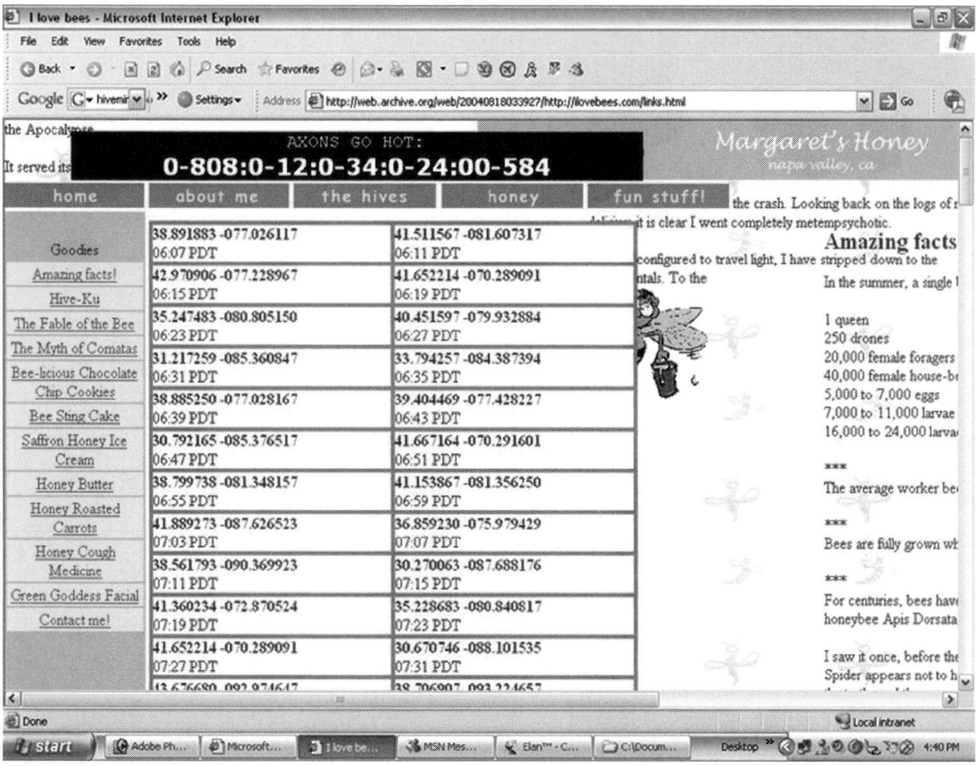

Figure 3
Screen shot of *I Love Bees* GPS coordinates puzzle. 210 GPS coordinates with matching time codes suggest to players hundreds of viable strategies (42 Entertainment, 2004).

in these distinct stages of highly collaborative game play: (1) *massively distributed content*, (2) *meaningful ambiguity*, and (3) *real-time responsiveness*. I offer these elements as a reproducible set of core design requirements that may be used to inspire future learning systems that support and ultimately bring to a satisfying conclusion a firsthand engagement with CI.

Stage One: Reconstructing a Hive Mind

The players of *I Love Bees* faced a single, open-ended challenge: "What happened to this site? Help me out here." To formulate a thoughtful response, the players first needed to understand the fictional world in which the game was being played. To do so meant putting together a story that had been shattered into thousands of pieces. This is the game-play stage I call *collective cognition*. During this stage, players collected, compiled, and analyzed game content, developing a cohesive theory of the game world and a shared language for discussing it. This initial period of intense collaboration provided the players with a sense of community, shared focus, and common knowledge. These social learning gains would later provide context and support for resolving more complex interpretive conflicts and for coordinating increasingly challenging parallel efforts.

Figure 4
Photograph of *I Love Bees* pay phone game play. Local teams of *I Love Bees* players met at pay phones weekly to intercept messages, talk to game characters, and complete real-world missions.

The distributed narrative of *I Love Bees* played out in highly "deconstructed" form. It was revealed in clue-sized pieces over the course of four months across hundreds of Web pages, dozens of blog posts, thousands of e-mails, and over 40,000 live MP3 transmissions. Some of these content fragments could be found by anyone who looked closely enough. Others loaded only on the Web browsers of players logging in from IP addresses linked to specific geographic regions (see figure 4). Still others were sent as private, personalized e-mails or phone calls to a single player out of the hundreds of thousands of total players. Because of this massive distribution of content, responsibility rested on each and every player to come forward with any and all discoveries, so that the entire collective could access and process as complete a data set as possible. As one *I Love Bees* player remarked during the game: "This is really beautiful. In order for any of us to move forward WE ALL have to move forward."[29]

These massively distributed puzzle pieces were tracked down and documented by individuals, but compiled and analyzed by the group. Once a new piece of content was turned over to the collective, it then would be analyzed by thousands of players on dozens of different community forums. A single new clue detected on Dana's blog, for example, resulted in 2,401 new comments from players within days of being found.[30] On one of the primary Internet Relay Channels used for *I Love Bees* speculation, players logged an average of 33,000 lines of chat daily discussing the story.[31] One particularly popular message board for *Halo* fans working on the *I Love Bees* mystery clocked in at a mind-boggling fifty new posts every thirty seconds during the first week of clue gathering.[32] Several other host servers were temporarily shutdown and massively upgraded to handle the rapid exchange of facts, theories, and speculation.[33] In total, in the first ten weeks of game play, players who had subdivided into core discussion groups of several hundred or thousand players each produced over a million message board posts in the quest to compile and dissect the narrative evidence.[34] The players' production of written analysis of *I Love Bees* content was nothing short of prolific. More importantly, each individual could be assured of a massive audience for his or her contributions. The first *I Love Bees* player-created story wiki, for example, received 1,157,951 page views in the first two weeks.[35]

In addition to the traditional online communications platforms of forums, blogs, Internet Relay Channels, and personal Web sites, the players used a range of online collaboration tools to compile and discuss the distributed content: wikis, group-moderated blogs, and multiauthored mailing lists, collaborative spreadsheets to list-servs, and toll-free online teleconferencing systems, to name just a few. These networked platforms enabled individuals to instantly update the entire player base with found data and novel interpretations. At the same time, by engaging these platforms, players generated a personal fluency in important emerging technologies. Playing the game meant flexing their muscles as literate users of this complex, participatory information space.

What did the players finally discover after all of this narrative search and analysis? When put together, the story clues presented a series of dramatic events leading up to the opening scene of *Halo 2*, when a race of hostile aliens land on Earth. The extremely complicated narrative premise developed by Stewart is summarized best by the players' collectively authored wiki-based "walkthrough guide" to the game. This wiki tracks players' understanding of the story over time. For instance, after gathering and sorting through the first weeks' worth of hundreds of pieces of narrative clues hidden on www.ilovebees.com and in e-mails, the player community tentatively posted a collectively authored interpretation of over 500 of those fragments on a wiki. The fragments were broken bits of poems, such as "*MAYDAY MAYDAY MAYDAY It happened one day, about noon, going towards my boat, I was exceedingly surprised with the print of a flea's naked foot on the shore, which was very plain to be seen on the sand.*" The summary also addressed over 150 found lines of futuristic programming code found scattered around the pages of www.ilovebees.com, such as *grope: !probe extern proc 0 crypt strong*. The players tentatively surmised:

> MAYDAY TEXT: we can collect all the maroon text into one coherent narrative, written by someone (or something) nicknamed The Operator. The Operator is lost, away from home, and has been shipwrecked—hence the Mayday. . . . COMPUTER CODE: we have no way of knowing if we've put all the fragments in the right order yet, but looking at the code seems to give us some clues. We can see that something is broken, but most of it is meaningless at the moment.[36]

Later, as they gathered more pieces and conducted more analysis, the players evolved their understanding, until they concluded that the following passage best described the game's plot:

> A military spacecraft named the Apocalypso from the *Halo* universe has crashed, and somehow it's controlling A.I. [artificial intelligence] has ended up on Earth. The A.I. controlling the craft, named Melissa (informally known as The Operator by her crew) . . . was very badly damaged and spent a while in delirium, not knowing where it is. The Operator apparently managed to transfer itself to a computer

in the Bay Area. It then took over a beekeeping website, ilovebees.com, from which the Operator is trying to signal any survivors from the crew on the planet.[37]

As this summary shows, the players concluded that the psychotic "hacker" was in fact a damaged AI program that had taken over an amateur beekeeper's Web site and was leaking memories and code onto the otherwise ordinary Web pages in an attempt to put itself back into working order.

But why would a *Halo* AI land on a beekeepers' Web site? What did bees have to do with the fictional world of *Halo*, players wondered, in which a future alien race attempts to annihilate humanity with outrageously powerful weapons? The answer, as players came to realize through their collective analysis, is "Nothing." Bees were chosen as a plot point by *I Love Bees'* creators not because of a natural connection to the existing game world, but rather to evoke the game's CI goals.

In a 2001 essay, "The Cyberspace Dialectic," digital theorist Michael Heim described proponents of CI as "network idealists." He wrote: "The network idealist builds collective beehives. The idealist sees the next century as an enormous communitarian buzz."[38] In the *I Love Bees* plot, we find a literal representation of what Heim identifies as the network idealists' ardent desire to see "the worldwide networks that cover the planet from a global beehive."[39] When Lee first explained the project to me in April 2004, he acknowledged that the metaphor implied by "www.ilovebees.com" was intentional. "It absolutely was meant to make players think about themselves as a hive mind."[40]

The players quickly picked up on this gesture toward collaborative gaming, demonstrating a general awareness of the concepts of hive minds and CI. An early post read: "I think one of the reasons 'The Operator' chose to invade a site about bees was to contact us.... It needed a hive intellect, or as we'd call it, a collective detective."[41] Another player suggested: "I think that this won't be an entire game about bees... but the hive mind or collective mind comparison may prove to be intentional."[42] Indeed, the players showed a conscious awareness of the designers' use of metaphor to shape the community. One player wrote: "The creators of this... have definitely put some thought into the storyline, and they definitely consider us SOMETHING. I wouldn't be surprised if we ARE supposed to be the bees."[43] As they discussed what to call themselves, the players embraced the bee-inspired metaphor: "I'd call us The Hive or HiveMind... after all, we are a collective."[44] The community excitedly embraced the metaphor. One player wrote simply: "Dude, that means that WE are the bees!"[45]

Not all players were familiar with these concepts, however, and so some individuals took the lead in explaining them. One player attempted to explain all of the hive mind references:

You know how an individual bee isn't too intelligent, but the entire hive acting as a whole can display a remarkable cohesiveness—becoming more than the sum of its parts, so to speak? And you know how an individual silicon computer chip can't do a darn thing, but if you put enough of them together in the right way, whoa, you get the Internet?[46]

Through its rather conspicuous allusions to a hive mind, *I Love Bees* encouraged players to develop self-awareness. It not only inspired collectively intelligent behavior, but also gave the players a language for talking about CI. Developing fluency with the concept and terminology of CI, therefore, was an important part of the overall story design. It enabled what literacy theorist James Paul Gee calls "metalevel reflection" about the learning that was taking place.[47]

The "axons go hot" clue, which appeared above the list of GPS coordinates and time codes, is an excellent example of how a language of CI was embedded in the content of *I Love Bees* in order to facilitate metalevel reflection. Early on in the game, many players on different forums linked to the Wikipedia entry for "axon" as part of their effort to unpack the phrase. Their most widely circulated reference was the following definition obtained from that entry: "An axon, or nerve fiber, is a long slender projection of a nerve cell, or neuron, that conducts electrical impulses away from the neuron's cell body or soma. Axons are in effect the primary transmission lines of the nervous system."[48] For weeks, players considered what this message meant literally and metaphorically, until one player suggested an interpretation that spread very quickly and gained widespread acceptance across the player community. He wrote: "The countdown phrase 'Axons go hot' in relation to an AI would put one immediately in mind of a *neural net*. Could this be a neural net that Melissa is building?"[49] This insight resonated strongly with the narrative puzzle the players had already solved: that Melissa was a broken AI, attempting to repair itself.

The players thus came to consensus that the GPS coordinates were silicon axons, part of an AI's effort to build a neural net using an ubiquitous computing infrastructure. The actual structure of a brain, of course, is an important metaphorical tool for thinking and talking about CI. As Thomas J. Malone observes: "Collective intelligence has existed for a very long time... we could even view a single human brain as a collection of individual neurons or parts of the brain that collectively act intelligently."[50] In this way, the Operator's in-fiction efforts to create a neural net paralleled (and therefore served as a conceptual model for) the players' own construction of a CI network. Like a Russian doll, the theme of CI in *I Love Bees* nested inside itself: an AI program rebuilds itself, axons go hot, players form the hive mind.

And so it was through the narrative context of CI constructs that players confronted the central puzzle of the game: What should they do about the axons? Now that they had created a shared context for action, what was the appropriate collective response to the GPS coordinates, time codes, and countdown?

Stage Two: Making Meaning

When the 210 pairs of GPS coordinates were first discovered, there was no consensus among players regarding what to do with them. Even after the players agreed on a narrative context, the 210 points of data represented a highly ambiguous call to action. Their efforts to work together to explore this ambiguity marked the second phase of CI game play. I call it the *cooperation* stage. In this stage, players individually formulated hypotheses, presented them to the group, and then solicited help in testing and refining them collaboratively.

During the course of *I Love Bees*, the GPS coordinates page was visited by nearly a million different users, and discussed by hundreds of thousands of players on many dozens of forums. Here, I want to focus on the GPS puzzle-solving work of just one particularly well-organized group of approximately 4,000 players, who called themselves the Beekeepers. Their efforts to solve this problem, and the 2,850 forum posts they collectively scribed to keep track of these efforts, were followed closely and referenced frequently by the majority of other player forums.[51] As such, their work serves as an excellent microcosm of the larger, sometimes seemingly chaotic, cooperative speculation and data processing that took place during the weeks leading up to the end of the "Axons go hot" countdown on August 24, 2004.

At first, the number of plausible strategies for processing the GPS data proposed by the Beekeepers seemed infinite. Some thought that the coordinates were a code for a verbal message. A player using the handle Nightmare Tony wrote: "What if the coordinates are merely giving us letters, such as the first names of each city or town, and THAT is the actual code phrase?"[52] K proposed, instead: "I thought the time gap between the coordinates might be to do with Morse code—the three minute gaps correspond to a dot, and the four minute gaps correspond to a dash. Not sure how you'd separate letters, though."[53] Others suggested that plotting the coordinates would reveal the solution. Emouse wrote: "Connect the dots?"[54] Swissben wrote: "Do we have a way to get the actual altitude of these positions through maporama or their sites? Maybe we need to add a third dimension to these points. . . ."[55] Lorre wrote: "What if we calculate the distance between the points (pairs) on a routeplanner?"[56]

Some thought that visiting the real-world locations would reveal more clues. A Beekeeper named Spgheddy wrote: "These GPS coordinates are very precise—down to 15 ft in each direction, which is about 10 steps in each direction. We need to go to the locations and look at things that are within this precise area."[57] Many others looked for a common thread in the locations identified by the coordinates. Guest_Beekeeper wrote: "Can these coordinates somehow be arranged into numbers of IP addresses?"[58] Jbd wrote: "Maybe they're Wi-Fi locations."[59] BoonIsha wrote: "Radio stations? Have we checked radios broadcasting frequencies for these locations?"[60] John Incognito wrote: "Are there any traffic cameras at the GPS locations in the towns about cell towers?"[61] MrToasty wrote: "Could these possibly map to cell tower locations?"[62]

And yet others wondered if the GPS coordinates were posing a map-based mathematical puzzle. Nola wrote: "Can we determine a point that is equidistant to all 220 locations?"[63] Xyzzy wrote: "Time, time, time. Everyone's so concentrated on the points themselves that time is slipping under the rug. What is the significance of when each Axon goes live? Has there been a mathematical look at the possible patterns there?"[64] Will Bushman wrote: "Since this is in a large part an AI game, and has some familiar AI terminology in this puzzle, axons from neural nets, why not treat it as an old AI problem, the traveling salesman problem. Essentially try to determine the shortest path which goes through every point, but doesn't go through any point twice."[65]

As the days passed, and as individuals looked for ways to contribute ideas that hadn't already been proposed, the players began to proffer interpretive frameworks that could only be classified as highly speculative. Mayday wrote: "Not sure if it amounts to much, but I reversed all the longitudes (changed them from negative to positive) and they all fall in China. Seems a little coincidental."[66] Oecumenix_temporary wrote: "Originally I thought that maybe the new format could be used to look up biblical passages or something (like book 38, chapter 53, verse 30)."[67] Theorizer wrote: "These coordinates in fact aren't relative to earth, but to Space instead. So I definitely don't have the technology to check this. But if someone could check if Space has coordinates like this, and also if there are, see if they can find where they are."[68]

For more than two weeks, the Beekeepers took obvious pleasure in generating progressively more creative readings of the data set. But to advance the game on August 24, they would need to take a more rigorous approach. How could they test as many of these hypotheses as possible, and narrow the interpretive field to a single collective solution before the "axons go hot" countdown hit zero?

After a flurry of several hundred wildly diverse hypotheses, the Beekeepers decided to organize into three different teams for further analysis. At this stage of meaning making, the player group began to embody Levy's ideal of CI, which supports specialization and a recognition of diverse perspectives. Each group established a dedicated forum thread and a unique analysis mission statement. The goal of this self-differentiation: to group like-minded analysts together, allowing multiple competing threads of well-researched interpretation to emerge. The three groups were named the "literal thread," the "relative thread," and the "numerical thread." Each composed its own mission statement to define clearly its approach—and to recruit more player-analysts to its side. The first group argued:

The *literal thread* is for those who believe that we are just supposed to show up at these locations when the Axons "Go Hot." This theory has pretty much been shot down by some players since some of the locations have been found to be on private property, in front of the Sears Tower (think: a group of online dweebs gathering w/ their GPS en masse when the countdown ends... don't think the city of Chicago's gonna like that), and even one in a forest. However, I don't think this theory can be thrown out completely, as it hasn't been completely disproven.[69]

Another group proposed a more conceptual approach:

The *relative thread* supports the faction which believes that the coordinates are literal places, but the surrounding buildings/landmarks/streets/wifi/etc. are the key to the solution. This thread would be a good place to discuss our findings at the locations (and those at the wiki) without bothering the mathematicians.[70]

And the third group took a very abstract, data-crunching tact:

The *numerical thread* encompasses all those who believe the coordinates can be solved mathematically. Either by: A) disregarding that they are coordinates and using them as a series of numbers to find a hidden message, B) assuming they are coordinates, but using the locations to find new coordinates or a hidden message, C) finding a graphical representation of the coordinates which communicates a message or points to a new location."[71]

Once the players had divided themselves into groups according to analytical interests and skills, they were able to get down to some serious data processing the collection of supporting evidence. They cooperatively churned through the possibilities, reporting their findings, posting helpful compilations of data, and asking for backup.

Sherpa, a player working in the numerical group, offered up a database of preliminary calculations to the group: "In the 'scientific method' camp, here's an Excel sheet which has the co-ords, distances, pairings and addresses in it. No conclusions as yet—it's meant to be a tool to help people experiment, rather than have to dig through 30 pages and several websites to get the data. Enjoy."[72] Xasper reported his own work on the database and awaited backup: "I've been playing with the sum of the digits in the postal codes as a cypher for letters, and had some weird results.... I'll watch this thread for other attempts and hopefully we can all use the information offered."[73] Extrasonic did the same:

I did the calculation for the speed required to go from the first point to the second point in 4 minutes. The speed required was Mach 7 (7 times the speed of sound at sea level).... I only calculated the speed required to go from the first coordinate (DC-area) to the second (Cleveland-area) in order to prove to myself that it wasn't feasible for something physical to make the trip (ruling out military aircraft and space-based objects). Other points might yield different, more interesting results or a pattern might emerge—I'm not trying to discourage additional investigation.[74]

At the same time, the relative thread explored the potential meaning of the GPS coordinates by seeking any common thread they could find. Drizjr wrote:

I looked up my own IP on geobytes. Took the lat/long from there and pushed them through MapQuest. While it is not where I'm sitting at my computer, it matched the map from Row 103/Col 01... off by only six city blocks. To me, it's close enough to say that Melissa is tracking us down through the emails."[75]

They rallied around promising theories. Handfulofhoneybees wrote:

Drizjr, I agree that a hit so close to home gives you that tingling sensation of confirmation.... but we need some data to flesh it out a bit. So once again, I implore the beekeepers! Locate yourself using any IP locator tool you can dig up on Google! Report *perfect* hits promptly, but near-perfect hits only when it seems like we've run out of options. Happy hunting.[76]

The relative analysts modified the shared databases and documents generated by the numerical thread with new fields to allow for even more directions of simultaneous analysis. DanteGA wrote:

Some of the patterns have already been remarked upon: Universities, Malls/shopping centers (and don't forget the many points along 'the Mall' in Washington!), other landmarks (San Diego Zoo, airports).... what I think is more intriguing is the fact that many, many of the names of the roads share similarities. The clearest example is that many of the points are either literally on Main Street (in one case, Maine Dr, which really caught my attention), or are on the 'main' street in the town.... I am attaching a version of the coordinate spreadsheet with two columns that I've added. In the last column is my interpretation of the MapQuest locations. Some of my locations may seem like a stretch, but I am hoping that they can be corrected.[77]

When online investigation failed to produce a unified theory, the thread organized a series of massively cooperative scouting missions, posting results to collaboratively authored documents. Dorkmaster wrote:

This is an urgent appeal from a beekeeper for some organization and some determination from my fellow players. We appear to be stuck in the mud on this GPS/axons puzzle. Here is what we need to do: VISIT all of these locations—OR at the very least, find out via the internet or whatever (in no small detail) what is at each one. Post your findings [on the wiki]... We've been brainstorming for days on the data we have and have come up with nothing. I think this is because we have to go out and gather MORE data. The coordinates tell us where to find it.[78]

The specificity of each coordinate meant that a player located near an unchecked data set could play a hugely important role in the analysis, even if he or she had not originally contributed the strategy of investigating locations. As mike3854 wrote: "Finally I might be able to stop being a lurker and help. As soon as I can, I'll take my camera with me and check the Kissimmee FL locations, seeing as how they are close to my house. If there is anything important there, I'll make sure you see what I see."[79]

In the end, however, the literal group won out with its most persuasive analysis that players should prepare to be at the locations on August 24, 2004, when the countdown hit zero. The success of their argument was only possible as a result of evidence collected by the relative thread and, in the wake of the numerical approach being ruled out, was directly sparked by some of the location scouts' observations. Giskard writes: "Something that just hit me... there's a lot of mention of coordinates being in malls, stores, airports, etc. Could it be they are locations of public phones? That would be awesome... if all of them got a call on august 24."[80]

Beekeepers used their earlier work during the cognitive phase to corroborate this interpretation. Cedmond writes: "what if these are all locations of public phones (as previously suggested)? There is a great amount of text in the poems and code about the entity trying to speak, find it's voice...."[81] Xhylph writes: "'Axons go hot' could be the same thing as 'pathways of information are accessed,' which would support the phone theory."[82]

Literal players combined narrative analysis with further location scouting. Peccable wrote:

I grabbed some maps off the 'net of the Philly position and I'm almost entirely certain that there's a set of payphones on that *precise* (northwest) corner. Melissa's new rant includes the fact that she wants to create a voice for herself. My theory: At 5:07pm EST (I believe that's when the AXON countdown ends) on August the 24th, the phones at the various coordinates will ring, and Melissa will speak. Like I said, I'll check tonight if there *is* an actual set of phones there, but I literally live around the corner from there and I'm pretty familiar with the area. Anyone have supporting data? Or non-supporting data.[83]

Members of the group used the tools compiled by the numerical and relative players to reinforce their own work. Atomant411 wrote:

Using both the road map and the satellite image map from the excel spreadsheets on the WIKI, I decided to drive by the Garland point today after work. If the maps are accurate on the spreadsheet, the point is actually in front a United Artists movie theater (enticingly close to a row of payphones) in the shopping center on the Southeast corner of Garland and Beltline... I've been a lurker throughout this entire puzzle, and haven't had much to say on the matter, thus the reluctance to post, but I thought this was important.[84]

In all of these ways, the players actively wove the three self-differentiated threads of investigation back together, drawing on their initial story work to arrive once again on common ground. And so as the August 24 date loomed nearer, player vpisteve vocalized what the majority of Beekeepers had collectively agreed upon:

[T]he fact that the coordinates are specific to the .000xth degree tells me that they do in fact mean a physical location in the real world. If this were merely a numeric or graphic puzzle, the PMs wouldn't have been that pinpoint, they could've just as easily made a puzzle to the .0xth degree.... Somehow, something will be *transmitted* (as tagged in the source code) to these actual, physical locations, something that will make Melissa "wide awake and physical."[85]

Ultimately, the players converged on this single interpretation, backed up by many thousands of visits to GPS coordinates and hundreds of thousands of viewings of the field players' digital photo reports and verbal summaries of what was observed on location. But did the players who had not originally backed this "literal" reading of the coordinates feel left out or unsuccessful? By all accounts, no. Ultimately, participation in the search for the solution was what mattered most. As a player named Sherpa observed: "There're a lot of trees to bark up the wrong way before hitting on anything."[86] And indeed, for a game as open-ended and initially chaotic as *I Love Bees*, all of those trees must be barked up to arrive at a single interpretation through process of elimination. For search and analysis players, failing to solve a puzzle in this kind of massively collaborative network does not mean failing to make any kind of contribution at all. Instead, it means successfully eliminating a framework so that others' resources can be redirected to still viable analytical tactics. As both Levy and Vinge argued, CI as a problem-solving pedagogy is extraordinarily inclusive. It engages a set of players that is as broad and diverse as possible in order to work through problems of unprecedented scale and complexity.

What is it about scale and complexity that supports inclusive participation? How, in the case of the *I Love Bees* GPS coordinates, can a single data set support such a vast range of interpretations and yet also directly inspire such a rigorous course of collective analysis? I would argue that the primary puzzle of *I Love Bees* embodied a *meaningful ambiguity*. That is, the data set lacked the clarity of formal interactive instructions, yet maintained a distinctively *sensical* nature. That is, the choice and ordering of the coordinates did not seem *non*sensical.

Instead, its arrangement was structured and seemingly intentional enough that it promised to mean something, if only approached in the right way. This meaning was implied through the specificity, volume, and overtly designed presentation of the data.

Moreover, this abundance of pliable data provided inexhaustible ways for players to take differentiated action, whether it was to perform calculations, make maps, conduct Web searchers, or visit real-world locations. In the GPS data set, there was enough perpetual ambiguity that there was always something more for a member of the Hive Mind to do. There were no limits on plausible actions to take. At the same time, there was enough structure and specificity of data to make the application of data processes a challenging, time-consuming affair. So there was never a shortage of supporting work to be done.

How important was ambiguity to the formation of a CI? It was absolutely crucial for two reasons. First, ambiguity creates a *critical* and *constructive* relationship with digital media and systems. It serves a psychological function, to draw players into the collective. Computer–human interface researchers William W. Gaver, Jacob Beaver, and Steve Benford argue in their scientific article "Ambiguity as a Resource for Design"[87] that "ambiguity . . . is a resource for design that can be used to encourage close personal engagement with systems."[88] They write: "Ambiguity can be frustrating, sure. But it can also be intriguing, mysterious, and delightful. By impelling people to interpret situations for themselves, it encourages them to start grappling conceptually with systems and their contexts, and thus to establish deeper and more personal relations with the meanings offered by those systems."[89] The GPS data set was intentionally designed to thwart easy interpretation. And as Gaver et al. observe, "By thwarting easy interpretation, ambiguous situations require people to participate in meaning making."[90]

For the players of *I Love Bees*, this grappling with ambiguity was meaningful not only on a personal level, but also on a collective level. On a discussion thread that was still active months after the game concluded, one player defined the emergent CI specifically as a search for meaning in the chaotic system of the game. "We experienced being part of a collective intelligence . . . participating in a search for, or perhaps creation of greater, shared meaning" (Phaedra).[91]

By asking players to cooperate to make meaning out of an ambiguous system, the game-based hive mind celebrates individual perspective even as it embraces the larger, intricate intelligence that emerges only at the scale digital networks afford. This ability to value both simultaneously is a fundamental lesson that search and analysis games work to impart, in addition to the practical technological skills of how to use collaborative software and communicate data and theories to the network. As Levy writes, "I am not interchangeable. I have an image, a position, dignity, a personal and positive value within the knowledge space. All of us have the right to be acknowledged as a knowledge identity."[92]

To underscore the importance of this message, I want to return here to Vinge's imagined CI curriculum of the year 2025. *Rainbows End* is not only optimistic about the future power of massively collaborative networks, but also realistic and insightful about the challenges they pose to the individual's sense of self-worth. In one scene, a Search and Analysis student admits how insecure she is about her ability to contribute to the collective. "There was a kind of frightened look in her eyes [as she asked]: 'But some people are better than others. . . . Or maybe others are just sharper. . . . What happens if we try our hardest, and it just isn't good enough?"[93] The inclusion of meaningful ambiguity in *I Love Bees* expressly addresses this concern. The plausibility of so many diverse interpretations empowered players of all kinds of skill levels, natural abilities, inclinations, and interests to achieve success. This kind of massively inclusive engagement is increasingly vital as we think about the future of learning. It ensures that no player is left out of the game, no individual discouraged or excluded from the opportunity to contribute to participatory culture.

It is true that ultimately there was only one best solution to the GPS puzzle—scout the GPS coordinates in advance of August 24, 2004; find all of the nearby pay phones; arrange to station players near all of those phones at the appropriate time code; and make sure the players show up at the right time and place. But in the bigger picture of the game, the many "failed" analytical frameworks suggested by players in the weeks before the countdown hit zero played an important role. In the twelve weeks that followed the first ring of a pay phone, over one hundred new puzzles appeared on www.ilovebees.com. These post-countdown puzzles required players to use Morse code, mapping, sophisticated math, research into scientific literature, physical modeling, advanced classification schemes, anagrams, and other wordplay, and more—in short, as many of the popular emergent frameworks that had not succeeded in solving the GPS puzzle that could be squeezed into the game. The game was designed to reward the creative, exploratory work and lateral thinking of the hive mind by creating ongoing opportunities for their experimental strategies to be applied successfully.

Next, as Gaver et al.[94] argue, ambiguity "allows designers to engage users with issues without constraining how they respond... It gives designers the ability to suggest issues and perspectives for consideration without imposing solutions." This is the second critical function that meaningful ambiguity plays in enabling a CI to emerge. The final results of a CI effort cannot be prescribed in advance by a design team consisting of a half-dozen people. CI must emerge from the massive collaboration of hundreds, thousands, or more. Therefore, the full solution *cannot* be predesigned. The puzzle of a search and analysis game must be ambiguous, and therefore open-ended enough to allow the players' emerging CI to suggest more complex solutions. The designers, through ambiguity, must cede control over the final scope and dimensions of the game's solution to the players. Gaver et al. write: "The artifact or situation sets the scene for meaning-making, but doesn't prescribe the result. Instead, the work of making an ambiguous situation comprehensible belongs to the person, and this can be both inherently pleasurable and lead to a deep conceptual appropriation of the artifact."[95] Indeed, the players' appropriation of the intentionally ambiguous game content led to the third and final phase of CI game play, the coordination stage.

Stage Three: Evolving a Collective Intelligence

Meaningful ambiguity promoted wildly diverse interpretation. In the case of *I Love Bees*, the players' interpretations far exceeded what the designers could have anticipated and created responses for in advance of live game play. In order for meaningful ambiguity to support CI effectively, therefore, the system had to be flexible enough to incorporate the myriad unexpected uses and ingenious attempted interactions resulting from its open-ended challenge. It had to support *real-time redesign* that enables the hive mind to evolve over time.

In the production of traditional computer games and video games, a formal line exists between the construction of the game and the play of that game by an audience. The vast majority of digital games are fully developed and finalized before they ever reach the players. They are shipped to stores or made available online for download as completed products, not works in progress. The programmers of *Halo*, for instance, do not create secret new levels after the video game has been shipped to consumers. They do not tweak the fighting algorithms of various enemies in order to make the game more difficult for players who have mastered it. Nor do they add new weapons to the players' inventory based on the expressed desires of fans on public *Halo* forums. It is true that eventually the same design team may produce a sequel that provides more play and different play—hence, *Halo 2*. However, the sequel is a different product altogether. The original game itself is not fundamentally flexible to players' emergent strategies, desires, and skills. Ultimately, the work of the game designers and developers ends the day the game reaches the players' hands.

The opposite is true for a game like *I Love Bees*, which is produced to a significant degree in *real time*—that is, in live procedural response to players' interactions with it. When *I Love Bees* launched in July 2004, approximately sixty percent of the final content had been created. The other forty percent was partly planned, but a great amount of design space was left entirely open. 42 Entertainment's team of behind-the-scenes writers, programmers, story directors, and game-play stage managers was assembled to create post-launch content that would build on what the players created. As cultural critic Steven Johnson observes, when it comes to producing the stunning interactive effects of traditional computer and video games, "it's all just a bunch of algorithms behind the curtain."[96] In other words, most digital games are closed systems of preprogrammed rules and prepopulated databases. When it comes to a real-time search and analysis game like *I Love Bees*, however, it's *not* just algorithms behind the curtain—it's a team of live game designers, repopulating the databases and rewriting the rules as the game is being played. As lead community designer for *I Love Bees*, I had the job of monitoring the interpretive and problem-solving efforts of the player community so that we could adapt the game to their evolving collective profile. Each day, after scouring player forums, blogs, and e-mails, and lurking in their chat rooms, I reported their most interesting new theories and strategies to the other lead designers. In turn, the other designers crafted ongoing game challenges, as well as the climax of the interactive story, in response to the skill sets and the investigative framework the players themselves had developed. Through this real-time, flexible design, we worked to encourage the existing *Halo* fan base to hone and strengthen their CI powers. This evolutionary phase is the third and final stage of CI game play, which I call the *coordination* stage. It consists of an *iterative*, or cyclical and repetitive, attempt to solve similar problems with increasingly sophisticated strategies and increasingly powerful techniques. Lead writer Sean Stewart describes this iterative process as a "call-and-response, jazz-style interaction. . . . It increases the ownership of the players in the game enormously."[97]

The creation of over one hundred post-countdown puzzles to incorporate "failed" analytical frameworks of the hive mind was an important part of this call-and-response game design. Consider a non-GPS-related example of a challenge that was created post-launch. In designing the central hacked Web site for the game, technical director Jim Stewartson had invented a fictional, object-oriented programming language through which various artificially intelligent programs communicated with each other. Among the programs that used this language were programs named the System Distributed Reflex Peril (the SPDR) and the Pious Flea. Throughout the first twelve weeks of the game, Stewartson dropped bits and pieces of this futuristic code into Web pages and e-mails sent by the programs, including the 150 lines of code that players initially collected and interpreted.

Stewartson never provided players with any direct translation or explanation of the fictive programming language. However, players discovered early on that it was possible to discern the meaning of specific lines of code by observing their impact on other characters and on the composition and functioning of the Web site. In doing so, they would be able to translate progress into narrative. The players therefore took it upon themselves to collect and to translate every line of code, in the hopes of gaining a functional fluency in the language. From their compiled examples they created a wiki-based guide to the language, which they themselves named *Flea++* (in playful reference to the actual present-day computer programming language *C++*). An example of *Flea++* code as translated by players appears below.

This dialogue, composed by the players out of fragments of found code, was actually quite a climactic one in the overall story. As the player providing this translation correctly surmised, the final pieces of code document the death of the Pious Flea, the very character for whom the players named the language.

In a postgame chat between players and the puppet masters of *I Love Bees*, Stewartson revealed that, as the game progressed, he worked directly from the players' *Flea++* guide to write new game content. He admitted: "to be perfectly honest, after a while, I started to

Code:

```
grope: seeker > !attach Princess
```

Remember that > is a question in most instances.

This means "Can I attach to you, Princess?"

Code:

```
fail "msg: SPDR-5.14.3
```

"No? SPDR-5.14.3?"

Code:

```
evade evade evade
```

"Crap. RUN!!!!"

Code:

```
!probe extern proc 1
```

"What just tried to attach to me?"

Code:

```
rogue proc
```

"You're not anything I recognize, you're foreign, not friendly at all"

Code:

```
!bite rogue proc 1

Recurse
```

"I'm putting a stop to this."

"And I'm not going to stop attacking you until I'm sure you're dead."

use the syntax cheat sheet from the [player-created] wiki."[98] Indeed, the players took such ownership of the language that they played with it extensively outside the formal challenges of the game. The players excitedly told Stewartson in the postgame chat, for instance, about "Flea++ apparently becoming a geek-trendy lingo, similar to [gamer] 1337speak," or "elite speak."[99] One player explained that players exiting chat rooms at the end of the night would say "!grope pillow" instead of "I'm going to sleep."[100] Another informed Stewartson: "I translated Edgar Allen Poe's 'Tell Tale Heart' into Flea++."[101]

Together, the formal documentation, successful translation, and creative use of *Flea++* signaled that mastery of the fictional programming language was a key component of the players' CI. Stewartson therefore decided to create a crucial *Flea++* game mission in the final weeks of the game. During this mission, he manned an e-mail account that players discovered

Code:

```
!splotch

clean confidence 100
```

Flea: "OH I AM DEAD"

SPDR: "Yes, you are."

had been hijacked by an AI program fluent in *Flea++*. In real time, hundreds of players sent bits of code to the character; Stewartson made live updates to www.ilovebees.com to reflect the impact of their code, as if the commands had been directly implemented by the character. As the players quickly learned not to cancel each others' commands through conflicting e-mails and to combine lines of code to achieve their desired result, they demonstrated an emergent command of the language that they themselves had helped formally to compose. Indeed, as Stewartson told me in a personal interview,

> Before the players put together all of the code on the wiki, I wasn't sure the language really made sense. They were the ones who made sense out of it. If they hadn't come up with their own standard version,

I never could have pushed them so hard on the final Flea++ challenge. They made that puzzle, really, because the solution came straight from the wiki they wrote.[102]

The *Flea++* mission shows how real-time game designers can create new content on the fly to encourage and reward the players' emergent CI, simply by paying close attention to the skills that develop in the audience and looking for opportunities to capitalize on them. But even more importantly, there must be formal mechanics for real-time design built into the interactive arc of the game. As Vinge's fictional Search and Analysis teacher reminded her students, "synthetic serendipity doesn't just happen. By golly, you must create it." In *I Love Bees*, a twelve-week cycle of calling pay phones every Tuesday was implemented in order to create this kind of organized serendipity, in which the game design emerged as perfectly coordinated with players' levels of ability and expertise. None of the pay phone challenges were designed before the game launched. Instead, the entire team collaborated on their design each Monday night after receiving my latest report on the players' most recent efforts and discussion.

By the time the countdown hit zero on August 24, the players were ready for far more than we expected. They showed up at the GPS coordinates laden with every form of digital communications technology and personal media devices you could imagine. They were prepared for virtually anything. They had compiled databases of each others' cell phone numbers in case they needed to relay information to or from the field. They had stationed significant numbers of players online in case real-time research was necessary to complete the mission. They brought large numbers of friends and family with them in case a group performance was necessary. But what they were, in fact, asked to do once they arrived on site (as it turned out) did not require any of those improvised supplies, allies, or information systems.

Instead, at each coordinate, at the appropriate time, a pay phone rang. If players located and answered the ringing pay phone, they were asked a prerecorded question by Melissa, the Operator. (The first question: "Who is the enemy of mankind?" The answer: "The Covenant," the enemy alien race in the *Halo* games.) If they answered correctly, they heard thirty seconds of a *War of the Worlds*–style radio drama. Their mission? To intercept as many pieces of the drama as possible and to report back to other players what they had heard. Players heard thirty different bits of drama that day; all were successfully intercepted in at least one location, and players met back-up online to put the narrative pieces together. They fulfilled their mission perfectly.

But by creating such a robust communications infrastructure and coordinating extensive mobile computing supplies, they had performed at a greater capability than we had expected. We felt as if they were asking us to ask more of them. They were directing us to direct them to do something specific: put their extreme coordination skills to the test.

Because August 24 was the first of twelve weeks' worth of GPS missions, we could do just that. In the weeks that followed, the coordinates page updated on a biweekly basis, and the number of coordinates posted per week jumped from the starting count of 210 until a total of over 1,000 were posted during the final week of game play. Ultimately, over 40,000 phone calls were made to over 1,000 pay phones around the world. To handle this increased distribution, players posted over 12,000 messages and weekly phone maps to a board called "Axon Coordination."

We started adding randomly distributed live phone calls with more complicated, live activities—precisely because the players showed us they were capable of succeeding at more challenging kinds of interaction. We also started calling the phones in combinations that made it increasingly difficult for local groups to coordinate effectively. For example, we regularly rang a dozen pay phones in Washington, DC's Union Station, which were spread out throughout the massive train station. At the start of the game, phones were scheduled to ring one at a time, with enough minutes spaced out between them so that the DC team of players could move from one to the next, methodically answering all of the calls and collecting all of the content. By the end of the game, all dozen phones were ringing at precisely the same second, forcing players to divide and conquer, while communicating in real time with each other via mobile phones to compare answers to the questions and report any live challenges that were given.

As the players pushed themselves to succeed at every challenge, we were forced to present them with a problem that we ourselves weren't sure they could successfully solve. We called it the "relay mission," and it was designed to make or break their CI. Shortly after sunrise on a Tuesday late in the game, we directed the voice actress playing Melissa the Operator to start making live calls to phones on the East Coast. She asked whoever answered the phone tell her something personal—for instance, a five-word phrase that described something he or she is very, very good at. The Operator then informed the player that she would be calling another pay phone somewhere in the world, as soon as one hour from that moment. Whoever answered the phone needed to repeat back to her the same five-word phrase. Then she hung up, providing no information about which phone she intended to call.

Our plan was, over the course of the day, to repeat this relay mission up to a dozen times, shortening the time increments until we would posed our final, seemingly impossible challenge: to relay an improvised personal message worldwide with only a fifteen-second time differential between the first call and the second. But we were fairly certain the players would never get that far. We had designed a number of failure responses so that we could reward players for however close they came, fully expecting them eventually to hit a wall past which they could not coordinate and perform.

The players, however, never hit that wall. By using their early axon coordination spreadsheets—they knew which players lived near which phones, and had their mobile contact information—and by consulting the timeline of GPS coordinates for that day, and cross-referencing those data against their knowledge of which pay phones the Operator had favored in the past for live calls, they were able to deduce which phones were likely to ring, and who was most likely to answer those phones in the time window the Operator presented. They then set up a relay team of online players broadcasting each secret five-word phrase as it was invented to all players known to be in the field; hundreds of players online called hundreds of players at pay phones so that they could update each other virtually instantly.

In the end, the iterative design of our pay phone events gave us powerful flexibility to help the players' CI evolve. From the outset, the game was designed to allow for a dozen redesigns. And as the game changed, the players' strategies evolved, creating a positive feedback loop of CI. As the players became more collectively intelligent, the challenges became more complex. And as the players invented smarter strategies and honed their coordination skills to meet these challenges, the designers were pushed to imagine future challenges even more difficult and confounding. Before we saw what the players were capable of, we never imagined that a massively multiplayer team of young *Halo* fans would be capable of building, in one day, a worldwide, instantaneous, mobile broadcasting platform. The idea to ask them to do just that was only possible after the players' brilliant coordination efforts emerged.

This real-time flexibility, I believe, is the true power of a puppet-mastered search and analysis game. Ultimately, the game can be designed beyond the scope of anyone's initial expectations—not only the players' expectations of what they can accomplish, but also the designers' *and* the public's perception of what the hive mind can achieve. The players themselves create the unprecedented context for achieving previously unimaginable goals. As these emergent goals are met by the players, the stakes of the game grow: no longer is it merely teaching the players CI. The game is also empowering players to teach the world what such a CI is capable of.

Conclusions

As the leading edge of research, industry, politics, social innovation, and cultural production increasingly seek to harness the wisdom of the crowd and the power of the collective, it is urgent that we create engaging, firsthand experiences of CI for as wide and as general a young audience as possible. Search and analysis games are poised to become our best tool for helping as many and diverse a population as possible develop an interest and gain direct experience participating in our ever-more collective network culture.

In *Convergence Culture*, Henry Jenkins considers the role that popular culture should play in cultivating CI. He argues: "Right now, we are learning how to apply these new participatory skills through our relation to commercial entertainment . . . for two reasons: on the one hand, because the stakes are so low; and on the other, playing with popular culture is a lot more fun than playing with more serious matters."[103] Jenkins predicts that, as a society, we eventually evolve our CI interests in the direction of real-world, rather than fictional, concerns. However, I am suggesting with this case study that, for young students learning about CI for the first time, popular culture and online entertainment will remain the most effective spaces for learning how real-world massively collaborative participation works.

In *Get There Early*, Institute for the Future researcher Bob Johansen argues that immersive gaming can prepare players for future changes in network culture. He writes: "Immersion helps get a feeling for what's possible. Immersion helps you try out different ways of acting, so you can develop your own agility."[104] Indeed, as I have documented with this *I Love Bees* case study, the immersive aspects of search and analysis gaming provide a visceral, first-person, hands-on experience of collaborative cognition, networked cooperation, and real-time coordination. Players develop a familiarity with CI techniques through direct experience. They gain confidence and fluency in emerging technologies and CI strategies by playing with new network platforms and multiuser applications in increasingly complex scenarios. Search and analysis games, with their iterative real-time redesign, are perfectly structured to provide such scaffolding challenges—a key aspect to mastering new modes of problem solving and cultural participation.

As massively social experiences, search and analysis games are also especially well-suited to encouraging metalevel reflection on the skills and processes that players use to meet new challenges. Being a part of a massively multiplayer game community means sharing your thoughts and experiences with your fellow players. Finally, and perhaps most importantly, as learning systems, collective gaming encourages risk-taking learning in a low-risk setting. As Johansen observes: "Learners get to dive in and learn in a first person way, without playing for keeps until they are ready."[105]

I want to conclude this case study with a letter from an *I Love Bees* player, for I believe the gamer's personal experience speaks best for itself. Several months after *I Love Bees* ended, I received an e-mail from "Rose," a mother who played the game with her fourteen-year-old son, a high school student and an avid video gamer. In the letter, she described the game as a powerful tutorial in networked collaboration for both of them, one that made them feel excited about participating in CIs in the future. She writes:

> It is really important to me that you, and other people, understand the differences that alternate reality gaming has made in our way of thinking. It has powerfully affected our attitudes about what is possible. The game for me has been about gathering a first hand knowledge of how a large community can function, including the role of technology. I know that large scale communities can work and be extraordinarily effective. I am not afraid of the complexities.[106]

Notes

1. Thomas W. Malone, What Is Collective Intelligence, and What Will We Do About It? Edited transcript of remarks at the official launch of the MIT Center for Collective Intelligence, October 13, 2006. http://www.webcitation.org/5K9ZqKlVU.

2. Unfiction Forums, Archive: The Haunted Apiary (Let Op!), *Unfiction.com*, July–November 2004. http://forums.unfiction.com/forums/index.php?f=200.

3. Pierre Levy, *Collective Intelligence: Mankind's Emerging World in Cyberspace*, trans. Robert Bononno (Cambridge, MA: Perseus Books, 1997), xxiv.

4. Ibid., 17.

5. Ibid., 9.

6. Wikipedia, http://www.wikipedia.org. Accessed December 1, 2006.

7. Yahoo! Answers, http://answers.yahoo.com/. Accessed December 1, 2006.

8. Google Image Labeler, http://images.google.com/imagelabeler/. Accessed December 1, 2006.

9. MapHub, http://www.maphub.com/. Accessed December 1, 2006.

10. SFZero, http://sf0.org/. Accessed December 1, 2006.

11. Hollywood Stock Exchange, http://www.hsx.com/. Accessed December 1, 2006.

12. World Economic Forums' Global Risks Prediction Market, http://weforum.newsfutures.com/. Accessed December 1, 2006.

13. Malone, What Is Collective Intelligence.

14. Ibid.

15. Seminal work in this emerging space of collective intelligence design includes James Surowiecki's *The Wisdom of Crowds* (New York: Doubleday, 2004), which identifies diversity, independence, and decentralization of participants as the three fundamental requirements to produce CI, and Howard Bloom's *Global Brain* (New York: Wiley, 2000), which argues for a strategic balance of conformity and diversity among CI participants, along with core interactive mechanics that allow participants to internally evaluate and revise strategies, to reallocate resources, and to compete externally with other CI groups.

16. Henry Jenkins, *Convergence Culture: Where Old and New Media Collide* (New York: New York University Press, 2006), 245.

17. Vernor Vinge, *Rainbows End: A Novel with One Foot Set in the Future* (New York: Tor Books, 2006), 60.

18. Levy, *Collective Intelligence*, 13–14.

19. Ibid., 13.

20. Sean Stewart, Alternate Reality Games, Personal essay on Web site, June 11, 2006. http://www.webcitation.org/5KP38jg59.

21. *I Love Bees* Home Page, July 24, 2004. http://web.archive.org/web/20040723031712/http://www.ilovebees.com/.

22. *I Love Bees* Links Page, August 11, 2004. http://web.archive.org/web/20040723031712/http://www.ilovebees.com/.

23. Emergency Exit, *I Love Bees* Blog, July 25, 2004. http://www.webcitation.org/5KP7zsFmV.

24. Because players are not required to register any personal details in order to play a game like *I Love Bees*, obtaining precise demographic data is extremely difficult. As the primary community researcher for the game, however, I estimate that approximately 20 percent of players were eighteen years old or younger, while another half were under the age of twenty-five. My rough demographic estimates here are based on an analysis of personal details mentioned by players on *I Love Bees* forums and in e-mails written to game characters; profile information on player-created blogs and forums; and my direct observation of player ages at live events. The number 600,000 is derived from proprietary Web traffic data and statistics collected by 42 Entertainment.

25. Elan Lee, This Is Not a Game, Design track lecture for the Game Developers Conference, San Jose, CA, March 19–24, 2002.

26. Sean Stewart, Post-Game Chat with the *I Love Bees* Puppetmasters, November 7, 2004. Chat log archived at http://www.webcitation.org/5KP7wONpF.

27. Elan Lee and Sean Stewart, Surfacing, E-mail message from manbehindthecurtain@visionary.net, July 24, 2001. http://www.webcitation.org/5KP8KZUIZ.

28. *Halo 2* Game Detail Page, http://www.webcitation.org/5KP8xDL8w.

29. Unfiction Forums, #109437.

30. The Extraordinary, *I Love Bees* Blog, August 24, 2006. http://www.webcitation. org/5KPBXKpT7.

31. Jane McGonigal, Interaction Statistics, 42 Entertainment Community Report, August 27, 2004.

32. Ibid.

33. Louis Wu, Forum Improvements, *Halo Bungie Forums*, July 27, 2004. http://www.webcitation.org/5KPBcYsjj.

34. During the live game campaign, I tracked and documented forum posts on forty-seven forums that were playing *I Love Bees*. Posts on these specific forums hit the million mark ten weeks into the four-month-long game, after which point tracking the increasingly distributed player discussions became too challenging and time-consuming a task to pursue.

35. http://www.bees.netninja.com/wiki. This Web site is currently offline. Statistics were measured on August 17, 2004.

36. *I Love Bees* Development Wiki. Summary, November 1, 2004. http://www.webcitation.org/5KPCUaMcs.

37. Ibid.

38. Michael Heim, The Cyberspace Dialectic, in *The Digital Dialectic*, ed. Peter Lunenfeld (Cambridge, MA: The MIT Press, 2000), 37.

39. Ibid.

40. Elan Lee, Personal interview with author, April 3, 2004.

41. Unfiction Forums, #43966.

42. Ibid., #43995.

43. Ibid., #73194.

44. Ibid., #45132.

45. Ibid., #44925.

46. Ibid., #44898.

47. James Paul Gee, *What Video Games Have to Teach Us About Learning and Literacy* (New York: Palgrave Macmillan, 2003).

48. See http://en.wikipedia.org/wiki/Axon. Accessed December 1, 2006.

49. The Extraordinary, *I Love Bees* Blog.

50. Malone, What Is Collective Intelligence.

51. Unfiction Forums, Archive.

52. Unfiction Forums, #43209.

53. Ibid., #58518.

54. Ibid., #52332.

55. Ibid., #55751.

56. Ibid., #55092.

57. Ibid., #55602.

58. Ibid., #55498.

59. Ibid., #53198.

60. Ibid., #56432.

61. Ibid., #55378.

62. Ibid., #52959.

63. Ibid., #55424.

64. Ibid., #57902.

65. Ibid., #55184.

66. Ibid., #52546.

67. Ibid., #58078.

68. Ibid., #55138.

69. Unfiction Forums, Archive.

70. Ibid.

71. Ibid.

72. Unfiction Forums, #53411.

73. Ibid., #56930.

74. Ibid., #57269.

75. Ibid., #54981.

76. Ibid., #55058.

77. Ibid., #56698.

78. Ibid. #54376.

79. Ibid.

80. Ibid., #52543.

81. Unfiction Forums, #52502. August 10, 2004.

82. Ibid., #52615.

83. Ibid., #52568.

84. Ibid., #58001.

85. Ibid., #55150.

86. Ibid., #55820.

87. William W. Gaver, Jacob Beaver, and Steve Benford, Ambiguity as a Resource for Design, in *Proceedings of the SIGCHI Conference on Human Factors in Computing Systems* (New York: ACM Press, 2003), 233–40.

88. Ibid., 233.

89. Ibid.

90. Ibid., 235.

91. Unfiction Forums, #111201. December 7, 2004.

92. Levy, *Collective Intelligence*, 13.

93. Vigne, *Rainbows End*, 60.

94. Gaver, Beaver, and Benford, Ambiguity as a Resource for Design, 1.

95. Ibid., 78.

96. Steven Johnson, *Everything Bad Is Good for You* (New York: Riverhead Books, 2005), 45.

97. Stewart, Alternate Reality Games.

98. Post Game Chat, 17:15.

99. Ibid., 17:17.

100. Ibid.

101. Ibid., 17:14.

102. Jim Stewartson, Personal interview with author, November 20, 2004.

103. Jenkins, *Convergence Culture*, 246.

104. Bob Johansen, *Get There Early* (San Francisco: Berrett-Koehler Publishers, 2008), 102.

105. Ibid., 78.

106. Rose, Letter to a Puppet Master, Personal e-mail correspondence, received August 3, 2005.

Game Credit

I Love Bees, director Elan Lee, lead writer Sean Stewart, technology lead Jim Stewartson, community lead Jane McGonigal (Emeryville, CA: 42 Entertainment, July–November 2004).

Halo 2, director Joseph Staten, executive producer Pete Parsons, art director Marcus Lehto (Redmond, WA: Microsoft Game Studios and Bungie Game Studio, 2004).

Education Unleashed: Participatory Culture, Education, and Innovation in *Second Life*

Cory Ondrejka

Linden Lab

Introduction

In the four decades since the start of the silicon revolution, the computational power of individual computers has increased by ten million times,[1] and computers have moved from prohibitively expensive scientific devices to an ubiquitous part of everyday life. During the same period, connections between computers have increased from the first packet-based transmissions of ARPANET to the saturation of the Internet and the World Wide Web.[2] These technological transitions drove two additional transformations: the rise of online computer games and the dominance of networked computers for information transfer and communication. These, in turn, have enabled a new media form: the virtual world. Like the computer games with which they share technology and terminology, virtual worlds take their participants to new places beyond the physical and geographic limitations of the real world. Yet virtual worlds go far beyond games in their leveraging of social connections and learning principles.[3] This mix of fantastic possibilities and social educational opportunities has virtual worlds poised to transform basic approaches to learning and communication, as well as innovation and entrepreneurship.

In an increasingly technologically linked yet socially fragmented world,[4] virtual worlds demonstrate the power to bring people together.[5] They bypass the historic impacts of geographic,[6] professional,[7] and generational[8] distance by allowing their residents to create knowledge[9] and identity[10] in collaborative spaces. Although a passionate minority of game players—those who play massively multiplayer online role-playing games (MMORPGs) like *World of Warcraft*, *Everquest*, and *Lineage*[11]—has already experienced some of the impacts of virtual worlds, it is the transition away from traditional game forms that allow virtual worlds to address a far broader audience. Instead of playing through a fiction provided by the game creators, virtual world residents collaboratively learn how to solve problems in the creation of their own worlds. The resulting culture of participation infused with pervasive learning makes virtual worlds dynamic learning environments.[12]

Within the possibility space afforded by virtual worlds, residents become engines of creation themselves, working as the producers of content in the world, designing and reshaping the space around their own ideas and interests.[13] Developers no longer produce all of the content; instead, this task is given over to the residents of the world. The virtual world *Second Life* was created based upon this premise, and has proven that, when given the correct tools, residents can create compelling and interesting content. Empowered by the ability to create, residents act with dedication and purpose, often overcoming tremendous obstacles to acquire new skills and knowledge in order to make the world their own. In *Second Life*, interactive 3D content is created via the process of atomistic construction, described later in this chapter. Yet, the actual act of content creation is only a part of the overall process of building, particularly given the challenging nature of the tools. Access to the tools reinforces the culture of amateur-to-amateur education as residents move beyond content creation to take on peer-to-peer teaching roles. This network of knowledge and practice created not only encourages more building in the world, but also establishes *Second Life* as a robust learning space, powered through peer-to-peer pedagogy.

Starting with the section "Participatory Culture and Media Creation," this chapter will focus on how features of *Second Life* align well with educational theory. These features both enable the emergence of different approaches to education and engage traditional, large-scale educational institutions.[14] *Second Life*, beyond simply acting as a method of distance learning, has become a tool that extends the reach of both credentialed professors in classrooms and amateurs teaching for fun.[15]

The power of virtual worlds to convey information, and potentially to reduce the cost of learning within them due to pervasive connectivity and social networks, means the same technologies and techniques that apply to education also lead to changes in business process and entrepreneurship. Combined with the far lower capital expenses inherent in digital worlds, in *Second Life* hundreds of thousands of residents try out new roles, learn new skills, and approach learning with a passion and excitement they may not have possessed in school. This ecology is creating a new highly trained and flexible workforce not necessarily tied to national, ethnic, racial, or age boundaries. In the past year alone, sixty-five companies employing a total of over 220 people started within *Second Life* before moving into the real world.[16] This group of innovators is leveraging education every day and building skills that also apply to the real world[17] as they manage distributed employees from all over the world. What are the implications of this changing approach to work, where the most capable and effective people may not classify their activities as work at all? Instead, they may describe how they spend their time as "play" or "fun."[18]

Virtual worlds like *Second Life* are on the leading edge of a new set of technological and experiential transformations that will impact how people communicate, play, and work. It is not surprising that this change is due to learning. Advances in educational theory, economics, and cognitive science mean more is understood about the process and impact of learning than ever before. So what are virtual worlds, and why do they educate so effectively?

Virtual Worlds, Not Games

The formal study of games is a young field,[19] and the study of video games is even younger.[20] However, even as researchers and educators are creating workable frameworks for the study of video games,[21] technology is enabling a new category of digital experience: virtual worlds.

It is easiest to begin by focusing on what virtual worlds are not. They are not massively multiplayer online role-playing games (MMORPGs). MMORPGs are currently the dominant form of online game, with at least fifteen million players worldwide.[22] These games trace their heritage back to Bartle's MUD, itself a descendent of *Dungeons & Dragons*.[23] This family tree results in recognizable signal characteristics, including strong game fictions and leveling. Strong game fictions mean the games take place within relatively cohesive settings that discourage intermingling with the real world. Fantasy motifs are common, but certainly not the only option. Leveling is the process of measuring progress via increases in experience points. These experience points are gained by activities appropriate to the level, and each new level grants the player access to new abilities or game features. When judged against Salen and Zimmerman's definition that a game is "a system in which players engage in an artificial conflict, defined by rules, that results in a quantifiable outcome,"[24] MMORPGs clearly are games, with the conflict, rules, and quantifiable outcome all keyed to the leveling progression.

Virtual worlds are something different. While still massively multiplayer, meaning that thousands of players simultaneously experience the world in a shared space, they possess neither strong fictions nor leveling. Instead, their defining characteristic is the ability of residents to generate creations of value within a shared, simulated, 3D space. Strong, predefined fictions are not appropriate, as they limit the design space available to the residents. Instead, residents create their own fictions and communities, imbuing them with meaning through interaction.

For example, within *Second Life*, a group of stroke survivors have created a space dedicated to poststroke cognitive recovery, collaborating with other residents to generate the funding and expertise required for the project.[25] Just as strong fictions would interfere with the resident-driven design of this space, the limited features initially available via leveling would prevent new residents from being able to act fully within this space. By freeing themselves from the limitations of MMORPGs, virtual worlds enable a far broader design space to be shaped and transformed by residents.

An observer might view the entire World Wide Web as a virtual world. After all, users have certainly built a tremendous amount of content and there have been attempts at 3D Web pages. However, it is important to recognize the basic differences that exist. In particular, virtual worlds generate simultaneously shared spaces. The Web is built around sequential, solo access to content. While two, three, or hundreds of people can read a Weblog, or collaboratively participate in generating a definition for Wikipedia, posts are made sequentially. This is a very different experience than a real-world discussion. Instant messaging comes closer to capturing this, but—like phone and video conferencing—loses the physicality and place so critical to communication. Virtual worlds demand an environment where multiple participants can interact in real time to create collaboratively, sharing not only space, but time.[26] This feature of virtual worlds makes them especially suited for amateur-to-amateur learning, and is one reason many are already using virtual worlds to experiment with the future of education.

Virtual worlds are the newest offshoot from the game tree, and the least understood. While they are not games, they share game technology, vocabulary, and—in many cases—customers. They also have proven remarkably adaptable and useful in supporting most every aspect of human behavior. In order to see this potential, it is useful to view the history of several key developments shaping the state of virtual worlds today.

A History of Virtual Worlds

Four broad areas paved the way for virtual worlds: the World Wide Web, virtual reality, massively multiplayer online role-playing games, and avatar worlds. Each of these areas explored ideas key to virtual worlds and helped build solid technological and cultural foundations. Together, these technologies demonstrated that residents make significant time and economic commitments to online spaces. They proved communities can build large and complex digital creations, do not have to be modeled on fantasy motifs, and showcased the power of shared spaces for creation. While the histories of all four technologies have been well documented elsewhere, a brief review of each helps explain how these histories formed the foundation for the conception of virtual worlds as robust learning spaces.

The Internet and the World Wide Web

From their beginnings as ARPANET in the late 1960s,[27] the Internet and Web have grown to connect people to a degree unprecedented in human history. Over one-and-a-half billion people worldwide now have the ability to communicate online. This communication often takes the form of networked peer production. Although Web sites are the most obvious example, Wikis and Weblogs form the core of an explosion of collaborative creation.[28]

Collaboratively authored creations are special because, unlike much of the Web, they are maintained. Despite low marginal costs, decay impacts digital creations just like physical ones. Community and collaboration have proven to be effective preservation tools. Wikipedia has become the default exemplar of this kind of networked peer production.[29]

Medium and technology both influence creation. In the case of the Web, most creations use text due to the ease of development, transmission, storage, and display. Unfortunately, the use of text compounds the Web's three significant flaws as a communications medium: it is generally asynchronous, it lacks place, and it is descriptive rather than experiential.

Contrast this with the real world, where communication is synchronous and interactive. This is true even when the conversation is largely one way (speeches) or nonlocal (telephone). Practiced speakers react to their audiences, adjusting their presentations on the fly, while telephone conversations allow speakers to react to each other. It is worth noting that telephone conversations share the Web's lack of place. Compare a conversation at a cocktail party to a phone conference with several people speaking at once. At the cocktail party, 3D audio and visual cues help to separate conversations, while overlapping phone conversations are often unintelligible. Place plays a part in providing the nonverbal cues critical to human communication. Relative location, movement, manipulation of objects, and body position are all lost when using text or voice media for communication.

Beyond the loss of place, Web sites are generally not experiential. A description of an airplane allows the reader to imagine flying it. Pictures, audio, or movies may cue the imagination, but the medium does not let the reader actually fly the plane. Physicality and simulation are not built into Web sites. So, while the Web supported peer production, it needed more. The next technology, virtual reality, attempted to fill this need by building on place.

Virtual Reality

Virtual reality has an extensive, albeit checkered, history.[30] Research into methods to allow interaction with virtual scenes has been going on for over forty years and has largely focused on head-mounted displays and haptic interfaces. The goal has been a natural viewing of virtual spaces and manipulation of objects within them. Overcoming tremendous technical and physiological challenges, virtual reality rapidly improved in the late 1980s. These improvements led to the idea that interaction with virtual models during construction would be a superior design and development tool. In particular, this would be the case when multiple users were in a shared space. Three-dimensional spaces—with creation, collaboration, and interaction between multiple users—would transform engineering and design.[31]

Unfortunately, research focused on the interface rather than on the collaboration. Head-mounted displays and haptic interfaces soaked up engineering effort and capital, with limited successes. Concurrently, computer-aided design continued to improve, but with little attention paid to shared spaces.

Only recently have engineering organizations been able to share modeling and simulation tools and data fully. Not yet in widespread use, organizations have begun to recognize the benefits of collaborative creation, allowing both creators and managers to share, visualize, simulate, and freely manipulate data. Automobile companies, for example, are starting to explore new and creative ideas while using modeling and simulation to determine the performance and costs of development. Collaborative creation is helping organizations design and build superior products.

However, large-scale computer-aided design and fabrication technologies are still extremely expensive and generally quite challenging to use. Until recently, only a small number of people have had the opportunity to experience online collaboration. Massively multiplayer online role-playing games changed that.

Massively Multiplayer Online Role-Playing Games

MUD1 opened in 1979 and was the first major online world in which people played together. Inspired by both *Dungeons & Dragons* and *The Lord of the Rings*, *MUD1* created the online game standards that have been followed ever since, and spawned countless text-based online worlds with which a generation of developers grew up. When technology improved sufficiently, these developers converted their text worlds into graphical spaces, beginning with *Meridian 59* in 1996. *Meridian 59* was soon eclipsed by two hugely successful games, *Ultima Online* and *EverQuest*, heralding the birth of the MMORPG. Pulled by the novel combination of culture, economies, and game play, millions of players moved into MMORPGs.

True to the inspiration of *MUD1*, MMORPGs retain the signal characteristics of leveling, strongly themed worlds, social organizations, and player behaviors.[32] MMORPGs have resulted in the growth of secondary markets for the value created within them, including virtual currencies, items, and characters. The global market for these virtual game items has been estimated at $880 million per year, despite attempts by developers to eliminate it via end-user licensing agreements (EULAs) that unequivocally prohibit transfers and sales of virtual items.[33] Players, spurred by time pressure, the desire to play with higher-level friends, and perhaps even the need to consume conspicuously, generate sufficient demand to keep secondary markets in operation despite efforts to close them.

Leaving aside debates about wealth generation and ownership, the markets for digital goods in virtual worlds are large and growing. More importantly, these markets drive commoditization and, within MMORPGs, commoditization is a problem. MMORPGs are enormously expensive to build, due primarily to the enormous cost of creating hundreds of hours of content. In order to keep the experience engaging, developers carefully map out the consumption paths for this content. Unfortunately, if players can commoditize content and shortcut these paths, players may consume the content far too quickly, rendering valueless the millions of development dollars invested in content creation. As a result, although some games are testing newer economic and game play models, MMORPGs generally have not integrated real-world digital item markets.[34]

MMORPGs brought millions of people online and taught them the power of real-time collaboration. Unfortunately, game play, design, and economic decisions limited their ability to move beyond the thematic and style roots of *MUD1*. One final experience was needed.

Distributed Avatar Worlds

The first broadly available, graphical virtual environment was *Lucasfilm's Habitat*. Launched in 1986 on the Commodore 64, *Habitat* introduced the avatar as the graphical representative of the player in a collaborative space. Users could interact with each other and customize the over 20,000 places within *Habitat*'s world. Although *Habitat* drew from multiple sources, including text games and science fiction, it made the critical decision to move away from a fantasy motif. More importantly, *Habitat* demonstrated the failure of detailed central planning to create truly immense and complicated places.[35]

While *Habitat* was successful, the avatar worlds that followed were commercial failures. Although many of them still operate due to the passion of their residents, most do not. Social interaction was clearly a necessary but not sufficient feature of digital worlds. Residents needed more things to do.

Active Worlds, introduced in 1995, attempted to provide building tools for users so that they could create additional content. Many users took advantage of these tools and demonstrated enormous creativity. Unfortunately, *Active Worlds* included neither the social nor the economic forces required to incentivize the creation and maintenance of large-scale and compelling content. Although still running, *Active Worlds*' population has waned.[36]

The lineage of *Habitat* through *Active Worlds* proved that online worlds not based on the fantasy orientation of *Dungeons & Dragons* were viable. They reinforced the idea that users could be tapped as incredible sources of innovation and creativity. While users enjoyed creating 3D content, this content was not compelling enough to draw in new users. Insufficient motivations existed to generate sustaining behavior. Despite this, the pieces were now in place to change virtual worlds forever. *Second Life*, launched in 2003, combined these four basic technologies, and added the power of collaborative creation via atomistic creation. The result has been an explosion of creativity and learning still accelerating more than three years after it launched.

Moore in the Valley

The increase in a computer's abilities to store and process data has greatly impacted how games and virtual worlds are made.[37] Despite the fact that hit digital entertainment launches generate larger first-day revenues than movies,[38] the cost of development greatly limits options for creating virtual worlds,[39] especially worlds targeted at niche markets like education.

Most game and virtual world projects are commercial and practical failures. Even with the best funding and most talented developers, creating virtual worlds that solve the myriad technical and social challenges related to bringing thousands or millions of people together is an extremely difficult task. These challenges are compounded by the risks in developing projects that require tens of millions of dollars to complete.[40]

In the early days of virtual worlds, the primary cost driver was the underlying technology, the computer code required to simulate and represent the world and its residents. Over the last ten years, newer and more powerful computers have allowed far more realistic depictions of environments and characters. In many cases, the display quality approximates computer-generated movies of only a couple of years ago. At the same time, the costs of creating those environments and characters also rival those of Hollywood.[41]

This should come as no surprise, since the tools and techniques for making art assets are fairly standardized, whether the artist is working on a movie or an online game. The only real difference is the extra difficulty of creating game assets, since—unlike movies—the content must be interactive. Imagine the difference between building a real town versus the facade of a movie set. In the real world, all the buildings would have interiors. Plumbing and electricity would have to work, problems like traffic flow and garbage removal would need to be addressed, and the building materials would need to survive decades of use.

These are the problems faced by game artists and designers. Content built for games must be used and reused in experiences and quests compelling enough for hundreds or thousands of hours of play. Whenever possible, games take advantage of Hollywood tricks and build facades or limit the path of the player, but these tricks are less useful in online games or virtual worlds. Instead, more content must be created, even after the game is launched, in order to keep the players engaged. The cost of content creation now exceeds that of technology development for many online games, and will continue to grow as a percentage of overall development.[42]

The long history of increased development costs has led to an increasingly risk-averse publishing model and fewer innovative games. Instead, more products are sequels and "me, too" titles. For the educator looking to use games or virtual world spaces as learning tools, this presents a real problem. Insufficient virtual world variety exists to provide enough choices for education and research. The problem becomes worse if educators want to build their own virtual worlds.

Virtual world development costs vary, but estimates range between $12 and $20 million.[43] While research projects of this magnitude certainly exist, this kind of spending exists outside the range of most researchers. Moreover, even if a school is able to marshal the resources required, it will face an even larger problem.

The Vast Majority of Games and Virtual Worlds Fail

Although in the commercial world, failure is defined economically, it is equally valid to examine it from the standpoint of use. Virtual worlds fail when they are insufficiently compelling for large numbers of residents to spend considerable time using them. If an educator or researcher spends millions of dollars building a virtual world and nobody shows up, that project is doomed to failure.

The problem continues to intensify as content costs soar. With the majority of development costs tied to content, traditional methods for building cheaper virtual worlds will not work. Middleware and full game engines are the most common approaches taken. Middleware is software designed to solve specific problems related to virtual world creation. Physical simulation[44] and foliage generation[45] are two classes of problems well-suited to middleware solutions. Similarly, full game engines have been built to reduce technical risk and cost.[46] Even if middleware and engines were able to reduce the technical development costs to zero, more than half of the development costs would remain, due to the cost of content creation. Of course, in the real world, middleware and engines still cost development time and budget, so in reality they create only an incremental change in development costs.

A natural response to this is to create markets for shared content resources. Success in this space has proved elusive. While numerous companies provide stock photography and sound effects, the specialized nature of real-time 3D rendering and the specific art needs of individual virtual worlds have combined to reduce the usefulness of shared 3D assets.[47] Worse, much content creation cost goes beyond the production of individual components. Complex creations, such as quests, scripted scenes, or even entire games, are particularly ill-suited for sale to multiple virtual worlds.

Fortunately, the World Wide Web has demonstrated the potential of user-created content. While participation levels still remain relatively small, with less than 25 percent of U.S.

Internet users adding content to the Web despite the emergence of easy-to-use tools like Flickr, the numbers are growing.[48] The challenges in applying the power of peer production to virtual worlds lie both in the tools provided to the residents and in the environment required to support high levels of exploration and use.

Atomistic Creation

While everything in the real world is built of atoms, they are generally not convenient tools for human construction. Nanotechnology, where products are built at the atomic scale, is expensive, difficult, and potentially risky. Construction at the macrolevel requires large expenditures of time, raw materials, and energy. Large-scale, real-world creation of artifacts like cities require economies of scale that generate undesirable outcomes like traffic and pollution. Unlike the real world, *Second Life* uses building blocks specifically designed for human-scale creation.

This is the principle the designers of *Second Life* call atomistic construction. Primitives are the atoms of *Second Life*. Simple primitives are combined to build interesting structures and behaviors, and are designed to support maximum creativity while still being simple enough for everyone to play with and use. To understand how atoms work, consider building a piano first in *Ultima Online* and then in *Second Life*.

In *Ultima Online*, a user can purchase a large number of objects, ranging from checkerboards to cloaks. With careful stacking and a lot of patience, it is possible to create something that looks like a piano. Of course, it is not really a piano and the user could not use it to compose music, although it might serve as decoration.

In *Second Life*, the resident would start building the piano in real time, simply creating primitives as needed. These primitives would be scaled, textured, colored, and combined to create a piano. Sound would be added to the keys, so it could be played. A symphony could be composed on it. Rather than simple decoration, this *is* a piano.

Of course, since it is built of primitives, the piano could also fly or follow the resident around like a pet. Copies of the piano could be given away or sold with practically no marginal cost of reproduction. When the piano was no longer needed, it could be removed from the world and stored for later use.

By endowing every primitive with physical and behavioral properties, primitives become the basic building blocks of everything from hats to houses, from cats to cars. Instead of the real world's hundred different atoms with complex interaction rules, *Second Life* is made up of several simple primitive types with the flexibility to generate a nearly limitless set of combinatorial possibilities.

These primitives exist in a physically simulated world, resulting in fairly predictable behaviors. Create a physical ball in the air, and it will fall. Build a square table with three legs, and it will fall over. Simulation allows residents to leverage their intuitive understanding of the real world. Although primitives are flexible enough to allow exceptions, the real world metaphor acts to orient new residents. Even more importantly, so much of this creation occurs in public that residents are constantly inspired. When a particularly spectacular motorcycle roars by, residents are able to ask immediately how they might build one, to explore and experiment on their own.

Primitives are manipulated and combined within *Second Life*, a construction process that does not rely on external programs. A resident does not have to build his model of a house in Maya, a complex 3D design program, before importing it into *Second Life* for use. Instead, the building of the house occurs directly within the world, and other residents can be invited to help in the process. Thus, default creative methods are collaborative and synchronous, rather than individual and asynchronous. Collaboration can be as simple as asking someone for help or an opinion, or as complex as dozens of residents building a city from a set of master blueprints.[49] Feedback is instantaneous, and communication a natural back and forth, rather than following the asynchronous, sequential mode of a blog or e-mail. Collaboration, as a key mode of interaction, drives the way residents learn within *Second Life*.

Second Life residents from all over the real world have learned to create at every scale, designing clothing to full-scale games, including MMORPGs built within *Second Life*.[50] The creative power of the digital melting pot is astonishing. This power also drives the economic forces within *Second Life*.

Economics

Like the real world, creations built by the application of time, effort, and innovation are worth more than their constituent parts. In *Second Life*, primitives have almost no cost beyond the computing, memory, and bandwidth resources they consume. For individual, temporary primitives, these costs are effectively zero. As primitives are combined and left in the world, their costs increase. For residents to maintain permanent artifacts in world—their houses for example—they need to own virtual real estate within *Second Life*. This ownership allocates computing resources and balances the load generated by usage evenly across the computers simulating the world.

The vast design space available to creators using primitives means there are a myriad of ways to meet similar needs. Creators who apply more innovation, skill, or time to their creations generate more valuable artifacts. Markets within *Second Life* allow consumers to define value in different ways, from efficiency and effectiveness to scarcity and beauty.[51] Some residents purchase space in order to create shopping malls while others create gardens and green spaces.

The flexibility and ease of collaborative creation drives tremendous variety and experimentation. For example, in November 2006,[52] 500,000 distinct residents spent time in *Second Life*. Those residents exchanged over 500,000 items in ten million resident-to-resident transactions with a total value of US$17 million. Although the transactions were made with the "Linden Dollar," or L$, it is possible to assign U.S. dollar values to these transactions because the L$ is freely traded against the US$. In November 2006, the value of those transactions exceeded US$2.7 million and maintained an exchange rate of approximately L$270 to US$1. As with physical simulation, trade and economic activity provide an important context within digital worlds. Residents learn about the potential to make money from other residents, so some choose to explore this opportunity. The power of the economy should be expected, as *Second Life* leverages factors long associated with economic strength and growth: property rights, the cost of learning, and decentralization.

Property rights are a key enabler of innovation and therefore per capita economic growth. Without ownership, property is not fungible and retards economic growth.[53] This was one of the key ideas behind *Second Life*'s decision to grant residents ownership of their creations. The growth of quality and quantity of user-created content in the three years since that decision is a significant proof point. However, precision here is important because digital artifacts are intellectual property (IP) rather than property.

The IP domain governs digital artifacts. This is important because although IP helps to steer innovation by creating excess value through temporary monopolies, it is the cost of learning that drives the rate of innovation.[54] Strong copyright, like the approach currently being applied in the United States, hampers innovation due to the increased learning costs. It also legislates areas of innovation rather than allowing less structured exploration, compounding the damage.[55]

Fortunately, digital worlds and atomistic construction have several advantages over the real world with regard to the cost of learning. First, atomistic construction allows anyone to reverse-engineer or improve on the ideas of others, rather than limiting those options to large corporations. Copyright still holds, providing creators with legal protections, but the freedom to tinker increases the opportunities for useful knowledge to spread as new and competitive ideas enter the marketplace. Second, digital worlds have the opportunity to give their creators IP regimes that better support innovation by reducing learning costs.

Decentralization is the final important economic factor.[56] The steady reduction of communication and transportation costs in the real world has allowed many businesses to explore increasingly decentralized approaches. Many open-source and collaborative projects, such as Apache and Wikipedia, use these techniques.[57] In the real world, decentralization can run into limits when the time comes to production. Marginal costs and the need for specialized skills and materials limit the degree of decentralization.

Digital worlds with atomistic construction evade this limitation. Although personal skills will still vary, any resident with an idea or need has the tools to create a solution, and many do. During October 2006, residents in *Second Life* spent 240,000 user hours per day in-world and 25 percent of their time was spent actively creating. Thus, every day 60,000 user hours are spent creating, the equivalent of 30 user-years per day. That is the equivalent of an 11,000-person content development team. It would cost over $1 billion per year to hire a team of that size! Even with Sturgeon's Law,[58] it is a team of 1,100, and this approach scales as the user base grows.

This decentralized creative team is closer to the community's needs and wants than any developer could ever be, allowing creation and innovation to be efficiently applied. For the same reasons that open-source users are often the best positioned to improve their products,[59] *Second Life* residents are constantly improving their world.

Participatory Culture and Media Creation

It is generally accepted that, for a given medium, rates of consumption will radically outweigh rates of creation. For example, far more people purchase music than play instruments, few television viewers create video podcasts, and only a small percentage of game players create mods of their favorite video games. Even when the technology and knowledge barriers to creation are low, creation is the exception while consumption is the norm. Despite the well-documented proliferation of Weblogs on the Internet, fewer than 7 percent of Web users have created Weblogs.[60] Wikipedia, often cited as the pinnacle of distributed user-created content on the Web, has contributions from less than 0.2 percent of its readers.[61] So, conventional wisdom is upheld, with creators as members of an unusual, separate class from the masses of consumers.

Conventional wisdom fails to tell the whole story, however. History has repeatedly demonstrated that adopters of new technologies act to distinguish themselves from the old, separating amateurs from experts by a gulf of jargon and certification.[62] While human performance clearly varies across any measured parameter, educational theory provides no theoretical framework for the narrow segregation of a population into designers and non-designers, into expert and amateur.[63] Although current research around emerging uses of technology points to greater overlap between producers and consumers, a strong example was needed. The virtual world *Second Life* provides this example.

Using a diverse collection of built-in tools, residents create the objects, clothing, characters, script code, and experiences to fill the world. Despite the steep learning curve of many of these tools, *Second Life* has remarkable participation rates. Within any thirty-day period, over 66 percent of the residents who used *Second Life* created something from scratch. For example, a resident might create a 3D model, such as a car or a house, using the modeling tools. This is a task generally considered to be in the domain of professional 3D modelers. Another example would be creating behaviors, such as making the car fun to drive, by using the embedded scripting language. Far from drag-and-drop visual programming, *Second Life*'s scripting language is as complicated as C, a programming language challenging to teach and to learn. Despite these hurdles, fully 15 percent of *Second Life*'s residents experiment with scripting every week.

Second Life's demographics make these statistics all the more remarkable. Rather than the expected young male audience, *Second Life* has a nearly balanced usage by men and women, a median age in the early thirties, with women slightly more likely to continue using *Second Life* than men. Moreover, the older the residents are, the more likely they are to continue using *Second Life*.[64] Given that some of the previous examples, such as Wikipedia, almost certainly possess diverse audiences as well, heterogeneity of users is clearly insufficient to explain the observed rates of participation. What other mechanisms could be at work? While there is no certain answer to the question, in addition to the economic component discussed earlier, *Second Life* is a particularly good environment for learning. Though no hard data supporting this claim yet exists, the kinds of learning taking place within the world are worth examining. In much the same way that James Gee, Jane McGonigal, and Kurt Squire explore the learning strategies intrinsic to games elsewhere in this volume, *Second Life* may be viewed as an educational space.

The learning potential of *Second Life* becomes even more exciting when examining the next generation of content creators. Thirty-three percent of online teens share self-created media on the Web and nearly 20 percent maintain blogs.[65] Teens between the ages of thirteen and seventeen use *Teen Second Life*, a separate part of *Second Life*. During the preparation of this chapter, the author and fellow volume author Barry Joseph discussed the possibility of surveying residents of *Teen Second Life* about their participation and learning. A full analysis of the survey data is beyond the scope of this chapter, but after receiving 384 responses, a few data points jumped out:

- Seventy-five percent of the respondents were male;
- Sixty-seven percent had written at least one program using the scripting language;
- Eighty-seven percent had customized their appearance;
- Ninety-eight percent had created objects using the creation tools;
- For questions related to customizing appearance, designing clothing, and writing scripts, the most popular source of information was "friends"; and
- Twenty-three percent had created Web sites about *Teen Second Life*.

Finally, the survey itself was administered via an object created within *Teen Second Life*. The object—and the program to operate it—was created by a fourteen-year-old girl.[66]

Amateur-to-Amateur Education

Residents spend a great deal of time in-world educating each other in both direct and indirect ways. Educational events, such as "Introduction to Scripting" or "Building 101," are available nearly every day and provide new arrivals to *Second Life* with a fun and inviting way to learn about the tools and possibilities available to them.[67] Residents also spend a disproportionate amount of time in the "Welcome Area," where new residents arrive. The "Welcome Area" is often full of residents displaying their newest and most impressive creations. While sometimes confusing to new arrivals, these displays provide a powerful demonstration of the power of *Second Life*, and often lead to the most critical of questions: "How did you do that?" This question is particularly important within *Second Life* because the answer can almost always be immediately demonstrated. Rather than redirecting the questioner to the solo experience of reading a Web site or learning a new piece of software, the demonstration is a social and collaborative experience, creating context and social bonds. More importantly, information is transferred "just in time," or "on demand," at a point when the learner wants the knowledge, rather than during an arbitrarily paced tutorial or lesson plan. This type of learning is one of the powerful features of games, and *Second Life* residents leverage it as well. This is one part of what learning specialists refer to as "situated learning," a point discussed by Gee and others elsewhere in this series.

Second Life has proven so effective at displaying and communicating information that educators at all levels are choosing to expand their classrooms into the virtual world.[68] From drama departments and architecture to computer science and entrepreneurship, the ability to create exactly what is needed for a specific curriculum, class, or student is a revelation to many teachers.

Examining the lessons of *Second Life* in regard to the creation of an innovative, peer-to-peer learning environment is very important. Conventional wisdom about the rarity of content creators is clearly misleading in this context. Domain experts must recognize the potential of amateurs as teachers and learn to welcome their efforts. While collaborative learning has long been well understood as an important and effective component,[69] particularly in informal learning settings, *Second Life* provides an environment wherein such learning takes place on a daily basis. Residents have multiple ways of learning, including content creation, which casts many of them as teachers.

Everyone a Teacher

While this phenomenon is not limited to *Second Life,* the nature of the tools and lack of overt game goals within the world provide huge opportunities for residents to experiment with creation as a mode of engagement. Given that the actual mechanics of building are extremely challenging, the question that must be asked is: "How do people learn to use *Second Life*?"

While the answer to this question is complex, at least part of it lies in the ability for all residents to teach in, and more importantly to teach within, *Second Life*. Most creations in *Second Life* are built using the atomistic creation tools discussed previously—the avatar editing tools and the scripting language. For residents, because the building occurs in-world—in public—it is easy to show someone both what is being created and how the tools are being used. This has led to a culture of educational events in which residents take time to teach others. Sometimes these teachers charge residents for their efforts, but in most cases residents hold classes because they perceive teaching to be a fun, social activity and a great way to meet new people.

Different communities within *Second Life* have taken on education as well. An excellent example is *Shock Proof*. This is the previously mentioned space for stroke survivors to work together toward cognitive recovery.[70] Several stroke survivors discovered *Second Life* independently, and together decided to build a space specifically designed to help their fellow survivors. In the aftermath of a stroke, a key indicator of long-term recovery is how engaged the survivor is in using the brain to communicate, solve problems, and practice fine motor skills.[71] In the real world, especially if mobility-impaired, finding these opportunities can be very difficult. *Second Life* offers many different ways to approach these problems. *Shock Proof* is not only filled with activities, but also has areas for the older community members to teach and work with the new arrivals. Another is the *CyberOne* law class being taught at Harvard Law School. Taught simultaneously in the real world and in *Second Life*, *CyberOne* has provided both local and remote students an opportunity to study law in new ways.[72] Or consider the virtual summer camp run by Global Kids, discussed elsewhere in this volume.

Examples like these abound, with communities using the tools of the world to educate newer members. Education has become a basic part of the culture. Perhaps more importantly, that education does not look like education in a classroom.

Virtual Vygotsky

The idea that education is strongly impacted by communities is certainly not new. Some of the earliest thinking on the topic was done by the psychologist Lev Vygotsky, who spent his brief adult years writing about play, internalization, and relationships between language and learning.[73] Vygotsky introduced generations of education researchers and instructional technologists to the basic concepts of learning by doing, arguing that education is best understood within the context of the surrounding culture and social interactions.[74] Designers, educators, and technologists like Seymour Papert[75] and Mitch Resnick[76] from MIT picked up on these theories in pursuit of developing constructivist tools for kids,[77] and the children's software movement discussed by Ito in this volume has its roots in Vygotskyian pedagogy.

A deep analysis of Vygotsky's theories is beyond the scope of this chapter, but understanding the breadth of influence of his ideas is helpful, because—unlike so many other technologies that have been applied to the classroom and education—virtual worlds strongly align with his basic theories. Rather than increasing the separation of surrounding social groups from education the way the computer often has, or decreasing the amount of time spent on actual hands-on activities as in the case of more passive media forms like television, virtual worlds both provide engaging playgrounds for experimentation and immerse these playgrounds within social networks.[78] This combination, enabled by the simultaneous collaboration model of virtual worlds, results in a striking alignment between play and authorship in virtual worlds, along with a variety of basic learning principles.

Legitimate Peripheral Participation

Legitimate peripheral participation (LPP) is an educational idea virtually unheard of outside education and literacy circles, yet it is arguably the most natural and effective learning technique available.[79] LPP is the idea that people learn best when they spend time with people who have mastered the skills they wish to learn. Most commonly seen in apprenticeships, LPP provides the basis for learning and training in many fields today,[80] including medicine, military service, and journalism.

More specifically, LPP enables new learners to approach complex information in stages. For example, in journalism, a new employee may first work at final layout and proofreading, two tasks that require relatively small amounts of training. However, as the new employee masters these new jobs, he or she is also exposed to the particulars of journalistic writing style, content, story construction, and other elements which need to be mastered before moving on to copy editing or writing original stories. This immersive process ensures that when the new journalist does move on to more difficult tasks, he or she is already prepared.[81]

While not all tasks in virtual worlds are so neatly subdivided, new residents are first able to spend time watching how more experienced residents customize their appearances, acquire information, and manage their businesses. Much of the initial, experimental creation performed by residents in *Second Life* occurs in "sandbox" regions designed for free building. These explorations take place around more experienced builders, so the neophyte is able to observe the tips and tricks required to build successfully. Even more importantly, they are able to contextualize why they want to acquire these new building skills because they can see the results around them. This is situated learning.

Situated Learning

Situated learning is the idea that better learning occurs when the reasons and motivations for learning are clear. Rather than the "skill and drill" of assignments followed by testing, situated learning is more like on-the-job training, where the acquisition of skill is introduced in the context of use.[82] Situated learning often provides an incentive to learn, an idea crucial to understanding the viability of virtual worlds as learning spaces.

In *Second Life*, residents constantly come into contact with people who may inspire them with their avatar design, possessions, businesses, or other skills. Although every resident is able to explore design space flexibly as they desire, these social interactions provide contexts and reasons for mastering skills they might not yet have. These incentives to learn make it clear, for example, why some mastery of the scripting language in *Second Life* is needed in order to make great jewelry. Or why practice with the avatar creation tools can lead to superior avatar design. Residents develop their skills as they build their knowledge around the possibilities the space provides. Residents not only model practical knowledge for each other, but provide opportunities for imagination to take hold and inspire new creation.

In addition, the desire to mold technology to individual needs can be further enforced within specific communities. Time spent visiting the International Spaceflight Museum in *Second Life* may inspire an educator to attempt a completely new approach to teaching about the history of spaceflight.[83] A habit of visiting jazz clubs may lead to an interest in music.[84] Because such flexible tools are available, the explorer has every opportunity for inspiration to lead to learning events.

This is reinforced by the on-demand nature of peer-to-peer learning in *Second Life*. When a potential student discovers a need to learn something new, the fact that nearly everything made within the world has been created collaboratively means residents are able to teach

each other. Unlike other mediums, the development platform of *Second Life* is both the distribution and experience platform. When a resident wants to see how to build a car, another resident can show how to do it right then or can refer the interested resident to one of the hundreds of classes a week being taught in-world.[85]

Suddenly, residents are free to explore design space, to experiment, and to try, secure in the knowledge that bumps in the road caused by incomplete knowledge or skills can be overcome. With minimal delays between the desire to acquire knowledge and the opportunity, learners remain motivated and excited.

Heterogeneous Learning

These excited and motivated learners are also not all alike. For many students, classroom education can be an incredibly homogenous experience, with classrooms populated by students of the same age, nationality, and socioeconomic backgrounds. Such homogenous learning fails to take advantage of what a more heterogeneous environment offers[86]—a place where irregularities in skills, knowledge, and experience create systems rich with differences.[87] In such systems, students must constantly make comparisons between elements, discovering strengths and weaknesses of each, and learning from the kinds of consensus and conflict that is created through the diversity of perspective.[88] Such a classroom is, in some sense, an ideal classroom. It becomes a place where people of different ages, experiences, and cultures come together to collaborate, share, and play. Virtual worlds can achieve such scenarios, bringing together learners of all ages into a single, shared space where each produces and shares knowledge.

This situation enables profoundly different learning and teaching opportunities than at any previous point in human history. For the first time, geography is not the primary determining factor in who can learn together or who can teach. Instead, affinity groups and communities of practice create the structures and methods needed to teach and to learn.

Schoolhouse Rock

Real-world educators are already taking the first steps to leverage the power of virtual worlds in education at every level. With over 150 universities and 1,500 educators already using *Second Life*,[89] a growing corpus of knowledge is being created around what it means to teach and learn in virtual worlds.[90] This knowledge is being shared, both within *Second Life* and via traditional Web structures like mailing lists and Wikis, so new educators can learn from each other.

For example, the 2006 *Second Life* Community Convention featured an educator's workshop and published proceedings that are now available online.[91] These proceedings detail a tremendous array of experiences within *Second Life*, from reports from the students themselves all the way to the initial steps taken in leveraging virtual worlds across large, public universities.

The tremendous possibility space offered by virtual worlds continues to emerge as a powerful theme. Groups of universities have joined together to create visually impressive spaces within *Second Life*,[92] with classrooms and lecture areas that are immediately recognizable for those new to virtual worlds. These spaces can act to extend the classroom by adding a holodeck to the blackboard or by allowing students to join the classroom from all over the world.

And this, of course, is just the beginning. Virtual worlds allow teaching to go beyond the classroom, extending learning beyond the limitations traditionally imposed by geography.[93] Musicians throughout the world have already begun to discover how virtual worlds provide new ways of engaging audiences. The ability for audience members to interact with each other, building communities that continue conversations after the performance, offers new opportunities for musicians, beyond the now traditional technologies of Webcasts and net radio. How long will it be before educators discover the same benefits?

In China, 1 percent of the population is urbanizing every year. This is the largest migration in human history, as thirteen million Chinese move to cities in search of jobs, education, and hope. In the midst of trying to build two New York Cities per year, China is facing an education crisis, as schools are overwhelmed and unable to keep up with growth and the demand of a generation of kids hungry for opportunity and knowledge. Given the power of virtual worlds, it is relevant to ask in what ways China's burgeoning interest in distance learning programs and online curriculum can be extended through the implementation of such programs within virtual worlds. It is clearly a smarter economic decision to deliver broadband to thirteen million people than to try to move them physically.

Small steps toward this virtual classroom model are being taken each day, with projects like Harvard Law School's *CyberOne* class, being taught jointly in the real world and in *Second Life*. The class is taught across worlds, with questions and information flowing freely between both, and is already offering up interesting lessons about teaching in virtual worlds. One unexpected discovery is that students have discussed how they are more comfortable asking questions when they attend class in *Second Life*.[94] While the full reasons are not yet known, the comfort and safety provided by pseudonymity and a virtual presence seems to play a part. With so much of education built around trying to reach students, are there ways for virtual worlds to remove some of the challenges of learning?

Group Learning

The ability for students to feel that they are part of an audience is important to facilitating a sense of shared learning as well. After all, in the real world, students can leave class and move off to study together. Traditional one-to-many communication channels like television or the Web do not allow receivers to build communities easily, or to find each other in order to continue the conversation. In virtual worlds, nearly every activity can occur within groups, so when the activity is education, participants already have a group of fellow students to lean on for additional discussion, learning, or study.[95]

Membership in multiple, parallel groups also encourages students to act as knowledge conduits between groups. Absent geographic limitations, virtual worlds provide an important mixing opportunity for students to spend time teaching and learning with fellow students outside of their immediate disciplines.[96] Many educators have long sought structures to help in creating cross and interdisciplinary study, and virtual worlds are poised to create contexts for such programs. If the ability to gain literacy across subject areas and disciplines is a key to innovation in the twenty-first century, then discovering ways of delivering such experiences is crucial.

In education, like other forms of knowledge creation, innovation is tied to the cost of learning.[97] The more isolated various communities of practice become, the harder it is for the critical cross-pollination so necessary for innovation to take hold. Education, by leveraging virtual world technology to teach and to learn, is on the leading edge of making more innovation possible. More than using technology to further education, the teachers mastering the space can build expertise that will flow far beyond the classroom.

Think Locally, Act Globally

The lessons and experiences of educators in virtual worlds will be invaluable as businesses[98] and governments[99] begin their own experiments. It will be critical for educators to keep the focus on learning—to avoid losing sight of the fact that, whether the goal is education or innovation, it is the lower cost of learning in virtual worlds that is transformative.

Any student of history can demonstrate that nations who educate their populations thrive.[100] Technology currently exists that allows research and development of education to benefit both education and business. After all, students are not just children aged five to eighteen, or those in college. *Second Life* shows that residents of all levels enjoy mastering new skills and are able to apply them in meaningful ways. As Schumpeter's "creative destruction" forces change on labor everywhere,[101] virtual worlds are another tool to help those caught in the transformation.

Within the United States, as elsewhere in the world, there are enormous educational and economic inequalities between geographic areas.[102] It should surprise no one that these same inequalities apply to innovation.[103] Spending money is likely to be a necessary, but not sufficient, solution to these problems. Virtual worlds, by allowing their participants to learn, to create, and to build communities across geographic and generational divides, are a critical tool in addressing these inequalities.

Projects like One Laptop Per Child and advances in cell phone technology mean that virtual worlds will soon have the same reach as the World Wide Web, but with the benefits over the Web already covered in this chapter. Even more importantly, virtual worlds bring markets with them. When examining the incredible impact of Grameen Bank on Bangladesh,[104] remember that this transformation was accomplished with microcredit loans of tens of dollars. As virtual worlds bring new markets, imagine the possibilities of marrying new ways of earning money with education goals. For example, if conducting immersion language training, why not hire local, virtual actors to supplement the educators? Normally, that sort of broad contact with a destination country is only found in exchange programs; virtual worlds could open the experience up to a much broader audience.

Suddenly, traditional media cultural imperialism is inverted. By allowing participants from around the globe to teach in their own ways, the value created for participants in virtual worlds is very different than traditional, one-to-many media. For many topics, the ability to learn from a local would be invaluable,[105] and virtual worlds provide both the markets to connect customers directly to providers and the platform for those interactions to be valuable in ways they never were before.

That value is created because the interactions take place between people. In the same way that online games rely on role playing as a core game mechanic, virtual worlds allow role playing to open opportunities that otherwise might not exist for participants. In the same way that students in virtual worlds are more comfortable asking questions of their law professors, role playing helps to reduce risk; to enable residents to cast themselves as learners, researchers, or experimenters; and to become more comfortable in those roles online before taking on those roles in the real world. This is a powerful idea, and it is fortunate that strong supporting evidence, such as the previously discussed *Second Life* development community, exists.

The Way Forward

The community and technology is here today for virtual worlds to become a basic building block of education for nearly every age group in most developed nations. Whether backed by established educators or not, this transformation is already happening as amateurs discover ways that virtual worlds can help them learn, communicate, and work. It is only a question of whether the mainstream will join them or get pushed aside.

That is not to say that this will be easy. Because virtual worlds have the potential to impact education in so many different ways, they will force the rethinking of curricula, of evaluation, and even of what it means to be a student. Schools that fail to embrace this change may find themselves increasingly on the outside of knowledge, increasingly outdated, and falling further behind as those who are mastering community and peer-to-peer education accelerate into the future.

And accelerate they will, for this is only the beginning. Nations and communities have no way to predict what it will mean to have education be—at every level—an international and multicultural process. What is known is that a general decrease in cost of learning between a more heterogeneous group of learners and educators will generate more innovation and change. The opportunity exists for teachers, schools, and universities to be driving that change, and they need to become part of the process today.

Businesses, communities, and nations that fall behind in a world accelerating along exponential curves may find it impossible to catch up.

Notes

1. Wikimedia, s.v. History of Computing Hardware, *Wikipedia*, February 19, 2007. http://en.wikipedia.org/w/index.php?title=History_of_computing_hardware&oldid=109380855.

2. Wikimedia, s.v. ARPANET, *Wikipedia*, February 19, 2007. http://en.wikipedia.org/w/index.php?title=ARPANET&oldid=109383208; and idem., World Wide Web, *Wikipedia*, February 20, 2007. http://en.wikipedia.org/w/index.php?title=World_Wide_Web&oldid=109604101.

3. Daniel Livingstone and Jeremy Kemp, eds., *Proceedings of the Second Life Education Workshop at the Second Life Community Convention*, 2006. http://www.simteach.com/SLCC06/slcc2006-proceedings.pdf. Accessed December 18, 2006.

4. Shankar Verdantam, Social Isolation Growing in the US, Study Says, *Washington Post*, June 23, 2006.

5. Wagner James Au, Everything Goes Better with Daleks, *New World Notes*, June 25, 2006. http://nwn.blogs. com/nwn/2006/06/everything_goes.html.

6. Idem., A Brother-HUD of Man, *New World Notes*, August 23, 2006. http://nwn.blogs.com/nwn/2006/08/a_brotherhud_of.html.

7. Andrew Scott, Pontiac's Road Map Leads to Second Life's Virtual Community. *Promo*, October 30, 2006. http://promomagazine.com/interactivemarketing/news/pontiac_virtual _community_103006/.

8. James Harkin, Get a (Second) Life, *Financial Times*, November 17, 2006.

9. Namro Orman, HeathInfo Island Update and Movies, *Infoisland.org Blog*, December 18, 2006. http://infoisland.org/2006/12/18/healthinfo-island-update-movies/.

10. Mark Wallace, Swedish Social Network Headed to Second Life, *3pointD*, May 12, 2006. http://www.3pointd.com/20060512/swedish-social-network-headed-to-second-life/.

11. Bruce Woodcock, *MMORPG Chart*, June 29, 2006. http://www.mmorpgchart. com/.

12. Wikimedia, s.v. Second Life Education, *Wikipedia*. http://www.simteach.com/wiki/index.php?title=Second_Life_Education_Wiki. Accessed December 18, 2006.

13. Wired Travel Guide: Second Life, *Wired*, 14, no. 10 (2006). www.wired.com/archive/14.10/sloverview.html

14. Wikimedia, s.v. Second Life Education.

15. Angela Thomas, My Teaching Semester in Second Life: Pitfalls, Challenges and Joys, *Second Life Arts Total Entertainment Magazine*. http://www.slatenight.com/index.php?option=com_content&task=view&id=107&Itemid=40. Accessed December 18, 2006.

16. Metaversal Myrmidons, Millions for Them, Not For Us, *Second Thoughts*, November 22, 2006. http://secondthoughts.typepad.com/second_thoughts/2006/11/millions_for_th.html.

17. Anshe Chung Becomes First Virtual World Millionaire, 2006. http://www.anshechung.com/include/press/press_release251106.html. Accessed December 18, 2006.

18. Henrik Bennetsen, Scalability of Fun, *Second Life Creativity*. 2006. http://slcreativity.org/blog/?p=25. Accessed December 18, 2006.

19. Wikimedia, s.v. Johan Huizinga, *Wikipedia*, February 12, 2007. http://en.wikipedia.org/w/index.php?title=Johan_Huizinga&oldid=107582369.

20. Raph Koster, Online World Timeline. *Raph Koster's Website*, February 20, 2002. http://www.raphkoster.com/gaming/mudtimeline.shtml.

21. Katie Salen and Eric Zimmerman. *Rules of Play* (Cambridge, MA: The MIT Press, 2003).

22. B. Woodcock, *MMORPG Chart*.

23. Ibid.

24. Jesper Juul, The Game, the Player, and the World: Looking for a Heart of Gameness, Keynote address presented at the Level Up Conference in Utrecht, The Netherlands, November 4–6, 2003. http://www.jesperjuul.net/text/gameplayerworld/. Accessed December 18, 2006.

25. Cory Ondrejka, A Random Walk Down the Long Trail of Innovation, *Official Linden Blog*, June 21, 2006. http://blog.secondlife.com/2006/06/21/a-random-walk-down-the-long-tails-of-innovation/.

26. Stephen Shankland, IBM's Virtual Pioneer, *News.com*, December 18, 2006. http://news.com.com/IBM+taps+into+broadband+into+our+brains/2008-1023_3-6144122.html.

27. Wikimedia, s.v. ARPANET.

28. Amanda Lenhart and Suzanne Fox, Bloggers, 2006. http://www.pewinternet.org/pdfs/PIP%20Bloggers%20Report%20July%2019%202006.pdf. Accessed December 18, 2006.

29. Jim Giles, Internet Encyclopaedias Go Head to Head, *News@nature.com*, December 14, 2005. http://www.nature.com/news/2005/051212/full/438900a.html.

30. Wikimedia, s.v. Virtual Reality, *Wikipedia*, February 1, 2007. http://en.wikipedia.org/w/index.php?title=Virtual_reality&oldid=104767035.

31. John Walker, Through the Looking Glass, 1988. http://www.fourmilab.ch/autofile/www/chapter2_69.html. Accessed December 18, 2006.

32. Richard Bartle, Paradigm Propagation, *Terra Nova*, July, 2004. http://terranova.blogs.com/terra_nova/ 2004/07/paradigm_propag.html. Accessed December 18, 2006.

33. Edward Castronova, Secondary Markets: $880 Million. *Terra Nova*, 2004. http://terranova.blogs.com/terra_nova/2004/10/secondary_marke.html. Accessed December 18, 2006.

34. Cory Ondrejka, Changing Realities, 2005. http://www.themisgroup.com/uploads/Changing%20Realities.pdf. Accessed December 18, 2006.

35. Chip Morningstar and F. Randa Farmer, The Lessons of Lucasfilm's Habitat, in *Cyberspace: First Steps*, ed. Michael Benedikt (Cambridge, MA: The MIT Press, 1991). http://www.fudco.com/chip/lessons.html.

36. Wikimedia, s.v. Active Worlds, *Wikipedia*, February 19, 2007. http://en.wikipedia.org/w/index.php?title=Active_Worlds&oldid=109196277.

37. Raph Koster, Moore's Wall: Technology Advances and Online Game Design, *Raph Koster's Website*. http://www.raphkoster.com/gaming/moore.shtml. Accessed December 18, 2006.

38. David Jenkins, Halo 2 Records 500 Million Online Games, *Gamasutra*, June 7, 2006. http://www.gamasutra.com/php-bin/news_index.php?story=9629.

39. Greg Costikyan, Death to the Games Industry: Long Live Games, *The Escapist*. http://www.escapistmagazine.com/issue/8/3. Accessed December 18, 2006.

40. Relmstein, MMO Failures, *The Many Relms of Relmstein*, July 25, 2006. http://relmstein.blogspot.com/2006/07/mmo-failures.html.

41. M. Wallace, AGC: Koster Says Game Industry Dinosaur 'Doomed,' *Gamasutra*, September 8, 2006. http://www.gamasutra.com/php-bin/news_index.php?story=10803.

42. Raph Koster, The Future of Content, *Raph Koster's Website*, December 12, 2005. http://www.raphkoster.com/?p=197.

43. BusinessWire, Red 5 Studios Grows with $18.5 Million from Benchmark Capital and Sierra Ventures, *Digital Game Developer*, December 12, 2006. http://www.digitalgamedeveloper.com/articles/viewarticle.jsp?id=88862.

44. Havok, Homepage, 2007. http://havok.com/. Accessed December 18, 2006.

45. SpeedTree, Homepage, 2007. http://speedtree.com/. Accessed December 18, 2006.

46. Wikimedia, s.v. Unreal Engine. *Wikipedia*, February 13, 2007. http://en.wikipedia.org/w/index.php?title=Unreal_Engine&oldid=107862088.

47. Dmitri Williams, Multiverse>SL>WoW, *Terra Nova*, November 9, 2006. http://terranova.blogs.com/terra_nova/2006/11/multiverse_sl_w.html#comments.

48. USC Center for the Digital Future, Online World as Important to Internet Users as Real World? 2007. http://www.digitalcenter.org/pdf/2007-Digital-Future-Report-Press-Release-112906.pdf. Accessed December 18, 2006.

49. Chip Pountine, *Virtual Suburbia*, April 4, 2007. http://virtualsuburbia.blogspot.com/.

50. Koden Farber, Game Reviews: #1 Living the Dark Life, *The Second Life Herald*, February 17, 2005. http://www.dragonscoveherald.com/blog/index.php?p=675.

51. SL Boutique, Homepage. http://slboutique.com/. Accessed December 18, 2006.

52. *Second Life* statistics were pulled from the SL databases by the author.

53. Hernando De Soto, *The Mystery of Capital* (New York: Basic Books, 2000).

54. Douglas C. North, Economic Performance Through Time: The Limits to Knowledge, 1996. http://129.3.20.41/eps/eh/papers/9612/9612004.html. Accessed December 18, 2006.

55. Reed Hundt, *In China's Shadow* (Kirkwood, NY: Vail-Ballou Press, 2006).

56. Thomas W. Malone, *The Future of Work* (Boston: Harvard Business School Press, 2004).

57. Yochai Benkler, *The Wealth of Networks* (New Haven, CT: Yale University Press, 2006).

58. Sturgeon's Law: "90% of everything is crap."

59. Ibid.

60. USC Center for the Digital Future, Online World.

61. Jakob Nielsen, *Participatory Inequality*, 2006. http://www.useit.com/alertbox/participation_inequality.html. Accessed December 18, 2006.

62. Carolyn Marvin, *When Old Technologies Were New* (Oxford: Oxford University Press, 1988).

63. Philip Ross, The Expert Mind, *Scientific American*, August, 2006. http://www.sciam.com/article.cfm?articleID=00010347-101C-14C1-8F9E83414B7F4945.

64. Again, *Second Life* stats were gathered directly from the database by the author.

65. Pew Internet and American Life Project, 57% of Teen Internet Users Create, Remix and Share Content Online, *Pew/Internet*, April 30, 2007. http://www.pewinternet.org/PPF/r/113/press_release.asp.

66. Raw survey results available online at http://survey.tslemporium.com/results.php. Accessed December 18, 2006.

67. See http://secondlife.com/events. Accessed December 18, 2006.

68. SimTeach, Second Life: A Virtual Resource for Educators and Academics, *Second Life Education Wiki*. http://www.simteach.com/wiki/index.php?title=Second_Life_Education_Wiki. Accessed December 18, 2006.

69. See James Paul Gee, Learning and Games, in *The Ecology of Games: Connecting Youth, Games, and Learning*, ed. Katie Salen (Cambridge, MA: The MIT Press, 2007), 21–40.

70. Ondrejka, A Random Walk Down the Long Tails of Innovation. Last visited August 2, 2007. http://secondlife.blogs.com/prompt/2006/06a_random_walk_d.html.

71. Wikimedia, s.v. Stroke, *Wikipedia*, February 18, 2007. http://en.wikipedia.org/w/index.php?title=Stroke&oldid=108988647.

72. CyberOne, Law in the Court of Public Opinion: The End of a Long Hiatus, October 29, 2006. http://blogs.law.harvard.edu/cyberone/2006/10/29/the-end-of-a-long-hiatus/.

73. Wikimedia, s.v. Lev Vygotsky, *Wikipedia*, February 15, 2007, http://en.wikipedia.org/w/index.php?title=Lev_Vygotsky&oldid=108262329.

74. Alex Kozulin, Boris Gindis, Vladimir S. Ageyev, and Suzanne M. Miller, eds., *Vygotsky's Educational Theory in Cultural Context* (Cambridge, UK: Cambridge University Press, 2003).

75. Wikimedia, s.v. Seymour Papert, *Wikipedia*, February 11, 2007. http://en.wikipedia.org/w/index.php?title=Seymour_Papert&oldid=107313031.

76. Mitch Resnick, *Turtles, Termites, and Traffic Jams* (Cambridge, MA: The MIT Press, 2000).

77. Seymour Papert, *Mindstorms* (New York: Basic Books, 1993).

78. Livingstone and Kemp, Proceedings.

79. Jean Lave and Etienne Wenger, *Situated Learning* (Cambridge, UK: Cambridge University Press, 1991).

80. Ibid.

81. Ibid.

82. James Paul Gee, *Situated Language and Learning* (London: Routledge, 2004).

83. Space Culture Blog, Space Now... Virtual, *Space Culture*, December 11, 2006. http://space-culture.blogspot.com/search/label/ism.

84. Sara Goo, Hear the Music, Avoid the Mosh Pit, *The Washington Post*, August 21, 2006. http://www.washingtonpost.com/wpdyn/content/article/2006/08/20/AR2006082000593.html?nav=rss_technology/personaltech.

85. Livingstone and Kemp, Proceedings.

86. Ivan Oransky and Anne Harding, Diversity in the Life Sciences, *The Scientist* 19, no. 21 (2005). http://www.the-scientist.com/supplement/2005-11-07/. Accessed December 18, 2006.

87. Mitchell Chang and Alexander Astin, Who Benefits from Racial Diversity in Higher Education, *Diversity Digest*. http://www.diversityweb.org/Digest/W97/ research.html. Accessed December 18, 2006.

88. Trish Lawrence, Why Diversity Matters, *The Scientist* 19, no. 21 (2005). http://www.the-scientist.com/2005/11/07/s20/1/. Accessed December 18, 2006.

89. Data collected by the author form Linden Lab databases, December, 2006.

90. Wikimedia, s.v. Second Life Education.

91. Livingstone and Kemp, Proceedings.

92. News Media Consortium, NMC Homepage. http://www.nmc.org/. Accessed December 18, 2006.

93. Grace Wong, Educators Explore 'Second Life' Online, *CNN.com*, November 14, 2006. http://www.cnn. com/2006/TECH/11/13/second.life.university/index.html.

94. Rachel Nolan, At Law School, 'Second Life' in the Cards and the Course Catalog, *The Harvard Crimson*, September 27, 2006. http://www.thecrimson.com/article.aspx?ref=514500.

95. CyberOne, Law in the Court.

96. SimTeach, Second Life Grad Student Colony, *Second Life Education Wiki*. http://www.simteach.com/wiki/index.php?title=Second_Life_Grad_Student_Colony. Accessed December 18, 2006.

97. North, Economic Performance.

98. Adam Reuters, IBM Eyes Move into Second Life 'V-Business,' *Second Life News Center*, October 24, 2006. http://secondlife.reuters.com/stories/2006/10/24/ibm-eyes-move-into-second-life-v-business/.

99. W. James Au, The Second Life of Governor Mark Warner, *New World Notes*, August 31, 2006. http://nwn.blogs.com/nwn/2006/08/the_second_life.html.

100. Juan Enriquez, *As the Future Catches You* (New York: Random House, 2000).

101. Wikimedia, s.v. Creative Destruction, *Wikipedia*, February 20, 2007. http://en.wikipedia.org/w/index.php?title=Creative_destruction&oldid=109597057.

102. Juan Enriquez, *The Untied States of America* (New York: Crown, 2005).

103. Ibid.

104. Wikimedia, s.v. Grameen Bank, *Wikipedia*, February 16, 2007. http://en.wikipedia.org/w/index.php?title=Grameen_Bank&oldid=108587610.

105. See, for example, the immersive language training experiment going on at Language Lab (http://languagelab.com/). Accessed December 18, 2006.

Why Johnny Can't Fly: Treating Games as a Form of Youth Media Within a Youth Development Framework

Barry Joseph

Global Kids, Inc.

When the tables are turned, video games become a medium for children's personal and creative expression. . . . Making a game and its rules allowed the game designers to be in charge and to determine the player's place in the world.

—Yasmin B. Kafai[1]

When kids program, just as when they write, they can learn to make their own claims about the world in the form of processes. Such a practice reframes videogame development as a rhetorical practice, not just a craft practice or a technical practice.

—Ian Bogost[2]

What's the Big Idea?

When Kristina was a high school senior, she spent a year participating in an afterschool program called *Playing 4 Keeps*, run by Global Kids, Inc. Trainers like me led the program, developing the youths' leadership skills around global issues.

Kristina learned how to play video games with a critical eye, and worked with her peers and the professional game development company, Gamelab, to make their own game. *Ayiti: The Cost of Life* challenges its players to educate an impoverished family of five in contemporary Haiti while keeping them healthy and out of debt. When the day came to release it online at theCostofLife.org, she presented the game to her school community at a special event attended by students, faculty, and even one curious security guard.

Afterward, I asked her how she felt sharing her game with others. She said, "I feel like you."

"What does it feel like to be me?" I asked.

She said, "It feels like being a trainer."

Developing a game about a global issue made Kristina feel like a leader. This is not unusual for youth who go through a Global Kids' program. What is unusual, however, is the path she took, playing and making digital games.

Many cast a cynical eye toward the idea that games offer anything of value, especially within an educational context. But not too long ago, comic books were viewed in a similar light. In fact, before the arrival of Art Spiegelman's Holocaust biography, *Maus*, who would have expected a comic book to win a Pulitzer Prize? Yet the medium, once seen as the corrupter of children's minds, had offered up the highest example of what could be achieved in literature. Expectations were revised. Life went on.

For years, video games have been blamed for turning children into mesmerized robots, agents of sexism and racism, and violent gun-toting psychopaths, concerns not far afield from those once lobbed at comics. Perhaps by the time you read this, the game equivalent of *Maus* will have arrived, winning its own Pulitzer.[3] Or the Nobel. But today, in spite of the absence of such a superstar, video games are emerging as powerful tools for preparing today's youth to enter a globalized workforce. Expectations are being revised. Life goes on.

There are now many voices describing the power of these tools, from James Paul Gee and his former colleagues at the University of Wisconsin to Henry Jenkins at MIT's Comparative Media Studies Program to others included in this volume. These voices have played a key role informing how Global Kids has incorporated the informal learning associated with games into a formalized afterschool setting.

In *Confronting the Challenges of Participatory Culture: Media Education for the 21st Century*, Jenkins[4] recognizes that "some have expressed skepticism that schools should or could teach young people how to play." He views this skepticism as confusion between "play as a source of fun and play as a form of engagement," arguing that the type of engagement offered by digital play—along with other forms of digital media—inducts young people into powerful learning environments, rich with opportunities for building and sharing knowledge. And yet, this learning need not be removed from a formalized educational setting. In fact, he writes that one of his goals is to "challenge those who have responsibility for teaching our young people to think more systematically and creatively about the many different ways they might build [new media literacy] skills into their day-to-day activities in ways that are appropriate to the content they are teaching."[5]

This is a challenge that we at Global Kids took very seriously when we decided to incorporate digital games into our programs. These new game-oriented programs were based, in large part, on Global Kids' previous youth media programs, like one in which teenagers made a documentary about the conflict in Northern Ireland, and another in which they developed a monthly radio show on youth-related health topics.

Introducing game development into our pedagogy proved more difficult than we had anticipated. Paradigms fundamental to youth media were soon challenged by the new ideas we encountered in the emerging fields of games and learning. Jenkins describes this split when he critiques media literacy advocates who fail to understand the changes created by new media technologies, viewing media "primarily as threats rather than as resources." He continues, "More focus is placed on the dangers of manipulation rather than the possibilities of participation, on restricting access . . . rather than in expanding skills."[6]

As we worked through the conceptual shift offered by this way of thinking about games and learning, we came to a new understanding of youth media and how digital games could be used to develop the next generation of global citizens. This chapter aims to describe this process and offers examples from our two games-based programs: the Microsoft Corporation–funded *Playing 4 Keeps* and the MacArthur Foundation–funded *Camp Global Kids*.

Raising Akiva (An Interlude)

As I write this, my son, Akiva, is about to turn eight months old. When he was barely two weeks, my wife and I went to a brunch where a friend asked, "So, do you have it down yet?"

Words failed me. Had we mastered raising a child? In only two weeks?

My wife was quick with a response. She said that learning to be a mom was like playing a video game. "Each day is a new level, with its own challenges," she explained. "By the end of the day you have a handle on them. But the next day you are faced with a whole new level."

Everyone laughed. Then she added, "Unfortunately, you can't return to an earlier level and try again."

My Day Job

Global Kids is committed to transforming urban youth into successful students and global and community leaders through its classroom-based, afterschool, digital media programs. We educate young people about international affairs, develop academic and leadership skills, and promote active engagement in civic life. We work in dozens of schools and other sites reaching over 14,000 teens and adults annually, mostly in New York City.

We approach teens and learning with what is now known as a youth development model. In its most general usage, "youth development" refers to any work with young people designed to improve their lives, whether playing basketball at a Police Athletic League or arguing on behalf of Madagascar in a model U.N. session. However, in the nineties, a very specific youth development model was articulated and adapted primarily by afterschool organizations around the country, with very specific practices and outcomes. This flexible and evolving pedagogy can be hard to pin down, but for Global Kids, it means creating interactive activities that are experiential, building on students' existing strengths, involving youth in the design of the programs, tapping into their interests and talents, and considering them not as "leaders of tomorrow" but as capable, passionate people who can better their world today.

Global Kids is unique in that we combine a youth development model with civic and global engagement within both classroom and afterschool contexts. I was hired in 2000 to develop the Online Leadership Program, with initial support from both the Academy for Educational Development and the Surdna Foundation. My mission was to use the Internet to extend elements of our youth leadership and global education programs, reaching a broad range of youth online and making the creation of these projects a leadership opportunity for Global Kids' youth leaders.

It was hard not to notice the increasingly visible role video games were playing in the lives of our youth leaders. Through a Global Kids' workshop they might become active in the struggle to eliminate the use of child soldiers, but return home to become active as virtual soldiers in a computer-based war game. Something seemed wrong with this picture.

At the same time, game elements had always been part of Global Kids' workshops. That's part of what makes them so engaging. Why couldn't the same educational aspects of games that were regularly employed in our school-based programs be coded into an online game? It seemed like a natural fit.

In the spring of 2005, we received a grant from the Microsoft Corporation's U.S. Partners in Learning program—which supports innovative technology and education programs—to develop an afterschool game development program. We named it *Playing 4 Keeps*. Just a few months later, the MacArthur Foundation granted Global Kids funds to gather the voices of youth around the topic of the role that digital media plays in their lives as part of their new Digital Media and Learning initiative. A core component of this work led us to develop a space in early 2006 within the virtual world *Teen Second Life* in a location we named *Global Kids Island* where, that summer, we held *Camp GK*.

How Not to Hail a Cab in Liberty City (Another Interlude)

A few years ago I walked into my local hotdog joint and watched a twelve-year-old play *Grand Theft Auto*. No one who followed the news could miss the controversy fueled by this game. Debates about its level of violence were frequently discussed and debated. I was intrigued finally to watch someone play it.

Imagine my surprise when I observed that the only thing the teen did in the game was to drive a taxi. It turned out there were multiple ways to play the game, and this young man's preference happened to be driving around the streets of Liberty City.

He had, however, developed an unusual method for being a cabbie. Rather than slowing down before picking up a fare, he would often run a person over, wait for him or her to get back up (as if nothing had happened) and climb into his cab, then drive away. I could just imagine how this might appear in a newspaper: "Teen Learns Violent Acts Have No Repercussions."

"Would you ever get in a taxi that ran you over?" I asked. Without breaking contact with the game the boy responded, "The A.I. is dumb," referring to the code controlling the behavior of his passengers.

This was my first of many "aha" moments as I delved into the world of games and learning. The teen was not learning to be violent. Rather, he was learning how to analyze the rules of a system and leverage its flaws.

As Ian Bogost has written elsewhere in this volume, when we play video games, "We explore the possibility space its rules afford by manipulating the symbolic systems the game provides."[7] By exploring *Grand Theft Auto*, this boy had discovered possibilities its designers most likely had never intended, and he was manipulating the system to his own advantage. More to the point, he very well knew it.

The Problem of Pedagogy

In the field of youth development, "youth media" refers to programs that help teenagers develop media skills, which they, in turn, use to express their thoughts and feelings and educate others. They might produce a video, or a Web site, or a book of poetry.

This strikes me as a conceptual offshoot of the general field of media literacy, which teaches consumers how to think critically about the effects (mostly negative) that various forms of mass media have on our minds and values, such as the influence of advertising on children. I can easily recall my first lesson in media literacy, in the cartoonish voice of Carol Channing, from the feminist-inspired children's album *Free to Be, You and Me*:

The lady we see when we are watching TV
The lady who smiles as she scours or scrubs or rubs or washes . . .
That lady is smiling because she is an actress
And she's earning money for learning those speeches
That mention those wonderful soaps and detergents and cleaners and powders . . .
So, the very next time you happen to be
Just sitting there quietly watching TV . . .
Remember, no one smiles doing housework but those ladies you see on TV
Your mommy hates housework . . . And when you grow up, so will you.[8]

That was a powerful lesson for an eight-year-old: Beware! Media pay adults to lie to you, to misrepresent the world to get you to buy products. It's little wonder that, as an adult, I was able to learn so easily how to develop youth media programs without access to any of the media's underlying pedagogical theory. All I had to do was watch other youth media practitioners and then try it myself to see that youth media's core paradigm concerns itself with the framing and addressing of two issues, which I will call the problems of *representation* and *manipulation.*

Most media do not accurately represent, when they attempt to represent at all, youth voices. To address this, one framework for media literacy challenges us to ask of any media message, "What lifestyles, values, and points of view are represented in—or omitted from—this message?"[9] When it comes to the specific voices of Global Kids' youth leaders, who tend to be youth of color from low-income neighborhoods, not only are their voices absent, but their representation to the public, and the issues that most concern them, are vastly distorted. Youth media positions itself as a necessary corrective, putting the power of media into the hands of the disenfranchised.

At the same time, media are seen to have a power that shapes our attitudes and desires, often without our knowing it. Media critic Noam Chomsky goes so far as to frame mass media within what he calls a "propaganda model," wherein the role of media is to mobilize support for the dominant interest groups to maintain their power.[10] They make children want fast food and adults believe in a connection between Iraq and the attacks of 9/11; they create a narrow range for holding public debates and deride all critical thought.

As such, youth media positions itself as an essential tool for a healthy democracy, developing citizens with the conceptual tools necessary to deconstruct the workings of media—whether television, movies, music, or advertising. As if against a virus, such programs inoculate youth against media's most virulent strains. Rather than become pawns of media, this training allows youth to maintain their independent perspectives and to be critical of the biases inherent in representation.

It was not much of a challenge to view Global Kids' new gaming programs from this perspective. Building games and critically playing games would empower the youth in our programs to use games as a means to express themselves and educate others while training them to be critical consumers of the games they already played. But we soon learned that a field of theory had developed specifically to address the vast learning potential these games—and other media within the popular culture landscape—afford.

We read Stephen Johnson's *Everything Bad Is Good For You*,[11] and learned that a new paradigm sees unparalleled learning opportunities in the increased complexity that exists in the forms of television and games, regardless of their specific subject matter. In a similar vein, Katie Salen and Eric Zimmerman, in their seminal game design textbook *Rules of Play*,[12] argue that games teach best when the core mechanic, the thing one learns to actually do to play the game, is itself the subject being taught, rather than a set of facts or figures. I saw the focus shifting from the content to the form, from the subject of a game to what it means to learn to play it.

We then read James Paul Gee and a number of others from the University of Wisconsin–Madison's Games, Learning, and Society group, who are articulating how digital games offer insights into key questions of learning and literacy.[13] As we learned about this, we did not have to throw out the old paradigm of youth media; however, we were challenged to reorient our framework toward the new problem that a games-based literacy often aims to address—the problem of pedagogy.

When I first began speaking with program officers at various foundations about games and learning, one of the first things I had to explain was that the world has moved far beyond Pong and Pac Man. Today's games have become increasingly complex, often supported by Web-based fora, complex guide books, and affinity groups.[14] They frequently offer various ways to play, as I learned from my encounter with the *Grand Theft Auto* taxi driver, and they force players to explore complex ethical decisions.[15] Games can teach players to develop critical thinking, comprehend sophisticated models of the world, understand complex systems theory, and more.

In fact, the learning found in today's video games, and associated affinity groups, offers a powerful model for resolving the conflict between, and limitations of, a permissive anything-goes progressive pedagogy (on the one hand), and a more traditional one focused on an expert imparting knowledge (on the other hand).[16] Gee refers to this as a "post-progressive pedagogy." Forget "No Child Left Behind," his work suggests. All children are getting left behind, trapped in a deficient educational model that leaves them ill-prepared for the globalized workplace of the twenty-first century.

Advocates of the educational use of games do not always dismiss media critics' concerns about the power of mass media—they just find that these critics often miss the point. Jenkins criticizes those whom he calls "critical pessimists," who "often exaggerate the power of big media in order to frighten readers into taking action."[17] This leaves a false impression that hinders those interested in leveraging the participatory power of new media. According to Jenkins, this exaggerated rhetoric "rests on melodramatic discourse about the victimization and vulnerability, seduction and manipulation"[18] of media consumers. Gee is in agreement, writing, "people are not dupes... necessarily taking from a video game... any one predictable message predetermined by the design of the game..."[19]

Rather than focus on "what media is doing to us," we should focus on "what we are doing with media,"[20] and learn how we can do so within, but not limited to or by, formalized learning spaces. This learning, according to Jenkins, is essential for today's youth to develop the skills they need to participate fully in the world of tomorrow.[21]

However, when Global Kids decided to approach games as a form of youth media, there were few examples of programs designed around such a games-based post-progressive pedagogy; there were no Carol Channings we could hum along with as our guide. How could an educator harness informal learning practices developed around—and through—vehicles of digital play, in order to build a formalized setting that would institutionalize this process? We had little choice but to apply these new ideas ourselves, and figure out how those like Gee's could be incorporated with those embedded in an already-familiar model of youth media literacy.

So This Guy Walks into a Situated Learning Matrix...

An important thing to keep in mind about Gee's work is that he is not necessarily arguing that games should be used for education. Rather, he wants to draw our attention to the powerful forms of learning already available in many games, regardless of their subject matter.

Gee calls upon those outside the gaming world to consider the kinds of learning theory that games support and to apply it in explicitly educational contexts, with or without the use of games themselves. Inscribed in Gee's thinking is a model he calls a Situated Learning Matrix, which defines the conditions required for good learning to take place (as currently modeled by good video games), described in his contribution to this volume, "Learning and Games." Rather than teach content directly, such as by listing facts on a board, in Gee's framework content is situated in a "goal-driven, identity-focused experience,"[22] and the content is encountered, interrogated, and absorbed in that specific context.

This leads to the question: How does this approach align with the youth development and civic engagement pedagogy used by Global Kids?

Playing 4 Keeps and the Birth of *Ayiti*

DeWayne, a junior at Brooklyn's South Shore High School, first learned of *Playing 4 Keeps* from an announcement over the loudspeaker explaining a new afterschool program about games. DeWayne often describes himself as someone who had been hanging out with the wrong crowd and doing things he ought not be doing. But that year he was ready for a change.

Over the course of the school year, DeWayne, along with Kristina and other youth leaders, met for two hours once a week in a computer lab at their school. For many, it would be their only time during the week in front of a computer. My colleague—Afi French—and I facilitated the workshops, often with the assistance and contributions of a number of designers from Gamelab. Over the course of the year-long program, we went from playing and critiquing games to exploring global human rights issues, to collaborating closely with Gamelab on the creation of what became *Ayiti*, to—eventually—launching the game online.

"We understand that there are a lot of different things going on in the world," DeWayne told me, "and poverty hit our mind quick fast." Why poverty? "Poverty is not just about being homeless and hungry. We want to get that out there to other people and let them know that it's in other places besides America." But why a game? "You can actually see how they are living. You can live like the family, work like them." So what does the game teach? "It lets you know that times are hard and people need help."

Games are being used in this context as a form of persuasive media "to change opinion or action"; however, *Ayiti* persuades not by harnessing the more traditional practice of verbal or visual rhetoric, but by what Ian Bogost terms *procedural rhetoric*, "through the authorship of rules of behavior [and] the construction of dynamic models."[23] As a popular online game magazine noted: "*Ayiti* . . . manages to deliver a strong political message without sacrificing strategy or entertainment, balancing real-life information with gaming convention."[24] In other words, students like DeWayne found their voices as engaged global citizens by creating a game that represented poverty as a dynamic system.

With online partners like UNICEF and TakingITglobal, within seven months of its release over 600,000 teens played the game (figures 1 and 2).

Do Avatars Dream of Virtual Marshmallows?

Camp Global Kids took a very different approach from that of *Playing 4 Keeps*. While the latter used the learning potential of game development, the former focused on the learning potential within virtual worlds. *Camp Global Kids* took place on *Global Kids Island*, a virtual space within the teen grid of *Second Life*.

Teen Second Life (*TSL*) is the growing online space for 13–17-year-olds within *Second Life*, a virtual world wherein millions of people create avatars and develop unique living environments and strong social networks. (For more on *Second Life*, please read Cory Ondrejka's contribution to this volume, "Education Unleashed: Participatory Culture, Education, and Innovation in *Second Life*.") By most definitions, *TSL* is not a game. There are no levels to achieve, no short- or long-term win states, no scripted fantasy narratives to explore. However, while not strictly a digital game, there is little doubt that *TSL* is still a space of digital play, offering many of the affordances available through digital games.

Global Kids developed a host of interactive experiential workshops for the *TSL* environment based on those used in Global Kids' offline programs. During these workshops—flying above the ground and dressed in inventive outfits—teen members discuss such topics as racism within virtual worlds, genocide in Darfur, global poverty, and the digital divide. We found that teens arrive on our island already possessing many leadership skills, often without an awareness of this fact. These skills are strengthened through the process of learning how

Figure 1
A screen shot of *Ayiti: The Cost of Life.*

to create their own avatars, objects, activities, and social narratives. Through our workshops, they learn to view themselves as individuals who can care about and help shape the world around them.

Camp Global Kids was the first virtual summer camp in *TSL*, taking place during the summer of 2006. This groundbreaking experiment gathered together a diverse group of sixteen teens logging in from three countries. Two of the teens were full-time interns, one in our office and one working remotely from his home in another state. Two others were assigned the role of "embedded reporters," documenting their experiences on our blog (HolyMeatballs.org). Within *TSL*, some teens reflected their real races, genders, and species through the design of their avatars; others chose, instead, to represent themselves as a "knife wielding teddy bear" or played with altering their races or genders.

In *Camp Global Kids*, we adapted our real-world educational workshops for use in *TSL*, both in concept and in practice, raising students' awareness of global issues like the impact of war or the genocide in Darfur, while helping them to realize what they can do to influence change in their world. While adapting these workshops was not a simple process, we eventually learned how to create experiential learning within the surreal physics, social networks, and unique youth culture of a virtual world.

For example, a workshop we often facilitate is called "Race to the Bottom." Participants are divided into teams and represent different developing nations, like Haiti. They then are pitted against one another in an attempt to curry the interests of a multinational corporation (played by the facilitators) as they have to balance the economic benefits of a new factory against the impact of reduced human rights and environmental standards. The politics are

Figure 2
Students playing *Ayiti* at the launch party.

didactic, but it is a fun workshop that clearly makes its point and allows for a vigorous postgame discussion.

In the real world, we simply don't have the time or resources to reproduce much of the simulation, such as the setting, props, or costumes. We leave these to the imagination. Yet this is not required in a virtual world like *Second Life*. In the real world, when we run the Race to the Bottom workshop, we don't bring students to a working factory and dress them in the outfits of people from the competing countries; to suggest taking such an approach for a forty-minute workshop would be absurd. But to suggest *not* doing so in *TSL*, in which the campers can produce all of the required elements, would be equally absurd. As such, the workshop took place in a simulation of a working factory, with one wall dominated by an industrial fan; the facilitators were dressed in sharp business suits; bidding was performed by piling up colored boxes to represent concessions offered to the multinationals. All elements just described, and more, were digitally designed and created by the campers themselves, in advance of the actual workshop.

After a few weeks of similar workshops, we challenged the campers to pick one topic and develop a method for educating their community about it. They chose one of the hardest topics we had discussed: child sex trafficking. To educate their peers and inspire them to take action, they built an elaborate maze, metaphorically representing the passage of a youth from being trapped in the system to one freed by the efforts of international advocates. Maze

Figure 3
Campers tour their finished maze against child sex trafficking.

visitors collected virtual issue-related freebies (e.g., a ball and chain that stated, "I wear this to bring attention to child sex trafficking"), they answered multiple-choice questions based on the information they learned, and they were teleported to a monument in the sky, dedicated to those still trapped in the system, which offered a variety of actions teens could now take.

In the first eight weeks after launch, over 2,500 teens visited the maze, with 20 percent donating money. As one camper reported after the program had concluded, "Before camp I never thought about issues in the world. Well, I did but I never thought there was anything I could do to fix them. But I've found out that I can help to make a difference" (figure 3).

Modding

Modding refers to the ability of game players to build new extensions, even completely new versions, of existing games. This has become so normal that many game designers depend on their players to create the tools and content that will maintain interest in the game over time. Modding became an important tool for our teens in *Second Life*—not only in how they participated, but in how they learned.

Gee contends that this aspect of video games "allow[s] players not just to be passive consumers but also active producers who can customize their own learning experience."[25] This lines up very nicely with viewing games as a form of youth media, while modding teaches youth—through building their own versions of existing media properties—to understand the framework within which games operate. At the same time, modding is a strong component of Jenkins's argument for a "participatory culture" in which youth engage with popular culture not just by consuming it, but by transforming it in the process.[26]

We knew this when we designed *Camp GK*. At least we thought we did. We knew the teens loved to build. It is the *lingua franca* of their virtual world, arguably nothing more than one giant, collective mod. To meet this need, the camp was structured to end with a final, collective build (what eventually became their maze). We soon realized, however, that was hardly adequate. They wanted to build every day. All the time. Even when we were not meeting.

They built the clubhouse where each day began and the campfire where it ended. They populated the former with chairs, plants, and lights, and the latter with marshmallows on sticks. They initiated and held their own competition to build a *Camp GK* logo and virtual T-shirt, then posted the design on the Web site CafePress.com where physical objects (like notebooks and coffee mugs) could be purchased. They were not content attending the program we had developed for them; they wanted, as Gee contends, to customize their own learning experience.

Why were we caught by surprise? Because we had forgotten our Gee! "In school," Gee writes, "the teacher is the insider and the learners are outsiders who must take what they are given as mere consumers." However, "game designers and game players are both insiders and producers—if players so choose—and there need be no outside."[27] The residents in *Camp GK* did so choose, the outside was erased, and we were caught unprepared.

Epistemic Learning

Gee's Situated Learning Matrix, discussed elsewhere in this volume, includes the notion of epistemic learning, which has been clearly articulated in the book *How Computer Games Help Children Learn*, written by his colleague, David Williamson Shaffer.[28] Epistemic learning looks to the ways that certain games afford their players the opportunity to step virtually into the shoes of a specific profession and, through game play, become familiar with its domains of knowledge, skill base, values, identities, and ways of thinking about the world.[29] As with Gee, Shaffer is interested in not only how games can offer this form of learning, but how educators can adapt it outside of games as well.

Global Kids developed *Playing 4 Keeps* before learning about the concept of epistemic learning. However, when we were first introduced to the concept and looked at our program from this perspective, we asked ourselves how well we were preparing the youth leaders to view the world as professional game designers. We realized we were coming up short. Sure, we were teaching them important skills, but only in a general sense. We were failing to provide them with the specific context, the context of the professional game developer, to tie it all together. And, as Gee writes, "learning out of context leaves learners with knowledge they cannot apply."[30]

We were no longer simply interested in teaching our youth skills in the classroom and providing them with opportunities to express themselves. We wanted to develop opportunities for them to be immersed in the world of this specific profession. We visited a game design office to see where game designers work. We went to a gaming conference to hear what game designers sound like. We brought in game developer magazines to read what game designers think about. We visited a "History of Games" exhibit in a museum to see what they selected and why. We created opportunities for the most articulate students to speak about the program at conferences—such as the annual Game Developers Conference—at a meeting on educational technology held at Microsoft, and even on a panel about games and learning alongside Gee and Jenkins.

It did not matter whether any of what the students saw made sense to them in any immediately practical manner. Often the discourse was, by its very nature, over their heads, as it was intended for other game designers and not outsiders listening in. But that was precisely the point: to expose them repeatedly to the epistemic frame of this field. So when we returned from a rather academic debate about the nature of game design, they did not report learning about, say, the gendered nature of play, but rather, as one youth leader noted (quite disappointedly), that "Game designers look like normal people."

As it would turn out, they were learning more than what it means to be game designers. By visiting our offices each week, traveling with us, learning from us, watching how Afi and I spoke to one another, observing how we dressed, and so forth, they also had an epistemic learning experience regarding what it means to be a Global Kids' trainer, as Kristina had so kindly brought to our attention.

So while a youth media model offers one framework for viewing the *Playing 4 Keeps* program, we can also see how exclusively doing so would ignore the epistemic potential of the program, just to pick one of many components within Gee's Matrix. We need not focus on one framework over the other; both have valuable things to offer. And both fit well within a youth development model, building youth voices by focusing on their current interests, abilities, and strengths.

21st Century Learning Skills

When I think about my baby son, or about any of my students, I can relate to the problems of pedagogy encountered by those grappling with games-based learning. Youth development programs share a similar concern, as we too attempt to develop critical thinking skills that are not necessarily designed for passing standardized tests. And we are not alone. A broader educational framework has been articulated, called 21st Century Learning Skills, detailing many of the educational objectives undertaken by most youth media, youth development, and games-based learning programs.[31] Developed, supported, and put into practice through funding offered by a broad range of high-profile foundations and corporations (including many who have funded our digital media work at Global Kids), companies like Time Warner, the Corporation for Public Broadcasting, the Microsoft Corporation, and the MacArthur Foundation recognize that we need to embrace new models for thinking about education.

21st Century Learning Skills puts into high relief the failed pedagogy built into the current "No Child Left Behind" model. As Gee writes, "Education has for well over a hundred years cycled between arguments for 'progressive' approaches to education and arguments for 'traditional' approaches to education . . . Good video games solve this dilemma."[32] And they solve it in a way that situates a games-based literacy as a strong addition to any program focused on developing 21st Century Learning Skills while challenging our current system to move toward this alternative educational vision.

In fact, Jenkins contends that since "schools as institutions have been slow to react" to these new opportunities, "the greatest opportunities for change is currently found in afterschool programs and informal learning communities."[33] Global Kids is cognizant of and inspired by the unique role it can play in this process, and it looks forward to collaborating with others to help bring about this change.

At a personal level, this gives me hope, both for Global Kids' youth leaders and the future education of youth like my son. Speaking of my son, you might recall I earlier mentioned that my wife found it convenient to use games as a model to describe the education she was receiving as a new mother. What interested me most at the time was that while my wife loves our son, she hates video games. She has not touched one in years. So even someone with no direct experience of contemporary video games, even one who hates to play them, could value and find useful the post-progressive learning theories embedded within them. Perhaps this is yet another example of expectations being revised. Perhaps it means a new praxis has been established, transmitting elements of the games and learning meme and signaling the arrival of a new paradigm that can deeply affect the future of education.

Perhaps somewhere, out there, Carol Channing is singing a new song.

Notes

1. Yasmin B. Kafai, Gender Differences in Children's Constructions of Video Games, in *Interacting with Video*, eds. Patricia R. Greenfield and Rodney R. Cocking (Norwood, NJ: Ablex, 1996)

2. Ian Bogost, The Rhetoric of Video Games, in *The Ecology of Games: Connecting Youth, Games, and Learning*, ed. Katie Salen (Cambridge, MA: The MIT Press, 2007), 117–39.

3. A month after I wrote this paragraph, I read the following in Arie Kaplan's excellent *Masters of the Comic Book Universe Revealed* (Chicago: Chicago Review Press, 2006): "In the 1960s, in the pages of a particularly lighthearted issue of *Fantastic Four*, writer Stan Lee jokingly announced that he and cartoonist Jack Kirby should be considered by the Pulitzer Prize Committee for their work on the *FF*. At the time, it was a joke: a *comic book* winning the Pulitzer? How ridiculous! With *Maus*, it's no joke."

4. Henry Jenkins, *Confronting the Challenges of Participatory Culture: Media Education for the 21st Century* (Chicago: The MacArthur Foundation, 2006), 24.

5. Ibid., 21.

6. Henry Jenkins, *Convergence Culture* (New York: New York University Press, 2006), 259.

7. Bogost, The Rhetoric of Video Games, 121.

8. Carol Channing, "Housework, Written by Sheldon Harnick." *Free to Be, You and Me* (New York: Bell Records, 1972).

9. Tessa Jolls, Jeff Share, and Elizabeth Thoman, *Five Key Questions That Can Change the World* (San Francisco: Center for Media Literacy, 2005), 3.

10. Edward S. Herman and Noam Chomsky, *Manufacturing Consent* (New York: Pantheon, 1988).

11. Steven Johnson, *Everything Bad Is Good for You* (London: Riverhead Trade, 2005).

12. Katie Salen and Eric Zimmerman, *Rules of Play* (Cambridge, MA: The MIT Press, 2003).

13. Examples of this work can be found at Academic ADL Co-Lab, the University of Wisconsin–Madison, at http://www.academiccolab.org/initiatives/gapps.html. Accessed June 19, 2007.

14. James Paul Gee, Learning and Games, in *The Ecology of Games: Connecting Youth, Games, and Learning*, ed. Katie Salen (Cambridge, MA: The MIT Press, 2007), 21–40.

15. In his earlier book, *What Video Games Have to Teach Us About Games and Learning* (New York: Palgave MacMillan, 2004), Gee refers to the form as the "Multiple Route Principle," and the latter as the "Cultural Models About the World Principle."

16. Gee, Learning and Games.

17. Jenkins, *Convergence Culture*, 259.

18. Ibid.

19. James Paul Gee, *What Video Games Have to Teach Us About Games and Learning* (New York: Palgrave Macmillan, 2004), 200.

20. Jenkins, *Convergence Culture*, 259.

21. Jenkins, *Confronting the Challenges*, 3.

22. Gee, Learning and Games, 26.

23. Bogost, The Rhetoric of Video Games, 125.

24. Jay Is Games, *Best of Casual Games 2006*. http://www.jayisgames.com/bestof/2006/best_of_simulation_results.php. Accessed June 19, 2007.

25. Gee, *What Video Games Have to Teach Us*, 194.

26. Jenkins, *Convergence Culture*, 162.

27. Gee, *What Video Games Have to Teach Us*, 194.

28. David Williamson Shaffer, *How Computer Games Help Children Learn* (New York: Palgrave, 2006).

29. Ibid.

30. Gee, *What Video Games Have to Teach Us*, 194.

31. An excellent resource is the Partnership for 21st Century Skills, http://www.21stcenturyskills.org. Accessed June 19, 2007.

32. Gee, Learning and Games.

33. Jenkins, *Confronting the Challenges*, 4.

Glossary

ARG. An alternate reality game (sometimes called a search and analysis game), it is an interactive narrative that uses the real world as a gaming space. ARGs most often involve player interaction with multiple media and game elements to tell a story.

Avatar. A game component controlled by the player.

Behaviors. Rules that describes the action of a game component. A game character might be able to run or jump, for example—two different kinds of behaviors. A door might be assigned an "invisible" behavior, which means that it cannot be seen on screen. Behaviors have certain qualities as well, like randomness, or a motion path, or intelligence. A behavior is, therefore, made up of an action and the qualities that define that action.

Challenge. An important way to shape the experience of play. If the challenge of a game is too high for a player's skills, he or she might become anxious or frustrated. If there is not enough challenge, boredom results. Ideally, games provide a balanced challenge at all moments.

Choice. Games present players with choices. Choices can be microchoices of moment-to-moment activity or macrochoices, which concern the long-term progress of the game. A game designer might give a player the choice to opt for the red or blue door, to discard or draw a card, to use a knife or a bow, to talk to NPCs or to ignore them. Designing choices is one of the biggest aspects of the design of any game.

Collaborate. To work together. Game designers collaborate with other game designers and members of their game design teams to design games.

Collective Intelligence. An intelligence that emerges from the collaboration and competition of many individuals. This is sometimes also referred to as *distributed intelligence.*

Competitive. All games are competitive in that players struggle against each other or against a game system as they play. Without this sense of competition, players would not be able to judge their progress throughout the game.

Conflict. All games embody contests of powers. Conflict is central to games, and arises naturally from interaction between components in a game. The player is actively pursuing a goal, and obstacles prevent this from happening easily. Game conflict comes in many forms. Conflict can be individual or team-based, cooperative or noncooperative, direct or indirect. Many games mix and match forms of conflict within a single game structure.

Core Mechanic. The experiential building blocks of player interactivity, which represent the essential moment-to-moment activity of the player, something that is repeated over and over throughout the game. During a game, the core mechanic creates patterns of behavior, and is the mechanism through which players make meaningful choices. Mechanics include activities like trading, shooting, running, collecting, talking, capturing territory, and so on. Game design relies on the design of compelling core mechanics.

Critique. To review or discuss critically. During playtesting, game designers ask players to critique their game designs, giving them feedback on what is and isn't working well.

Damage State. A game component's health status, indicating the level of damage (if any) it has currently sustained, and how close it is to elimination.

Decision Tree. A branching tree-style diagram that outlines all of the possible moves a player can make in a game. Decision trees are a common way of flow-charting interactive experiences. For example, if you are designing an interactive story that has a hypertext structure, you might draw a diagram that shows all of the links between the different parts of your story.

Degenerate Strategy. A way of playing a game that ensures victory every time. Usually, degenerate strategies are to be avoided in games, because they diminish uncertainty and the overall quality of play.

Design. The iterative process by which a designer conceives of and plans a system to be encountered by a participant, from which meaning emerges.

Discernable. Actions and outcomes in a game must be discernable, meaning that a player can perceive the immediate outcome of an action.

Dynamic System. Games change in response to decisions made by players and are, therefore, considered to be dynamic, interactive systems. The design of the rules that guide how, when, and why a player interacts with the system, as well as the kinds of relationships that exist between its parts, forms the basis of a game design practice.

Emergent Systems. A type of system that generates unpredictable patterns of complexity from a limited set of rules. In an emergent system, the whole is greater than the sum of the parts. For example, the limited set of the rules of grammar cannot account for all of the possible statements that might be made in a language.

Exploit. A weakness in a game's design, allowing a player to win every time.

Game. A system in which players engage in artificial conflict, defined by rules, and resulting in a quantifiable outcome.

Game Components. Games are made up of objects that make up a game world. Components include game characters or markers, the game space, the scoring system, and other objects defined as part of the game system.

Game Design. Game design is a complex, multilayered design activity, whereby systems of meaning (games) are created through the design of rule sets, resulting in play. Consider a game of Tag. *Without* game design, we would have a field of players scampering about, randomly touching each other, screaming, and then running in the other direction. *With* game design, we have a carefully crafted experience guided by rules, which make certain forms of interaction explicitly meaningful. *With* game design, for example, a touch becomes meaningful as a "tag," and whoever is "it" becomes the one to avoid.

Game Designer. A particular kind of designer, much like a graphic designer, an industrial designer, or an architect. The focus of a game designer is designing game play by conceiving and designing rules and structures that result in play for players. A game designer is not necessarily a programmer, visual designer, or project manager, although sometimes she or he can also play these roles in the creation of a game. A game designer might work alone or as part of a larger team. A game designer might create card games, social games, video games, or any other kinds of games.

Game Interface. The total sum of means by which players interact with the game. The interface provides means of *input,* allowing the player to manipulate a system, and *output,* allowing the system to produce the effects of the player's manipulation. In a board game, the interface includes the board and the tokens a player uses to move around the board. In a digital game, the interface is often graphical, allowing players to select areas of the screen to activate or to sort and organize inventories.

Game Theory. A branch of economics that studies rational decision making. It often looks at game-like situations, but it is not a general theory of games or game design.

Game Review. A written report describing a game, which includes strong and weak points, as well as information on genre, name of the designer, and date it was made.

Game Rules. See *Rules.*

Game Space. The area defining the space of play. In nondigital games, the game space might be the board or field on which the game is played. In digital games, the game space is the area in which game action occurs on screen.

Game Systems. Sets of components that can be used to design or play different games. Game systems can be digital or nondigital, like a deck of cards.

Game Tuning. The game design process, in which a game designer balances the degree of challenge in a game or across levels of a game.

Gaming. The sum total of activities, literacies, knowledge, and contexts activated in and around any instance of a game.

Gaming Literacies. Literacies made up of attitudes and forms of interaction that arise from the intrinsic qualities and characteristics guiding the types of learning gaming and games advance. These skills build on the foundation of traditional literacy, research skills, technical skills, and critical analysis skills taught in the classroom.

Genre. A game's classification or type as broken down into two broad subcategories: *turn type* (real-time, turn-based, asynchronous, etc.) and *category type* (action, strategy, sports, shooter, role playing, adventure, etc.).

Goal. The condition that must be met to win the game or beat the level. Choice is related to the goal of a game, which is often composed of smaller subgoals that a player must meet in order to win the game.

Integrated. Actions and outcomes in a game must be integrated, meaning that the outcome of a chosen action is woven into the game system as a whole. Game designers must design the rules of a game in such a way that each decision a player makes feels connected to previous decisions, as well as to future decisions encountered in the course of play.

Iterative Design. Game design uses a cyclical design process: that is, a game is designed through a repeated sequence of modifications to the rules and to the behaviors of game components. Game design follows a cycle of design—playtest—evaluate—modify—playtest—evaluate—modify. It is through iteration that game designers achieve the right balance between challenge, choice, and fun.

Level. A game level is a section or part of a game. Many console or PC games are so large that they are broken into levels, so that only one portion of the game needs to load at one time. To complete a game level, a player usually needs to meet specific goals or perform specific tasks; this allows the player to advance to the next level. In puzzle games, for example, levels may be similar, but more difficult, as the player progresses through the game.

Level Design. A game design activity involving the design of levels for a game. A game designer must work to create a system of levels that feel like they are part of the same game, all the while tuning or balancing the levels to manage the degree of challenge in each.

Level Designer. An individual game designer involved with the creation of game levels.

Level Editor. A software application used to design levels, maps, or campaigns for a digital game. Level editors are sometimes integrated into the game; at other times, they are separate parts of the game.

Literacy. New Literacies Studies defines literacy in this way. "... literacies crucially entail sense-making within a rich, multi-modal semiotic system, situated within a community of practice that renders that system meaningful in the first place." UNESCO defines it in this way: "Literacy involves a continuum of learning to enable an individual to achieve his or her goals, to develop his or her knowledge and potential, and to participate fully in the wider society." Within gaming, literacies encompass attitudes and modes of interaction with multimodal systems.

Loss Condition. Defines what game state causes the game to end. For example, time runs out or the avatar loses all available lives. Because all games must have some kind of quantifiable outcome to be considered games by traditional definitions, defining the loss state for a game is a critical feature of a game's design.

Lusory Attitude. The state of mind required to enter into the play of a game. To play a game, a group of players accepts the limitations of the rules because of the pleasure a game can afford.

Maze Game. A video game genre characterized by movement through a complex, puzzle-like space. Maze games often challenge players to manage limited resources, and may contain series of connected rooms.

Meaningful Play. Meaningful play in a game emerges from the relationship between player action and system outcome; it is the process by which a player takes action within the designed system of a game, and the system responds to this action. The meaning of an action in a game resides in the relationship between action and outcome.

Media. Games' presentation platforms as broken down into two broad subcategories: *digital* (PC, platform, Web-based, handheld, cell phone, etc.) and *analog* (board, card, miniatures, physical, social, etc.).

Mod. A game modification. Game designers often practice their craft by modifying the rules or content of existing games, as a way to gain more knowledge about how games work. Mods that add new content to the underlying games are often called *partial conversion mods*, while mods that create entirely new games are called *total conversion mods*.

Nondigital Game. A game made without digital technology. Nondigital games include board games, card games, physical games like *Tag*, social games like *Mafia*, and crossword puzzles.

NPCs (Nonplayer Characters). Characters that are not controlled by the player.

Outcome. The result or consequence of a choice (or set of choices) in a game. Game designers must consider the outcomes of choices they are giving players within the overall system of the game. For example, if a designer creates a game wherein the player can pick up a weapon or a key, he or she must consider what the consequence of this action might be: Does the key open a door? If so, which one?

Platformer. A video game genre characterized by jumping to and from suspended platforms or over obstacles. The most common unifying element to these games is a "jump" button.

Play. When rules are combined in specific ways, they create forms of activity for players, called "play." In a game, play occurs as the game rules are set into motion and experienced by the players.

Players. A game is something that one or more participants actively play. Players interact with the system of a game in order to experience the play of the game.

Player Character. A character controlled by the player.

Player Cooperation. Refers to games in which players all work together to achieve the stated game goal. Not all games exhibit player cooperation.

Playtest. Playing a game in order to diagnose its strengths and weaknesses. Playtesting happens throughout the game design process, and is fundamental to creating good games.

Postmortem. A document written after a game design is complete, documenting what went right and what went wrong along the way. The purpose of a postmortem is to communicate one's design thinking to other designers, so they can learn from the experience. A good postmortem gives specific examples of design decisions that were made, and discusses whether these were good or bad decisions for the game overall.

Procedural. Procedures (or processes) are sets of constraints that create possibility spaces, which can be explored through play. Games are procedural systems that generate representations out of the experience and logic of play.

Prototype. A version of a game that is in early development. Prototypes generally express the core idea of a game, and undergo playtesting to discover the strengths and weaknesses of the basic design before moving toward refinement.

Puppet Master. An individual involved in designing and/or running an ARG.

Puzzle. A puzzle is a special kind of game in which there is a single correct answer or set of correct answers.

Quantifiable Outcome. Games have a quantifiable goal or outcome. At the conclusion of a game, a player has either won or lost or received some kind of numerical score. A quantifiable outcome is what usually distinguishes games from less formal play activities.

Racialized Pedagogical Zones. Refers to the way that video games *teach* not only entrenched ideologies of race and racism, but also how game play's pleasure principles of mastery, winning, and skills development are often inextricably tied to and defined by familiar racial and ethnic stereotypes. (Concept by Everett and Watkins, this volume.)

Randomness. Degrees of randomness and chance are two tools that a game designer has at his or her disposal to balance the amount of strategic choice a player has in a game.

Real-Time Design. Game design in an open game system wherein the system (in this case, a game) responds to information received from players. Many ARGs (alternate reality games) utilize this design framework.

RPG. Role-playing game.

Rules. Rules are a fundamental part of any game. They provide the structure out of which play emerges, by defining what a player can and cannot do, as well as the relationships between components in the system. Defining the rules of a game and the many ways the rules fit together is a key part of a game designer's practice. Rules define interaction between game components and describe what happens when these components interact. Does the ball (component) bounce (rule) off the wall (component) or smash (rule) a hole (object) in it?

Rule Set. All of the rules that make up a game.

Scoring System. A game component that tracks the number of points earned by a player.

Second-Order Design. Because rules, when enacted by players, are embodied as the experience of play, game design can be considered *a second-order* design problem. In this type of design, a game designer only indirectly designs the player's experience by directly designing the rules of play.

Sequence of Play. The order in which things occur in a game.

Space of Possibility. The space of all possible actions and meanings that occur in the course of the game.

Special Abilities. A unique ability or behavior that is assigned to a particular creature or class of creatures.

System. A set of parts that interrelate to form a complex whole. Games are designed systems.

Systems of Meaning. Game design is the design of systems of meaning. Like letters in the alphabet, objects and actions within a game gain meaning through rules that determine how all of the parts relate. A game designer is responsible for designing the rules that gives these objects meaning.

Transformative Play. A special kind of play that occurs when the free movement of play alters the rigid structure of rules in which it takes shape. Not all play is transformative, but all forms of play contain the potential for transformation.

Turn Type. Describes how players interact with a game and with other players in relation to the element of time. Examples include real-time, turn-based, and asynchronous, to name a few.

Ubiquitous Computing. A design framework that rejects the notion that a computing technology should be separated from the environment. Computation is, instead, integrated directly into objects and systems like games, developing "things that think." Also referred to as *ubicomp* or *pervasive computing*.

Uncertainty. A key component of every game. If a game is predetermined, the player's actions will not have an impact on the outcome of the game. Designing uncertainty into a game means that a player always has the ability to affect its outcome.

Victory Condition. The game's goal or objective. That is, the game is won.

Win Condition. All games have win conditions, which indicate what must be achieved in order to win the game. Because all games must have some kind of quantifiable outcome in order to be considered games by traditional definitions, defining the win and loss states for a game is a critical feature of a game's design.

Workaround. See *Exploit* and *Degenerate Strategy*.

Zero-Sum Game. A game in which the winnings of the victor are equal to the losses of the loser. Games such as Chess, with a single winner and loser, are zero-sum games.

Games Index

50 Cent: Bulletproof
VU Games, Genuine Games, 2005
Console game; handheld game

Active Worlds
Active Worlds, 1995
Online world

Age of Empires
Ensemble Studios, 1997
Computer game

Age of Empires II: Conquerors
Ensemble Studios, 2000
Computer game

America's Army: Operations
U.S. Army/Secret Level, 2002
Computer game; console game

Animal Crossing (series)
Nintendo, 2001
Console game; handheld game

AstroPop
PopCap Games, 2005
Online game; mobile game

Ayiti: The Cost of Life
Gamelab/Global Kids, 2006
Online game

Barbie Fashion Designer
Mattel, 1996
Computer game

Bejeweled
Popcap Games, 2001
Online game

Beyond Good and Evil
Ubi Soft Entertainment, 2003
Console game; computer game

Bridge-Builder
Alex-Austin, 2000
Computer game

Bully
Rockstar Games, 2006
Console game

Burnout 3: Takedown
Criterion Games, 2004
Console game

Call to Power
Activision, 1999
Computer game

Chibi Robo
Nintendo, 2005
Console game

Civilization (series)
MicroProse, 1991
Computer game; console game

Countdown
Voyager, 1992
Computer game

Counter-Strike
The Counter-Strike Team, 2000
Computer mod

Def Jam: The Fight for NY
Aki Corporation/EA Canada, 2004
Console game

Def Jam Vendetta
Aki Corporation/EA Canada, 2003
Console game

Destroy All Humans
Pandemic Studios, 2005
Console game

Deus Ex
Ion Storm, 2000
Computer game; console game

Diablo (series)
Blizzard Entertainment, 1996
Computer game

DinoPark Tycoon
MECC, Manley & Associates Inc., 1993
Computer game
Doom
Id Software, 1993
Computer game
Dragon Ball Z: Budokai 3
Dimps, 2004
Console game
Droidworks
Lucas Learning, 1998
Computer game
Dungeons & Dragons (series)
Dave Arneson & Gary Gygax, 1973
Tabletop role-playing game

The ESP Game/Google Image Labeler
Luis von Ahn, 2006
Online game
Everquest
Verant Interactive, 1999
Online game
Thinkin' Things; All Around FrippleTown
Edmark, 2001
Computer game

Full Spectrum Warrior
Pandemic Studios, 2004
Console game

Gertrude's Puzzles
The Learning Company, 1983
Computer game
Getting Up: Contents Under Pressure
The Collective, 2006
Console game; mobile game
Godfather: The Game
Electronic Arts, 2006
Console game
Grand Theft Auto: Liberty City
Rockstar Leeds/Rockstar North, 1998
Console game; computer game
Grand Theft Auto: San Andreas
Rockstar North, 2004
Console game; handheld game; computer game
Grand Theft Auto: Vice City
Rockstar North, 2002
Console game; computer game
GuildWars
ArenaNet, 2005
Computer game

The Gungan Frontier
Lucas Learning, 1999
Computer game

Half Life
Valve Software, 1998
Computer game; console game
Halo (series)
Bungie, 1999
Console game

I Love Bees
42 Entertainment, 2004
Alternate Reality Game (ARG)
The Incredible Machine
Jeff Tunnell Productions, 1993
Computer game
The Island of Dr. Brain
Sierra On-Line, 1992
Computer game

JumpStart Kindergarten
Knowledge Adventure, 1994
Children's software
Just Grandma and Me
Brøderbund, 1991
Children's software

Karaoke Revolution
Harmonix and Blitz Games, 2003
Console game
KidPix
Craig Hickman/Brøderbund, 1991
Computer software
Kingdom Hearts
Square/Disney, 2002
Console game
Kriegsspiel
von Reisswitz, 1824
Wargame

Legend of Zelda: Four Swords
Nintendo, 2004
Console game; handheld game
Lego Island
Mindscape, 1997
Computer game
Lineage
NCsoft, 1998
Online game
LOGO
Wally Feurzeig & Seymour Papert, 1967
Programming language

Lucasfilm's Habitat
Lucas Arts, 1986
Online world

Madden NFL 06
EA Tiburon, 2005
Console game; computer game
Magic Artist 3D
Disney, 2001
Children's software
The Magic School Bus Explores the Human Body
Microsoft, 1994
Children's software
Major League Baseball 2K6
2K Sports, 2006
Console game
Mario Brothers (series)
Nintendo, 1983
Arcade game; console game; handheld game
Mario Kart
Nintendo, 1992
Console game
Math Blaster
Davidson/Knowledge Adventure, 1987
Computer game
The McDonald's Videogame
Molleindustria, 2006
Online game
Meridian 59
3DO Studios, 1996
Computer game
Microworlds Project Builder
Logo Computer Systems, 1994
Authoring Software
Midnight Club 3: Dub Edition
Rockstar San Diego, 2005
Console game; handheld game
MUD1
Roy Trubshaw and Richard Bartle, 1979
Computer game
Myst
Cyan, 1993
Computer game

NBA Ballers
Midway, 2004
Console game
NBA Street (series)
EA Sports BIG, 2001
Console game
NFL Street
EA Tiburon, 2004
Console game
Number Munchers
Minnesota Educational Computing Consortium (MECC), 1991
Computer game

Okami
Clover Studio, 2006
Console game
The Oregon Trail
Minnesota Educational Computing Consortium (MECC), 1971
Computer game

Pac-Man
Namco, 1980
Arcade game; console game; computer game
Pajama Sam (series)
Humongous Entertainment, 1996
Computer game
Planetary Taxi
Margo Nanny, Voyager Company, 1993
Children's software
PLATO
University of Illinois/Control Data Corporation, 1960
Curriculum-based computer-aided (instruction system)
Pong
Atari, 1972
Arcade game; console game; computer game
Print Artist 4.0 Gold
Sierra Home, 1998
Software

Quest Atlantis
Sasha Barab, 2001
Online game

Reader Rabbit
The Learning Company, 1989
Computer software
Rise of Nations
Big Huge Games, 2003
Computer game
Rocky's Boots
The Learning Company, 1982
Children's software

Rollercoaster Tycoon (series)
Hasbro Interactive, 1999
Computer game
Roller Typing
EdVenture Software, 2004
Educational software

Saint's Row
Volition, 2006
Console game
Second Life
Linden Lab, 2003
Online world
The Sims (series)
Maxis, 2000
Computer game; console game
SimCity (series)
Maxis, 1989
Computer game
SimTower
OPeNBooK Co., Ltd., 1994
Computer game
Space Invaders
Taito, 1978
Arcade game
Spore
Electronic Arts/Maxis, forthcoming
Computer game
Supercharged!
MIT Education Arcade, 2002
Computer game
Super Smash Brothers Melee
HAL Laboratory, 2001
Console game
SWAT4
Irrational Games, 2005
Computer game

Take Back Illinois
Persuasive Games, 2004
Online game
Teen Second Life
Linden Lab, 2006
Online world
Teenage Mutant Ninja Turtles
Konami, 2003
Console game; computer game
Tetris
Alexy Pajnitov, circa 1986
Computer game; handheld game; console game
Thief (series)
Looking Glass Studios, 1998
Computer game
Tony Hawk's Pro Skater (series)
Neversoft Entertainment, 1999
Console game; handheld game
True Crime: Streets of LA
Luxoflux, 2004
Console game

Ultima Online (series)
Richard Garriot/Origin, 1980
Computer game; online game
The Urbz: Sims in the City
Maxis/Griptonite Games, 2004
Console game; computer game

The Visual Almanac
Apple Multimedia Lab, 1989
Interactive CD-Rom

Where in the World Is Carmen Sandiego?
Electronic Arts, 1992
Console game
World of Warcraft
Blizzard Entertainment, 2004
Online game
WWE SmackDown! (series)
THQ, 2000
Console game

Zoo Tycoon
Blue Fang Games, 2004
Computer game